SAYING WHAT WE MEAN

Northwestern University
Studies in Phenomenology
and
Existential Philosophy

Founding Editor †James M. Edie

General Editor Anthony J. Steinbock

Associate Editor John McCumber

SAYING WHAT WE MEAN

Implicit Precision and the Responsive Order

Selected Works
by Eugene T. Gendlin

Edited by Edward S. Casey and Donata M. Schoeller
Foreword by Edward S. Casey

Northwestern University Press
Evanston, Illinois

Northwestern University Press
www.nupress.northwestern.edu

Copyright © 2018 by Northwestern University Press.
Published 2018. All rights reserved.

Printed in the United States of America

10 9 8 7 6 5 4 3 2 1

ISBN 978-0-8101-3622-9 (paper)
ISBN 978-0-8101-3623-6 (cloth)
ISBN 978-0-8101-3624-3 (e-book)

Library of Congress Cataloging-in-Publication Data
are available from the Library of Congress

In grateful remembrance of
Gene Gendlin (1927–2017),
colleague, mentor, friend;
subtle explorer of the most
intricate edges of human experience

—E.S.C. and D.M.S.

Contents

Foreword, by Edward S. Casey ... xi

Introduction, by Donata M. Schoeller ... xiii

Note on Abbreviations ... xxi

Part 1. Phenomenology of the Implicit

1. Two Phenomenologists Do Not Disagree ... 5
2. What Are the Grounds of Explication? A Basic Problem in Linguistic Analysis and in Phenomenology ... 22
3. Experiential Phenomenology ... 46
4. The New Phenomenology of Carrying Forward ... 80
5. Words Can Say How They Work ... 93

Part 2. A Process Model

6. Implicit Precision ... 111
7. A Direct Referent Can Bring Something New ... 138
8. The Derivation of Space ... 151
9. Arakawa and Gins: The Organism-Person-Environment Process ... 164

Part 3. On the Edges of Plato, Heidegger, Kant, and Wittgenstein

10. What Controls Dialectic? Commentary on Plato's *Symposium* ... 175
11. *Befindlichkeit*: Heidegger and the Philosophy of Psychology ... 194
12. Time's Dependence on Space: Kant's Statements and Their Misconstrual by Heidegger ... 225
13. What Happens When Wittgenstein Asks "What Happens When . . . ?" ... 237

Part 4. Thinking with the Implicit

14	The Responsive Order: A New Empiricism	253
15	Introduction to *Thinking at the Edge* (with Mary Hendricks)	282
	Acknowledgments	295
	References	297
	Index	301

Foreword

Edward S. Casey

I first met Eugene Gendlin over twenty years ago at a meeting of the Society for Phenomenology and Existential Philosophy (SPEP) at Northwestern University. His reputation had preceded him; mutual friends had assured me that he was truly one of a kind—someone who not only spoke his mind with candor but had arresting and original things to say on many contemporary philosophical issues, especially those inspired by Continental philosophy. Before I had a chance to ask him about his research, he asked me point-blank: What are *you* working on? He wasn't so much interested in what I had written and published before that moment as what was happening in my thinking *now*, at that very moment. Once I said that I was writing a book on memory, he proceeded to explore with me a given memory of my own so as to better understand its meaning in crisply descriptive terms. He asked incisive questions that, in the space of fifteen minutes, led me to rethink my entire project.

This was the first of many such conversations we had over the ensuing decades—in New York City, Paris, and Spring Valley, New York. In each of these talks, I marveled at Gendlin's ability to pursue the subject matter under discussion in ways that were at once unanticipated and refreshing. Our encounters included sessions in which we pursued Focusing and Thinking at the Edge. For the most part, however, our talks were resolutely philosophical, and I recognized in my conversation partner a thinker who, like Socrates, had a genius for getting others to understand the implicit, not-yet-spoken meaning of what they were thinking at the moment. But instead of getting to a level of insight that is intact but concealed (as Socrates supposed), Gendlin's practices help people to detect and carry forward a bodily felt sense of what wants to be said—a sense that, once articulated, generates new and surprising forms of insight into their intricate order.

Gendlin wrote and published extensively in the field of philosophy as well as psychology. In addition to his eminence in psychology—for which he has received many major awards, including that of being named the Distinguished Professional Psychologist of the Year by the American Psychological Association—he steadily gained recognition as a premier thinker in philosophy whose work is at the cutting edge in several major areas. In fact, he thought of himself as primarily a philosopher. He earned a Ph.D. in philosophy from the University of Chicago, and taught for many years in both the philosophy and the psychology departments of that university. His first book, *Experiencing and the Creation of Meaning* (1962), proposed an innovative model showing how human beings create meaning in the interaction of symbols and schemes with ongoing experiencing, how meaning exceeds literal or formal parameters, and how our tacit awareness of meaning in all its complexity can be explicated in endlessly diverse ways. Since then, he has published a series of highly original essays that are distinctly philosophical in tenor, addressing both classical and recent issues in philosophy in strikingly novel ways. The result is an extraordinarily rich and diverse contribution that illuminates human experience—and beyond—at every significant level.

This volume collects a number of these remarkable essays—those that Donata Schoeller and I consider to be at once most representative and most provocative. It is the first such collection in any language, and its contents were chosen with an eye primarily to their philosophical interest. Two of the most important essays are previously unpublished. Our hope is that this collection will bring Gendlin more fully to the attention of the philosophical as well as the psychological world. An earlier volume edited by David Kleinberg-Levin included essays by contemporary authors on Gendlin's contributions to philosophy: *Language beyond Postmodernism: Saying and Thinking in Gendlin's Philosophy of Language* (Northwestern University Press, 1997). The present volume is the first to gather a broad sample of Gendlin's own explicitly philosophical writings in one accessible book. We consider these writings to be exemplary of the author's written work in philosophy over the past several decades. They bring together what is essential in his thought: the responsive order of nature that always gives back "more" than can be explicitly stated, and the amazing precision of this implicit "more." They exhibit Gendlin's abundantly generative mind at its groundbreaking best, and at the same time they complement his masterwork, *A Process Model* (2017), which will appear simultaneously with this volume. Taken together, we believe that these two volumes demonstrate that Gendlin is an altogether unique figure in philosophy as well as psychology. They show him to be one of the most challenging and creative thinkers of our era—someone whose work will make a decisive difference in how we construe experience and meaning at every level of human experience.

New York City
October 2016

Introduction

Donata M. Schoeller

> Where others see indeterminacy, we find intricacy—an always unfinished order that cannot be represented, but has to be taken along as we think. It is a much finer, more organic order that always provides implicit functions, whether we attend to them or not.
> —Gendlin, "The New Phenomenology of Carrying Forward"

Eugene Gendlin was trained as a philosopher at the University of Chicago, and his work from early on inquires into the implicit functions of our bodily-felt sense of situations. He discovers that such embodied experiencing is not at all vague or imprecise. Unlike contemporary debates on the qualities of experience, Gendlin's work does not convey yet more descriptions or arguments for or against experience's qualities, but demonstrates the responsive, meaning-making roles of embodied experiencing in the use of language. This new move in thinking complements the linguistic turn of philosophy in important and unparalleled ways. Gendlin shows us that we always think with *more* than ideas, concepts, observations, cognitions, positions, conditions, propositions, or arguments. His philosophy demonstrates how to think and how to say the *more* that we *take along* with every explication. From his very first articles and books to his latest publications, ranging over half a century, his theories of meaning investigate the functions of what we think, speak, and also act *into*. He is able to craft concepts that can *function* in what in the past and today could only be designated as the "excess" of experience, the "preconceptual," the "background," the "tacit dimension," the explication of which has seemed logically impossible. Gendlin does not describe or analyze what words or phrases such as these indicate. His concepts engage what they think into, thus opening it up, making it deliberately workable. Thus he acts as a powerful reminder that thinking, researching, and philosophizing are *more* than the discourses they engender.

Philosophers such as Wilhem Dilthey, Edmund Husserl, Martin Heidegger, Maurice Merleau-Ponty, and John Dewey discovered a blind spot in philosophical and scientific methodologies that consists in their inability to account for the organic-experiential and meaningful processes from which systems of knowledge arise. Today, philosophers and scientists from different schools (for example, Hermann Schmitz, Thomas Nagel, Francisco Varela, and Terrence Deacon) note with similar concern an analogous point: the incompatibility between what seems real, relevant, and meaningful from a first-person perspective and what seems real, relevant, and meaningful from the third-person approach of scientific methodologies.

Facing this split, our culture suffers severe forms of crisis that deeply affect our environment and our collective life. Gendlin's philosophy of the implicit finds subtle and yet powerful ways to provide new grounds for thinking. He does not just give one more critique of the shortcomings of dualistic approaches. Nor does he merely describe the importance of ordinary or qualitative experience. He finds ways to explicate the vital and precise functions of the experiential process *within* symbolic conceptualization, and he shows how to think systematically with first-person intricacy. Gendlin's thinking and practices move across the body-mind split, expanding the field of experience and thinking beyond so-called subjective or objective approaches in order to cultivate an awareness for the preciseness of what he calls a "responsive order."

Gendlin's move to the edge of conceptuality has the distinctive virtue of suggesting a new philosophical practice that others (most notably Pierre Hadot and Jacques Derrida) have called for but did not themselves fully deliver. His new practices teach us the ability to access and deliberately reflect the *finer organic order of an experiential process and its implicit responses to what we think and say in ordinary living, in research, and in creative work.* Today these practices are being applied in many different fields.[1]

Finding ways to think into or "at the edge" of formulations, Gendlin sensitizes us to notice the experiential *effects* of (not only what can be logically inferred from) observations, cognitions, truths, descriptions, and the like. Using a certain word or phrase, for example, can unpredictably widen, specify, clarify, or change what has been said. This kind of change is not logically predetermined. The most "serious use of a formulation," Gendlin says in chapter 10 of this volume, "is in further thinking," when, through the formulation one "discovers new aspects by running into trouble with them." In thinking in detail about a responsively precise

INTRODUCTION

dynamic of thinking and speaking that works implicitly in order for us to conceptualize something, Gendlin has opened a new terrain for philosophy. This is apparent in the kinds of concepts he introduces that require a radically self-reflective style of thinking to show their powers. Gendlin's work is an encouragement, and a training, in how to do so.

In the preface to his first book, *Experiencing and the Creation of Meaning*, Gendlin summarized his project as follows:

> The project is to *enter into* how concepts (logical forms, distinctions, rules, algorithms, computers, categories, patterns . . .) relate to experiencing (situations, events, therapy, metaphoric language, practice, human intricacy . . .). Or, we can phrase it: *how experiencing . . . functions in our cognitive and social activities.*
>
> Of course one cannot stand outside this relation in order to conduct such an examination. The relations to be examined will obtain in the very process of examining. Experiencing will play some of its roles in the process of speaking about—and with—them. This philosophy is therefore constantly reflexive. It can say what it says only as what it talks about also functions in the very saying. And since it tells how the experiential side always exceeds the concepts, this also happens in the concepts right here. The "functional relationships" and "characteristics" set forth in this book are themselves specific ways in which their own formulation can be exceeded. The curiosity about how this might be possible is an appetite I would like to rouse in my reader. (*ECM* xi)

With the present volume we would like to do just this: to excite an appetite for the extraordinary thinking of Eugene Gendlin and for the effects of his concepts as well as his practices that, in paraphrasing Adorno, "open up" the phenomena they make thinkable. By learning the lesson of becoming experientially more self-reflective, the reader will be able to employ logical thinking within the wider order of human sense-making. The reader will learn how it can be possible to speak and think with the way schemes for understanding exceed their conceptual structure even as (and precisely as) we employ these very same schemes.

In the first part of this anthology, titled "Phenomenology of the Implicit," we witness the complex challenge posed by Gendlin's approach. In this part, the author circles around slightly different entries and approaches to the responsiveness of what we speak, write, or think *into*. This first part also shows how consistently and patiently Gendlin *sits with* his phenomenon. Step by step, his work becomes more and more creative in finding a use of conceptual language that works to differentiate, functionally, what he conceives as the nonnumerical, multischematic nature of experience (in his later work, this is referred to as "implicit multiplicity"). He thus shows how, in referring to experience, experience responds in turn, and how in using language one can say more than concepts say. As he writes in chapter 3 of this book, "We will find that, in the process of being *further* schematized, experiencing has no definite units, is responsive to any scheme, and is capable of being schematized by any other experience. Experiencing is 'nonnumerical.'"

These first articles also shed light on what Gendlin conceives as a turnaround of the "usual philosophical order." In the usual understanding of order, conceptual structures are assumed to take the lead. Experience of the world needs to be put into place according to our categories, logical rules, and systems. There is no way to come to, let alone speak of, what seems "given" in experience without already applying concepts in thinking and perceiving. In this opening part, Gendlin does not reiterate this old problem or take sides in its discussion. Rather, we witness the process of turning this order around: continuously discovering new ways to do what had seemed impossible: to demonstrate and to understand the vital and important precision and the implicit functions of an experiential or implicit order that is *not* identical with a conceptual order. This is not meant as a metaphysical claim. Gendlin's work is not concerned with rendering propositions about what the structure of experience is. As he says in chapter 1 of this volume: "Here then, is 'the' structure of experiencing, not indeed as it 'is,' but as it is in regard to the next, or any further symbolization!"

His close-up studies of what happens in the transitions between sentences, between one formulation and the next, enable Gendlin to think across different philosophical schools and methodologies such as linguistic analysis, existential phenomenology, psychology, epistemology, philosophy of language, and so on. Thereby, he forges his methodology and his conceptual tools to be able to "instance" (instead of represent, construct, analyze, or describe) what he calls the "responsive order." This order begins to unfold before our eyes in the various ways Gendlin thinks and writes, demonstrating what it takes to consider speech and thought acts as lived processes to be interacted with when we think and formulate them, always involving more than can be empirically observed or logically deduced from the third-person perspective. Paraphrasing Brandom, one could say that "making it explicit" always implies the interactional richness of experiential intricacy functioning *in* the explication. This cannot be identical with explicative assessments and inferences themselves. It is rather the lived interaction of body-environment with a vast past implicitly functioning in every explicated and experienced now. With every explication of the implicit, Gendlin shows that we do something new.

INTRODUCTION

The second part of this book, "A Process Model," presents glimpses of Gendlin's later inquiry, providing a new epistemological basis for the embodied grounds of thinking. The articles summarize and point to Gendlin's magnum opus: *A Process Model*. Gendlin has written and conceived this model for more than two decades. The epistemological perspectives he lays out in this highly original work tackle the challenge of his earlier work from a different side. Speaking with Kant, he conceives of the "conditions of possibility" for the implicit precision of experiencing which his philosophy of meaning brings to the fore. In his thinking of the living process *as a model*, Gendlin's basic concepts overcome the dichotomies and theoretical cuttings of post-Cartesian thought. To think only in these latter structures and their implications has stultified philosophical thinking about language, meaning, intentionality, and consciousness, trapping it like flies in a fly-bottle, as Wittgenstein famously notes. Gendlin's anchoring of meaning in the "implicit intricacy" of body-environment interaction significantly contributes to showing how thinking can find its way out of its own traps.

The approach unfolded in the second part of this book builds on one major condition. This is not to conceive body and environment apart from each other. The interactional happening of body-environment makes for new concepts that preclude splitting along the lines of habitual binaries such as inside and outside, body and mind, subject and object, past and present, conceptual and nonconceptual. Bodily process always already exceeds the skin-envelope, always already involves the environments which it also co-generates. Experiencing (and feeling) the living we are is thus to be conceived as interactional, interaffective, and situated—from the start. Gendlin spells out new distinctions that grasp and work in this basic relationality:

> I propose that the active organism does something I call "implying."
> It implies the environment. The environment may or may not occur somewhat as the body implies. Implying and occurring are two interdependent functions that create one process. *Instead of body and environment being two things, let us distinguish between* implying and occurring and spell out how their functions require each other. (136).

In *A Process Model*, Gendlin introduces major innovations by creating new conceptual distinctions that empower us to think an organic development of meaning in ways that never lose the experiential intricacy involved, at any level. They make bodily implying accessible to thinking. Nevertheless, his concepts retain the precision of logical thinking. This makes for a reflective practice that involves the entire somatic-semantic continuum. His major concept of direct reference is itself a methodology and a practice. Such reference cannot be reduced to a scheme. Conceptual thinking that is never only schematic is the methodological thread tying together the two first parts of this book. In his later work, Gendlin demonstrates in careful steps the powers of a new kind of *systematic thinking* that does not need to discount the embodied, first-personal doing that is involved in thinking and meaning.

The third part of this volume, titled "On the Edges of Plato, Heidegger, Kant, and Wittgenstein," presents the originality of Gendlin's relation to other thinkers. We chose essays by him on Plato, Kant, Wittgenstein, and Heidegger. It is interesting to note that for a very long time Gendlin was not willing to read Heidegger because of his Nazi affiliations. When he finally did, he was surprised how well he already understood Heidegger's thinking, mainly through the lenses of Merleau-Ponty, Sartre, and others. In the article in this volume, he lays out a concept of Heidegger's idea of *Befindlichkeit* that is embodied. As Gendlin has emphasized in the previous internet version of this article, one should not mistake his interpretation of this notion to be identical with Heidegger's, even though Gendlin's reading of this concept deepens our understanding of Heidegger. Few people know that Gendlin did a considerable amount of translation work. He translated Heidegger's "What Is a Thing," and wrote a commentary on it that was lauded by Heidegger himself. He also translated Aristotle's *De Anima* and wrote two volumes of line-by-line commentary on it (available from Amazon.com). But engaging with thinkers in the past was not for Gendlin a scholarly end in itself. In part 3 one can see that previous thinkers are a resource for Gendlin, one that sharpens his own approach and allows him to think further.

The fourth part of this volume, "Thinking with the Implicit," presents Gendlin's introduction to the practice of Thinking at the Edge (TAE). In creating this practice, Gendlin does something that makes him truly singular in the academic world of philosophy: he transforms his method of accessing implicit meaning into practical steps that are eminently teachable. His passion for devising such a method (as well as his earlier method of Focusing) has something to do with a special political conviction. Precise and creative thinking that arises in the interface of thinking and symbolizing should not be the privilege or the obsession of a few highly educated and, as Emerson put it, "stubborn" people. It should be brought into the world and made available to all who might benefit from it. Gendlin never ceases to find ways to help others to think more deeply, more authentically, more originally. He constantly encourages us to improve our understanding of situational living and to express what matters in uniquely new ways. This is what makes first-person experience so valuable. This experience is not replaceable or repeatable. The intricate precision that is immanent in the knowledge we have gained in ongoing experience can be shared in professional, scientific, and private contexts by means of Gendlin's methodology of TAE.[2] Gendlin's practices teach us how to engage different systems of knowledge without being dominated and incapacitated by them, and thus to be able to cultivate and discover in thinking what Stanley Cavell characterizes as one's "own voice."

The very last essay integrates a radically self-reflective approach into an understanding of science as an explication of "The Responsive Order." This essay opens up a striking understanding of objectivity with a novel account of creative theoretical advances in science. In Gendlin's view, scientific methods rely on the responsiveness of conceptual/experimental procedures and their objects, interactively co-generating each other, emerging, stabilizing and shifting together, yet never in arbitrary ways. Among other things, Gendlin's understanding of objectivity can be read as an elaboration of a more inclusive practice of research: to engage, reflect, feel, and experience a wider, implicit order of interaction and its intricate responses to and in everything we find, analyze, describe, and do.

Notes

1. D. Schoeller, "Somatic-Semantic Shifting: Articulating Embodied Cultures," in *Thinking Thinking: Practicing Radical Reflection*, ed. D. Schoeller and V. Saller (Freiburg: Alber, 2016), 112–36; T. Satoko and M. Kida, *Qualitative Research with TAE Steps: Thinking at the Edge; Theory and Applications* (Hiroshima: Keisuisha, 2011); G. Walkerden, "Researching and Developing Practice Traditions Using Reflective Practice Experiments," *Quality and Quantity* 43, no. 2 (2009): 249–63; H. Deloch, "Das Nicht-Sagbare als Quelle der Kreativität: E. T. Gendlins Philosophie des Impliziten und die Methode Thinking at the Edge," in *In Sprachspiele verstrickt; oder, wie man der Fliege den Ausweg zeigt: Verflechtungen von Wissen und Können*, ed. S. Tolksdorf and H. Tetens (Berlin: De Gruyter, 2010), 259–84; G. Walkerden, "Felt Knowing: A Foundation for Local Government Practice," in *Social Learning in Environmental Management: Towards a Sustainable Future*, ed. M. Keen, V. A. Brown, and R. Dyball (London: Earthscan, 2005), 170–87; G. Claxton, "Thinking at the Edge: Developing Soft Creativity," *Cambridge Journal of Education* 36, no. 3 (2006): 351–62; Alvin Mahrer, *The Creation of New Ideas in Psychotherapy: A Guidebook* (Ross-on-Wye, Eng.: PCCS Books, 2006); *The Folio: A Journal for Focusing and Experiential Therapy* 19, special issue on "Thinking at the Edge" (2004).

2. One of the editors of this volume, Donata Schoeller, has had considerable firsthand experience with TAE, teaching it to graduate students at various universities in the United States and in Europe.

Note on Abbreviations

At various points in the essays collected in this volume, two of Gendlin's most important works are cited: *Experiencing and the Creation of Meaning* (Northwestern, 1997) and *A Process Model* (Northwestern, 2017). The former work is cited as *ECM*, the latter as *APM*. *ECM* is cited by page number. *APM* is cited either by the page numbers of the edition published by Northwestern University Press in 2017, or by the book's internal divisions of chapter-section-subsubsection, using hyphens to separate the subdivisions: for example, "*APM* VII-A-e" means chapter VII, section A, subsection e. Other standard abbreviations in this book are these: *BT* (Martin Heidegger, *Being and Time*, trans. John Macquarrie and Edward Robinson [New York: Harper and Row, 1962]); *BN* (Jean-Paul Sartre, *Being and Nothingness*, trans. Hazel Barnes [New York: Washington Square Press, 1966]); and *PP* (John Austin, *Philosophical Papers* [Oxford: Oxford University Press, 1961]).

SAYING WHAT WE MEAN

Part 1

Phenomenology of the Implicit

1

Two Phenomenologists Do Not Disagree

Heidegger wrote: "That which is to become phenomenon, can be hidden. And just therefore, because the phenomena are immediately and mostly *not* given, phenomenology is needed" (*BT* 60). Phenomenology is partly "-logy," logos. "The logos lets something be seen," and logos is or includes speech: "Speech lets something be seen" (*BT* 56). It is clear from these quotations, and from Heidegger's whole work, that phenomena are directly there for us, but only after they are uncovered by phenomenological assertions. "What is it, which in an outstanding sense must be called 'phenomena'? . . . Obviously just such as immediately and mostly does *not* show itself" (*BT* 59; trans. modified here and elsewhere).

The italics are both times Heidegger's, for the word "not" in the above. Phenomena do not at first show themselves, at least not the phenomena we are concerned with in phenomenology. It is "the function of logos" to enable a "simple letting be seen" (*BT* 58).

But if the self-showing of phenomena thus depends on our linguistic formulations, two questions arise: (1) Are our formulations constitutive of phenomena, are phenomena totally dependent upon formulations? Or do they have some kind of independence? (2) Is there still a difference between phenomenology as Heidegger does it, and any other serious philosophy—since any philosophy bases itself in *some* way on experience? In other words, is there really such a thing as phenomenology?

I will answer both questions affirmatively. But the answer is not simple. We can be sure that Heidegger did not make a simple mistake either in his insistence in italics that phenomena do not show themselves without our assertions, or in his insistence that what he did was phenomenology.[1]

I

Rather than imposing assumptions for a convenient account of "experience," phenomenologists begin with experience as we actually have it, and articulate that. Whether a sentence does or does not articulate experience is not entirely up to the sentence and its own meaning. Heidegger writes: "Each originally drawn phenomenological conception and sentence, as a communicated assertion, stands in the possibility of degeneracy. It is passed on in an empty understanding, loses its groundedness, and becomes a free-floating thesis" (*BT* 61).

For a sentence to be phenomenological, something more is involved, since the same sentence and its conceptual meaning can lack its phenomenological ground if it is understood only conceptually. To say that such "empty understanding" is possible shows this additional role of the phenomenon. The phenomenon shows itself as a result of the sentence. But this means that once the sentence is grasped, the phenomenon *itself* must still appear. *It* must come and be seen. The sentence and its conceptual meaning are not simply constitutive of the phenomenon; the sentence and its meaning can be used without looking, so to speak, or can fail to lead us to something we then see directly.

The experiential aspects which phenomenological philosophers point to are held to be universal: any person should be able to corroborate any phenomenological assertion directly. What any phenomenological sentence points to should appear directly, as an experiential aspect so distinct and separate from the mere sentence and its meaning, that it could be there or not be there, a totally distinct addition to the sentence and its meaning.

If this claim of phenomenology were simple and obvious, then phenomenologists would never differ. A phenomenon would always corroborate every phenomenological sentence that was used phenomenologically, and no phenomenologist *could* differ with it.

On the other hand, if this claim is denied, if it is merely that some assertions fit experience but other assertions contradict them and fit as well, then there is no such special thing as phenomenology. But phenomenologists do differ, and nevertheless the claim to some type of independence of phenomena is not nothing. It follows that we must investigate much more exactly the relationship or relationships between phenomenological *formulations* (words, symbols, sentences, conceptual models) and phenomena. (The use of this very word can only become clear if these relationships become clear.)

But did not Heidegger and also Husserl do exactly this? Were not sections 31–35 of Heidegger's *Being and Time* and large parts of Husserl's *Logical Investigations* and *Ideas* exactly about the relationship between experience on the one hand, and words and various kinds of attention on the other? And yet these two phenomenological philosophers differ from each other, and from others, even in their account of this basic relationship, as well as on other topics.

What is worse, they do not apply their account of the relations between formulation and experience at each step of their discourse. They choose and use formulational models such as actuality-possibility, form-matter, knowing-feeling-willing, particular-universal, without stopping to look at just what the choice of formulation does to experience, and exactly what some alternative choice would have done.

Therefore we are not in a very good position to know what to think when, for example, Heidegger phenomenologically speaks of the "what for" as basically constituting the object, while Husserl speaks of the willing or value aspect as if it were obviously and experientially different from the start, and added on to givenness, while Sartre uses Hegel's categories (in-itself vs. for-itself) to "describe" phenomenologically.

None of them turn to look at just how their own steps are, each time, grounded (and, in what respects not grounded), nor do they tell us how one would check each step against a phenomenon, except for the general indifferent assertion that there always is one, being lifted out. Clearly not every aspect of their sentences is corroborated thereby. These thinkers do not tell us how their formulational terms interact with experience. Clearly, this "grounding" doesn't mean that the phenomena are simply identical with everything the formulation is. Perhaps there are different kinds of formulational effects. Perhaps some formulations intend to point, only, and would then enable further reformulation; perhaps others intend to represent or render, or create new aspects. Perhaps, too, the effect of a formulation or a further reformulation is not a simple either/or: merely, to show or fail to show the same phenomenon. Perhaps a "same" phenomenon can still give rise to further and different aspects. It is not all so simple. For phenomenological philosophers there *are* specific ways in which universal experience *is* involved in how they reach each conclusion. There are several specific ways in which direct experience *can* function as a ground in each step of formulating. To say exactly how opens up a whole new field of inquiry.

Heidegger poses this problem, but only on the side of formulations. He says that any statement always already involves a metaphysics, a certain "approach" to phenomena. Once we recognize this, we do not wish to fall back into just some one approach, a metaphysics if we attribute our approach to phenomena. But, he asks, what would be an approach which is not just another approach? Heidegger says that he does not answer this question. A whole future generation shall answer it.

In posing this problem in this way, he is still looking only at the old problem of relativism: how can we proceed at all since any way in which we do will still only be one of a variety?

So formulated, however, the puzzle assumes exactly that which it tries to overcome, namely that the answer must be an approach, a type of formulation, and that reality is somehow fundamentally like some approach, so that as soon as we can have more than one we are in difficulty.

If, instead, we study the formulating process itself, and the roles of experience in it, we may find how experience can ground different formulations differently, so that we might then be glad (and also specific, and knowing) about different formulations.

It is far too general to say simply that formulations are constitutive of phenomena, but also too general to say that phenomena lie there, nicely sorted into essence-piles, waiting for formulations to pick them up. Both statements lift out something but they are poor statements, nevertheless. Instead of these generalities let us study exactly how, in specific respects, phenomena are affected by a given formulation, and differently affected by another. Let us also see exactly in what respects they have some independence during the steps of formulating. In this way we may discover more exact aspects of what Heidegger and Husserl pointed to. We may also develop the phenomenological terms in which to say what we phenomenologists do, when we take a step of formulating. And there may be different kinds of such steps.

Elsewhere I have formulated three bodies of such observations. There can be a long list of noticeable *signposts*, which mark when one is phenomenologically proceeding as against when not.[2] For example, phenomenological statements have many logical implications which the philosopher does not intend. Something other than the statement is always involved: something the reader must see, find, discover, experience. The next step of phenomenological procedure does not necessarily follow especially from the statement here. One will not be able to follow how the procedure gets to its *next* step, unless this more-than-statement, this experience, has been gotten, as *this* step. The next step may logically disturb the literal meaning of this statement, or it may seem to jump rather than follow. Logic is no longer the only guide from step to step.

None of these signposts would be willingly accepted by anyone whose procedure is more orthodox. They are quite uniquely the marks of those who ground their steps experientially. (The above was only a little from a much longer list of signposts.)

Another set of findings concerns different *types of experience-formulation pairs*. Formulations do not always attempt to say what an experience is. Sometimes they point ("Do you know *what* I mean?" "I will say *this* another way."). Sometimes they metaphorically generate some quite new likeness between different things, rather than formulating either thing. Formulations and experiences can be found in rather different kinds of parts. And one *can* always move from one pair to another! (For example, one can always move from having rendered to pointing again, and from pointing to a new rendering.)

Still another set I must abbreviate here consists of the peculiar *characteristics which experience exhibits when one moves from one formulation-experience pair to another.* It seems then that experience has not given units, and can respond to different schemes rather than having just one of its own. New aspects can always be created from any experience to relate to any other. And yet, also, an experience is always just this, and responds not at all as we might wish, to our formulations, but just as it will. I am going to say more about this.

I hope I have sketched out this new field, the study of experientially grounded steps of formulating, sufficiently, so that I can now engage in a fresh and much more limited discussion: two phenomenologists do not disagree.

At first this seems very simple. Some phenomenon—some aspect capable of being experienced—is lifted out, or related to, at every point. Two phenomenologists, let us say you and I, disagree: there are two possibilities: either you and I are really describing two different phenomena, or we are describing the same one with two different formulations. If it is two different phenomena, we will soon agree. You will show me the phenomenon you are describing, and since it is a universal human experience your description can lead me to it. My description will show you the one I have been describing. We may have to improve our descriptions a little in response to each other's misunderstandings, but soon we will realize that we are talking of two different phenomena, and each will see what the other points to. We are each grateful to the other for having been shown a new phenomenon, and we walk out arm in arm.

Or, if we are describing the same phenomenon, but our difference lies in the vocabulary, concepts, logical model, with which we approach it, then there are again two possibilities:

Either we soon realize that our differing formulations refer to the same thing, and now we can proceed together from here on. Although you may not like my formulation as much as you like your own (and I might prefer mine, although I could now like yours better, either way), we find that what we are lifting out is the same. So we can go on together. After all, it is via the phenomenon that we get to a next step, and so it does not matter that we spoke of it differently. We proceed on from this point arm in arm.

Or, we find that our two different formulations lead to two different further steps, even though in some sense the phenomenon we described was "the same." Formulated as you did it, the phenomenon turns out to have an aspect which does not appear when I say it. This aspect leads you to something further, to which I don't follow you. And my formulation, too, may show something yours hides. The two formulations reveal two different aspects of the "same" phenomenon. Their difference was not "only" logical or verbal. Now again, you can show me the experienceable aspect your formulation lifts out from our phenomenon, and I can show you mine. So this is simply another instance of two different phenomena, this time two aspects of the "same" phenomenon. Different aspects, if experienceable, are again two phenomena. Again we agree.

It cannot all be so simple, but there are some great advantages even in this simple version. If we were to consider at each step of our procedure, just what experienceable aspect makes us want to hold on to our formulation, then (even though every phenomenon is always formulated or attention-held in *some* way) we could always find just what experienceable difference either formulation makes. The exact aspects of the difference made, which we care about, might again have to be formulated variously. Again we could see what if any difference might be lost or gained. If we disagreed again, it would not be the same issue. I assume, here, that we would not each be privately committed to some logical model which we would reapply stubbornly to each sub-aspect. Rather, as phenomenologists, we would be committed only to the phenomena or experienceable aspects, not to any model. The sub-aspects would not themselves be mere instances of our issue, because experience is not a scheme of particulars under one set of generalities. Therefore, even if we do again differ on how to formulate the sub-aspect which is our difference, and even if the further difference matters to us, it will not be the same issue.

It is in exactly this sense that Heidegger and other phenomenological philosophers must be understood. It is in exactly this sense that they intended to be understood. There are always many spots in these philosophers where they tell us not to take the model aspects of one of their formulations too literally. How then do they want us to take these formulations? In terms of the experienceable aspects which the formulations reveal—and not at all as implying the loss of any other experienceable aspects which other formulations might reveal.

But doesn't this do away with formulation altogether, as if logical inconsistencies are all right, and the whole point of thinking clearly might be lost? Not at all! Formulations, and concepts and logic have their use precisely in the power to be precise, to make logical differences, and by differences to point at something experiential that is being missed.

In emphasizing the difference between logical formulations and experiential aspects I am emphasizing the need for both, and the irreplaceable role which each plays in regard to the other.

Only after we have specified the experienceable aspect, can different formulations which don't affect it be considered equivalent for the time being. Or, if the different formulations make differences in "it," the discovered further aspects will again need specifying. This does not only resolve the difference so that we can proceed, but rather it gives us the experiential aspects which our assertions really aim at. Only after that, is there the systematic possibility of considering different formulations equivalent, rather than endlessly pursuing them and losing what we were really concerned about.

That we can set two different formulations at an equivalence in respect to some *directly referred to* aspect is a principle of importance. I call it *functional equality*. It applies only at some given point in a discussion or line of thought, and continues to apply only as long as no experienceable differences made by the two formulations matter. We may think now that they don't matter, but they may later on in a discussion or line of thought, and then must be dealt with. Or that may never happen. For a given point or line of thought the two formulations may function in the same way, in respect of some "same" phenomenon, or aspect.

I also point to the basic phenomenological willingness to forgo implications that are *only* logical or conceptual. I assume two thinkers who will always be willing to drop "merely formulational differences or implications" in favor of what the experienceable aspect itself implies. Is such a distinction really possible, and clear?

At any point in any line of thought it is possible to proceed in two different ways. For example, if you have just said something I think is nonsense, there are two ways I can respond: I can point out to you at length why what you said offends various truths or logical relations. Or I can ask you to say differently the sense you thought you were making, since obviously you did not experience yourself talking nonsense. In the second case you will come up with a different formulation than the first one which failed to work for me; it will be a fresh alternative formulation of the sense you were trying to make. If this succeeds and a new aspect of experience is now given me, we can leave it for another time to determine if your first formulation did offend truth or logic, or if it was a matter of my limitation that the first version did not work for me.

Similarly, I myself may find that some formulation keeps a hold of some important experienceable aspect for me, even though I already see that the formulation otherwise offends various other concerns, which I also retain. Shall I discard the experiential aspect which this untenable formulation holds on to, for me? No, I will not think the experienceable aspect lost, just because this formulation cannot long stand. I will limit the formulation just to pointing, and if I can really not devise a better one (which should always be possible), I will apologize for it and warn others away from its erroneous logical implications which I don't intend.

But if I were following the logical, rather than the experiential next step, I would be led away to that which I don't intend.

Every formulation has conceptual implications which one does not intend, and if seen, would warn others away from. (This does not mean that *all* its logical power is unused, as I shall show in a moment.)

Public discourse is much given to the rule that logic *alone* entitles one to further steps. When someone is shown that a set of statements offends logic, it must be withdrawn. Of course, privately the person may retain the original sense, and especially from a phenomenological viewpoint, the person can know that the form has been scuttled, not the point. But the usual rules do not permit answering: you have sunk my statement, but not my point.

For example, my own initial conceptual approach here was in terms of two distinctions: "formulation vs. experienceable aspect" and "same vs. different." But now, in discussing what was implied in my simple version and in "functional equality" and in proceeding from an experienceable aspect, what has become of my same vs. different model?

Is a given experienceable aspect really either "same" or "different"? It can be *same* for some time and then turn out to have importantly *different* aspects lifted out in it. It is both the same and different. If I were doing dialectic, this would be the occasion to move to a new *conceptual* distinction. But I rather point to the *more specific sub-aspects* we each have. These make our phenomenon neither the same nor different. Once we see them we will not disagree, because: there they are. We will then also see how each affects our discourse, or is irrelevant. Sameness and difference do not univocally apply to experience in the process of being formulated.

Are two different *formulations* the same, or not? It depends on whether there is an experienceable aspect to which they both refer, and which leads to the same next step. If so, they are "the same," although different.

Clearly, I have not let my logical categories determine my own steps, but rather my steps have changed the logical categories "same" and "different." I have given several different experienceable cases to which they can differently refer.

Thus we can always let the experienceable aspect lead us, and if different formulations let us have the same aspect leading in the same way, we can leave it to more traditional philosophers, or to another time, to examine further the formulational differences for their own sake.

But formulations and logical implications must not be taken *too* lightly. If different verbal and conceptual formulations really came down to totally the same thing, if they did not each have their own type of meaning-power, then they could not effectively lift out phenomena. It is only because of their peculiar conceptual precision that a given formulation can do something, others not or differently. In regard to this aspect of "different" formulations, we need their differences sharp. The activity of clarifying them for their own sake is important also for experiential thought. But that doesn't mean that we cannot use their very sharpness to let us see, by the experienceable aspects they lift out, which of their differences needs to be pursued, and which (always many) others we can ignore, to let you and me get to each of our experiential points.

Thus my own first set of logical categories, "same" and "different," have now received the kind of reference to specific experienceable aspects, which should let us see at least some respects in which we do and don't need to assert that different formulations and phenomena are different, or can be the same.

My other conceptual distinction was "formulation" versus "experienceable aspect." These never were clearly distinct in my discussion, since I began by asking what the degree of their independence might be. So we need not be surprised if these two also have come to refer variously to more specific experienceable aspects, rather than being two conceptual meanings. Nevertheless I spoke of "them" and organized my discussion of the problem with "them."

These were of course never simply independent; rather, I asked what the degree of their independence might be. I began by saying that if there are disagreements among phenomenologists at all, then phenomena are not simply independent, just to be looked at and reported on. But if they are totally dependent on formulations, then there cannot be such a thing as phenomenology. But these two categories did not determine my discussion; rather, my discussion can now aid us in defining these two better.

What we are seeking are the experienced respects in which they are dependent and independent upon each other.

If one can have an experienceable aspect even with an untenable formulation which mostly points, and some of whose logical implications must be disregarded, does this mean that one has the experienceable aspect quite alone and independently? It certainly seems to be most convenient for my argument, if that is so. However, we point by means of this otherwise inadequate formulation. Pointing, too, is a function which words serve in regard to experienceable aspects, if only the word "this." It is a kind of formulating (see *ECM*, chap. 4).

The independence of the experienceable aspect is at any rate possible only after it has been lifted out by some formulation. (I want to argue that events too, not only words, can "lift out" an experienceable aspect, and such events perform a formulating or symbolizing *function*. To pursue this would lead us to think about formulations as instances of a larger class. I cannot deal with this direction here.) *Once a formulation has lifted out or specified or pointed to an aspect, then we can devise other formulations to do so as well, and we can see if different sub-aspects of importance are made thereby.* In both regards *the aspect demonstrates its independence* to this degree, from its initial formulation which gave birth to it: *it can function in other formulations, and it can also give rise to sub-aspects which the initial formulation could not have led to.* Such aspects could arise from a different formulation, or even from the aspect itself as soon as it is found. We might be grateful to the formulation which first led us to the aspect, but the formulation cannot limit what the aspect can further lead to. I have done just that many times in this discussion already.

It is in the power of the *movement of steps* from one experience-formulation pair to another that the independence respect of an aspect lies. We need not assume, therefore, that experience comes packaged in aspects. Formulations, events, attention, affect what will be found as aspects and sub-aspects. Nevertheless, experienced aspects have exactly this kind of independence: *they* can lead to steps, to sub-aspects, which *their own first formulations* cannot lead to, and they can lead to other formulations than the initial one could lead to.

So long as one only moves one step, supposedly from experience to formulation, as is so often claimed in phenomenology, any independent grounding by phenomena must seem simple-minded, as a claim. Only if we examine kinds of *steps*, can we see the experienceable phenomenon exerting independent grounding functions, determining what a formulation just now means (meaning by "means" how it functions in relation to experienceable aspects one moves to, and from), what formulations are equivalent, and if different, what the differences are, which result, as steps further.

II

I must now give some examples and convey much more directly what an experienceable aspect is, and how it is always capable of leading to many more and different aspects.

Also, I spoke of the possibility, which always obtains, of formulating whatever one of us is saying in some different way. Another person can always say: "Yes, I've got what you mean, but I don't like the way you're putting it!" thus showing the difference between experienceable aspect and formulation. And we can always reformulate "it" and then also see what different aspects that further makes, or loses.

The inherent capacity of anything experienced to lead to further and different aspects is grossly underestimated in most discussions.

Especially today in an urban society, the usual routines of personal interaction and language are usually insufficient to deal with most of our situations, so that almost anything we experience far exceeds the existingly formed actions and phrases.

Let me ask you for a moment, in a personal way, to recall one of your own situations in which you are not sure what to do. Whatever you have said to yourself about it, it has also more. What you have said may be quite accurate, but it leaves—does it not?—some felt sense of unresolvedness or confusion which is of some importance. Your actions when you take them, or some next thing you say or think *may* resolve this felt sense of "more," or it may not. You would know the difference quite clearly.

Heidegger discusses such a thing under the heading of *Befindlichkeit* and Sartre calls it "nausea," meaning not what that ironic term implies, but our constant sense of ourselves in our world. These authors bring this up quite late in their treatment (Sartre only broaches it more than three hundred pages into *Being and Nothingness*). But isn't it quite basic to how every simple step is taken in phenomenology? Is it not present whenever we make any point? *No formulation captures all of what we mean, why we say it, why we say it just now, in this regard, and so on.* Even if it did, a little further discussion or further occurrences would reveal further aspects of it.

Compare now the potential complexity of this "more," which we experience, with the thinness of our usual discussions! Someone, for example, has introduced into ethics the distinction between "causes and reasons." It is argued that human conduct has reasons, not causes. We wish immediately to know exactly what aspects are intended to be different under these two words, isn't that so? Suppose now, it is said that causes follow by physical necessity, while reasons are ethical justifications. This difference can now lead us further. The intention probably was to mark out the field of ethics, leaving causes out. We might agree, depending upon where the argument leads. Even so (say we agree that ethics concerns "reasons" or justifications), we can also attempt to find further experienceable aspects within what is assigned to ethics as reasons: for example, it happens that at first we are unaware of why we want to do something, we feel "caused." We can still do it or not, so *in that sense* our doing it still has "reasons," not "causes." Yet, when we do it, and then later discover why we did, these reasons will feel different to us than had we known and chosen on that basis. So now we have another differentiated experienceable aspect, which "causes versus reasons" helped us find. It isn't the same as the one intended by the first formulator. We can rename it to keep ourselves clear.

But there are times, perhaps often, when there are not one or two reasons, but a whole texture of facets, more than can be sorted out.

Then there are not even "reasons," but a "texture": (I mean, when we are inclined to pursue a whole chain, such as: "and if I didn't do that, then I'd have to do this other which I don't want to because it never works for me, which I know is my own weakness, well not exactly, but part of it is I can't fake such and such, which has to do with this way that I get when I do, which is because . . ." and so on!)

Is it not clear how poor mostly are the concepts and formulations with which we try to substitute for experiencings?

And if formulations are "thin," and yet they partly determine what we find, then would we not want to return to and hold on, at each step, to the experienceable aspect? Only so can we determine whether we agree or not, at a given point, and just what is being said at a given point, and just what use will be made of what is being said at a given point. But an aspect *must come* as *it* will.

Also, in our present age of mass literacy, it is becoming possible for us to articulate our own unique experience. Until now, for most people, their own experience could be articulated and reacted to only by means of routine expressions, or even literary expressions made by poets and novelists, which did not at all describe the specificity of their own experience. That was always left as a felt darkness that had to remain an unknown "more." And yet, just therein are we the persons we are. One needs, and today can not only take a step from experience to language, but also back again, to see the difference made, the aspect found, which then is more specific than the bit of language, and whose further aspects can be further found.

III

I must now answer a number of possible objections, and in the course of doing so a number of further aspects of formulating experience will arise.

(1) Does what I have said imply that experience as such has no order of its own, this formulation lifts out this, and another formulation something else?

No, experience has *more order* than all our schemes put together, but it is an order of its own, different in kind, an "organic" order. If we wish, we can think of experience as already having the structure of the living body's life process, and of evolution's further elaboration of that life process, and culture's elaborations of that, to which must be added our own elaborations in our personal ways of living. So *it* gives us the aspect that *comes* in response to a formulation.

Thus there need not be a mystery why experience, even before we formulate in words, is not just any old putty but is more organized than any of our formulational systems.

(2) Did I say that this organization awaits us there, finished and packaged?

No, what we lift out is a product of the great order that is there, and our further lifting.

(3) Do formulations just drop on us somehow as a primitive other "pole"? Don't different formulational models themselves arise from experience in some way? Did I assume a basic two-pole model?

No, language and theoretical patterns of thinking, conceptual models, are also cultural products and develop as further elaboration of experience.

When we formulate experience, that is by no means the first time experience and language have met! Experience is the living process in the cultural world.

Although experiential organization is much broader than that of language, linguistic sequences are part of—and the means of—many distinctions of inter-human situations and interactions. Therefore, they are also part of our bodily feelings, and can reemerge from them.

(4) Did we destroy the universality that philosophy is concerned with? Are we not grounding ourselves always in just this person's unique experience of this unique moment in the discussion?

The very meaning of "universality" changes, is it not lost altogether? If a formulation, conceptual statement, i.e., something universal, can give rise to many different experienceable aspects, and "means" them, is anything ever universal?

And, if this is lost, do not "formulations" cease to have any use or character altogether, since "formulating" after all, implies for anyone hearing or reading it?

No—universality is not lost, but its nature does change:

The old meaning of "universality" was the notion of "classes" which include under themselves the "particulars," which are instances of the universal. The particulars are supposed to have no nature of their own other than the universal's nature, except that the particulars are concrete existents, embodiments, instances.

Husserl uses that model (early in *Ideas*) when he says that any experience can be considered as universal. One need only consider it as an instance of its kind.

I would retain Husserl's statement, but I would also go another step to another experienceable aspect: that one can take any experience as an instance of *many* kinds—all of them "'its' kinds." Always many can be quite new. Once a kind has been formulated, it can lead to other instances each of which can further instance many other kinds (*ECM*, chap. 5; see also "Experiential Phenomenology" in this volume).

The difference is, of course, that I am considering an aspect as a partly creative product (of an experience that has its own character and a formulation that also has its own).

This comes from not assuming that nature or experience are an already divided set of unique particular entities, units, univocal bits, a static set. And this assertion is not only a refusal to accept an assumption, it also points to an experienceable aspect for anyone who directly formulates experience, in steps (not just in one step), and moves from one to a further and still further aspect formulation of "the same" experience, which is thereby kept as "that" experience and also allows further aspects to arise from it.

Communication between people, it now seems, is not really a simple locating or reminding someone of some universal they already have. Rather, it is a process in which an aspect of experience comes to be, which was not before differentiated as such.

You create an aspect in me, and I in you, which we did not have before, as such. In fact, if communication always had to be only of what we already have—it would not be of much interest!

In this way universality is not lost, but it alters. Instead of being a static structure shared by everyone always already, it is *the capacity to become shared*. And it becomes shared by a creating in the other.

It now follows, startlingly: *the more unique* to you (private, swampy, autistic-seeming) the experience is that you formulate, *the more universally significant* it will be to all of us because your formulation will create more new aspects in us, and any other person.

(5) Are not "experiential aspects" and "formulation" now interchangeable terms? An aspect is always formulated, even pointing is a kind of formulating. And formulations are to be taken in terms of the aspects they lift out.

No, when we shift from a formulation to a pointing, and thence to a further formulation, then the aspect shows its difference from formulation (or also when we reformulate or go further).

(6) Does this not always push any decision out to an indefinite future? What the aspect is depends on the further aspects to be found, and so also the formulation depends on that? Could one argue that any decision is always only in the future?

No, just the opposite: a formulation can be used definitively, if one has the aspect to which it refers, or which it formulates, for the time being, for this juncture in this discussion. The method is one of stopping the endlessness, which non-experiential methods do not stop, but only ignore. (I mean that the thinness of the usual arguments does not deal at all with the further creative potential of experience, it simply substitutes thin patterns that come to their own end.)

(7) But now, is not everything dependent on what will be said to "matter," or be "relevant" to the present juncture of the discussion? What if we disagree on that, or are in doubt?

Whether an aspect is relevant, or not, just at this point, is again a question of experienceable aspects. If I can be shown what aspect of our topic this affects, and then you say it is relevant and I don't agree, we are working on different aspects of our topic. We can show each other the two topics. Or, you will have shown me how what I now care about *is affected*, since I did not at first see the relevance. I will have been shown a new aspect of *my* topic. Relevance works as phenomena do.

Truth and relevance are not only up to formulation, but also to the fact that in response not just anything but exactly this aspect is revealed; comes. This is *not* arbitrary, *nor* mere logic alone.

(8) But isn't it still true that different "models" or approaches or methods in philosophy or theory will give different results?

Yes—but if we keep a hold not only of these formulations, but also the directly sensed experience of what we are investigating, then we can each time see just exactly what aspects each model reveals.

If we wish, we can *then* formulate those aspects further in our own preferred type of model. And if that makes further differences, we can examine the relevance of these, as well.

I am radically asserting that formulations are *not* constitutive of phenomena in the simple sense that has been assumed in a relativistic viewpoint. What a model first shows me as something, need *not* be used to further formulate it. Both that aspect and the further aspects I find, can be formulated in any type of formulation (and the difference which may matter, can also again be formulated in any type). It has been falsely assumed that aspects of experience become the property of the type of formulations that show them to us, but they do not.

Once that is realized, one may work with many theories, many models, many types of philosophy, and expect always to discover some aspects one will be glad to have discovered. One can then formulate them in whatever single model one likes, or actually employ several, as one wishes.

(9) Did I emphasize the experiential at the expense of thought, logic, formulation communication, and conversation?

No! I have wanted equally to emphasize the independent power of both, or else experience could not thereby be discriminated. I have wanted to restore to thinking the immense world-building power that it has whenever it grips into what it is about, so that this is revealed in its concreteness.

It is not my intention that thought and formulation be downgraded, but just the opposite, that their effects should be attended to. Many people, seeing the thinness of most of our theories, choose to accept thin thought as the only kind. It was my intention to point out noticeable, experienceable marks of thought that overcomes this thinness.

An example of this is my looking forward to a discussion of these ideas. I know that the process of discussion, alone, can show me both how far I have really formulated what I think I have, and can show me aspects I would not want to miss. I want to improve thought and develop another self-conscious step of this human power. Throughout, I emphasize a process of steps, not just one step.

(10) Even if others disagree with me, will they not do so in the way I said? Therefore, did I not "lock" us into *my* formulation, now? Naturally, I will answer that it is only a first brief formulation and can be discarded while we retain what it pointed to—but doing this discarding and retaining will be in accord with *my* model, will it not?

You can further formulate what you retain and do it differently and with different further aspects. But isn't that now also part of *my* model? For example, you can formulate differently than my assertions about experience being organismic, and still deal with the same or different aspects of how experience and its environmental context are related, and yet transcend each other. But however differently you do it, won't it be just an instance of my saying that you can indeed do it differently?

But the point is not that we must find a model that isn't a model, or that we must be able to deny anything we ever said. Because of the difference between formulations and experiences, any *phenomenological* assertion is never going to turn out just plain false, but neither does that mean that further steps are then *nothing but* instances of such not-plain-false-statements. In phenomenology no model is ultimate in that way, nor totally nonultimate, and that is fine. Of course, even that statement can and should be gone on from, and much further.

Notes

1. This essay was presented at the annual meeting of the Heidegger Circle in Chicago in 1976. At that time, I was aware that much more would need to be said and explored before this method would recommend itself, and I looked forward to the circle's discussion both to clarify some points and to teach me some others. The present revision has indeed profited from the discussion at

the meeting. In this chapter I cite Martin Heidegger, *Being and Time*, trans. John Macquarrie and Edward Robinson (London: SCM, 1962). [As noted earlier, Gendlin sometimes modifies this translation to suit the context of his own discussion.]

2. Eugene T. Gendlin, "What Are the Grounds of Explication? A Basic Problem in Linguistic Analysis and in Phenomenology," *Monist* 49, no. 1 (January 1965): 137–64.

2

What Are the Grounds of Explication? A Basic Problem in Linguistic Analysis and in Phenomenology

In this chapter I will attempt to discuss linguistic analysis and phenomenology accurately so that the adherents of each can agree with what I say, and yet the discussion of each method must also be understandable to the adherents of the other. If I can really do that, the basic similarities will appear. I will attempt to state some propositions that apply to both frames of reference. The similarities which these propositions state are basic aspects of philosophic method, and they also pose a major problem.

The problem, as I see it, concerns the grounds of explication. In both methods the main assertions are founded neither on formal logic nor on observed relationships. They are based on an "implicit" knowledge (if we call that "knowledge"): on what is "implicit" in experiencing, living, and acting in situations. How are philosophic statements founded on something "implicit"? Such statements are called "explications." What is the basis for asserting and evaluating them? What criteria are possible for such statements?

The problem, as I will try to show, does not lead backward to a reassumption of "external" criteria or constructs, but rather opens a new area of philosophic study.

I will not generalize away the differences between various linguistic analysts and between different phenomenological philosophers. (In fact, these differences bring home the problem of criteria.) I will limit myself to specific formulations from one philosopher in each mode. Generalizations of a lowest common denominator are not really usable without their detail. On the other hand, even one bit of detailed discussion, if closely examined, displays the method. I will use a few excerpts from the writings of Austin, and then from those of Sartre.[1]

Propositions applicable to both methods will be formulated first as they arise from my excerpts of linguistic analysis. In this way the propositions will be connected to their detailed employment there, and yet phenomenologists will recognize them. Later, in my discussion of Sartre, I refer back to them. Thereby I may be able to show how the methods are similar and pose a similar problem of explication.

If indeed the methods are similar in the ways I try to show, then my later discussion of explication can be considered an instance of either method and should carry both methods forward into a new and central problem area. I realize that this is a considerable program, but if the methods are specifically similar in this respect, then the program is possible.

I

I turn first to that kind of philosophizing which proceeds from ordinary language. Austin approaches a question of moral philosophy as follows:

> A study of . . . "excuses" . . . will contribute in special ways . . . to moral philosophy in particular. (*PP* 125)

> When . . . do we "excuse" conduct? . . . In general, the situation is one where someone is *accused* of having done something. . . . Thereupon he, or someone on his behalf, will try to defend his conduct or to get him out of it. One way of going about this is to admit flatly that he, X, did do that very thing, A, but to argue that it was a good thing. . . . To take this line is to *justify* the action. . . . A different way of going about it is . . . to argue that it is not quite fair or correct to say *baldly* "X did A" . . . perhaps he was under somebody's influence, or was nudged . . . it may have been partly accidental, or an unintentional slip . . . briefly . . . we admit that it was bad but don't accept full, or even any responsibility. (*PP* 123–24)

In this excerpt Austin makes some discriminations: defense by justification of an action is distinguished from defense by disclaiming responsibility. Then different kinds of disclaimers of responsibility are distinguished.

The excerpt shows that the question of responsibility (think of the traditional question of "free will") is here discussed in a context. Linguistic analysis operates in the context of specific situations ("perhaps he was under somebody's influence, or was nudged").

CHAPTER 2

Proposition 1: *Philosophic terms are examined and used in the context of living and acting in the world. The use of each term marks a discrimination in that context.*

What one cannot do (is advised not to do) in this mode of philosophy is to work with abstractions purely theoretically. For example, "responsibility" cannot be discussed in the manner of the "free will problem" of some traditional philosophies: "voluntarily" and "involuntarily" are not "contraries" such that one of them always applies to any action.

> Given any adverb of excuse, such as "unwittingly" or "spontaneously" or "impulsively," it will not be found that it makes good sense to attach it to any and every verb of "action" in any and every context: for example, "voluntarily" and "involuntarily": we may join the army or make a gift voluntarily, we may hiccough or make a small gesture involuntarily. . . . "Voluntarily" and "involuntarily," then, are not opposed in the obvious sort of way. . . . The "opposite," or rather "opposites," of "voluntarily" might be "under constraint" of some sort, duress or obligation or influence; the opposite of "involuntarily" might be "deliberately" or "on purpose." (*PP* 138–39)

If you ask about a phrase in this chapter whether I wrote it "voluntarily," you imply something rather unusual about my professional circumstances or about my editor. But you don't imply the contrary (you imply something totally different) if you ask whether I wrote that phrase "involuntarily" (perhaps it slipped out and went unnoticed).

If we examine each term as tied to the circumstances its use discriminates, then we are not examining the terms as constructs. *As constructs* these two terms above would be contraries. *As used*, they discriminate different and not directly related aspects possible in living.

But what of the vast main body of actions which involve neither of these special aspects? Are they done "voluntarily" or not? Is one "responsible" in general for actions (as per "free will") or not? Obviously, the question is nonsense if one anchors the terms "voluntarily" and "involuntarily" each to their special contexts.

Does this mean that the famous and rich problem of human freedom has been avoided by a sleight of hand? Not at all. The problem has become many more specific problems, anchored to discriminations in the world in which we live and act. If we ground each term in the aspects it marks, we can also discuss "the detail of the complicated internal machinery we use in 'acting'—the receipt of intelligence, the appreciation of the situation, the invocation of principles, the planning, the control of execution and the rest" (*PP* 127).

If we proceed in this way, nothing need be lost.

But, using such distinctions, can one *conclude* anything on a question, for example, a question of moral responsibility? Austin offers an example: Finney, an attendant in a mental hospital, ran scalding hot water into a bathtub while a patient was in the tub, killing the patient. Was Finney "responsible"? Austin quotes his attorney:

> If the prisoner, knowing that the man was in the bath, had . . . turned on the hot instead of the cold water, I should have said there was gross negligence; for he ought to have looked to see. But . . . he had told the deceased to get out, and *thought he had got out.* If you think that indicates gross carelessness, then you should find the prisoner guilty of manslaughter. But if you think it *inadvertence* not amounting to culpability—i.e., what is properly termed an *accident*—then the prisoner is not liable. (*PP* 145)

For Austin the excerpt illustrates a "very free use of a large number of terms of excuse . . . several as though they were . . . equivalent when they are not," thus showing that "ordinary use" in people we observe often needs sharper discriminating. But the excerpt also shows that discussion *and conclusions* are based *on the discriminations marked by our uses of terms.*

One could now argue that "free will" is "assumed" in this excerpt, since it concerns the fact that Finney didn't "choose" the hot water tap knowing the patient was in the tub; we seem not to question here—but rather to assume—that, in general, a man *can* choose. Is there a general question of freedom "above and beyond" (or "underneath") the specific discriminations of various kinds of ordinary acting and responsibility?

By saying or asking about "voluntarily" we imply aspects of coercion in the situation *within* the ordinary human world (not some "underlying" constant coercion of "determinism"). By saying "deliberately," we discriminate something noticeable in an action (not some "underlying" construct of "freedom").

Proposition 2: *There are no entities, constructs, or determinants assumed to be "behind," "beneath," or "over and above" the world in which we live and act. There are no "external" principles or criteria.*

But if there are no more basic, underlying principles against which to evaluate language, must linguistic analysis simply accept the "prisons of the grammarians," the assumptions in how language happens to slice and render the world? Not at all.

To examine and evaluate assumptions, constructs, and "models" is a main task of linguistic analysis. But this critique does not invoke superordinate principles. Rather, the critique leads models back to (and limits their use to) the specific circumstances which their use can mark. For example, take the assumption (the "model") of "free will" and of "all actions."

> "Doing an action," as used in philosophy, is a highly abstract expression—it is a stand-in used in place of any . . . verb with a personal subject, in the same sort of way that "thing" is a stand-in for any . . . noun substantive, and "quality" a stand-in for the adjective . . . notoriously it is possible to arrive at . . . an oversimplified metaphysics from the obsession with "things" and their "qualities." In a similar way . . . we fall for the myth of the verb. (*PP* 126)

> We take *some very simple action*, like shoving a stone, . . . and use *this* . . . as our model in terms of which to talk about other actions and events . . . even when these other actions are . . . much more interesting . . . than the acts originally used in constructing the model. (*PP* 150)

> To say we acted "freely" . . . is to say only that we acted *not* unfreely, in one or another of the many heterogeneous ways of so acting (under duress, or what not). . . . In examining all the ways in which each action may not be "free," i.e., the cases in which it will not do to say simply "X did A," we may hope to dispose of the problem of Freedom. (*PP* 128)

Proposition 3: *Arguments are not conducted or evaluated critically on general theoretical grounds. Instead, assumptions and models are critically evaluated in terms of what they discriminate in living and acting in the world.*

An overextended use of an expression is called "misleading" even when perfectly sound logical implications were drawn from it by logical necessity. To formulate what the use of an expression discriminates, we are not led by its logical implications, but rather by the "implications" *of its use.* Not the expression as such, but its use, "implies" the discriminated aspects in situations.

Let p stand for an expression. We say p only when facets A, B, C obtain. Therefore, *when we say p*, we imply facets A, B, C.

Austin writes: "not p . . . but *asserting p* implies . . . By asserting p I *give it to be understood* that . . ." (*PP* 32).

Thus the main assertions of linguistic analysis concern an "implication" by an activity (*using* words).

Proposition 4: *The main philosophic assertions state "implications" of a different sort than logical implications. They state "implications" of an activity.*

And now the question of criteria: when (as in most of its central assertions) linguistic analysis states what aspects of the world the use of a word marks, that is, what the use "implies," how may we tell when such statements have correctly (or adequately, or well) formulated these circumstantial aspects?

The question is illustrated by a celebrated disagreement between Austin and Ryle in a case of this sort.[2] Ryle wrote: "In their most ordinary employment 'voluntary' and 'involuntary' are used . . . as adjectives applying to actions which ought not to be done. We discuss whether someone's action was voluntary or not only when the action seems to have been his fault" (cited in Cavell, p. 175). There is a contradiction in the fact that to "join the army or make a gift" (Austin's examples of when we use "voluntarily") are not actions "which ought not to be done."

What criteria are there for statements that explicate such "implications" as these?

Since not the word, but its use, does the "implying," our question of criteria depends on what sort of "implication" an activity like using can have. As we already said, it differs from logical "implication": "'implies' must be given a special sense" (*PP* 32). "It is not an 'analytic' implication. If it were analytic, then whenever x is y, y *must* be either a part of *x or* not any part of it . . . (as) *would* be the merest common sense if 'meanings' were things in some ordinary sense which contained parts in some ordinary sense" (*PP* 30).

The "model" of "analytic" implication is criticized by leading it back to just those situations it discriminates when used properly, situations where there are "parts" which can be "included." Austin calls it a "shabby working model" which *"fails to fit the facts that we really* wish to talk about" (*PP* 30). His italics in this sentence indicate that the circumstances of using a word do not have given "parts."

Proposition 5: *The activities whose "implications" the philosophy states cannot be assumed to consist of parts or units in some ordinary sense.*

But neither are these "synthetic" statements. They are not based on a survey of how most people use a word, nor would such a survey be pertinent. Most people (like Finney's counsel) use language sloppily, or not as sharply as it can be used.

Let us treat statements of "implications" of use like any other expressions. We want to examine the use of such statements by philosophers, so let us see what they do, and when.

What do linguistic analysts do with such assertions? They formulate "rules" for when we should use expressions. Who is entitled to formulate such rules? The answer is: the native speaker of a language. By "native" is marked the sort of learning which doesn't occur from a book but rather, learning in a context of living. We have learned language not as labels for rigid objects as might be pictured in a book, each with word below, but through living in contexts in which words are used. Thus, explication statements occur when "native" speakers spell out specific aspects of the contexts in which they have learned to use words. Such statements spell out a learning (or "knowing") which is not already cut up into the sort of "parts," or units or variables we use in "spelling out." The learning and "knowing" of language by a native speaker (his learning or "knowing" the circumstances) is "implicit": Austin calls this a learning of "semantic conventions (implicit, of course), about the way we use words *in situations*" (*PP* 32).

Thus the use of the word "implicit" in this context marks several aspects:

First, it marks a relation between an activity (like using) *and a statement*, such that what is called "implicit" is "in" the activity but not in the form of the spelled-out units of statement.

Proposition 6: *The statements are "implicit" in the activity, i.e., not in the sense that its verbal units, "unit-meanings," or "representations" are "in" it.*

Second, "implicit" marks a relation between activity and *world* again in a sense other than as concrete or represented things "in" it.

Proposition 7: *Aspects of the world (contexts) are "implicit" in the activity, that is, not in the sense that things (or images of them) are "in" the activity.*

Third, our *knowing* when to use a word (our having learned to use it) is said to be "implicit" in the activity of using the word (and in our habit or capacity to do so). This is the "native" knowledge which entitles us to make assertions about "when we should say . . ." If we did not call it "implicit," then the "knowledge" would be the sort we have after rules are formulated. But, we do not learn language by repeating explicit "rules" to ourselves.

Proposition 8: *We know "implicitly" what the main philosophic statements formulate, i.e., not in the sense of a knowledge separable from activity (or the capacity for the activity).*

We now see that explication statements are neither "analytic" nor "synthetic" for the same reason; "analytic" is used when there are already defined and separable units or parts (as in formal logic), and similarly, "synthetic" is used when there are already defined observation units (as in observing two "associated" traits). But we do not learn, know, or use language by knowing separate, defined, unitized "variables" of circumstances.

The linguistic analyst has learned what the use of a word might mark, but not as separate "synthetically" associated variables. He proposes exemplary sentences to himself in imagined contexts, and thereby he notices *newly specific* variables standing out, which may convince him that the example is right or impossible.[3]

Proposition 9: *Observation and experience cannot be assumed to be constituted of already given units, "variables."*

Austin emphasizes that explicating the circumstances of "use" is not merely a matter of observing already given variables. "Situations," "circumstances," "actions," the contexts in which we "use" language, are not given in already definite units (these would be reified verbal units). Austin says situations are capable of being "split up" along "various lines." For example, there is no hard-and-fast way of knowing what is "an" action: "what, indeed, are the rules for the use of 'the' action, an action, a 'part' or 'phase' of an action, and the like?" (*PP* 127). Austin indicates here that this problem must be dealt with by the same method as any other ("what are the rules for the use of 'the' . . . or 'an' . . . action"?). The criteria for unit actions would have to be found in the circumstances in which we use "the" or "a" or "an action."

But circumstances of using do not come in already defined unit variables. Thus, to explicate the "rules" (that is, circumstances of use) for units of action involves the same difficulty. Austin points this out and urges us not to take as our model-cases only those simple and relatively dull circumstances in which variables are already definite units, plainly and easily given:

> Is to think something, or to say something, or to try to do something, to do an action? . . . All "actions" are . . . equal, composing a quarrel with striking a match, winning a war with sneezing. (*PP* 127)

> What is *an* or *one* or *the* action? For we can generally split up what might be named as one action in several distinct ways, into different *stretches* or *phases* or *stages* . . . we can dismantle the machinery of the act, and

describe (and excuse) separately the intelligence, the appreciation, the planning, the decision, the execution and so forth. (*PP* 149)

It is in principle always open to us, along various lines, to describe or refer to "what I did" in so many different ways. (*PP* 148)

The method seems to offer no criteria to decide among those various "lines" along which to split up. Surely, we won't let it remain at this! Can it be that these philosophers uncritically use just whatever assumptions happen to creep into the "lines along which" they "split up" the circumstances of use and action?

Proposition 10: *The philosophical method has the problem that explications can be formulated along various lines. The explications depend partly on the given philosopher's mode of formulating, for which no justification is offered.*

Philosophic questions, after all, are just those which deal with the problems of the variety of modes of conceptualizing. Are we to say that ordinary language philosophy cannot deal with just this most properly philosophic type of question?

The problem is rounded out since "use" itself is *probably* an "action" (it depends on how we split it up!). Austin's treatment of action here is therefore an inquiry into the fundamentals of how one explicates use. Austin formulates some parameters along which use or action can be split up in a variety of ways: "stretch," "phase," "stage." But he does not intend to make this into a scheme similar to the many schemes philosophy already has.

Proposition 11: *No one scheme can be given to analyze the various parameters along which possible explications may differ. Such a scheme would only again follow models or constructs. The activities in their contexts are always more basic than any system of constructs or parameters.*

Austin wants us to notice that the context is not already "split up" into given, cut-and-dried variables.

When we examine what we should say when, what words we should use in what situations, we are looking again not *merely* at words . . . but also at the realities we use the word to talk about. (*PP* 130)

We need therefore to prise them [words] off the world, to hold them apart from and against it, so that we can realize their inadequacies . . . and can relook at the world without blinkers. (*PP* 130)

The world at which we "relook" is thus not assumed to be already structured out for us in some hypothetical way, or as words have seemed to cut it. In the direct examination of the circumstances when we use words, we "relook" without being bound by the prisons, cooky forms, and models of already given variables. Austin says we get "a sharpened perception" of phenomena "directly." The analysis of words' uses leads beyond the ways words *had* structured the world. We know the world "directly" and we say of this knowing that it is "implicit." Words have no "handy appendages," "meanings," or "denotations" corresponding to them (*PP* 29).

Proposition 12: *Since activities in context are more basic than constructs or pictures, the view of meaning and cognition differs from the traditional. No longer are contents, representations, denotations, pictures, objects as referents, considered basic. The representational view of meaning is overthrown. Neither world nor activities are assumed to be given already cut up into "handy denotations" or set, given "meanings."*

One cannot argue that we simply note what is "similar" in the different circumstances in which we use a word. Austin opposes the assumption that there is somewhere a denotion or "respect" in which situations are "similar" (*PP* 38). "The different meanings of the word 'head' will be related to each other in all sorts of different ways at once" (*PP* 43). And this is an argument not merely against real universals. It is an argument to show that the world of circumstances (in terms of which "use" is explicated) is not already split up into handily packaged variables or denotations.

A striking example is the case of "pleasure": "pleasures . . . *differ* precisely in the way in which they are pleasant. No greater mistake could be made than . . . of thinking that pleasure is always a single similar feeling, somehow isolable from the various activities which 'give rise' to it" (*PP* 41; Gendlin's italics).

There is no "similarity" given such that we might simply look to see what is "similar" when we use a certain word. For example, we must look "directly" to see the circumstances in which pleasure is termed one, and those in which it is termed by various subtle specific words. Thus, while our formulations of circumstances are not arbitrary (they are systematically related to our "looking directly"), neither are these formulations governed by given "similarities" or given variables of observation. The lesson is that the world cannot be given "similarities" or given variables of observation. The lesson is that the world cannot be assumed to consist of ready and waiting variables. Is Austin perhaps saying that our words and concepts do not necessarily conform to some *unknowable* nature of "things in themselves"? Just the opposite: he is saying that we may "relook directly" and that we know "implicitly."

Proposition 13: *The method involves a direct access to an experienced world not yet split into word-like or thing-like units or traits. The method systematically relates formulations of philosophy to this direct access.*

Is not this an attempt to leap out of the ancient problem of the variety of ways of construing anything? If we can "relook directly" at the circumstances words mark, and if thereby we think ourselves freed of presuppositions, assumptions, constructs, variables already isolated, etc.—if we insist that circumstances are not given with "intelligible essences" ("similarities") of their own—are we not at the mercy of whatever assumptions and selections creep into our formulations of this direct, "implicit" context?

How then can we evaluate a formulation (or worse: two differing ones)?

There is a seeming "vicious circle" in evaluating all terms and propositions by what circumstances their uses implies, and then basing statements of use-implications on what? On direct looking. But we assert that the world looked at "directly," "without blinkers," does not come marked out by heavy black lines into "variables," "kinds" of circumstance, "similarities." We assert thereby that direct looking cannot provide a foundation for the assumptions and varieties of formulations.

Proposition 14: *The ultimate statements of the philosophy are said to be "direct descriptions," formulating what is already "implicit" in certain human activities in the situational world. Yet, it is expressly denied that what we "look at directly" has the structure that various formulations employ. Thus one both asserts and denies that the structure and assumptions of descriptions inhere in the directly looked-at.*

But if no ultimate structure is "given," then why should we need for it to be? There must be a positive view of this seeming "vicious circle." We must accept that explication is not "based on" something "implicit," through a correspondence of structure, and we must examine what the relationship is which is here called: "based on."

To do so we must examine what we do when we explicate.

II

Phenomenologists will have recognized that each of my "propositions" is basic also to their method. But I have not yet presented phenomenology so that linguistic analysts could appreciate how these propositions apply in it. Also, I have not yet shown that the problem of explication statements is central also for phenomenology.

Linguistic analysts wish to limit discussions to precise formulations. Since the method (as I hope I have shown) centrally involves something "implicit," i.e., something not formulated, they find it difficult to describe their method. Phenomenologists choose the opposite order: they begin by pointing to something unthematized, pre-objective, preconceptual, experienced and lived but not explicitly known.

This difference in where the two methods begin leads to characteristically different common misunderstandings of each: linguistic analysis can seem "trivial," concerned only with extant words and linguistic conventions. Phenomenology can seem "fuzzy," concerned only with unspeakable unknowables.

These characteristic misunderstandings point up that these methods involve a *relationship between* formulation and the not yet formulated. One mode is misunderstood as using *only* what is already formulated, the other as using *only* the inveterately unformulable.

It is well, therefore, to say of phenomenology first that it formulates, explicates, "lifts out," renders in structures and discriminating description, aspects "implicitly known" to us, but not known explicitly till formulated.

Phenomenologists too, like to claim that their formulations are "direct descriptions." They like to say that they are not "explaining" (rendering in construct systems) but rather, "only" describing. Heidegger considered *his* formulations as explicating *the* basic structure "implicit" in living and acting, yet Husserl found them incorrect. Obviously not every aspect of these differing "descriptions" is directly founded on phenomena directly viewed by all (see Proposition 14).

Phenomenologists (like linguistic analysts) do not argue from theoretical models. All terms, propositions, and arguments are evaluated not by their theoretical structure but by what they "lift out" directly for us. If, as a result of the "description" we now notice something directly, the description has done its proper work.

Phenomenology depends upon our having, in addition to terms and constructs, something directly accessible ("phenomena") not assumed to be determined or patterned by assumed constructs. The method systematically relates philosophy to this directly accessible (Proposition 13).

What is the nature of directly accessible experience or phenomena? Husserl examined *only* "experience" but experiences are always "of" something. On phenomenological grounds Husserl rejected "psychic entities"—he just never found them. They were never directly noticeable. They are mere constructs of a certain kind of psychology. Experiences are always of what is seen, noticed, heard, aimed at, wanted, expected, desired, etc. Husserl found more and more that the whole human world is involved when one examines "only" experience.

It takes artificial constructs to say that our experiences are "in" us, that they are "subjective," that there is "another" world out there, in addition to "percepts" in us. Phenomenology is thus insistently not "subjective." The ordinary human world is "implicit" in experience. Heidegger and Sartre begin where Husserl gradually arrived. Experience ("consciousness") is "being in the world."

Sartre begins where our discussion of linguistic analysis ended, namely, the refusal to assume that our activities (action, use, thinking) or the world are constituted of thing-like entities, meaning-constructs, or representations.

> [It is an error to] make the psychic event a thing and to qualify it with "conscious" just as I can qualify this blotter with "red." (*BN* liv)
>
> We must renounce those neutral "givens" which, according to the system of reference chosen, find their place either "in the world" or "in the psyche." (*BN* li)
>
> Consciousness [of] pleasure is constitutive of the pleasure as the very mode of its existence . . . and not as a form which is imposed by a blow upon a hedonistic material. (*BN* liv)

The point—even the choice of an example—is similar to Austin's, as already cited. There are not already given meanings, units, or forms like "pleasure." Pleasure "is not a representation, it is a concrete event" (*BN* liv) (Proposition 12).

Sartre's emphasis is on the ongoing process, the activity. Representations ("objects of knowledge," "objects of reflection") occur only as "supported by" the concretely ongoing process. There can be consciousness of representations, but not representations of consciousness. All structures, concepts, representations, schemes, and laws are to be viewed as already involving a concretely ongoing activity, and thus they can never explain or picture it. "It is futile to invoke pretended laws of consciousness . . . a law is (an) object of knowledge; there can be consciousness of a law, not a law of consciousness" (*BN* lv). Thus the concrete activity remains always more basic than any representations or laws (had only through it) and hence no ultimate laws of it can be given (Proposition 11).

Sartre's constructs ("for itself" and "in itself," and various specific pairs of terms similar to this pair) stem from Hegel. They cannot be attributed to the very nature of consciousness or the world (except insofar as *with* these terms ... and with other terms, too ... we can "lift out" and bring to notice aspects of living which we *then* can see directly, that is, even without these terms).

You may therefore view Sartre somewhat as though he were a linguistic analyst who happened to like dialectical instead of British Empiricist types of terminology. Just as linguistic analysts are not party to British Empiricist assumptions although they often employ that philosophical tradition's terms, so Sartre is not fashioning an abstract dialectic although he uses dialectical terms.

But is there any phenomenological foundation for this choice of terms? If there were, would we not have to assume that there is something inherently dialectical (or, if we oppose it positively, something inherently nondialectical) in the phenomena and activities themselves? As we saw, no dialectical or other such "laws of consciousness" are possible. The concretely ongoing activities are always already involved even in the holding of such laws.

Thus there is no basis for the formulative assumptions and constructs with which the philosopher describes and discriminates (Proposition 10).

As we have seen, Sartre rejects thing-like "neutral givens," both "in the psyche" and "in the world." Phenomenologists assume no static "objects" or variables of observation "out there" or representations of them "in here." Hence observation is no mere "gaping at" (Heidegger's term) already given entities, variables, or perceptions which we need only "associate" (Proposition 9).

Activity-in-context replaces the view of given entities. Why not, then, fashion philosophic terms that are not static representations?

We must not call Sartre's type of term "ambiguous" if we are bothered only because it isn't a representational type of term. For this nonrepresentational character of human activity Sartre employs paired terms, designed for use in a movement from each to the other. Moving between these dialectically paired terms often has a paradoxical sound. Linguistic analysts should not miss their kinship to this mode of philosophizing because of a dislike for such terms. After all, linguistic analysts have not yet fashioned terms for this nonrepresentational aspect so central also to their method. Linguistic analysts bring home this same aspect, but they do it with examples—and these are also intentionally paradoxical, to point up the fact that activity in situations is not reducible to units, pictures, objects of knowledge, representations.

Both methods reject reasoning from constructs alone, and wish to

CHAPTER 2

evaluate constructs only in terms of what is done with them, how they are used, what they directly discriminate. It follows that we should not turn away from the type of constructs used before seeing what their use discriminates.

Sartre's dialectical terms do not make an abstract dialectical scheme. Traditional dialecticians object to Sartre's "dialectic" because it remains on the "first level" on which it starts. Sartre refuses to "raise" his contradictory terms to a "higher" (more abstract) synthesis. For Sartre, when Hegel's "being" and "nothingness" turn into each other and are then absorbed in a higher synthesis, they become "mere concepts" (*BN* 16).

A pair of Sartre's terms are never absorbed. In moving from one to the other and back, we discriminate an aspect of concrete living and moving that cannot be represented by single static representations.

Such a pair of terms gets at something Sartre finds in a great many aspects of human living: "scissiparity" (a word reminiscent of scissors, borrowed from biology where it is used for the amoeboid splitting of one organism into many). As Sartre uses it, *scissiparity* names something he sees over and over again: some facet of human activity which is really one, and yet appears to have two poles. The traditional misrepresentation of the activity represents the two poles as though they were entities or things, and the activity is thereby misconstrued or lost. Thus consciousness (an activity) always seemingly involves "*something* present to *something*," and there you have the temptation to describe it all in terms of thing-like contents in a mirror-like consciousness.

For example: "reflected–reflecting." When we reflect on our own consciousness, to be conscious "of" always involves also our ongoing process or activity. We must not take one term as just itself ("it isn't identical with itself," Sartre will say). Nor can we simply put both terms together, as two representations tied together. That gives only the poles, not the movement. The wish to have the totality *represented* must fail. The movement, the activity, the process, is being discriminated. "Thus by the sole fact that my belief is apprehended as belief, it is *no longer only belief*: that is, it is already no longer belief, it is troubled belief. Thus the . . . judgment 'belief is consciousness [of] belief' can under no circumstances be taken as a statement of identity" (*BN* 75). The phrase "no longer" illustrates the movement to which Sartre points with the pair "reflected–reflecting." These terms make no sense considered as separable somethings (as each "identical to itself").

On no account can we say that consciousness is consciousness or that belief is belief. Each of these terms refers to the other and passes into the other, and yet each term is different from the other. We have seen that neither belief nor pleasure nor joy can exist *before* being conscious (*BN* 75).

Sartre offers many other such pairs and with them he can characterize many detailed aspects of living, loving, smoking, doing, making, having, and so on. (Like linguistic analysis, phenomenology seems unphilosophical to some because of its many new discriminations of life detail.)

The pairs of terms avoid the pitfall of a representational analysis. But are not these pairs themselves representations? No, they are not. Are they the proscribed "laws of consciousness"? No, they are not. Applying the method to our own use of it, we have to accept that we use not what the terms picture but our own ongoing activity. This activity is not being represented by the terms. They "point to" this activity (much as examples in linguistic analysis do). Thus these philosophic terms are not "the" structure of consciousness, but "pointers" which newly discriminate concretely had aspects of what we do, have, notice. We ("implicitly") have and know what the terms get at, point to, and explicate. (Otherwise they would be again just another set of constructs, "laws," or "representations" of consciousness) (Proposition 8).

Our own concretely ongoing activity "sustains" concepts or laws or representations or structures or terms. It is always more basic than they and not made up out of them. "Consciousness is not produced as a particular instance of an abstract possibility but . . . it creates and supports its essence—that is, the synthetic order of its possibilities" (*BN* lv). These "possibilities" of action constitute the "self." We seem to have a "self," "interrogate ourselves," "refer to" ourselves inwardly, and "aim" questions at ourselves. But Sartre denies that "contents," "entities," or "meanings" characterize consciousness.

> Some wrongly hold . . . the "I" . . . to be the inhabitant of consciousness . . . through hypostasizing the being of the . . . reflected-on . . . these writers fix and destroy the movement of reflection upon the self. . . . We on the contrary, have shown that the *self* on principle cannot inhabit consciousness. It is an *absent–present* (note how this pair of terms operates) . . . the existence of *reference* . . . is clearly marked . . . (Consciousness refers) *down there,* beyond its grasp, in the far reaches of its possibilities. (*BN* 103)

> We refer not to something actually there but to something "absent," the "far reaches of its possibilities," but "this possible . . . is not present as an object . . . for in that case it would be reflected-on." (*BN* 104)

Most often we talk of the "self" as something unquestionably "present" inside us—which misses the peculiar way in which we must interrogate, seemingly to find out what we are, feel, and so on. The Freudian "ego" and "id" come directly from this interrogating and digging. Again, the

CHAPTER 2

poles of the activity are made into entities: the ego; the id. Sartre, phenomenologically, rejects both the constructs of a present and of an absent entity. It is the "absent–present," not as a paradoxical sticking together of both constructs, but as a delineation of what we do: we seem to "refer" to inward contents but—we find: for example, I am thirsty. What do I "refer to"? My "thirst" as a content, like "pleasure," an object "of" which I am conscious? Rather, it is the "possible" of drinking. Actions in situations are "implicit" in the way consciousness "refers" to itself qua "absent": "But this possible . . . is non-thetically (not like an object is given) an absent–present . . . The satisfied thirst which haunts my actual thirst (it "haunts": it is not baldly here nor not here, it is my desire or possibility) is consciousness of itself-drinking-from-a-glass and a non-positional consciousness" (*BN* 104).

Rather than "a thirst" as a "content," when we "refer" to and "interrogate" our "absent-present" self, we find the possibility of drinking from a glass—and this possibility of action in the situation is not given "in there" as an object of reflection. Rather, there is this "itself-drinking-from-a-glass" and a "non-positional consciousness" (the last phrase reminds us that it is *concrete activity*. If it were not, we would again interpret activity as representations, this time as representations of possible actions).

Actions in the situation (our possibilities) are "implicit" in this activity of "referring" to ourselves as "down there" in our feelings. Indeed, every explication of feelings always reveals not entities like anger, fear, thirst, pleasure, and so on, but anger at this and this situation, because it forces us to do so and so, and give up such and such, or fight with so and so. These are what we might do in the situation (Proposition 7).

How is it that we "refer" to what we bodily feel and thereby "make to be" such possibilities of situational action? The body is the "condition of possibility" (*BN* 338). We are bodily in situations. The ongoing activity of consciousness is this bodily being in the world. This bodily feel Sartre calls "nausea," but he indicates that it needn't have just that specific quality. It is your ever-present live sentient feel. He also calls it "coenesthetic affectivity." It is the body, again not as entities but as activity in context. That is what we "interrogate" when we "aim" questions "at" our self "down there"; the "feeling" which isn't a content but the "possibilities" of action: "Coenesthetic affectivity . . . provides the implicit matter of *all* the phenomena of the psyche . . . it is this which we aim at . . . and form into images . . . in order to aim at absent feelings and make them present" (*BN* 338).

And now, the problem of criteria: granted that we are looking "directly," without the "blinkers" of words or constructs, and granting that a good "description" leads us to notice newly discriminate aspects, nevertheless: do our descriptions not import a variety of assumption systems each with different consequences?

Consider that Merleau-Ponty—with similarly phenomenological intentions—argues strongly for a very different type of term and different assertions.

We have to grant that while philosophic statements "lift out" what is "implicit," "already there," "given," or "noticeable" directly, it is not there in the structured units and patterns that descriptions impose (Proposition 6).

These philosophers emphasize that "phenomena" or activities ("consciousness," "perception," "being in the world") are not constituted of given units, things, representations, meanings, etc. Thus it is not the question whether Sartre's or Merleau-Ponty's descriptive terms represent the really "given" units and structures. Both emphasize the prereflective and prethematic character of living activity (Proposition 5).

It follows that we must look more closely at how phenomenological descriptions are "based on" our direct looking and living. Obviously, "based on" here does not mark a correspondence of structure such that the formulation's structure corresponds to the structure of the given (although, why oh why is just this so often claimed?).

When a phenomenological philosopher offers his descriptions as "ontology," he claims only that we already know "pre-ontologically" everything he has to say. We know it in living, but without the explicit structure which he "lifts out" with his description (Proposition 4).

But, if descriptions are not congruent with the pattern already there (because what is there isn't given so patterned), then are they arbitrarily imposed? Are phenomenological philosophies mere speculative assumption systems no different from other such systems? Is the claim to phenomenological grounding merely an unfounded claim to special privilege for one's assumptions?

Just as linguistic analysts feel you are missing the point when you question the constructs and assumptions in their "descriptions" (of circumstances), so phenomenologists feel that the point is being missed when the variety of construct systems is questioned. The point is that as a result of a description (no matter how wild its terms) you may directly notice something you had not previously noticed. Do not evaluate the description as a set of constructs, but as a set of pointers. All constructs are evaluated by what they discriminate directly (Proposition 3).

But suppose we do not miss the point. Suppose we call a description "good" whenever it "lifts out" something for us. Even then, we must ask: can two different descriptions lift out the "same" aspect for our notice? If we say yes, we assume that the given activities come already cut up (such that there is a "same" aspect waiting there apart from the differing descriptions). If we say no, we admit that the supposed directly discriminated aspects are really a function of our descriptive "blinkers."

We must view phenomenological *explicating* also as an activity. Then we will not assume that it is determined by some system of entities or constructs that lies beneath phenomena. Hence no "same" aspects can be waiting for us there (Proposition 2).

But our activity (as much during explicating as any other time) doesn't only "sustain" representations (it isn't reducible to representations). It also "surpasses" them . . . it reorganizes, reinterprets, creates new alternatives, new possibilities. For example, Sartre does not believe in an abstract "freedom" such that I might be able to leap out of the situation I am in. (If I am a cafe waiter, this role doesn't define me. It is a representation which I sustain, but I cannot suddenly be a diplomat instead.) Activity surpasses representations in all sorts of ways, but not in just any old way: always in regard to the situation I am in: the "facticity" of the situation (Proposition 1).

The pair of terms: "facticity-surpassing" is another Sartrean pair. A situation's factual constraints cannot be described apart from my activity and possibilities. Its factual constraints are created by, posed for, and in terms of, my possible activities in the situation. Similarly, my activities always create new possibilities (and thereby aspects of the situation which it couldn't have been said to have, before and apart from me). Similarly, the world isn't given in just such and such a structure so that we might read it off. Rather, our activity creates, sustains, and surpasses the patterns we explicate.

But it is clear, therefore, that we lack any way to examine the various explications, how they newly "make be," "surpass," "split up," and describe, and their various unexamined assumption systems and consequences.

We cannot leave this problem in this shape: all claims of a phenomenologist's base for description are in question. We must ask: what then *is* the way in which explication is "based" on the implicit pre-structured?

III

The "implicit" factor is so central in these methods that we have already had to say a good deal about it, and about "explication." The propositions I offered constitute a treatment of explication, provided we now continue.

WHAT ARE THE GROUNDS OF EXPLICATION?

(a) We said that a "good" explication statement (we were asking for criteria for such statements) leads us to notice directly some aspect we had not previously noticed. This is actually a striking criterion (of a peculiar sort, to be sure) which sets successful "explication statements" apart from the many statements one can always formulate which do *not* succeed in bringing something new to direct notice.

(b) Furthermore, we don't always call a statement an "explication" when it leads us to a newly noticed aspect. One can always devise very many statements which (by objective criteria) state the many facts that were there and had not been noticed. One does not call these "explications." It is an "explication" only if we are "sure" that the new aspect "was implicit" before (i.e., we now insist that it was "known" to us, or "there" for us). This retrospective assertion of the newly noticed aspect is also something only few special statements bring about.

The new aspect (once noticed) must have this special relationship to what we do remember noticing (or feeling, or knowing) so that we now "insist" it "was implicit" in what we knew, felt, or noticed, and not just another fact in the situation.

(c) Once an aspect is discriminated and newly noticed, it cannot be made unnoticeable again. Of course, one need not pay attention to it, one can forget it, consider something else, etc. But once discriminated, the aspect cannot directly be made to merge away again.

(d) These three powers of a newly discriminated aspect are not totally dependent on the explication statement. The statement leads us to the newly discriminated aspect, but once it has done so, the aspect is noticed "directly." Also its quality of "having been implicit" in what we knew or did before doesn't come from the statement (usually cannot be reduced to formal relationships between statements of what we knew before and this statement). We may throw the statement out and still the newly discriminated aspect cannot thereby be made to disappear again.

Because of this partial "independence" of the discriminated aspect, we can say that there is "direct" noticing and not *only* various statements. If what is directly noticed depended *entirely* on the statement (not only for its being noticed, but also for its quality and for its remaining noticeable), then all discussions would again become a matter of various formulations related to, or clashing with, each other.

(e) But neither can we say that the newly discriminated aspect is *fully* independent of the variety of statements once we notice it. It would be convenient (though, in the long run it wouldn't be at all desirable) if we could say flatly that once we notice the aspect we can use various statements of it equivalently for this "same" aspect. At a particular juncture of some discussion or tasks, two very different statements might serve to discriminate the "same" aspect, but the very next step of the discussion, or the next difficulty in the task, might require that we discriminate further aspects, and we may then note that the two statements are no longer equivalent (or, perhaps they still are—but we must look).

(f) Because the newly discriminated aspect is the function and purpose of the statement, we need not argue from the statement as from a model: we *can* but we *need not* be bound by the logical necessity with which all kinds of logical implications follow from the statement.

Yet, if we were to deny the statement all logical character, it would cease to have any discriminating power. How do we decide what logical implications we use, as against those we ignore? We decide by noticing what the logical implication may further discriminate in the directly noticeable aspect.

This means that logically different éxplication statements with different models *can* always discriminate *different* further aspects of anything we directly notice. It is a decision, to consider these differing further aspects unimportant (for the present discussion, task, etc.)—a decision which has to be made at every step, since at each step these differing aspects may become important.

Thus the logical characters of different explications can neither be always accepted nor always ignored, but must be pursued to notice what is differently discriminated by them. Only so can we have explication statements that are not again mere formulative assumptions.

(g) I cannot go into it very far here, but because of the way one can neither drop, nor uncritically accept the logical structural aspects of explication statements, there is a whole field of such procedural choices we use and must examine (see *ECM*).

Either linguistic analysis and phenomenology are to be considered merely arbitrary play with arbitrarily chosen assumption systems, arbitrary ways of selecting and defining new distinctions, arbitrary imposition of formulative patterns, that is to say, either we consider these modes of philosophy to be no different (though less self-critical) than traditional philosophy, or we will have to grant the central role of directly had, not yet formulated experiencing.

Only because these methods involve the use, during philosophizing, of directly had, not yet formulated experiencing, is the appeal to phenomena or to "direct looking" more than a circular and invalid claim to special privilege.

But this raises, as a central problem, the question of how formulations may be related to directly had, not yet formulated experiencing.

Sometimes this directly had, not yet formulated experiencing is called "feeling." (For example, in this common conversation: *Question*:

"On what do you base your assertion that this rule explicates the use of this word?" *Answer:* "The use it states feels right to me. Doesn't it feel right to you also?") Either we take such assertions of "feeling" to be merely self-righteous claims, or we must really examine what sort of relationships a formulation may have to "feeling." (You might call it "sensing": "Ryle sensed trouble where trouble was," says Cavell).[4]

Notice also that such "feeling," "sensing," or not yet formulated but directly had experiencing *is used as we formulate.* Similarly, the few criteria and procedural distinctions given above concern the use of direct feeling or sensing (We "insist"... we are "sure" we have a direct sense that the newly discriminated aspect was involved in what we did notice earlier...). We can further explicate and give a logical rendition of any such instance, but this still involves the direct use of the experiential discrimination so that we may explicate *it* and thereby set up logical explicit accounts of how we have already proceeded.

Philosophy is not the only discipline in which this relationship between the directly felt experiencing and conceptualization arises. Another such discipline is psychotherapy.[5] There, too, an individual freshly discriminates and conceptualizes directly felt, not yet formulated experiencing. There, too, the individual backs his formulations up with insistence that it "feels right," and unless this be fatuous, much more is involved in this peculiar relationship between direct feeling and concepts.

And does it not seem now that these philosophic approaches have after all fallen back on a "private datum" or "content," much as they eschew such a view? Again, this will be the case only if we leave the relation between feeling and concepts unexamined. If we examine it, we notice that we deny the assumption that the whole sequence of explication (or behavior) is somehow folded into the feeling, like an accordion. We deny that feeling, as such, needs to be "checked" against (as in the spurious problem of the "private" supposed basis for first-person statements). We have already seen that feelings or "implicit" knowledge are not such as to permit checking their correspondence with what is said. Even if the feeling were not at all "private," even if it were an object on the table, it would not contain in itself explicitly the whole sequence of explications or behaviors. Explication and behavior occur in the world. Feeling ("implicit" experiencing) is not fully behaved, not fully explicated. As *not* fully behaved it does *not* yet contain the objective sequence. But it functions centrally (we must see how) in behaving or explicating, and when it does, there is no problem of observing its bearing in the world. For example, my six-year-old daughter, just before getting the mumps, had a pain and told me about it in an explicated and behaved way which needed no "checking": "Daddy, right here under my ear (pointing) it feels like a black-and-blue mark, but I looked in the mirror and there isn't any black-and-blue mark there!"

When not-yet-formulated experiencing plays its role in formulating and behaving, the way it bears on aspects of the world becomes quite clear and observable. Before it plays such a role, it is not yet all that. The activity of explicating or behaving doesn't just play out steps fully contained in pre-formulated experiencing. Rather, it carries experiencing forward, formulates and creatively shapes it further; and yet a given feeling won't function to support just any and all formulative attempts (as our "criteria" above show). Only *some* very fortunate formulations (often we fail to find *any*) obtain these characteristic responses from the directly felt.

Thus, on the one hand, the directly experienced "implicit" knowledge we feel doesn't fully determine the formulations and hence leaves us open to assumptions and contradictory possibilities. On the other hand, it doesn't permit any and all arbitrary formulations. It is therefore essential that we specify the kinds of support which the directly used "implicit" gives to formulations.

Such an examination must occur in terms of procedural choices which can be specified. The role of feeling in explicating can't be examined except in explicating. But there it must be examined, otherwise very different procedures in regard to formulational models will be mixed together, our use of them will be arbitrary, our accepting some logical implications of some models will be arbitrary and our rejection of other logical implications of the same models will also be arbitrary, we will have no way of dealing with contradictions between seemingly applicable "rules" or "explications," and we will have no systematic way of appealing beyond mere theoretical constructs to direct experience.

Elsewhere, I have attempted this examination.[6] Here I have been able to give only a few instances.

My main purpose in this chapter has been to show that both phenomenology and linguistic analysis employ not yet formulated, directly had experiencing in their methods. I have tried to show that this is no abstract or ephemeral thing, but something the individual must directly have and use, otherwise the rules and explications he formulates are merely arbitrary.

I have tried to show that this type of philosophy indeed breaks out beyond mere theoretical assumptions and constructs, that it breaks out toward directly had and used "implicit" experience, not yet formulated or cut up into neatly packaged traits, variables, denotations, and so on.

The vicious circle I pointed out was not intended to lead us back to the imposition (the reading in) of theoretical constructs as basic immutable assumptions. Instead, the problem leads forward to an examination of the relationships between the directly sensed "implicit" experiencing we use, and the variety of formulations and procedural choices we make.

Notes

1. Hereafter in this chapter, the abbreviation *PP* refers to J. L. Austin, *Philosophical Papers*, ed. J. O. Urmson and G. J. Warnock (Oxford: Oxford University Press, 1961); and the abbreviation *BN* refers to Jean-Paul Sartre, *Being and Nothingness*, trans. Hazel E. Barnes (New York: Philosophical Library, 1956).

2. Gilbert Ryle, *The Concept of Mind* (London: Hutchinson, 1949), 69. Cited in Stanley Cavell, "Must We Mean What We Say?" *Inquiry* 1, nos. 1–4 (1958): 172–212. Referred to as "Cavell" in next sentence of main text.

3. See D. Shapere, "Philosophy and the Analysis of Language," *Inquiry* 3 (1960): 29–48, for an illuminating discussion: "We seem forced to assume *both* that we know the facts, and so can discover the true meaning or real intention or true form of the proposition, *and* that we know the true meaning or real intention or true form of the proposition, and so can discover the facts" (42). The author leads up to the realization that the method involves *newly* differentiating and explicating *both* language and facts.

4. Cavell, "Must We Mean What We Say?" 181.

5. See *A Process Method*; see also Gendlin, "A Theory of Personality Change," in *Personality Change*, ed. Philip Worchel and Donn Byrne (New York: Wiley, 1964).

6. See Eugene T. Gendlin, *A Process Model* (Evanston, Ill.: Northwestern University Press, 2017); hereafter this work is cited as *APM*.

3

Experiential Phenomenology

In this chapter I will first outline a little of the basic approach of the philosophy of experiencing, and then show how its application has led to some research advances in psychology.

I will begin by formulating what I consider the basic unsolved problem of current philosophy. I will first discuss phenomenology and linguistic analysis from the vantage point of the philosophy of experiencing, but I hope to be both fair and clarifying. If I attribute to them certain explicit understandings which perhaps they often lack, it is because clarification is like that: what one clarifies is in a sense already there—in another sense, not.

I will then outline some systematic relationships between experience and verbalization, some characteristics of experience in the process of being explicated, and some few points of method. With these I will hope to have made a new phenomenological approach, one which solves the basic problem by approaching it quite differently.

I will then show the application of this new approach in psychology.

The Problem

In the Western tradition of philosophy, experience (and nature) has usually been interpreted as basically a formal or logic-like system. This was done through a philosophical analysis of the basic assumptions of knowledge or science. These assumptions were then attributed to experience. Experience "must be" such-and-so, the philosophers said; otherwise science or knowledge would be impossible. Philosophers have not agreed on their analysis of science or knowledge, and therefore also not on what they attributed to experience. For instance, those who held that knowledge is basically mathematical and consists of unit steps, each repeatable, considered nature and experience to be a system of that same sort. Thus the forms required by knowledge were read into nature and experience.

Some philosophers made this reading-in quite explicit, in which case experience was held to depend frankly on the nature of thought (Idealism, so-called); others preferred to present this reading-in backwards, so that experience was said to be the origin from which knowledge received its forms. Either way, experience (or nature) was inferred to have the kind of forms, relations, and connections which knowledge requires. Either way, therefore, the needs of knowledge (as analyzed) governed what was said of experience or nature. Since Schleiermacher, Dilthey, Husserl, Heidegger, Sartre, Merleau-Ponty, Wittgenstein, Ryle, and Austin, this approach has gone out of style. Instead, it is now widely held that experience need not, and in fact does not, have the same character as logic, science, or knowledge. Experience is not organized like a verbal scheme. What we say in philosophy should be based on experience, not read into it.

The crucial problem has two parts: (1) if experience is not like a verbal scheme and we do not wish to say that it is, then how can we say anything at all about it without imposing a verbal scheme?; and (2) if we wish, in some way, to appeal beyond logical schemes to a sense of "experience" not yet organized verbally, in what way do we have such "experience" present and available for an appeal, and in what way does experience give "yes" or "no" answers, so that some statements will be "based" on it and some statements not?

Although my major concern is with phenomenology, let me say a little about linguistic analysis in these regards, because both these philosophies stand or fall with this problem.

Linguistic analysis, following Wittgenstein and Austin, examines how words are used in the context of ordinary situations: these philosophers find the use of a word quite unlike the logic scheme the word embodies, and quite unlike its logical relations to other words. For example, although "voluntarily" and "involuntarily" are logical opposites, they are used in entirely different kinds of situations. One does not use them to mark the same thing in either its presence or absence, as opposites would do. Ryle says, rather, that "voluntarily" is a word of affirmation or denial ("not voluntarily") that we use when something "morally fishy" has been done and we want to assign or withhold blame.[1] "He did not do it voluntarily" means the morally fishy act was not his responsibility. "Involuntarily," on the other hand, belongs to muscle jerks, reflexes, or automatic behavior. A man might shoot someone not voluntarily but in self-defense; yet we would not use the word "involuntarily" unless the trigger was released by accident.

This kind of approach moves beyond logical and philosophical schemes and instead analyzes situations of ordinary living. Our living in situations is said to be a great deal more complex than any scheme. Situations, and how we differentiate and act in them, involve a great many distinctions which we "know," and which are marked in language use. But this "knowing" is not like knowledge or science; it is rather like "knowing how" to do something—perhaps how one does it cannot be explained, at least not easily. Yet one "knows" when to use a given word, and when it would be inappropriate. The complexity and distinctions of our situations have developed with language; hence linguistic analysts use language as the lead from which to discover these differentiations and to make explicit what situational characteristics are being differentiated.

Linguistic analysts, therefore, appeal to something beyond the logical relations of words, beyond the "models" implicit in them, and beyond any philosophical scheme of the kind formerly considered to be basic to experience. For example, the discussion just alluded to is in some way a philosophic discussion of will, choice, and responsibility, yet no scheme of "free will" or "determinism" is used. Neither are the purely logical relations of the words to be trusted. Linguistic analysts appeal beyond schemes and logic; they appeal to our knowing how to act, speak, and live in situations. But what sort of appeal, what sort of basis for an appeal, is involved here?[2]

Austin says our actions and uses of words in situations are organized very differently from the way a flat system of words is organized. He denies that a word has a "handy denotation" to which it refers.[3] For one word there is not necessarily one thing. Philosophy appeals beyond words to something that is not organized in a one-to-one relation to words, and does not have units and relations that are the same as words and their logical relations. Linguistic analysis only looks like an analysis of language. What is actually analyzed is something very different: namely, our "knowing how to use" words in situations.

This knowing how to use a word involves knowing all the complexities of the situations governing its use. It is possible to try to explicate what these are, and linguistic analysts attempt this. But in so doing, they inevitably give this "knowing how" a verbal scheme which the "knowing how" is not. They verbally organize the maze of situational detail in just certain ways, even while asserting that action-in-situations cannot be so organized. We can see this clearly in the way in which linguistic analysts differ among themselves as to when such an explication has been achieved. Austin did not agree with Ryle that our knowing how to use "voluntarily" was rightly explicated by saying that we use it in "morally fishy" situations to assign or withhold blame. Austin says that we do not use the word to determine whether the act is blameworthy or not: a child may give a gift "voluntarily," or because his mother made him give it; in neither case would his action be morally fishy. With this example to argue from, Austin changes much of Ryle's explication of how we use "voluntarily."

How is it that the same knowing how which grounded Ryle's earlier explication now grounds Austin's differing one? Clearly, the verbal organization of neither the one of these explications nor the other can claim to set out "the" complex organization of situational aspects implicit in our "knowing how."

This brings us to the second part of our problem. Even if we accept the fact that, although these philosophers set themselves the task of getting at experience rather than imposing a scheme on it, they end by imposing a scheme after all, we can still ask: Did they involve the not-yet-verbalized experience in some way? Did they merely impose a scheme, or did they use their sense of "knowing how"? How did they use it? In what way do they have this "knowing how"? Surely, not only in the form of the scheme and not only after they state it. Surely, they will tell us how they have this "knowing how" and use it to make their explication.

Even here we will get no satisfactory answer. The philosophers exhibit their "knowing how" to use a word by using it in action. When analysts try to explicate this "how," they talk about various situations. They propose examples, which force us to admit that some are possible and some are not. It is not possible to say, "He did the shooting under orders, therefore he did it involuntarily." The word seems to mean the right thing, yet in that example it doesn't. It sounds wrong. This means it feels wrong; it gives one a sour, discordant feeling. If someone now says, "'Involuntarily' belongs with muscle jerks or accidents, not with being compelled," this feels right. (Still, quite possibly it isn't right.)

Now, what is this "feels right" or "feels wrong," which seems to be the ultimate court of appeal? One intends to appeal to the situations directly, for the decision as to what words can and cannot be used in them, but actually one appeals to "what feels right" in them, or "feels wrong." Linguistic analysts do not actually go out and observe situations directly. They would not accept an empirical statistical study of the use of the word, because more people use words in a sloppy way than use them rightly. Can "rightly" mean only that it feels right?

Can "feeling" be used in this way? Isn't it a "private datum"? Isn't feeling a poor criterion for philosophy? Why and how does it work? Why and how does feeling seem to allow some organizations or schemes to be imposed upon it, and not others? (And some of these may be found "wrong" later.) What the philosopher organizes and defines (some of the situational details) was somehow, puzzlingly, "implicit" in the feeling. Does it really all come down to feeling?

Phenomenologists similarly hold that language and living developed together (and continue to do so), that experience and situations are together (just as our sense of "knowing how" to use a word and the situations in which we use it are together). In Heidegger's *Being and Time*, "being-in-the-world" is a way of defining humans as beings-in, as experiencing-in situations.[4] According to Heidegger, situations are differentiated with language, and linguistic distinctions are thus in the very texture of the situations with which we live.

Husserl and Merleau-Ponty discuss the experiential sense which guides our use of language, an "emotional sense" that "fills" verbal sound patterns (which are empty in a language foreign to us).[5] Experience, language, and situations are thus inherently connected.

Phenomenologists also hold that while language is part of the situations in which we live, experience and the life-world are not like a system of words or concepts. Phenomena cannot be equated with schemes, and it is an error to impose schemes on them. Thus, Heidegger argues that every statement, or truth, "stands in some kind of approach," and depends on it. That is to say, the world cannot be rendered as such, but only through some (historically developed) scheme.

To get beyond this, Heidegger seeks "an approach that would not be again merely an approach." Rightly, he envisions that, having gained perspective on the variety of possible schemes and approaches, and their historical development, we would not now simply settle for another scheme. But what else is possible? There Heidegger stops. This next step will be the work of a whole culture, he says, not of one man. It is a conundrum which affects every philosophy which refuses to equate experience or world with a scheme. On the one hand, it appeals to that experience in a way that should be corrective of schemes; on the other hand, the result has to be again a scheme, and thus attributes to experience the nature of a scheme.

Husserl may be said to be the first to base philosophy, quite explicitly and deliberately, on an examination of experiencing as we actually live, have, and are, rather than regarding "experience" as already imposed upon by the requirements of one view of science, as had been done traditionally. Husserl found, for example, that the notion that experience comes in colors, sounds, smells, and so on, is a notion already derivative from a philosophical scheme which analyzes experience into certain handy units. Ordinary experience is of trees, doors slamming, kids crying—not of colors and sounds. (Austin makes the same point many decades later.) Thus Husserl finds the whole "life-world" implicit in experience, even when he first brackets all questions as to what exists and seeks to examine only experience as such.

Although Husserl resisted schemes that have been read into experience, how could he himself organize his own analysis of experience? What about such schemes as cognition versus emotion versus conation (which he used)? What about noesis versus noema, or, simply put, process and object, as organizing notions in his work? What about the individual as the starting point (as compared, for example, to Heidegger's different starting point) and the ensuing difficulties about other egos? These are only examples of a larger fact: the phenomenologist has set himself a seemingly impossible task: that of examining and describing lived experience without imposing schemes upon it. But to "examine" and to "describe" are activities which inherently involve schemes.

Husserl was aware of this problem. Each period of his work is followed by a period in which he again undercut his own assumptions and schemes; as he said, whereas others built edifices, he only dug further into the ground, and he meant by this something both good and bad. Good because it was his self-set task to undercut schemes and assumption systems; bad because he knew that in some sense he was failing at this task.

He had to fail in this regard, since, on the one hand, he wanted to study the structure of experience without importing a scheme, and yet, on the other hand, any studying, describing, laying out in words and distinctions must, after all, employ some scheme and some organizing parameters. Could he claim that his distinctions and organizing parameters were themselves "the" structure of experience?

That we cannot grant Husserl such a claim is shown by the fact that other phenomenological philosophers set out "the" structure of experience quite differently. And again, is not each phenomenologist involved in a contradiction, claiming both that experience is pre-schematic and that the scheme arrived at is true of it?

The second part of our problem is also a problem for phenomenology. The second part is: Even if we grant that a scheme is being imposed, what, if anything, is a "phenomenological basis"? How do we have it and how do we use it? Are phenomenologists simply claiming unwarrantedly, in the most puerile fashion, that they have some kind of mysterious direct line into not-yet-verbalized experience, without being able to show us even a trace of it? Or is there something clearly explainable that can be called a "phenomenological basis"? Granted that experiencing is never to be equated with a verbal scheme, and granted that it does not contain some verbal "the" scheme, and granted that each phenomenologist does use, and thereby in some sense imposes, a scheme in his verbal descriptions, is there any difference left between phenomenologically grounded assertions and those which are not so grounded?

For example, if you say to me, "You are tired," then if you intend your statement phenomenologically, you will consider it false if I do not feel tired. On the other hand, if you are not proceeding on a phenomenological basis, you might still retort, "I can tell from looking at you that you are tired," or, "I know you have been working for eighteen hours now, and I know that anyone who has worked that long is tired." Roughly, these two assertions are based respectively on empirical observation and on logical deduction.

These three types of bases for statements—phenomenological, empirical, and logical—are not unrelated. For example, it is possible to say, "Because of what I saw you do, and because of what I can figure out, I think you will feel tired if you stop working and lie down for a while." Here a phenomenological basis is used (if I don't feel tired then, you will admit that you were wrong), but it is asserted in the future and predicted because of the inherent connectedness of situations, logic, and experience.

Our example is much too simple. Also, it raises some well-known problems about just whose experience shall be a phenomenological basis, whether such direct experiences are "private," how these can be grounds for assertions, and other questions. But the example illustrates how a statement may be phenomenological if one seeks to make some direct experience the court of appeal for its correctness or falseness.

In order to assert truth and falsity these philosophers *seek* to appeal to direct experience, beyond schemes and assumptions. Can we say more than that? Can we say that in some way this appeal works?

We know the appeal does not work univocally, since these philosophers frequently disagree with each other. How then, does it work? Husserl discusses: "Expression and what is expressed [are] two layers that are congruent, one covers the other. . . . One must not expect too much from this image of layers, expression is not something laid on . . . rather it affects the intentional underlayer."[6] Clearly, here Husserl gets at something beyond the image of layers that he uses in saying it. How can you tell that this is so? How can you tell if it is right? How can you tell that the image of layers is wrong?

Husserl says expression "is congruent" or "covers" what is expressed (and for this the layers image does nicely); but it also affects what is expressed (and for this the layers image fails, he says). Thus Husserl himself says right here that the verbal schematizing he uses is wrong. Something more than the verbal schematizing is operating, or else we would have nothing more than a statement which is at the same time being called wrong.

Notice that we have more than just the sentence, so that we do not lose everything when we discard the sentence. How do we have this experience of what Husserl is getting at by "an expression covers"? How do we have this experience of what Husserl means by "expression . . . affects the intentional underlayer," in a not-yet verbally schematized way, so that we can first agree to the scheme of layers and then also agree that the scheme of layers is wrong? How are both of these agreements possible, despite the fact that "covers" really contradicts "affects": if the expression changes what it purports to be congruent with, how then is it congruent with it? Clearly the verbal scheme or metaphor fails, and yet we have something more.

Without a further, much better, treatment of these questions we can only say that we *feel* how an expression fits when it succeeds in expressing; we can say only that we also often *feel* a change in what we are expressing in the process of expressing it. But would one want to make "feeling" the final judge of philosophic discourse? After so much careful thought, will we say that whatever we feel to be right, is right? Since so much of what the other fellow feels is obviously wrong, we can only view this kind of basis with doubt.

This passage just quoted from Husserl is not only an example of appealing beyond the verbal metaphor one uses; the passage is itself about the fact that verbalizing "affects" an experience.

The basic unanswered question of current philosophy, then, seems to be: how can lived experiencing be a basis for assertions? Both major current philosophies claim such a basis, claim that this basis lies beyond the verbal and logical schemes of assertions, claim to correct schemes by means of it, and yet have shown neither how we have and use this lived experience as a basis for assertions, nor how the result is more than simply another imposed scheme.

It is scandalous that current philosophy appeals to something beyond verbal schemes, and yet claims that its assertions are "merely" read off, or that they "merely" state this something. It is as if, having said that direct experience or knowing how is not a scheme, contemporary philosophers pretend that it shows its schematic organization on the very face of it.

But as we have seen, when looked at more closely, these philosophers do go by something other than schemes made or found, just as they claim to do. But because these philosophers fail to examine just what their basis is and how they use it, therefore they have left it in this unexamined state of mere feeling.

But can there be a solution to this problem? If saying involves schematizing and organizing, how can it not impose scheme and organization? If experience is used as a basis and is not a set statable structure, must it not be merely vague and felt?

A New Beginning

To arrive at a solution and a successful phenomenological method, we must make a fundamental turn, and a new beginning. We must look at the situation sideways, make a ninety-degree turn, so to speak. Instead of standing only on statements, deploring that we can speak about experience only through them, let us stand to one side and look at both statements and experience as they affect each other.

Let us free ourselves from that perspective in which experience is to be rendered without the statement having an effect upon it. Obviously, we cannot state experience, as it is unstated. Let us take the bull by the horns and study the ways stating can affect experience. In this way we make a field of study out of what was an embarrassment.

We cannot study experience as it is when it is not studied; we cannot state it as it is when it is not stated. What we can do is to study it in the process of being stated. From this new approach we take our standpoint neither in statement, nor in an experience that we can say nothing about. Rather, we study both experience and statement as they occur in the process of affecting each other. What many different effects may they have on each other?

I will try to show in the following section that this turn, this new approach, has borne fruit.

Situations, Language, and Feelings

We have seen that external situations, language, and feelings are intimately related, yet each may independently establish truth criteria. Thus a sentence might be called true or false either because it stated or failed to state a definite empirical observation, or because it followed or failed to follow logically from other statements, or because it explicated or failed to explicate a directly felt experience. It is often useful to make quite clear the basis on which a sentence is intended to rest. However, these three types of truth criteria are not independent of each other, really, since situations, words, and feelings are inevitably interrelated.

Thus, while phenomenologists intend their sentences to rest on their success or failure to explicate direct experience, they should make it clear (and I have tried to show that they often *do* make it clear) that feelings, situations, and language are inherently involved in each other. Thus, although Husserl began not with these interrelations but rather with direct experience, he soon found these interrelations in that experience.

Wittgenstein's argument against "private data" was that the use of words is governed by situations and our actions in them, not by what it feels right to say. The way in which the word is objectively used is the criterion for its use. "Look on the language game as the *primary* thing, and look on the feelings, etc., as you look on a way of regarding the language game."[7] This means not that I do not have feelings, or that they are not complex and organized, but rather that Wittgenstein asks us to make the behavior in situations the criterion for feelings, rather than the reverse. Linguistic analysts first honor, then disobey this dictum, since they first assume that what feels right to say is governed by objective situations, and then proceed to state the marks of these situations, by using what feels right to say in them as the criterion.

Experience is always already organized by, or in, situations. Language is used to distinguish situations and to differentiate aspects of them. When we want to study experience and statement in relation to each other, it must be clear that they are always already related, and that both are related in turn to situations. Thus we will not be studying "pure" experience as if it were some kind of putty; rather, experience is always organized by the evolutionary history of the body, and also by culture and situations organized partly by language. Although language is always involved in the complex organization of experience, it is never all that is involved in it. The role of language does not get at all of an experience. But neither are you relating statement to experience for the first time when you explicate. Language is already involved in experience.

For example, the different rooms in a house and the activities that go on in them are developed and differentiated along with the words and phrases used in these activities. Even the house cat experiences each room and its activities differently. Although the cat does not use the words that go with these differences, nevertheless these words are, in a way, implied in the different experiences the cat has with the different rooms. Observable situations are related both to the cat's experiences and to the words that for us structure some of the aspects of these experiences.

Thus when direct experience serves as a basis for statements, it does not do so apart from situations: situational structure is implicit in it. But we can also *further* structure situations with feelings and words, and in explication we do so.

The argument against private data has been mistaken by some to imply that one's statements about one's own feelings are incorrigible, that they cannot be found to be in error (or true, therefore). But this is a misunderstanding. We will show that one can both be mistaken and can later correct what one said and believed about one's feelings. But when one states (or corrects) a feeling, one states aspects of the situations in which one has the feelings.

But just as feelings do not have some simple verbal-schematic structure, neither do situations. The complex and arguable nature of the marks for when we use a simple word have already shown that. It may be quite an objective matter, but it is not one that can simply be observed. To delineate situations involves simplifying and further organizing, imposing further patterning upon what is already very complexly patterned. The situations we live in do not come in "handy denotation" packages, nor in any single set of already cut-out units.

We must therefore assert both that experience is already organized in part linguistically and situationally, and that in using experience (or situations) to ground statements upon, we further organize it. We must assert *both* that this further organizing is not the pattern of the experience, *and* that it does have something to do with the way the experience is already organized. To state this in the reverse order, the organization of experience is not the kind which we set out in a verbal pattern, although what we do set out in such a pattern has something to do with the experience's own kind of organization. (And, since these are related, with the situation's own kind of organization.)

We must examine and explicate situations, feelings, and language in their relations to each other, realizing that explicating gives them a still further relation.

Functional Relations and Characteristics of Experiencing

In *Experiencing and the Creation of Meaning* I set out seven functional relationships between experiencing and words.[8] I will cite four of these briefly, to show that we can study these relations in action, and to clarify our later discussion.

(1) **Direct reference** is a use of words to set off, separate out, set up some "aspect" of experience which can thereby be called "this" or "that" experience, or "an" experience. The words used may very well be demonstrative pronouns—or they may be somewhat descriptive. Yet what they say is so obviously vague and untenable literally that it is clear that they only "point," if they do anything.

For example, when I spoke of "that feeling" which an inappropriate explication gives one, I was directly referring to your having such a feeling. If you did not have it and had never had it, I might arrange to give it to you, but the phrase "that sour feeling" would not in itself give it to you.

Thus direct reference is a use of words such that *an* experience is thereby set out. But the words alone do not convey or call out the experience: one must know already with what approach and in what situation to look, and the directly referring phrase must have a result which is definitely not simply that phrase. The result must be a distinguishable aspect of experience which now stands out, so that one can say, "Yes, I know what *that* is." (You might now say, "But I wouldn't call it 'sour' . . . ," and you might propose another word that I might agree is a better word. Still, my phrase would have succeeded in directly referring.)

It is perfectly possible for the direct reference to either fail or be misunderstood. Though words do structure experience further (into "this" or "an" aspect), nevertheless the experience is not totally the result of schematizing, entirely up to how schematizing proceeds. It is not the mere result of schematizing, since the direct experience may appear, or it may not. If not, then you have *only* the words. If it does appear it talks back—which may lead you to discard the very words that let it emerge.

We see now, that, far from there being a "pure" pre-organized experience which might first be verbalized, even the existence of "an" experience such as "this" one is already a further organizing we have made. To be sure, it need not be words, exactly, which do this, although it can be words. It could be a certain pointing and differentiating attention; we feel "this" and "this" and "that." Hadamard says he often uses dots rather than words, putting a dot down for each separable aspect as he separates them.[9]

(2) **Recognition** is my term for the way in which words seem to have "their own" experience, which they call out in anyone. (Or, we might say that if one is in the kind of situation that gives one that feeling, one then finds that the word comes.) The word seems to call out the feeling, and if we fail to get it we fail to "recognize" the word. The feeling seems to call for that word. If one has the feeling, then the word comes. (One has the feeling in a situation, so the word seems to explicate the situation as well.)

The relationship between words and experience appears here to be a one-to-one relation—the word says the experience, the experience calls for that word. Actually, the experience is much more complex and much different, and if you directly refer to a "recognition feeling" which seems paired with a word, you will find that you could use a great many other words to say what it is. Similarly, there are quite complex situational aspects which give us this feeling and make this word come. But to try to state the recognition feeling differently is quite another relationship between experience and words. For the moment, we want to set out this very ordinary, seemingly one-to-one relationship of words and "their" recognition-feelings, so that each gives you the other.

CHAPTER 3

To make this quite vivid, suppose you are in some situation and feel a certain way for which you know there is a word. You might find yourself unable to think of the word. You then have only "that feeling," to which you can directly refer, but for which you are unable to think of the word. (You can describe this aspect of experience in a roundabout way, seeking to give another person the same sense of the situation so that he might come up with the word. This is again another relation of words and experience, one in which you seek to create the experience in others, not by calling it out with the word, but by putting them, actually or vicariously, through many events until they have it.)

(3) **Metaphor** involves novelty. Here words are used in such a way as to create a new experience. The metaphor or simile is literally about some other situation or experience but is now used about this situation or experience. A metaphor requires direct reference; you must be able to point directly to the experience the metaphor is now about, and permit the metaphor to apply to it. Understanding the metaphor requires a recognition of the usual use of the words. Then, if the metaphor succeeds, some new aspect of the present experience should emerge.

Some people would like to say that such a new experience (and new aspect of a situation, for as usual these are together) is not really new, that the similarity already existed between the present situation and the one that the metaphor derives from. But this is to assume that the world consists of already cut-up, handy "similarities" that only await noticing. Rather, the metaphor involves a further creative organizing, as in direct reference. An aspect of experience emerges, and in the case of metaphor, a new one. Many such new aspects could metaphorically be made to emerge, if one brought many other areas of experience to bear on the present one.

(4) **Comprehension** occurs when an experience or feeling has no regular words, when these must first be made. Usually such words cannot be made up anew, but must consist of new arrangements of extant words, used in a fitting way. As we have seen, if a metaphor is presented to you, it creates a new experiential aspect. But now, let us say you already have the experience and you seek to make words for it. To fashion a new verbalization of an experience or a feeling, you must perform the metaphoric task (so that the old words make a new experiential aspect), but this new aspect must be very close to the one that you already have. Comprehension thus involves direct reference (to *this* experience you want to verbalize), as well as recognition (the experience or feeling the words usually arouse), and also metaphor (the use of these words to create a new experiential aspect). All three functional relationships are used in such a way that the thereby-made aspect shall be the one you already have, which was to be verbalized.

This is the relation in which words are said to "feel right" or "sound right"; but note how much more complex it is, once the various relations of words and experience are set out. By no means do we need to let it remain at a "feeling right."

There are a number or aspects involved in "feels right," which have just been explicated here. Unless the other relationships are clearly set out, this one cannot be understood. Even without understanding, that is to say, even if you reject my description of each relationship, it is helpful at least to separate the direct reference power of a statement, if it has any, from the (usual or novel) recognition power the words may have. Thus a statement purporting to state some aspect of experience may have direct reference power. It may only half succeed, but by its context, and by what you already have, you may get the experiential aspect it sets out. And yet you may want to reject—not that there is such an aspect—but the way in which the sentence formulates it. This distinction enables us to keep the experiential aspect a statement refers to, at the same time rejecting what the statement says ("I know what you're getting at, but you can't put it that way").

Our earlier examples—"that sour feeling" of an inappropriately used word, and Husserl's "an expression covers"—were attempts at comprehension. In both instances we kept the experiential aspect referred to, but rejected these statements as comprehension.

This short presentation of four relationships in which verbalizing affects experiencing shows that there is a fruitful field of study here, and may invite you to look at the fuller treatment of these relationships.

Experience is never entirely caught in any one relationship to words. It is always possible to refer directly to the experience, to apply patterns from other areas of experience to it, and to permit new aspects of the experience to emerge. Thus there are usually a series of steps or successive versions in an explication.

Neither the first verbal patterning nor the second, and neither the first set of "aspects" of the experience nor the second set, *is* exactly the experience. Experience can never be equated with our assertions. Rather, we can say something about experience in relation to the fact that one can always schematize further and get, or fail to get, certain experiential results. What character does experience have which is revealed in this fact that we may always schematize further in these different relationships?

To be able to be further schematized is a very striking characteristic of experience. In *Experiencing and the Creation of Meaning* I examined this possibility of further schematization under nine headings. Here I will use only three: we will find that, in the process of being *further* schematized, experiencing has no definite units, is responsive to any scheme, and is capable of being schematized by any other experience.

Experiencing is "nonnumerical." We can see this from the fact that direct reference can be made in many ways, each of which sets out some further "this" or "an" aspect. Experiencing does not come as a unit, or set of units, already cut in it. If it does, still quite other units can be set out from it. Although the recognition a word calls forth (or the situation which calls for a certain word) seems superficially to be packaged as a unit by that word, a situation is always potentially multiple. It can always be further differentiated, cut up, unitized.

Experiencing is "multischematic." Something unique (and not just anything you like) will emerge when you apply any scheme. Even if you keep a directly referred aspect "constant," it will respond differently to different schemes. Even when a scheme already seems to do well to organize an experience, other schemes can be applied and will have different results.

Experiences are "interschematizable": I mean by this that any experience (you need direct reference before you have "an" experience) can schematize any other, or be schematized by any other. This is hard to believe and needs examples. You can use any experience as a way of patterning another. Thereby commonalities will, as it were, fall out. With these, you can talk about either experience.

For example, consider what you were doing just before reading this, and use that activity to schematize our discussion. Perhaps you were on a bicycle ride with a friend. Yes, some parts of our discussion were uphill struggles, just as were parts of the bicycle ride, and some were easy and smooth and downhill. (Note: once you apply this bicycling experience to our discussion, you get just certain parts of it which were uphill and just so many. You can't have it just any one way; unfortunately you can't have it all downhill. Any scheme applied gives you just certain results.)

Isn't it near madness to claim that any experience can be a scheme for another? Does this mean everything is everything? And it seems mysterious that any experience already contains something that will fall out as common with any other experience. Isn't this a metaphysical assertion? But, no. All we are saying is that a common aspect *can be created* in the process of schematizing one experience by the other; we don't say such an aspect *was* there, before.

We are discussing experience in terms of what *can be created*. What, then, *is* experience? The word "is" applies to experience only as held static, symbolized in some way, and hence it applies only to both experiencing and its symbolization as a compound.

Here then is "the" structure of experiencing, not indeed as it "is," but as it is in regard to the next, or any further symbolization!

Nonnumerical, multischematic, and *interschematizable* together make up a type of order obviously different from the logical kind. But now, do not these three terms themselves constitute a scheme? Yes, of course. But their value lies in what they say we can *do*: we can directly refer and unitize; we can apply a scheme and see what we get; we can apply another experience and then schematize and see what we get.

It is quite true that "this" aspect of experience which I am setting forth here, and naming "the character of experiencing," could be formulated very differently than I did above. Not necessarily three but more or fewer characteristics could be set out. One could merge the "non-numerical" and "multischematic," since they imply each other; one could merge the distinction between extant schemes and schematizing by another experience, thus merging the second and third characteristics. One could then apply some other scheme or experience to lay it out again, and differently. This is one fact we are finding as a characteristic of experience.

The problem now is whether we must think of this fact as a limitation on thinking, or whether there is not, here, the beginning of a more powerful method, closer to the nature of experience and living, which we may develop.

In *Experiencing and the Creation of Meaning* I presented eight points of method. Here I can only briefly touch on method.

For example, if I directly refer to, and then formulate, some aspect of experience, my formulation will have many logical implications. Must I be trapped by them all? Must I, on the contrary, lose all logical precision? Neither.

I can use any formulation and see what effect it has. If it makes me lose hold of what I wanted to formulate, I will retreat from it immediately. If, on the other hand, it makes new "aspects" of the experience stand out, and especially if these aspects seem important or troublesome, I will hold on to them. It may take a lot of fruitful work for me to find another way to formulate these new aspects, and to examine how my second formulation alters them and whether the difference is important to me, just now.

Two different formulations may be equivalent in regard to some directly referred-to aspect of experience—but only equivalent for the moment and in regard to the present point I want to make. One more step of thought, work, or action, and I might have to retract the asserted equivalence, for now the difference may be important.

I can even insist, in the case of two equivalent formulations, that since their words differ they must be capable of schematizing something different for me, and this can be pushed until it happens, and pushed further until it happens usefully.

Although most thinkers do not intend their schemes to be used in this way, any scheme can be employed as an open scheme—that is to say, it can enable us to refer directly to aspects of experience which may be formulated in a different, and possibly a better way, with many further aspects emerging.

One can be systematic and precise about which of these sorts of steps one takes at any given juncture in one's thinking.

Signposts of the Explication Process

Let us return to our previous example, which, as we have said, was much too simple. You say that I am tired. If you consider your statement to be phenomenological, you will consider your statement wrong if I do not feel tired.

Your statement invites me to see if I am tired. How would I do that? Not by reviewing how long I have worked, and not by looking in the mirror. I can attend to my body directly and see if I find there what is called "tired." This is direct reference. Until you asked me, I paid no attention. Now, in reaction to your words, I seek to set up such "an" experience as we call "tired." If I cannot do so (and, note, this is not a matter of choice), your statement was wrong. Let us suppose that I agree I am "sort of tired."

Let me show how much further we can go than when we first considered this example.

Now suppose I say, "I am not exactly tired, but I *am* getting a little weary." It is clear that here you were definitely right in some way. Your words succeeded in "directly referring." They were also close in what they conveyed; they were pointing in the right direction. (I might have said, "No, I have a slight toothache.") We do not know as yet why I prefer "weary" to "tired"—they seem to be indistinguishable. "Weary" might perhaps include along with "tired" some sense of some long, drawn-out cause for being tired, and indeed we have been working all day and all evening. (It is this sort of experiential sense of how a word is used, which the linguistic analysts explicate.)

We must note that I probably did not feel tired until you said so. Your saying it made it true by leading me to create, specify, set out, distinguish (these words are equivalent here) "an" experience. Before I tried to refer to it, it wasn't there; now that I do, it is.

Yet, the feeling must be there; I do not just make it. Trying to refer to it, trying to see if I am tired, doesn't always make that feeling. Since now it did, for me, I would want to say that it *was* there before, only I didn't notice it. Of course, as a "this feeling" it certainly was not there before. (Yet the case is different than if you had suddenly made me tired, perhaps by telling me some heavy news. There is a continuity between how I remember being before, and my direct reference now to this tired feeling; thus the tired feeling is a newly set-out aspect *of* the overall experience I was attending to.)

Suppose I now continue to explicate why "weary" seems to be true for me, and "tired" doesn't. I may say next, "Well it's sort of not tired, but tired-of. That's why I said 'weary.' I don't feel like going on to this next job we have to tackle now. It's too tough."

Having said this, which is a more exact version of how I feel (as well as an explication of the use of the word I preferred), I might say, a moment or two later, "I feel like going out and having a good time. I am *not at all tired*—just so we don't have to get into this next job, it's too hard to do."

Now I am actually denying flatly what seemed above to be "in the right direction," though I really feel no different. I am still talking about "the same thing," and, despite the flat denial of what I said, I hold that what I say now is what my feeling really "was."

As I continue now to say just what it is about the next job that seems so tough, I may say, "Well, it isn't exactly hard to do, but what *is* hard is that I know they won't like how I'll do it." And then, *"The job is really easy."* And, again, further, "It isn't so much that I care what they think of it; it's just this one way I care, and that's a way that they're right, really. Gee, *I don't care at all what they think!* But this one criticism they'll make, I know they're right about that. It's really what *I* think that I care about." And, further, "I could help it, but I would have to take a day off to study up on how to do it right, and I don't want to do that." And, again, "Really, *I do want to.* Every time I hit this sort of thing I wish *so much* that I could take the time off to learn how to do it, but I just can't give myself the time off. It would seem like a whole day with nothing done. I don't feel any trust in myself if I go and do something that isn't a part of the routine we call work, just doing something because I'd like to do it." And, later, "Hell, I'll do it tomorrow."

This aspect of experience—its vast capacity to be further schematized and unitized in relation to verbalization, and thereby revealing aspects which, we now say, it most truly "was," has not been recognized at all in philosophy until now. Therefore no systematic method has been devised for the various kinds of steps involved in explication.

It is clear from the example that one's own feelings *can* be stated falsely by oneself, and later corrected. There can be several steps in such correcting.

How may we get at the truth criteria involved in calling such steps a "correcting"? Both feeling and situation are internally complex and capable of having this complexity explicated verbally in various ways.

It is an error to think of situations as already cut up neatly and tidily, so that they need only to be observed and stated, just as it is an error to think of feelings as featureless masses unrelated to situations or words. We have feelings in and of situations. Conversely, situations are not physical facts but predicaments for people's living, desiring, and avoiding. Situation and experience cannot be separated, and both have the characteristic I attributed to experience: they can (and often must) be explicated further.

Thus, again considering our example, I can neither make anything I wish of my feeling and situation, nor can I regard them as given in a defined way. I must structure the situation further. This further structuring must go beyond the way in which the situation is cut and defined—at least in situations that are a problem for me. On the other hand, I must remain in accord with something about the situation—or else no realistic, feasible course of action will emerge. The sense in which I must remain in accord with the situation can be stated as its *nonnumerical, multischematic, and interschematizable character.*

Although in this chapter I deal chiefly with the relation of words and experience, I must say here that speaking and thinking are special cases of action. Experience and situation are always already organized, but are capable of being further schematized and organized not only by verbalization but also by actions. Again, such further structuring can occur in a variety of ways, but it is never arbitrary. For any given action you will get only just what you get, not merely anything at all. In phenomenological explication, as in ordinary action, you must not only interpret a situation, but you must also apply your organization if you are to live in the situation further. That is very different from merely imposing some logical or attractive way of organizing it, and then being able to leave and let it go at that. Thus explication differs from mere deduction. One deals with not only the words and statements but also the experience and situation, and what is or is not revealed in them.

The relationships between experience and verbalization show this character of explication: each relationship involves not only words but a certain effect in experience which they elicit or fail to elicit. One cannot simply wish for the words to have this effect. For example, although I might wish my phrasing to have the power to create an experiential aspect in you, it might fail to have that power. I may wish a word to produce a certain recognition feeling and "be the word for" that, yet it may not be. And, of course, I may from the start wish that my statement not be accepted but be used only for its direct reference power; yet it may fail to have such power for you, even in the context and with all you know. Thus each of the relationships I have cited is, in a way, its own truth criterion—if it happens at all.

Therefore, if we can be sure that a given chain of thought or speech is a true phenomenological explication, then we can at least be sure that it will move a step forward in some way. Thus there are truth criteria not for a single statement alone but for a kind of process, a kind of step, each step in relation to an earlier one.

To restate what we have already said, the following *signposts* help us to recognize when phenomenological explication is going on and when it is not. When phenomenological explication occurs:

(a) Precise defined meanings of words and the defined aspects of situations are used, but they can be further structured and redefined in ways that would not follow from the extant definitions.

(b) Something more than what is defined is employed. A not yet cognitively clear sense, feeling, or experience is used. This experience enables one to be dissatisfied with the words and definitions one has. Without it one would have only the statements and would have to either accept or reject them. In explication, on the other hand, a statement often serves to enable a step to be taken, and yet the statement cannot be accepted. Something directly referred to is involved in addition to statements.

(c) Aspects, and aspects within aspects, of this experience can be found.

(d) Demonstrative words such as "this" or "it" are used importantly, and yet such words alone convey little or nothing.

(e) Several different descriptive words may be used for the "same thing," despite the fact that literally they mean different things. Such different words can have quite different effects even in regard to the present experience, and one may ignore this, or pursue it.

(f) Previous assertions which enabled important steps forward may later be flatly denied.

(g) Whatever one now says is held to be what the experience "was" all along.

(h) Earlier false steps are believed to have been in the right direction, despite the fact that they are flatly contradicted now.

(i) What is at first simply physically "felt" becomes explicated in words that are about situations and world (not in feeling-tone words such as "dull" or "sharp" or "intense").

(j) Despite revealing new aspects and despite its changing, what is talked about is held to remain "the same" (not *literally* "the same"; it is obviously capable of various organizations and aspects).

If we accept the explication process of steps instead of a good or bad, single-step statement, we are in the position of caring less about "what" the statement says and more about "how" it relates and affects the experience: we are interested in the effects of the statement.

We have already cited some characteristics of an explicative step.

Although its ultimate truth value is not firm, but depends on what subsequent steps will reveal, its characteristics as explication (or not) are quite firm.

In regard to our initial problem, we have denied that explication statements simply describe, state, or read off experience without changing it. Instead, we propose a method in which a statement can be used as exactly relative to the change it makes in the experience, or—more fairly said—to the kind of relationship it has with experience in the process of being further schematized. There are several such relationships that need to be distinguished. Each enables us to determine a statement's use as relative to that relation. Thereby certain specific methodic moves also become specifiable.

We rejected "feels right" or "sounds right" as a criterion, and instead found the several specific relationships involved. Explication always involves direct reference—and may succeed relative to that relationship—yet it may fail to achieve verbalizations we can accept. Far from being right if it feels right, such a statement is likely to succeed in directly referring and yet fail quite obviously in what it formulates. Even if the failure is not obvious, there is always the possibility of further differentiation of new aspects, as well as further formulation.

This phenomenological method makes the process, relationships, and steps of explication (rather than any given statements) basic. As I will now try to show, this shift from what is said to how it is related to experience has basic applicability to many fields.

The method may seem as if it launches us on an endless progression, but even here there are methodic ways of knowing when a desirable stopping point is reached; again the stopping point is not a final statement *of* an experience, but rather a way of structuring words or situations adequately so that some living, some action, or some intellectual task may be carried out. With respect to the final nature of experience there is no stopping point to statement, because the nature of experiencing vis-à-vis further structuring is precisely that it can be further structured, and in several different ways. There are steps rather than statement.

I have tried to show that this avenue can lead to a systematic analysis of relationships between verbalizations and experience, a systematic characterization of experience in these relations, and systematic rules of method.

The strategy of looking at the "how" of a process, rather than at the "what" of single-step statements, has many applications. Let me cite one. In ethics, for example, it is said that a person has "reasons" for his actions, even if these are not always apparent to him. But what an oversimplification it is, then, to adduce these reasons—without taking into account the nature of experiencing characterized here!

In ethics, one must first recognize this character of experiencing. One must then see that any "reasons" stated may bear the several kinds of relationships to experience that we have outlined or alluded to. Further steps of explication are always possible. It will be better, for a philosophical ethics, to turn ninety degrees, and instead of calling some reasons good and others bad, to characterize the kind of decision-making process that arrives at "good" results. There is much adulation of spontaneity and feeling-expression today, but only some actions and speakings are related to feeling-experience in this good way. A different kind of relation obtains in impulsive behavior which is worse and less grounded than thinking alone. Still a third type of relation obtains for people who have explicit "reasons" that are not even explications of the experiencing leading to the action. Even a fourth relation is possible: one may truly have explicit "reasons" for an action (truly, that is to say, not as a rationalization or disconnected cover for experienced reasons) that are experiential and yet have nothing to do with what the reason is or says—as when a person tries to act in accord with some principle not for its own sake, but because he wishes to be loyal to a certain group holding that principle. Here we would need to explicate his experience—not of that reason and not the experience leading to the action, but of what led him to such loyalty to that group.

I cannot discuss ethics here. The single paragraph above illustrates, however, that the strategy of a ninety-degree turn may be fruitful in a variety of fields. The strategy is one of characterizing the "how," and of allowing the "what" to change step-by-step—being very precise, however, about these steps.

I will now discuss the application of experiential philosophy to psychotherapy research and psychology generally.

Psychotherapy Theory and Practice

In psychology too, the shift has been a basic and fruitful one: from the consideration of only structures and patterns to the consideration of the structure-experiencing relationship. This crosscutting type of variable, the phenomenological consideration of the relationship of statements or thoughts to experiencing, has been found fruitful in psychological research.[10] I want to report in detail one chain of such research which has become important in that field.

In psychotherapy it is common for a patient to work on a direct referent, "an" experiencing he feels quite strongly and yet does not cognitively understand. The kind of sequence illustrated by our example of "tired" is quite common. Not one, but a whole sequence of explicative statements occurs, each step bringing a shift in this so-called same experiencing. The change wanted in psychotherapy is not some final true statement but the continuation-and-change in the bodily-felt experiencing which occurs in such steps.

All psychotherapists and psychotherapy patients know the difference between statements that are merely true and—much rarer—statements which make an experiential difference. Every psychotherapist has found that interpretations are often ineffective even when they are quite correct. One can say something about oneself which one understands quite well, and which one feels ought to be different; yet there is no change. One's feelings and behavior remain as they were, even though one can now explain the problem, trace its origin, and show why and how the change is desired. Freud discusses the fact that the intellectual acceptance of an interpretation does not necessarily make a difference in the way a patient feels and acts. The task of psychotherapy is not to devise correct interpretations, but as Freud said, to "work [them] through," to concretely live and experience the trouble and its change.[11] Freud said that this was the most crucial part of any analysis, but he said very little about how to make it happen. We are told that it happens in transference, that is to say, in the relationship between patient and analyst, but the process is left as a rather obscure struggle. Most of Freud's writings concern *what* human beings typically find in these explorations, what interpretations may be about, but he says very little about *how* interpretations may be effective in this process of working-through, and why so often they are not.

Fenichel, who systematized most of Freud's work, is more specific: an interpretation, to be effective, he writes, must be given only "at one immediate point":

> Namely, where the patient's immediate interest is momentarily centered, . . . interpretation means helping something unconscious become conscious by naming it at the moment it is striving to break through. In giving an interpretation, the analyst seeks to intervene in the dynamic interplay of forces, to change the balance in favor of the repressed in its striving for discharge. The degree to which this change actually occurs is the criterion for the validity of an interpretation.[12]

The phenomenological approach is, of course, much more familiar with the problems of dealing with direct experience. Phenomenologists reject the Freudian explanatory concepts (such as theoretical "forces"), and therefore would reject the above explanation of why some interpretations are effective. But in rejecting the Freudian concepts (of "forces" and of the "unconscious"), phenomenologists are not quite able to account for all the observations Freud was concerned about. Some interpretations are effective and elicit material seemingly not there before, which, however, in some way, is experienced also as always having been there. However, with the philosophic method I have outlined, a more powerful phenomenology can both reject Freud's explanatory scheme and still hold to the direct experience and observation he described. In every effective psychotherapy, the patient feels an experiential shift as a result of (some few) effective interpretations, whether made by analyst or patient. Many other statements have no such effect.

If we look phenomenologically, but with our new method, at what Freudians mean by the "unconscious," we note that—at least in the above instance—they mean the common occurrence in which a person will for a time have confused but quite conscious feelings, which then later "shift" and "open up into" statements which seem to state what the earlier confused feeling really was.

To so restate the "unconscious" is to restate it in terms of a relationship between experience and explicatory statements. Let us further delineate psychotherapy by using terms that concern the relation between experiencing and statement. It is one task of philosophy to criticize the concepts used in science and to fashion new and better kinds of concepts. Let us see if we have done so.

As we have seen, it is very common in psychotherapy for a patient to have a difficult and confused feeling for which he cannot find the proper words—at least not for some time. Not only can he not find words, but the feeling itself is also confused and partly closed to him. He would not say, "I know what I feel but I can't find words." He would say, "I am not sure what I feel, but I sure feel it . . ." He might call it "that funny feeling I get when . . ." or "this knot in my stomach," or he might use some other such phrase which in itself cannot convey any specific feeling. Yet it is clear that the patient uses the phrase in order to hold on to the specific feeling or sense he has. We recognize this as the relation between experiencing and statement that we earlier termed "direct reference."

Direct reference (along with statements or with a pointing attention, such as Hadamard's, as already noted) is likely to affect the experience. If the patient will keep referring directly (and this may be somewhat difficult to do), specific aspects of this feeling will form, and although this, of course, is a major change, he will say that he now has his feeling more clearly. Perhaps he now can say it. The words he fashions are usually metaphoric, but are designed to convey the specific aspect to which he directly refers (we called it *comprehension*).

Quite often the process is not so swift. Both patient and therapist may make many true and trenchant statements valid in their own right, but without any felt effect. Psychotherapy can be defined as a search for the few statements—about 5 percent—that do have such a directly felt effect.

A statement which does have an immediately felt effect leads, as I have already said, to a further explicating of a somewhat changed texture of situational detail. Now the patient can say a more specific "this" and "that," usually in terms of situations—how he lives, feels, and acts in them. Such comprehension further shifts his experiencing. Unless the difficulty was resolved in one such step, which is rare, he soon feels again the incompleteness or difficulty he is working on—only the confusion he now feels differs from what it was before. He moves into his next step, where he may again stay for some time.

The steps in this process are like the steps in our example, which led from feeling "sort of tired" to not wanting to do the next task. Such a step, as we saw, often leads one to entirely different situational concerns from the ones thought to be relevant to the last step. Had we not gone on with the directly felt experience, we would have been stuck in long discussions about the considerations which seemed relevant at each step. We would have discussed how long the person was working, instead of what was hard about the next task. Or we would have discussed why that task is hard to perform, when at the next step the problem turned out to have nothing to do with its difficulty. We would have discussed how "they" will react and whether "they" are wise and fair or not, when again at the next step that would have turned out not to matter. Thus it is wise to return after each step to the directly felt experiencing of whatever difficulty is left, rather than engaging in statements not related to the direct experiencing of the moment.

A psychotherapy is phenomenological, according to my theoretical reformulation, if its words and vocabulary are used in relation to experiencing. Unfortunately, many therapists of all persuasions prefer to argue with their patients, rather than constantly referring to their concretely-had experiencing, rather than foregoing each, however interesting, set of considerations for the revised interpretations of the next step.

Research

For many years, the leading research problem in psychotherapy has been the measurement of whether or not effective psychotherapy is taking place. In the past twenty-five years many cases have been tape-recorded, but the many attempts to define the differing problems that patients verbalize, or methods therapists use, have failed to show any relationship to outcome. Methods emphasizing different, supposedly "basic" psychological factors show about the same degree of success. Different orientations of therapists concentrate respectively on sexual problems, infantile experiences, life styles, self-concepts, interpersonal relationships, or other kinds of "basic" contents. These differences do not seem to matter. Some therapies are successful and some fail, with or without any of these content areas. The resolution of this problem along phenomenological lines lies instead in studying *how* patient and therapist talk, rather than *what* they talk about.

The usual method in research was to give the patient psychological tests before the therapy began and after it ended, and then to establish whether or not change resulted. Sometimes it did, and as often it did not. But there was no way to study psychotherapy directly, and hence no accounting for why each method and emphasis sometimes succeeded and sometimes not.

Nor was it possible to measure the outcome of *psychotherapy*, since *psychotherapy* could not even be defined. One could measure the before-and-after change in a great number of cases and in different methods, but all that these cases had in common was that therapist and patient *intended* something undefined, called psychotherapy, to happen. It was clear that the ongoing process itself needed defining, but how to do so? Whenever those factors that most writers held to be basic were tested, it was found that they did not necessarily provide for a successful outcome. Interpretation, transference, discussions of supposedly basic contents did occur, but sometimes the outcome would be successful and sometimes not. About the only finding relating outcome to what occurred during psychotherapy was that those patients who later showed the most change made more positive statements about themselves in the later interviews than in the earlier ones, a finding that is clearly about the result and not the source of therapeutic change.

Using the relationships between experience and statement earlier cited, and the signposts of experiential explication they led to, it became possible to define and make operationally observable the kind of verbalizing that effective psychotherapy involves. The train of thought and steps of statement in effective psychotherapy clearly differ from narrative (and then this happened, and then that happened . . .) or logical deduction (and so it follows that such and such must be so). Instead, effective steps of verbalization are connected through relations to directly felt experiencing and, as we have seen, move in the kind of steps we defined. How such steps follow each other is understandable, but not by situational narrative, since the relevant situational considerations differ after each step of experiential explication. The steps are understandable, but not logically; in fact, there is often a seeming flat contradiction and denial of what was affirmed earlier. One may see this, for example, in such transitions as the one from "I don't want to" to "I do want to, but . . ."

Working from signposts such as those already listed, and others, it was possible to devise an Experiencing Scale, consisting of descriptions of specific aspects of verbalizations that can be observably noticed in tape-recorded psychotherapy.[13] Using this scale independently, different individuals have arrived at measurably close scores.

A whole series of studies has now shown that, indeed, those cases that score high on the Experiencing Scale during psychotherapy result in successful change.[14] Successful outcome can be predicted from a surprisingly small number of short excerpts, in some studies merely from four, four-minute segments, so consistent, apparently, is the presence or absence of the experiential mode of doing psychotherapy in a given case.

As we have seen, the Experiencing Scale measures *how* the patient works in psychotherapy, not *what* he says, or what areas of concern he works on. He is successful to the extent that he refers directly to, and explicates, what he directly feels, and follows the steps through which experiential explication leads. He fails to the extent that he *only* explains or narrates (although everyone does some of these latter).

This measure is currently the only gauge which enables us to determine whether or not effective psychotherapy is currently taking place. The findings strongly imply that these experiential signposts are indicative of whatever makes therapy effective.

Possibilities for further research have also been greatly enlarged, because we now no longer need to wait until the termination of therapy in order to measure individual cases. Previously, if an investigator wanted to test whether a given procedure or factor was related to a positive outcome, the tape recordings of completed cases had to be collected. Now one can test the effect of the factor by using the tape recordings of just a few interviews before and after the introduction of the procedure (or with, or without, the given factor); one can test swiftly whether or not the factor makes for an effective therapeutic process.

To further show what this scale measures, let me cite an example.

Low on the Scale:

Client: I'm trying to rewrite some of these papers, before I send them out with my Vita to find a job. It's only December, and it ought to be ok to spend two weeks rewriting them—nobody is going to give me a job over Christmas anyway. But I sit there and I can't let myself start. It seems

EXPERIENTIAL PHENOMENOLOGY

like it's so urgent I ought to send them out today, right away. I can't work on them so I'll have to go and send them in the shape they're in.

Therapist: Well, maybe you could give yourself one week? Do they really need rewriting, or is it perfectionism?

Client: No, I can't even give it a day. But there are some plain, obvious bad spots in the papers that I know how to fix. I just have no confidence at all that I can get a job. (*Long conversation lost in details of papers, time, and hiring policies.*)

High on the Scale:

Therapist (*picking something that he wished the client would have an experiential sense of and go into*): Is the urgent feeling that you don't think you'll find a job?

Client: Yeah. No. Well, something like that. (*Keeps quiet a while.*) I'm so mad at myself.

Therapist (*thinking he's angry at himself for not being able to work and fix the papers*): It's urgent, and you're mad at yourself for being tied up.

Client: No, I'm just mad. (*Long silence.*) It's like, I *should* send the papers out in bad shape, because that would serve me right. I didn't do them right and now it's too late. It's my father—you didn't do it when you should have done it, so now go take your punishment. (*Shakes his head.*) Well, now I can work on them, but isn't that something?

Therapist: You've still got his kind of ethic in you—you didn't do it right, so suffer.

Client: It has something to do with his dying last year, I would say it must have something to do with that.

Therapist (*not wanting to get off on the dying part, which seems extraneous*): It's a punishing, critical, go-suffer kind of angry.

Client: Yes, it's him. (*Long silence.*) It's because he died.

Therapist (*understanding the connection now*): It's your way of hanging on to him.

Client: No, he's hanging on to me. That's the only relationship he had to me.

Therapist: It's the bond between you.

Client (*emphatically*): Yes, that's the way it feels. (*Long silence, then with mixed hate and love and slight tearfulness.*) You old son of a bitch, why, you old son of a bitch.

This bit of psychotherapy illustrates the signposts that are a constant feature of *psychotherapy*: What is being worked on is an experiential "something," the nature and change of which takes surprising turns. Remaining on the initial level of attitudes and circumstances makes for no therapeutic change (though it can be valuable in other respects). The felt, directly-referred-to, experiential sense of what is troubling the individual produces a series of steps whose verbal statements follow our signposts of explication. What seemed to be the subject matter changes, is even opposite to what had been thought—yet there is the continuity of a "same thing." The experiential process has steps which, in retrospect, have the peculiar "was" structure of explication (despite what I said then, what I say now is what it "was" all along).

The therapist, be it noted, is as often wrong as right, but the statements are used phenomenologically, to point to what is being experienced. Lengthy explanatory schemes could be introduced at every point, but these would only hold up psychotherapeutic movement and would not produce the next step.

It can be seen that the scale is interdenominational; it will fit any school of psychotherapy, whatever its vocabulary. Even "behavior therapy," which is usually contrasted to psychotherapy and uses behaviorist language in its theories and with patients, has been found similar on these indexes.[15]

There is one other area of psychological research to which the Experiencing Scale has been applied: old age. People in their seventies go through a process called "life review," wherein they attempt to cope with the meaning to them of all that has happened in their lives. Some ten years ago, in a major project at the University of Chicago, old-age-home residents were given five quite simple questions: "What is it like when you feel happy?" (sad, lonely, and so on). When their answers to this questionnaire were recently measured on the Experiencing Scale, it was found that those who were high on the scale had significantly more often survived into their eighties than those who were low on the scale. We interpret this to mean that "life review" is similar to psychotherapy, that both involve the same experiential process, that is to say, an organismic and bodily process whose manner affects life in a bodily concrete way.

Psychotherapy is not the only field in which the signposts of experientially related verbalization are important. We may want to measure the extent to which children in a classroom are engendered to think out their own experience of subject matter they are encountering. We may want to know which kinds of children, fields, or methods of teaching maximize this process and which minimize it. Can the same indexes measure this? No, the actual measure has to be devised freshly for each new field and context, but the *kind* of indexes to be used are the same. Thus, in measuring the effectiveness of almost any activity, one may ask: are there observable marks to indicate whether or not what is going on is experientially related and engenders experientially concrete steps? This form of question is likely to lead one to an effective research instrument through a shift from studying *what,* to studying *how,* a shift from an emphasis on the patterns of speech and action to an emphasis on what these patterns do or do not do in regard to concrete and ongoing experiencing.

For example, suppose we wanted to measure authenticity of choice and decision making. It is unlikely that this can be done by studying what people choose, or what value-conclusions they arrive at. It is likely that authenticity will become definable in terms of *how* an individual arrives at a value-conclusion, rather than what it is. Has the person experientially explicated various feelings and unclear commitments, loyalties, fears, and wants, and thus arrived at a value-conclusion? Was it taken over knowingly from some respected source, arrived at a value-conclusion? Was it taken over knowingly from some respected source, but without as yet relating to the person's own experiencing? Or has the person succumbed to a confusing and not clearly known pressure or wish to appear in certain ways to others? These three possibilities, if measured, would predict very different behavior and results, even though the value-conclusion itself might be the same.[16]

Creativity, an area that has been widely studied in psychology, also involves indexes of this type. What characterizes it is "how" it occurs. The uncreative individual has been characterized negatively as "stimulus-bound," that is, not able to let go of the usual or given form of something so that a novel one may arise. There is now some experiential research that offers positive definitions of what one does do when one does not hold to an extant form. A person's own description of how he proceeded would reveal whether or not he referred directly to experiential aspects, and whether the first bits of structured form he obtained were or were not related to his experiencing in the ways I have defined. To measure this, one would need to devise specific indexes in accord with the range of comments people make about their own thinking. It is, however, already somewhat clear that those who are creative are able to focus their attention directly on what is being experienced but is not yet cognitively clear, just as the successful patient does in psychotherapy, and the successful phenomenologist does when he explicates.

Again I want to emphasize that specific signposts need to be formulated for each different process. I do not wish to say that the same process occurs in all these different settings What is the same is the study of the *relationships* between what is structured, patterned, formulated, or explicit, and the ways in which experiencing is affected by these relationships. Such an approach, I find, is a more effective research approach than studying the patterns and contents as such. Either way, one studies formed and patterned observable data, but the marks or signposts one seeks, the "variables" one defines and counts, differ. Advances in research do not usually come from merely relating already existing variables; new observations must first be defined and set up as demarcated variables. In this respect observation is at first as "implicit" as feeling. It has been fruitful to define observable variables by means of the philosophy of experiencing, which raises this type of question: how does whatever we seek to study differ observably when it is in certain relations to concrete experiencing, as against when it lacks these relations? This is a shift from *what* to *how*.

Other Theoretical Issues

In our discussion of the psychoanalytic views of "unconscious" and "interpretation," with direct reference to experiencing, instead of as part of an explanatory machinery, we have employed a shift in theoretical formulation.

How to conceive of the "unconscious" has long been a problem. One view is that it consists of unobservable ideas lying somewhere outside a person's thought. But these cannot be measured so that they might then be compared with what is later *said*, so that we may know if what is later said is what was unconscious before.

Phenomenology and empirical research are similar in discarding merely imputed constructs which do not at any point lead to experience. Therefore, the concept of the unconscious has not been very useful in research, nor is it usually accepted by phenomenologists. But the method we have developed allows us to reformulate the unconscious theoretically. Instead of considering it in terms of a hidden place, or unthought ideas, we reformulate it according to relationships between statement and experience and steps of explication. In this way we define the specific observable differences which mark what a Freudian would call "something unconscious breaking through." For, while the unconscious may be unobservable, the signposts are observable: they distinguish from other statements those that now say what an earlier confused experience "was," and refer to or comprehend directly the experiential effect of such statements. I am sure that such statements can be mimicked even without experiential effect, but such mimicking is not usual and would require a good actor, poet, or seasoned patient. Theoretically, the implication is neither simply that there is no unconscious, nor that the unconscious consists of complete thoughts and experiences that happen outside of consciousness. Rather, experience can be understood as

EXPERIENTIAL PHENOMENOLOGY

a process in itself and thus as capable of further structuring which has not yet occurred. The capacity of experience to be further structured (in thought and action) is "the unconscious"—the not indeterminate, but also not finally formed character of experience. Thus the unconscious includes bodily, evolutionary, cultural, verbal, situational, and personal aspects which have much to do with what can or cannot be further said and done but are not sayings and deeds.[17]

We should not allow phenomenology to be so shallow as to simply deny the unconscious. Phenomenology need not be limited to one-step descriptions of some experience.[18] However elaborate and interesting such descriptions can be in themselves, they take off from experience but do not return to it. The important criteria for phenomenology lie not only in beginning with experience, but also in returning constantly to it and allowing it to have the corrective force which the occurrence of experiential effects gives it. When one explicates a difficult text, it is not enough to take off from some line and spin an interesting interpretation; one must return to the text and see if the interpretation sheds light on other lines in the text, whether it solves or shifts difficulties. If it has no such effects, then the interpretation of the given line was simply a digression, interesting for its own sake perhaps, but not attributable to this text. Thus a phenomenological psychology need not be baffled by the very real problems to which the theory of the "unconscious" is such a poor answer. It need only concern itself with steps of explication, rather than remaining fixed at one point.[19]

Steps of explication and their signposts give criteria for the truth of the next statement, only in relation to the previous. But then neither are there final statements in ordinary science. The next discovery may overturn previously well-established statements. Phenomenological explication steps have criteria which can be called criteria of continuity. The relationships I have outlined do not simply produce abrupt changes in what is experienced. On the contrary, despite change and despite contradictory statements, the individual will have the insistent sense that "this" is now "really" what that earlier experience "was." Thus there is continuity: there is neither flat identity nor an abrupt new thing. Experience has its own kind of order, different from logic and defined events. Experience can always be "carried further," but not in just any way, only in some ways. These ways may have to be found or invented, but until they occur, the explicative continuity does not exist.

Thus, it is possible to make some seemingly convenient statement, explication, or value-conclusion which might state what one feels or wishes or desires, but which lacks the signposts of experiential explication. In this case it is quite likely that much of what is felt (and thus much that is important in living in situations with others) has not been carried further. What one says is not continuous with the many considerations that are "unconscious." Actually one can feel many of these, with awareness if one wishes, but cognitively they are unclear and only later come to have specifiable aspects.

A phenomenological ethics, for example, cannot do without experiential explication and its signposts. It is both a methodological and a moral error to say that authentic choice is nothing more than individual choice. What matters is *how* one does it. One may base decision on "experience" in the sense in which it is already identified and defined (for instance, as a desire to do such and such). Or one might simply follow the strongest passion, speaking and acting in ways that have poorer grounding than if moral precepts were used, however insufficient these might be. It is better for speech and action to be based on "experience" than on thought alone—but only if they are "based" in such a way as to give us more than do formulated thoughts alone. This will be the case only if the thinking is explicating and continuing the experiencing. Without specific criteria to help us recognize when this is so, everything becomes arbitrary.

Notes

1. Stanley Cavell, "Must We Mean What We Say?" in *Ordinary Language*, ed. Vere C. Chappell (Englewood Cliffs, N.J.: Prentice-Hall, 1964).

2. Eugene T. Gendlin, "What Are the Grounds of Explication? A Basic Problem in Linguistic Analysis and in Phenomenology," *Monist* 49, no. 1 (January 1965): 137–64.

3. J. L. Austin, "The Meaning of a Word," in *Philosophical Papers*, ed. J. O. Urmson and G. J. Warnock (Oxford: Oxford University Press, 1961), 29–30.

4. Martin Heidegger, *Sein und Zeit* (Tübingen: Niemeyer, 1927); English translation, *Being and Time*, trans. John Macquarrie and Edward Robinson (London: SCM, 1962); hereafter abbreviated as *BT*.

5. The terms in quotation marks are borrowed from, respectively, Maurice Merleau-Ponty, *Phénoménologie de la perception* (Paris: Gallimard, 1945); English translation by Colin Smith, *Phenomenology of Perception* (New York: Humanities, 1962). Edmund Husserl, *Logische Untersuchungen*, 3rd ed., 3 vols. (Halle: Niemeyer, 1921–22), vol. 2, part 2, investigation 6; English translation by J. N. Findlay, *Logical Investigations* (New York: Humanities, 1970).

6. Edmund Husserl, *Ideen zu einer reinen Phänomenologie und phänomenologischen Philosophie: Erstes Buch* (The Hague: Nijhoff, 1950), par. 124; English translation, *Ideas: General Introduction to Pure Phenomenology*, trans. W. R. Boyce Gibson (New York: Humanities, 1931; paperback ed., New York: Collier, 1962); here the translation is slightly modified.

7. Ludwig Wittgenstein, *Philosophical Investigations* (New York: Macmillan, 1953), 656.

8. Eugene T. Gendlin, *Experiencing and the Creation of Meaning: A Philosophical and Psychological Approach to the Subjective* (Evanston, Ill.: Northwestern University Press, 1997), 91–137; hereafter cited as *ECM*.

9. J. Hadamard, *The Psychology of Invention in the Mathematical Field* (New York: Dover, 1945), 76–77.

10. Eugene T. Gendlin, "Galvanic Skin Response Correlates of Different Modes of Experiencing," *Journal of Clinical Psychology* 17, no. 1 (1961), 73–77.

11. Sigmund Freud, *Beyond the Pleasure Principle* (New York: Bantam, 1959).

12. O. Fenichel, *The Psychoanalytic Theory of Neurosis* (New York: Norton, 1945), 25–32.

13. M. Klein, P. Mathieu-Coughlan, D. Kiesler, and E. T. Gendlin, *The Experiencing Scale Manual* (Madison: Wisconsin Psychiatric Institute, 1969).

14. Eugene T. Gendlin, J. Beebe, J. Cassens, M. Klein, and M. Oberlander, "Focusing Ability in Psychotherapy, Personality and Creativity," in *Research in Psychotherapy*, vol. 3, ed. J. Schlien (Washington, D.C.: American Psychological Association, 1967), 217–41.

15. B. Weitzman, "Behavior Therapy and Psychotherapy," *Psychological Review* (1967).

16. Eugene T. Gendlin, "Values and the Process of Experiencing," in *The Goals of Psychotherapy*, ed. Alvin R. Mahrer (New York: Appleton Century-Crofts, 1967).

17. Eugene T. Gendlin, "A Theory of Personality Change," in *Creative Developments*, ed. Alvin R. Mahrer (Cleveland, Ohio: Case Western Reserve University Press, 1971).

18. Eugene T. Gendlin, "Expressive Meanings," in *Invitation to Phenomenology*, ed. James M. Edie (Chicago: Quadrangle, 1965).

19. Eugene T. Gendlin, "Experiential Explication and the Problem of Truth," *Journal of Existentialism* 6, no. 22 (1966): 131–46.

4

The New Phenomenology of Carrying Forward

In this chapter I show a new approach to what phenomenologists call "phenomena," a deliberate way to *think and speak with* what is more than categories (concepts, theories, assumptions, distinctions, and so on). Some categories are always implicit in language, and language is always implicit in any human experiencing. So what I just called the "more" cannot be separated from implicit categories and language. This is well known. What is little known is that experiencing always goes freshly beyond the categories and the common phrases. I have been establishing a deliberate way to think with more. This is crucially needed in philosophy, but it has seemed impossible. We can reformulate the problems it involves.

Most philosophers gave up on phenomenology long ago, because it was recognized that neutral description is impossible. Description involves categories. Sartre's dialectical categories differed from Merleau-Ponty's functional approach, therefore their "descriptions" differed from each other's and from Husserl's. It was soon said that phenomenology finds no phenomena at all, only the same philosophical issues that have always been contested. The phenomena seemed to depend entirely on the categories (through history, culture, and common language forms). Philosophers were tempted, like Heidegger in the years after *Being and Time*, to deal with categories apart from phenomenology, from the top down. Everyone can now see that working with the categories alone is not at all hopeful. None are ultimate and their use always involves an "excess" which fits neither within categories nor can it be had separately. This impasse has led to the dead-end aspect of postmodernism. It frees us from any privileged set of categories, but leaves us only with an aporia, still only on the level of concepts. But if one recognizes that language is inherently metaphorical and not controlled by concepts, then there need be no dead end.

It is now evident that philosophy needs to employ more than conceptuality, but the current "return" to phenomenology need not be a retreat from postmodernism. Phenomenology need not back away from the problem of the relativity of descriptive categories and approaches.

We have ways to think with the so-called excess. I have shown that it is much more than a texture of old concepts. What I call "experiencing" is not separable from concepts, but it plays crucial, directly demonstrable roles in ongoing thinking. It performs functions that concepts cannot perform.

The "excess" is our situated experiencing in the world, in situations with others. It does not utterly depend on categories. History and culture are insufficient to handle even an ordinary day. The common phrases do not limit our next steps of action and thought. Applying different categories does indeed bring forth different phenomena, but the direct experiencing of whatever we study always responds very precisely, always just so and not otherwise, and always with more than what could follow just from our categories. Experiencing is a "responsive order," as I call it.[1] This order is always unfinished in regard to further conceptual form, but always more finely organized than any conceptual forms. If you are willing to think with the "excess" rather than leaving it behind, you can attend to it directly at any juncture of thinking. Then you can notice that it will not permit you to say most of the cogent things you can easily say. It will stay opaque, stuck, and mum unless and until just certain sentences "come" to open it. Such freshly formed, often metaphorical sentences show that language is deeply rooted in experiencing and not controlled by extant concepts or categories. If we think from where these arise, we can examine and redirect some of the functions which implicit experiencing provides at that particular juncture of thought.

I am summarizing what I call a "reversal of the usual philosophical order" in my philosophical work. Philosophies have long claimed a basis in experience, but "experience" was always construed according to the concepts and categories of that philosophy. The concepts were always read into experience. This is still done today when the "excess" is understood as just a texture of old concepts. Only a phenomenology can employ the functions of experiencing beyond the variety of concepts. In works I summarize here, one can find a philosophical way to show and directly employ some of its functions in thinking and speaking.

We find neither objectivism nor indeterminacy. Where others see indeterminacy, we find intricacy—an always unfinished order that cannot be represented, but has to be taken along as we think. It is a much finer, more organic order that always provides implicit functions, whether we attend to them or not. I will try to show some of these functions in the first part of this chapter.

To speak with and from what is more than the categories, we employ the capacity of language for new sentences. This capacity of language is rooted in the human body as reflexively sensed from inside. The reflexivity is currently being missed, because *attention* is understood along the lines of perception, as if a neutral and unexamined person over here directs a neutral beam at some already separate object over there. If we attend to experiencing directly, we find that we live with situational bodies which always sense themselves in sensing anything else. So the first half of this chapter concerns the functions of what is more than categories, especially the inherent interrelations of language, situations, and the human body. The second half of this chapter concerns the reflexivity of attention, self-consciousness, and first-person process.

Phenomenology, as I understand it, determines its own use of language. It can develop new categories of description. It can examine and direct the use of logic and theory. Phenomenology for me is not the small phenomenology which understands itself as only describing conscious experiences cut off from the universe, from other persons, and from the "unconscious" depths of person and body. I will touch on these topics to show that they are not beyond phenomenology as I have always understood it. Phenomenology is small when it accepts a small corner within the world-picture of the reductive sciences.

A philosophy that can think with more does not assume the science picture. It does not assume, in Russell's words, that logic is the "furniture of the world." We want to derive and understand the great power of logic and science, and grasp how these are embedded in more than themselves. We badly need to add a new and different kind of science to augment that world-picture. Husserl's refusal to assume the reductive ontology was sound, and we can go much further in the direction he opened. We can derive this and also other ontologies in and from phenomenology.

In use, all concepts involve more than their clean logical patterns. But if we do not pay more attention to this, then we seem to have nothing left when the concepts fail. There is no new road, only arbitrariness where the concepts break. We find ourselves in a welter of conceptual possibilities, a mix of all the concepts and theories we have read and thought. We can move in all sorts of possible directions, old and new. Many analytic distinctions can always be made, and need not be foolish. In this plethora what we choose to say is arbitrary.

Where I wish to point is a little further. The welter of old concepts is here, but they do not alone determine what we find. Let me ask you: when no concept seems to work, what more do you find here? I think you find that *you* are still here, of course, in the midst of your situation, and you can still find your hope for something from your foray into the topic. Perhaps you were pursuing an unclear lead, the sense of something promising. In that case this is also still here. Along with this you feel implicitly all you ever learned and thought, but not as a welter, but rather as it relates in a focal way to what you are tracking. None of this goes away.

What you find is not disorder, not limbo, not just flow, not some concept together with the opposite of that concept. Rather, you find an intricacy, pregnant, implicitly ordered, perhaps partly opaque. From this intricacy you may at times be unable to go on, at least for a while. This implicit intricacy is quite different than the welter of analytic concepts and possibilities.

There are phenomenological variables at this "edge." Sometimes the sense of such an edge is already there, calling for our attention, but usually we need a quiet minute of attending to where it can come. And when it has come, if we leave it even for a moment, then we only remember it. We need another quiet minute to find it again. When it comes, it may be open to be spoken-from. Or it may be closed and opaque, requiring us to return repeatedly before it opens. It may be a diffuse sense from which many strands can be articulated. Or there may be one single focal implying like a felt lead or an insistent sense of something. In *Experiencing and the Creation of Meaning*, I found interesting relations among these variables. Much work has since been done on this kind of datum.

I have been speaking about concepts breaking down, but even when they work well, we can always go to the implicit intricacy. It is a more *organic order*, a more *precise* and more demanding *kind* of order, a very finely *determined* order, very *different* from logic, yet responsive to logic. It contains a great many implicit distinctions and entities, but you can easily assure yourself that it has much more order than these, and an order of a different kind.

Now I must point to the mode of language I have already used here. Can I really use words such as "organic," "order," "precise," "kind," "determined," and "different" to speak of more than conceptual distinctions? These words seem to mean certain conceptual distinctions. Does not "order" always consist of discrete entities and patterns? Does not "organic" refer to certain defined entities? But in my sentences the words have not remained within their old meanings. When we speak from the intricacy, the sentences can add to the meanings of the words. We notice this especially when we have trouble finding words. Then we can sense the physical strain as the implicit words rearrange themselves in our bodies, so that when they come, they arrive newly arranged. Words can acquire more meaning when they come in sentences that come freshly at the edge of the implicit intricacy.

You need not be a philosopher to find yourself at such an edge. You might be tracking a half-formed new observation in any field. Or you might be in the midst of writing a poem. Or you might find yourself in a

CHAPTER 4

troubling situation which no obvious action can resolve. With the usual view of the body as a machine, it may seem surprising that the body can feel a situation, and what is more, can imply and demand a next step of speech or action that has never been seen before. But we are familiar with this bodily "knowledge" from many practical situations. We know that we cannot base our actions just on what we can conceptualize. We have to use our implicit bodily sense of the whole situation. We may find a way that resolves our bodily unease, or not. We decide when we must, but perhaps a large discomfort remains hanging there. This bodily discomfort "knows" some of the intricacy which the decision did not take account of. But when a decision does sit right in our bodies, how well we sleep that night!

Right now, for example, where do you sense your reaction to what I am saying? If you have not stopped to articulate it, then it is still only a physical sense of implicit meaning, perhaps excitement, perhaps discomfort, at any rate a bodily sense which only a philosophical body could create. It is not an emotion, not a mere feeling *about* this discussion, but an implicit intricacy, a cluster of implicit philosophical thoughts.

But I am getting too far ahead. Let me choose one example and go into some detail. I hope the example will let me point to the close relation between language and the body. In my example you will note the *physical* "coming" of words. The example should also show how we can find where the implicit intricacy opens. Third, it should show how we recognize when we did *not* speak from the implicit intricacy, and when we did.

Say you are writing a poem. You have six or eight lines but the poem is not finished. It wants to go on. In an implicit way you feel (sense, have, live, are . . .) what should be said next, but you do not know what to say. The phrases that come do not precisely say it. You reject one phrase after another. How are you able to do this? You do not know what to say, but you recognize that these phrases do not say it. Something implicit is functioning in your rejection of them. Lovely phrases come. Some are so good, you save them for another poem. But THIS demanding implicit sense still hangs there.

You may be distracted for a moment. Now the demanding sense is gone. You quietly reread the poem so far, and there, at the end of what you have, there it is again! And you still cannot say it.

What or where is "that," which is there again? It is so stubborn and precise. Your body understands the phrases that come. It knows the language and demands—I say implies—something more precise. Your hand rotates in midair, your body knows what needs to be said and has never as yet been said in the history of the world (if it is a good poem). Eventually the right phrases *come*! What does the word "come" say here? How do words come to us? This "coming" needs to be studied. How do the right phrases come and how are they recognized?

As a poet you need not worry over these questions. Poets work in what Husserl called the "natural attitude." But as philosophers and phenomenologists we want to think with, from, and into this unclear but more precise demanding edge, and think into this coming of words. When we then speak from there, these three words "language," "concept," and "body" will have acquired more meanings.

As philosopher observing yourself as poet, you find that THIS, which needs to be said, is more precise than the common phrases. How or where do you have this? Your rotating hand almost says it. Your whole body demands (implies) THIS. But now the word "body" speaks from your body as sensed from inside, not only your externally observable body.

The implicit meaning does not exist before or without language. In animals the inwardly sensed body exists before language. But the human body is never before language. But the implied meaning is not the result *only* of language. The relation of language to the body is more intricate than just with or without. Your body understands well the language and the more intricate than just with or without. Your body understands well the language and the phrases it rejects. But it can generate a bodily implying that goes beyond what the already-shared common meanings could imply. The body knows the language, and it always moves on freshly again, beyond the already existing meanings.

The body physically rearranges the same old words, so that they come to us already arranged in new phrases and sentences. This is so in all ordinary speech, not only in fresh thinking. We do not look up single words and paste them together. If we hear ourselves saying the wrong thing, we can only stop, regain the implicit sense of what we were about to say, and wait for another set of words to come.

The "coming" of words is bodily, like the coming of tears, sleep, orgasm, improvisation, and how the muse comes. But here we have to be careful. The higher animals also sleep and have orgasms, and very complex lives even without language. But language is implicit in the whole human body (not only in our brains). Language is implicit in our muscular movements and in every organ. It is implicit in what rouses or spoils our appetites, and in what disturbs our sleep. The language is part of culture and history, but the body is always freshly here again, and can say "no," even when culture and reason say "yes." If you enter there, you find a finely ordered cluster of strands, far more intricate than culture. The body can insist on some new and more sophisticated way that has never as yet been found, and may never be found. We often need to find our way beyond the cultural forms. Similarly, improvisation and the muse come in a bodily way beyond the already existing forms.

Although what we called "you" does not control what comes, the implying is not an otherness (not an "alterity"), not another self, not unreachable. Rather, what *comes* in this way feels more deeply and uncensoredly *from yourself* than anything that you could construct. Now the words "you" and "self" tell of degrees of selfness, since we are *most ourselves* when there is a fresh and surprising coming through the body.

There has been no established word for this kind of bodily datum. The words "perception," "idea," "emotion," "feeling," "affective," "kinesthetic," and "proprioceptive" all mean something else. Do not call it by an old word; people will not be able to find it. Let it generate an odd fresh phrase. It is a felt meaning, a felt sense, the direct referent, the implicit demanding.

All known concepts are available, but their patterns are not what we find here. If we had nothing else, we would be in limbo. But we have much more than the concepts—we have language forming freshly and oddly to say all this. And we have what language can freshly speak from, which is anything but indeterminate. What comes in this way from the intricacy is more finely organized, usually on a new plane, skewed and around the corner from the common meanings. Now let me consider the great question which must obviously be asked here: how are we able to recognize when we are speaking from the implicit intricacy, and when not? We want to grasp how. The fact that objective observers can reliably distinguish it is now well established. We have a good deal of research to support this claim.[2]

But how do we recognize carrying forward? How does the poet recognize the right line when it comes? The poet in the "natural attitude" need not explain this, but it is now our turn as philosophers to speak from this. Implicitly we "know" the answer, but we cannot easily say it. People say that the words "match" the feeling, but words and feeling have no common shape like two congruent triangles. When people in the natural attitude say "match," this is sufficient for them to "know" what they mean, but if we examine what they mean, we find that this word "match" does not speak from what happens. It speaks from the usual concepts of representation, of a match or copy which is impossible here. A sentence is not a copy of a feeling.

But can we say what does happen? Or can we only negate the old notion of representation? Do we have more here than the old concepts? Of course we have more here. We have what happens, and also the power of language which can speak freshly from what happens. Let us permit the language to do this, and also observe how it does this.

Instead of the word "match" we invite fresh whole sentences. The poet rejected the many lines because the more precise implying *continued to hang there*. None of those lines could *take it along*. Now it *no longer hangs there*, because that special line has *carried the implying forward*.

Was the new line already hidden in the implying? No, the line *came from, but was not in* the implying. The pattern we spoke of as: "came from but was not in" is more complex than representation. We are speaking from it; we are taking it along.

Does the implying become explicit? No, not at all! The implying does not become words, even after the newly phrased words arrive. The implying never turns into something explicit, as if now it is no longer there. If the implying were no longer there, the poet would not know to prefer just these words. Rather, *these words carry the implying along with it. They bring it. They carry it forward. They take it along*. They bring this implying with them, which is how the poet knows to keep just this line.

At last the poet knows what the implying "was," but is this quite the same implying that was there before? We cannot say yes because the poet didn't quite know what was implied. We cannot say no because then there would be no connection and no reason to keep these lines. Here again the old concepts break, and again I point to the more intricate pattern we find, and to the power of fresh language to speak from it. We can do much more than deny that the implying is the same or different. As philosophers we recognize the "same and different" as the arch principles of the logical use of concepts.

In commenting on my philosophy, Mohanty wanted to divide carrying forward. He wanted to know which part was there before and which part is new and different. Instead, let us speak from the pattern that we do find here.[3]

The fresh language of "no longer hanging there" and "carried forward" now becomes a new concept, but also an instance of a new way to use concepts. Fresh language leads to a new concept when there is a pattern, something we can see also in many other places. I think you will find yourself using the concept of "carrying forward" at many junctures. *There has been no way to speak from this relation between implying and words, but now there is.*

As a concept, "carrying forward" does also have the usual kind of pattern, a structure, a kind of diagram in empty space. It contains the spatial pattern of forward (and backward), and also the pattern of "carrying," i.e., something taken and moved by something else. But this

CHAPTER 4

alone says very little. The concept means our use of it *at this juncture*, where words (it could be actions) let a precise implying no longer hang there, but take it along. Without taking this juncture along, the concept does not say much. So it does not substitute for the role which the implicit intricacy plays here. We do not substitute the concept for the intricacy; rather, we take the intricacy along so that the concept can *speak-from* this intricate juncture.

But is not something a "concept" only because its pattern goes free from the juncture at which it first arises, so that it is applicable elsewhere? But the pattern of this concept is not only a separable spatial diagram. The pattern is also its relation to the carried-forward intricacy. When we apply "carrying forward" elsewhere, we apply this juncture. Let me explain how such a concept is applicable at other junctures.

Concepts that carry their implicit junctures with them are much more precise. They mean what they do at that juncture in that situation. When applied elsewhere they bring their first implicit juncture *into* the new implicit juncture. So they do not have the same effect there, nor just a different effect, but again more than same or different. Can language say what we do find? The concept's first implicit juncture "*crosses*" with the new juncture, to produce just this next change at this new juncture. We can enter into its effect. Then we find that crossing opens every concept so that it can do more than before. We also find that it opens each new juncture so that there is more there than before. The crossing of two junctures does not bring the lowest common denominator but rather a great deal that is new to both of the two that cross.

In a logical order every additional meaning is a further limitation of the result. It decreases the "degrees of freedom." But intricacy has the responsive order in which, the more requirements have been formulated, the *more* further possibilities are thereby opened. I was able to show this in *Experiencing and the Creation of Meaning*.

When two patterns function only logically, they do limit each other down to their lowest commonality. Our capacity for logical patterns is an enormously valuable human power, but we do not lose it if we also use the kind of pattern which happens with intricacy. "Carrying forward" and "crossing" are two more-than-logical concepts I have introduced. In the crossing of two intricacies, each becomes implicit in the other insofar as it can. This is an extremely precise implicit process. When we enter into this implicit effect, we find that the new possibilities are much more precisely differentiated than what we had before (see my article "Crossing and Dipping" for this philosophy of language and word use).

For example, earlier I distinguished experiencing from the arbitrary analytic plethora. This distinction has its meaning just at that juncture, in order to find both. I said only: "If you go further, what do you find you have there?" Other than for the sake of finding them, I did not distinguish them. Even so I had to say that the analytic one is already implicit in the experiential one. So this was not the separable pattern of "two." When we apply this odd dyad elsewhere, we can expect it to do more there, than can follow from it here. But concepts really always bring their intricacy along. When we apply any concept elsewhere, we can enter the intricacy to find what effect it has had there.

Things do not come separately with external relations between already-cut units. Experiencing precedes units. We create units. We fashion them retroactively, and thereby gain the powers of logical inference. We can create logical theory without assuming a reality that consists of logical units. And we can always reenter the intricacy after any logical inference.

It has long been known that concepts bring their implicit junctures and are not the same in different contexts, but this was always considered a terrible limitation which has to be ignored if we want to make sense. Concepts were therefore said to "drop out" all their intricacy, as if the actual intricacy consisted only of "particulars" subsumed under them. But concepts do not drop out their intricacy, and the intricacy does not consist only of subsumed detail. When concepts are treated as empty patterns, they seem to close the intricacy which is always there and can always be entered. Although this closing is vital for logic, it has given concepts a bad reputation as if they must always close us to more. This is not so.

In contrast to spatial patterns which have no inherent value-direction, we find that experiential implying has a life-enhancing, forward-moving character. The implied new steps (of language or action) are in a life-forwarding direction. What we usually call the "direction" is defined by some external aim or mark. The externally defined "direction" can change at each step, but in its implicit intricate meaning we say, looking back, that the surprising steps of carrying forward were in "the same" direction all along. The body's organic direction is prior to the externally defined "direction." As a society we must be careful that the great progress of the logically reductive sciences does not lead us to lose this little-understood characteristic of body process.

We see that language, body, and situational interaction are a single system together. Every situation consists of hundreds of possibilities for actions and speech-acts. Those are culturally given routines, but an individual body can sense not only the routine patterns, but also new life-enhancing steps beyond the forms and routines.

Experiencing is always *a sequence*. If we apply "carrying forward" to a whole sequence, the concept has a new effect. We can think of the sequence as a constant carrying forward of implying into new implying which is in turn carried forward into still newer implying. This process is a "zigzag" between what is implied on the one hand, and statements or actions on the other. Implying and occurring respond to each other.

If we employ the zigzag, we can monitor whether we are speaking from the implicit intricacy, or not. Suppose you have some half-formed new ideas for a paper, and now you have a chance to talk about it with someone. You have a rich implicit sense of what you want to say, but nothing written. Talking about such an implicit sense may kill it. You seem to have had only two dull ideas. But we know that talking about it can also maximize and expand it. Then you are amazed to find so many strands, all still developing. What does this depend on?

My point here is: you need not wait till you get home, and either deplore speaking prematurely, or happily laud the power of dialogue. If you keep returning to the implicit, you can check step by step whether the implicit is being carried forward. If it shrivels, quickly discard the statement. Better words will come.

This example will now help me to discuss a far-reaching conclusion: whether you will say retroactively that you "had" a rich idea or a thin one depends not only on what you had, but also on whether it was carried forward or not. Carrying forward has two past times, both the recorded time behind it, and the retroactive past looking back from now. In the recorded past you might remember how it seemed before you began speaking. In the retroactive time you now say what the implying really "was." Neither is invented. Both are very precisely just what they are.

The carrying-forward sequence gives us a new concept of time. For example, the new line lets the poet know what was "really meant" by the previous lines. Now they may need revising, but this will be a sharpening, not just a change. The process has reached back behind itself to carry forward what the previous lines "meant." Retroactively one can now explain just what it "was" in the earlier lines that has led to this new one. There is not only the remembered past, but also a new past, a second past which is experienced from the present, back, but very precisely, not arbitrarily.[4]

I call the carrying-forward sequence "non-Laplacian." Laplace said that if he could know all the particles and their velocity at any one moment, he could tell us everything about the past and the future. The zigzag stands in contrast to the Laplacian logic. We need both. Logical inference is indispensable and arrives where nothing else can. You might often want to pursue thirty-nine purely logical steps in a row, but after that, or at any point, you can institute the zigzag process in which each step can revise the whole.

Action and speech acts *occur into implying* so that it becomes a next implying. The present is constantly also the going back behind itself to bring the past implying into the newly implied future. This pattern is more intricate than linear time. It is a time of internal relations, rather than the usual time which consists of perfectly present positions that are not related to each other unless an observer externally relates them.

What I have presented are small samples, small bits from a philosophy. My intention is only to indicate a new way in which we can do phenomenology of language, phenomenology of the body, and phenomenology of concepts.

I could show only a little here. We have become able to employ and (by means of the employment also characterize) many of the ways in which the intricacy functions in thinking, in language, and in action, as well as in logic and science. In addition to "carrying forward" and "crossing" we have developed other such more-than-logical concepts, for example, "implicit governing" and "unseparated multiplicity."

We have also found certain characteristics of more-than-logical processes. The one I mentioned is that more conditions increase the degrees of freedom. I have already mentioned *A Process Model*, in which the carrying-forward process exhibits itself and develops concepts with which to understand itself. These non-Laplacian concepts are both internally and logically connected. They are inherently phenomenological, but also have the powers of logical inference. They consist partly of the implicit functions themselves, but they can also serve as purely logical concepts which can apply to the data of the reductive sciences. This makes it possible to augment the latter so that we can think also about living things and human beings.

This philosophy provides a new way to go on from where most philosophers stop. Of course, they all employ the intricacy. Philosophy sharpens and usually repositions the main terms, which can happen only because terms work in the intricacy. Some philosophers also point to the intricacy. We can stand on their shoulders and go on from their work, both because we can enter the intricacy, and because we can let fresh language speak from it in new sentences and with new patterns. In this way we can employ a philosopher's contribution more effectively.

Notes

1. Eugene T. Gendlin, "The Responsive Order: A New Empiricism," *Man and World* 30, no. 3 (1997): 383–411, reproduced in part 4 of this volume.

2. See www.focusing.org for an overview of the research. Twenty-seven successive studies have shown that higher levels on the Experiencing Scale (applied

to the tape-recorded interviews) correlate with more successful outcome in therapy. The philosophy has led to widespread applications in psychotherapy and other fields.

3. See my "Reply to Mohanty," in *Language beyond Postmodernism: Saying and Thinking in Gendlin's Philosophy*, ed. David M. Levin (Evanston, Ill.: Northwestern University Press, 1997). See also Eugene T. Gendlin, "Crossing and Dipping: Some Terms for Approaching the Interface between Natural Understanding and Logical Formation," *Minds and Machines* 5, no. 4 (1995): 547–60; and Eugene T. Gendlin, "Thinking beyond Patterns: Body, Language and Situations," in *The Presence of Feeling in Thought*, ed. B. den Ouden and M. Moen (New York: Peter Lang, 1992), 25–151; also available at www.focusing.org.

4. For the new time model, see *APM* IV–V.

5

Words Can Say How They Work

Heidegger knew he had changed the philosophical terrain. He didn't think he could go on from that change. "A philosopher cannot jump over his own shadow," he said.[1] He wrote to Frings, pleading with us not to call our meeting "the Heidegger Circle" but rather the "Circle for the Question of Being." He wanted his work deeply considered, but above all he wanted people to go on, to think freshly.

The purpose of this chapter is to save and carry forward some of Heidegger's crucial insights, especially about the openness that is not a form or a formed thing. But to go on as he did not, some points may have to shift. I will state two such shifts, but I am not concerned with the exact line of difference. Rather, please ask: is this a good and viable way to go on?

The Loss of the Openness

My objective is to think with more than conceptual structures, forms, distinctions, with more than cut and presented things. What is more than form is not just a faraway outer edge. We can find it and let it play a vital role in our own thinking.

Through its role in our thinking we will be able to reestablish the great openness, what Heidegger called the "source" that is not itself formed, but conceals itself in every form and formed thing. This is what he was most concerned about at the end. Currently it seems impossible to think or speak about what is more than form, because of a great current error: what is not clear and distinct is said to be simply indeterminate, a limbo, merely a negation of determined form. Now Heidegger's great openness seems mere indeterminacy.

Derrida can lop off this great openness. He says honestly that he just does not find it. We can conclude that it could be important to find it, rather than leaving it as something lovely and freeing that we merely posit. Should it not be findable? I will show how we can find the openness everywhere in anything.

CHAPTER 5

I will introduce two shifts:

(1) I argue that *Being and Time* could open an avenue for philosophical thinking to go on within what Heidegger called "being-in." I develop a kind of thinking that philosophy can employ drawing upon what he calls *mood* or *situatedness*. I will show that such a thinking is more than form, and can think and speak about more than form. It can think and speak about itself.

(2) I include the body within Dasein. With these two shifts, we will reestablish the openness.

The Problem

It seems we cannot talk or think about more-than-form—at all. How could Heidegger have talked about more than form, when all talking involves conceptual and linguistic forms? How could he escape the schemes inherent in the language? He struggled with that question for more than thirty years in his middle period.

On the one hand, the conceptual patterns are doubtful in various ways: they come in a mutually exclusive variety. They change in history. Each breaks down if pursued. Clean logical patterns cannot even define what clean logical patterns are or would be. They do not work only logically. Thinking is always situated (affected by mood, experience, bias, interest, practice, the body, events, situations, one's place in the world......).

On the other hand, we cannot avoid forms and concepts; we cannot think only what is more than cuts and presentations. If we talk about what is more, we cut and present that. We talk about what is more than concepts, but how? In concepts.

Suppose I lecture on the discussion method of teaching. I want my class to learn how one learns more through active discussion, so I lecture about it. You notice something wrong.

Similarly, my word "more" brings the conceptual pattern of the quantitative more and less. Am I not ridiculous? I say "more than conceptual patterns," but "more than" is a conceptual pattern. This is the problem I will attempt to resolve.

Even to state the problem, we use various distinctions. We assert that the same statement can have different implicit meanings in different contexts. In saying this we distinguish statement from context, and "explicit" from "implicit." But then we still have only what we said explicitly, it seems. Or we say that language does more than it says. This distinction renders the more as a doing (not saying), but it seems we still have only what we say, not what our saying does. Therefore Wittgenstein rejected all explanations of what language does. Therefore Heidegger could not say; he could only "point" (in his dialogue with a Japanese scholar).[2] But can we defend him in saying even that? "Pointing" brings the scheme of a thing in space to which we can point.

The conceptual patterns are doubtful and always exceeded, but the excess seems unable to think itself. It seems to become patterns when we try to think it. This has been the problem of twentieth-century philosophy. In one version or another, philosophy led to this problem and then stood still before it.

So far it has been understood only as a problem. I will turn it to advantage. What seemed like a problem becomes a power. We need not deplore the fact that concepts are never only clear patterns, nor that the more is inseparable from patterns. It is a good thing that the more is always there as well. Since we always think with both, we can do so deliberately. We can employ their inseparable togetherness by letting the concepts mean how they work within and about the situatedness. Let me show how that is possible.

Heidegger on Mood and Understanding

The late Heidegger tells of a kind of thinking he calls "dwelling" (*wohnen*). He says it is his new term for what was called *Befindlichkeit* in *Being and Time* (part 1, sections 28–31). *Befindlichkeit* is translated both as *situatedness* and as *mood* (also rather badly as *state of mind*).

In German, *Wie befinden Sie sich* is ordinary language meaning, "How are you?" This "are" fits what Heidegger says of humans: we have the kind of being that is involved in situations, projects, and worries. *Befindlichkeit* is how you are, how you find yourself just now, how you are situated, and it is therefore also your "mood." It is one of three parameters with which he defines the human mode of being. The other two are understanding and speech.

Heidegger said that our mood (our how-we-are) always contains an implicit understanding, and that this understanding is always moody. Let me put these together and speak of "moody understanding."

Your mood knows what you have been trying to do and why, what you are trying to avoid and why, how you have perhaps not avoided it and why. You might not know all that explicitly, but the mood contains an understanding of how you came into this situation and therefore into this mood.

Heidegger says that even if you don't know what to say about it, your moody understanding inherently involves speech. He did not say just how it does, only that it is already articulated in a way that can make speaking from it possible. I will say more.

Heidegger insisted that these two notions—*understanding* and *Befindlichkeit* (situatedness or mood)—are not concepts or categories. But how not? Are they not gatherings, kinds? Categories separate. Perhaps he was emphasizing that these three are implied in each other. But many ordinary concepts are implicit in each other (for example, Kant's "autonomy" and "freedom").

Since there is no common definition of "concept," and since in some sense these surely are concepts, let us more modestly ask: how are they not just concepts? If we cannot answer, does it mean Heidegger told about what is not just concepts—in concepts?

Heidegger said that the mood's understanding reaches "further than concepts can reach." It "far exceeds cognition."

In *Being and Time*, how could we understand these terms? How could we agree that the mood's understanding far exceeds cognition?

An immediate answer is possible. We understand these terms with a moody understanding. Thereby what we understand far exceeds what cognition can reach.

Without a moody understanding of these terms, we would have only their conceptual patterns and the role he gives them in his argument. We could still read how the mood is from having acted in the past toward a future we want. We could read that Heidegger posits some sort of more-than-cognitive understanding, but it would be a black box. We could grasp only the conceptual pattern of something supposedly more than conceptual. Here is the problem of twentieth-century philosophy.

But if we understand with a moody understanding, we use what the two terms are about, in order to understand them. They are not just concepts because they involve what they are about.

Of course, this succeeds only insofar as we actually have a moody understanding of those terms. We must have a mood and also that it contains an understanding of what we have been trying to do or avoid in some situation, that we do not know all of that and yet it is somehow understood in our mood. Such a mood is familiar, but what Heidegger says about it is not. He says that in the mood we understand more than we know. How can we "understand" what we don't even know? With the usual understanding we cannot understand what the word says here. What the word says must actually happen in how we understand the word.

We think such terms not only with conceptual patterns, but also with that which exceeds the pattern. Such concepts are about how their pattern is exceeded. If they make sense about that, then they no longer say what they would mean alone. Now their meaning is what they say in and about what exceeds them as patterns.

Now let us expand this so that we can take all concepts this way. All concepts bring more than their patterns. Rather than wishing it were not so, we can deliberately allow the pattern to work in and about the more. The more is always available whenever we think or speak. We can enter it and let our phrases make sense in it, if they will.

For example, now we can take my word "more" in both ways: it says the quantitative pattern more and less, but also how the moody understanding is more than the pattern. Without the moody understanding we would have only the conceptual pattern of "more" but not more. But if both are in play, then the pattern "more" is said in and about what is more than the pattern.

I have long argued that we can think in this way, not only about these two terms, but about anything.[3] If moody understanding reaches further than cognition, wouldn't we want philosophy to reach further than cognition from now on?

To go on, it is not enough to think and write in a moody or poetic way. Yes, the concepts bring more than a pattern, but they can also be about how the more functions, how it exceeds the pattern. Thereby the concepts can tell how they themselves work—in and about what exceeds their patterns. If they make sense about it, they say how they work—they are language that can say how language works.

This type of conceptual precision lets us enter a realm that was closed until now: the realm of what functions implicitly.

Instances

The kind of concepts I have been describing can be made directly from situations—instances. Let me cite an instance:

You see someone you know coming down the other side of the street, but you don't remember who it is. This is totally different than seeing a stranger. The person gives you a very familiar feeling. You cannot place the person, but in your body there is a gnawing feeling. That gnawing feeling does know. Your body knows who it is. It is ....., a whole sense in your body.

Your body also knows how you feel about the person. Although you don't remember who it is, your ..... has a very distinct quality. If you had to describe it, you might say, for example: "It is sense of something messy. I feel a little as if I'd rather not have much to do with that person, but there is also mixed in with it some odd curiosity that doesn't feel too sound, and uh ......" If you went on further into it, you could find more and more, both about the person and about yourself. But the whole felt sense cannot be put into words. However well you express it, there is always more left in it than you said. Even to say some of it, you have to make up new phrases because it does not fit into the usual phrases and categories. It is uniquely your sense of that person. Any other person would give you a different body-sense.

By focusing your attention on the ....., you may suddenly remember who the person is. Now you might be surprised. You might say "I didn't know that I felt that way about the person!"

But how can we understand this? Does your body have its own opinions of the people you know? And if it has, why does it keep its opinions to itself, instead of telling them to you right along?

Here is an instance I have given before: consider a poet, stuck in the midst of writing an unfinished poem. How to go on? The already written lines want something more, but what?

The poet rereads the written lines. The poem goes on, there, where the lines end. The poet senses what that edge there needs (wants, demands, projects, *entwirft*, implies .....). But there are no words for that. It is ah, uh, ... The poet's hand rotates in the air. The gesture says that.

Many good lines offer themselves; they try to say, but do not say— that. The blank still hangs there, still implying something more precise. Or worse, the proposed line makes the ..... shrivel and nearly disappear. Quick, get that line out of the way. The poet rereads the written lines and ah ....., there it is again. Rather than that line, the poet prefers to stay stuck.

The ..... seems to lack words, but no. It knows the language, since it understands—and rejects—the lines that came. So it is not preverbal; rather, it knows what must be said, and knows that these lines don't say that.

Heidegger was right: speech is inherent even without words. The implicit implies speech. When we cannot find words, we poignantly feel that we cannot find words. Language is implicitly working in the ...... Language is—.....—in pain in it. And to describe it so would be a case in point. In the ..... the language is reworking, rearranging, re-creating itself.

The ..... knows with a gnawing, like something forgotten, but what it knows may be new in the history of the world.

How Could Our Words Here Say What We Said?

Now I need to intrude on your privacy in a personal way. Although I don't know some of you, I do know one of your secrets. I know you have written poetry. So I can ask you: Isn't that how it is? Isn't it so, that in order to go on with a poem we must ..... use, directly refer to, focus on, feel, experience, physically sense, have, be ..... a ..... where the lines stop and the poem continues?

As you check my assertion, you refer directly to this direct referring. It is not just a theoretical term. You have it, you are being it, there. Right?

Certainly the word "refer" brings an old scheme that seems to make the ..... a thing in space to which we point. But "directly refer" is not merely a scheme. This kind of concept deliberately includes your referring. Thereby you understood implicitly that "referring" speaks of what you are doing, which exceeds the scheme. Now the scheme of referring says how it is exceeded—by your referring.

Now we can defend Heidegger's pointing. We can answer that something similar had to happen to that word when he said he could only "point" to the openness. Otherwise he could not have said even that, since the scheme of the thing in space would have hidden the openness to which he pointed.

But since the scheme in "refer" or "point" is exceeded by what you actually do, need it be a referring? I did not use the word "refer" alone. It came with a string of other words. I said we "must use" (directly refer to, focus on, let a role be played by, feel, experience, physically sense, have, be .....) the ...... The different schemes in those words would boggle and cancel each other, if taken as just schemes. But they are not just schemes. Each is exceeded by—and now says something in—the ...... There the words all work. After them all, the ..... implies and shapes a next step of thought more finely than a scheme can.

I said "experience, physically sense, have, be ..... the ......" We could pursue how the famous word "be" changes here, if it made sense to you in this spot, if you moodily understood it. Here it says (at least) that being is not only this or that form but it is (and we are) rather as the ..... is at the edge of an unfinished poem—or at the end of a string of alternative words.

What happens to "referring" and "pointing" can happen to all words about how language works. Such words work in what exceeds them. They say how they work, how their pattern is exceeded by what functions implicitly. A philosophy of language is possible since words can say how they work.

Isn't it surprising that throughout our century words have not been permitted to say how they work? The need has certainly been recognized. It was painful that philosophers could not say what they were doing.

CHAPTER 5

From long history it seemed that if language could say what it does, it would involve the claim that the explication equals what is implicit. No, those are never equal. It is precisely because the implicit continues implicit, that it enables words to say some of (only some of) what they do. They can say something about the implicit only because the implicit is part of their saying. The implicit always plays crucial roles in how words work, and with its roles they can say how they work. That words can say how they work is the most important message of this chapter.

A third instance:

A ..... comes not only in forgetting and in poetry, but also at the edge of all writing—yes writing—and all fresh thinking. Heidegger said poets and thinkers draw from the same openness.

We think not only formulated thoughts, just this and just that and just that other. Cumulatively our steps of thought arrive; they make a point. At the end you say "See .....?" You expect me to see (feel, have, understand, grasp, be .....) not just this and that and that other, but ...... What makes the difference between getting the point, as against not getting it? It is the ..... which performs that role.

And if I don't get it, then you have to say your point another way. You pause; you recollect your point, and new phrases come to lead to it. So your point is not the first set of phrases, nor the second. Your point is what you focus on to try for new phrases. The fact that you can try to rephrase it shows that what we call the point—is not a formulation; it is a ......

And of course, when we think, we don't just arrive. Quite often something continues where the words stop. We reach an edge where we sense more, but we cannot yet say that. We know not to pass by there. Of course we could move on in familiar ways, but no; we prefer to stay stuck at that edge. We even glory in it—we say "I'm on to something! Something new can come here!"

Functions of the Implicit

My three instances showed some crucial functions that only something implicit can perform. Just from what we said, I can list the following:

1. Something implicit lets us know that we forgot something.
2. It also lets us know when we have remembered.
3. It lets us know when a new step of thought is implied.
4. It functions to reject otherwise good proposals if they leave the ..... hanging there, still implying something more precise.

5. Something implicit can understand a situation directly.
6. What we want to say forms implicitly, and also
7. implicitly rearranges the language, so that
8. quite new phrases form implicitly, and come.
9. It lets us know when "the right" phrases have come.
10. The cumulative effect of a chain of thought is implicit.
11. To understand—to grasp—anything is an implicit function. We say "Oh ....., yes, I see what you mean."
12. Having a point is a ......
13. Even just to try to put differently something we have already said (as when someone doesn't get it) requires us to refer to the .....—the implicit sense of what we wanted to say.
14. Something implicit lets a new use of a word make new sense.
15. Words say how the implicit functions, if we take how the words make sense in and about that.
16. Taking the same word or sentence in various ways is made possible by the implicit. How do we know which way we took it? The difference does not lie in the sentence; only the implicit lets us take the sentence this way rather than that way, and lets us think on from having taken it this way, rather than going on from it, taken that way.

These functions are so ubiquitous, and each is so specific, why did people ever think of them as some sort of fuzzy exceptions to an otherwise form-distinguished universe? How could one think that what is not cut out and presented before us is indeterminate?

A New Kind of Concept

In stating implicit functions, the conceptual patterns are exceeded and altered by some of those functions. But they still sound the same. Can we go further? Can we change the conceptual patterns as well?

If the usual patterns were right, these instances and functions would be quite impossible. Since they don't instance the usual concepts, what changed concepts do they instance?

The implicit functions more intricately than patterns do. If we enter and say (some of) how it functions, we arrive at new conceptual patterns. Of course, those don't replace—they still require—the implicit functioning—but they set out some characteristics of how something functions when it is implicit.

"Carrying Forward"

The usual concept of "implying" means something folded under but already there. But when we say a ..... implies a next step, we know implicitly that the word does not say that. Neither is the next step simply not there. But the word says more than mere paradox, since implicitly it says however the ..... does it.

Now let us go on. The implicit functions more intricately than patterns, more intricately than there or not there. When the right phrases come, they don't copy the blank. A set of words looks different—it cannot be the copy of a blank. The right new phrases come only in the explicating, but to say that they "were implied" does rightly assert a special relation between the phrases and the blank. If we keep this implicit relation and enter it, we can devise new patterns to say some of it.

With the special phrases, the blank is not lost, altered, or left hanging. These special phrases carry the blank along. But now that they have come, the phrases say more. They are a kind of continuation of it. They carry it forward into more. "Not left hanging," "continuation," "carry with them," and "forward into more," those are schemes of course. But if we keep what the ..... does with us, the new schemes in "carrying forward" carry this implying forward.

"Crossed Multiplicity"

What about when there is no ....., when the next moves come smoothly in ordinary speech? A great deal functions implicitly also when there is no pause and no ...... We can see some of it if we do pause, but of course not quite as it functioned without pause. We want neither to read a ..... in where there isn't one, nor deny that a great deal functions implicitly also without a ...... Our concept "carrying forward" can say this: the very formation of a ..... is a kind of carrying forward, and then our lifting out (differentiating, synthesizing .....) this or that is a further carrying forward.

When we know we forget something, there is a ...... When you remember the person on the street, your ..... suddenly opens. All about the person floods back. You don't need to take time to enter and lift out this and that. But if you do, you find that the ..... implicitly contained your whole history with that person, also what you hope for and worry about with the person, what that person rouses in you, some of your own unresolved troubles. It contains the intricate way you do and don't like the person, and much more. All this functions together. You can lift out four or eight things, but there are far too many to think each one. Most of them remain an implicit many that have never been separate. How they all function changes the scheme in the words "they" and "all."

The phrase "too many to think each one" says the implicit kind of plural, a never-yet-separated multiplicity. Let us enter this intricacy and formulate a new pattern.

This kind of multiplicity is not just a merger. It functions more intricately than separated things. It is neither an enclosure by logical form, nor just rupture and limbo, but a more intricate way of shaping the next move.

Now that you remember the person, you go over and say an appropriate hello, not too warm, not cold, not long but not too short, your slight smile fittingly governed by all that multiplicity. It won't come out that way if you say to yourself: "Now smile, smile."

As formed determinants, one of these factors would make you smile broadly, another frown, and another hit the person. But when they function implicitly, they are always already crossed. Each opens the would-be determining of each of the others.

"Restored Implicit Governing"

For example, in a sport, say golf, an instructor tells you to keep your left arm stiff. You didn't know whether it was loose or stiff. Now you realize that it was loose. Your arm becomes salient for a while. Your game is thrown off, which shows that there was an implicit governing that is now disturbed.

After some time the stiff arm becomes "natural." The implicit governing of the arm is restored. It rejoins all the other factors that mutually modify each other and together shape the next move. Then your score is better than before.

In explicating we first separate something, but then we must also restore it to the implicit governing. That makes it available both as explicit and as implicitly crossed.

For example, it helps to explicate the metaphysical forms that trap us—but not if we end by having nothing but those. We gain the advantage of explicating only if we don't lose the implicit, if we rejoin its implicit governing of our further moves.

The concepts I propose make sense only in and with how the implicit functions. So they explicate and also restore themselves to its functions. They are concepts about how the implicit functions—more intricately than patterns.

There is a way to say—we have been saying—how the implicit functions. The attempt to say is not foolish.

How the Word "Body" Works in the .....

We have been speaking of the implicit (mood, understanding, situatedness, experience, bias, interest, practice, events, situations, the body .....). We could pursue how the conceptual patterns in each of these words change here. We could enter the implicit intricacy and arrive at better concepts. Let us do that with one of them, the word "body."

Of course the meaning of the word changes, if I say that the body provides the functions I listed. Now the body senses itself from inside, and that provides the new sense of the word (and the new sense of any newly used word).

When I say that the implicit functions are bodily, the new sense of the word can explain what a ..... is, how the bodily ..... can know so much, how it can be more precise than we can say, and how it can perform the functions I listed. But then how "body" works here will also explain the word "explain" in a new way.

I have a long work on this topic (see *APM*). Here I will only sketch four concepts of such a body:

(1) If moodily knowing the forgotten person is a bodily quality, then the body knows people and situations directly. Usually we don't say the body knows the situation; we say that we know it, and our bodies only react to what we know. Of course they do react to what we think, but not only to that. Our bodies know (feel, project, *entwerfen*, are, imply .....) our situations directly.

This implicit function can change our concept of the simpler organisms. How shall we rethink all living bodies, so that one of those could be ours? Can we think that animal- and plant-bodies know their situations?

Yes, we can. A plant lives in and with soil, air, and water, and it also makes itself of soil, air, and water. Now the word "is" also changes if we say: a living body is its environment. Similarly, the word "knows" changes if we say a living body "knows" its environment by being it.

Of course, its environment is not just something lying there waiting to be photographed. Living bodies have the intentionality that Heidegger worked out between Dasein and world. As Dasein knows the world, the plant-body knows the air, soil, and water implied and crossed in its life process.

Now we can know and understand how it is possible to know and understand by being the moody understanding. The ..... knows by being our living-in our situation.

Let us set up this concept: we have situational bodies.

(2) The body's being-knowing is not something spread out before the body. It is not a percept. This knowing is not perception. If a plant-body could sense itself, it would sense its environment in sensing itself, quite without the five senses. It would sense itself expanding as water came in, and it would sense itself implying water when it is lacking. It would sense itself using the light in the photosynthesis that the plant-body is.

I speak of a plant because it doesn't have the five external senses. Those only elaborate how a living body is environmental interaction. The body is not behind a wall as if it could know the environment only through five peepholes.

Another concept: we humans have plant-bodies.

(3) In Western science everything is passive, organized by externally imposed relations. A formalized "observer" connects and interrelates it all. But if we want to study the actual observers, we cannot attribute the interrelating to still another observer. Somewhere there is a self-organizing process. Let us say that a living body is a self-organizing process.

With how a ..... implies we can say that all living bodies do their own implying of their next bit of life-process. A plant or animal body projects (*entwirft*, structures, organizes, enacts, expects, is ready to go into, implies .....) its own next step. The concept: a living body implies its own next step.

(4) The next move of living that the human body implies is often something that we want to say. Speaking is a special case of further bodily living.

If we think of speaking this way, then the subtleties of language and situations do not float. Humans expedite their food-search partly by speaking. The plant absorbs from the ground; animals interpose food search between hunger and feeding. Behavior is a special case of body-process: each bit of food-search is a special version of hunger implying the eventual consummation of feeding. But in animals the plant-body has been elaborated so that now it needs far more than food. Animals need each other, groom each other, pick each other's fleas—and not only because the fleas bite, but to comfort each other. Animal bodies imply many more bodily consummations than plants do, and we humans even more. Our interposed behavior, no less than the animal's, carries a bodily implying forward. The body implies what we want to say and do.

Therefore the most sophisticated details of a linguistic situation can make our bodies uncomfortable. From such a discomfort the body can project (imply .....) new steps to deal with such a situation. Such a ..... can exceed and rearrange the common phrases until we can speak from it. The body is not just an inferred precondition as Merleau-Ponty had it. Rather, our bodies perform the implicit functions essential to language.

That is why our next words just "come" from a body-sense of a situation which we need to change by speaking, just as hunger, orgasm, and sleep come in a bodily way, and just as food-search comes in an animal.

Let us set up this concept: our bodies imply our linguistic and situational meanings, and can carry them forward.

Do these concepts explain the .....? But it is from and with the functions of the implicit that we have restructured the concepts. These functions continue to exceed these concepts.

Can We Reestablish the Openness?

It will always be a vital human power to take patterns as patterns, purely logically. Then the role of the implicit is not attended to. But the logical taking is an implicit function.

We cannot think only with conceptual patterns, nor without them. It is not a calamity that thinking does not enclose and is always situated. It is not the end of philosophy. Nor is it cultural-historical relativism. What is implicitly crossed does not confine. Neither implicit concepts nor history, social class, and our personal ways, no implicitly functioning determinants confine our next move to remain consistent with them. Nor, when they fail to enclose, do they leave us in limbo, or in a paradox of enclosing and not enclosing. The openness is not indeterminacy. It is more determinative than explicit forms.

What functions implicitly shapes the next move, but in a way that can imply something quite new and more intricate than could follow consistently from any of the crossed determinants. Such a next move is anything but arbitrary; it may be so demandingly and precisely implied and so difficult to devise that it may not come at all. Still, we prefer the pregnant openness to the easy moves.

Situatedness does differ individually and historically, but that does not mean there is no human nature. People who differ from us can make us understand them. Goethe wrote: one travels, then one brings home what is valuable from other cultures.

Dilthey said it more exactly than Goethe: "Anything human is in principle understandable." When we read, we understand authors better than they understood themselves, he said. Let us understand this better. Let us explicate it further than Dilthey did:

Cultural forms do not enclose. They are implicitly governed in the vastly more intricate crossing of bodily living.

Of course, one can misunderstand a culture. But the "marginal" person who has lived in two cultures can accurately explicate each in ways that cannot be done from one culture alone.

To understand is not a mix or merger that partly distorts. If one does not understand a culture, statement, or text exactly, one misunderstands. No, we understand exactly. But to understand is an implicit function. Our own experience (history, events, situations .....) crosses with the text; they implicitly govern each other. With all this functioning implicitly, of course we can explicate in ways the author could not. But we also understand ourselves better than before, and in new ways.

When our personal experiences and historical determinants function implicitly, they do not confine. They do not limit our next steps to remain consistent with them, as explicit logical forms seem to do. What functions implicitly together is always already crossed.

In crossing each of the many is not just itself, and has never been just itself. As just itself each determinant would constrain everything subsequent to be consistent with itself. In crossing each is not itself but crossed and governed by the others. This explains the openness in spite of so many determinants. Indeed, since each undoes the enclosure of the others, the more determinants the more openness.

Each of the many has already opened the enclosure of each of the others. The result is open for further crossing. This crossed openness for further crossing is a universal human nature. Human nature is beyond both rationalism and culturalism.

Now the word "nature" has changed to include the role of the implicit. We could pursue how this has changed the concepts that the word usually brings. To do it we would use more words whose schemes change. Each would say something new in and about how the implicit functions. There is no end to this.

Notes

1. Martin Heidegger, *What Is a Thing?* trans. W. B. Barton Jr. and Vera Deutsch (Chicago: H. Regnery, 1968).

2. Martin Heidegger, "Dialogue on Language between a Japanese and an Inquirer," in *On the Way to Language* [*Unterwegs zur Sprache*], trans. Peter D. Hertz (New York: Harper and Row, 1971), 1–56. The dialogue is a reconstruction of an actual meeting Heidegger had in March 1954 with Tezuka Tomio (1903–1983), a Japanese scholar of German literature who visited him in Freiburg.

3. See *ECM* and also Eugene T. Gendlin, "Thinking beyond Patterns: Body, Language and Situations," in *The Presence of Feeling in Thought,* ed. B. den Ouden and M. Moen (New York: Peter Lang, 1992), 25–151.

Part 2

A Process Model

6

Implicit Precision

An organism is an environmental interaction that continuously regenerates itself. It does not follow from the past, but it does take account of it. We can show that the regenerating is a kind of precision. We call it "implicit precision."

What the organism brings to the present interaction has been called the "background," though the background has previously been considered as if it were a static thing rather than part of a regenerating process.

There is general agreement that the background is "implicit," but what "implicit" means has remained mysterious. It is often said to mean "unconscious," but of course not really unconscious as from a blow on the head. But if we approach the implicit background *as part of the present process*, it may become evident *how it functions* in that process. I want to show exactly how something implicit functions *and* that it functions precisely, *as well as* exactly how regenerating takes account of its past.

There are two kinds of precision, a logical and an implicit kind. They are inherently connected and can be understood in relation to each other. This inherent connection can be seen in how the organism's accounting for its past generates new logic. The organism's taking account of its past is a *regenerative* process; this regenerative process *is* the implicit precision.

Implicit precision is not *un*logical. It *generates logical precision.* Logical precision depends on defined units—objects—with *necessary relations*, as in mathematics. In contrast, the implicit precision functions neither as units nor as a whole, but as *a process*, to which body and environment always both contribute. This process generates and regenerates the background objects and their relationships, including logical scientific units. We can move between the two kinds of precision, keeping the science of logical units steady, but also considering the wider process of generating such units.

There is need for an alternative model to change some old assumptions. The old model starts from "perception" which is a "here" about an "over there," something supposedly "inside" the body about something "outside." Perception leads us to assume the split between organism and environment. But organism and environment are always inherently *one interaction*, starting with primitive organisms before perception ever develops. The alternative I propose is *a model of process*. I have developed this model in detail elsewhere; here I use it to discuss three questions in the current philosophy about neurology.[1]

1. Three Current Questions

Question 1: *What is the environment of the active organism?*

The organism seems confronted by an environment that is strange to it. Things it cannot deal with may strike it. But it responds very appropriately to a large variety of things. The question as usually stated is: how does the organism *select and interpret* what is relevant to it?[2] The question applies not only to humans, but to animals, trees, and single-cell organisms.

Selection and interpretation would not be necessary if by *environment* we meant the organism's own, which it actively participates in generating. Recently some authors speak of organism and environment as mutually causing each other.[3] We need distinctions so that we can use the word *environment* in several ways.

Currently it is said that the organism is "active in its own formation." I think this is a great advance. But we can ask: Just what is the active role of the organism in relation to its own environment? How are they originally linked, and why do they seem to be two things?

Question 2: *The background is said to be "implicit," but how does something implicit function?*

To explain what the organism makes of the environment, some authors invoke a "background," but this consists of entities that do not really occur. Past experiences function in some way, but not by occurring again. The background includes a great number of experiences and items of knowledge, many more than could ever be enumerated. How does the organism *take them into account* without running through them all again each time?

The background may seem to be a "holistic" merger as if without distinctions. But we find an organism's process always stubbornly precise; just this particular intricacy and not something else. It functions *neither as separate occurrences nor as a merged whole.*

The background is said to function *implicitly*. We need to spell out what this means. How does something function when it functions implicitly?

Michael Polanyi wrote that the "tacit" (the implicit) is like a skill, like *knowing how* to ride a bicycle.[4] It is like knowing-*how* to do something, not like knowing-*that* such and such is so. Since we don't run through the "internal" contents again each time, some authors argue that only what is *external* functions in action.[5] I think these authors might mean rather that every kind of knowledge *does* function, but *like* a skill, that is, implicitly. But can we spell out how something functions implicitly?

Question 3: *How can a body have cultural patterns?*

Currently many authors feature our human interactions as the source of what we know and feel.[6] I think this is another great advance. But if our interactions are attributed to "culture," we may seem culturally programmed since we are born into a world of language, art, and human relationships. Culture may seem imposed on human bodies.[7] But we can ask: how can a body have cultural patterns such as speech and art, and how can it act in situations? If we can explain this, we can explain how culture was generated and how it is now being regenerated further and further.

These questions cannot be answered in the current concepts which are built along the lines of a system that assumes the body divided from the environment.

2. Where the Split between Body and Environment Comes from; the Perceptual Split

The currently underlying conceptual system leads us to assume that what exists is always something that can be *presented before us*. So there are always two, what exists and also us, the before whom. Contact with anything real is assumed to be by perception. Perception (or even more narrowly, sensation) is supposed to be the beginning.

Perception involves a split between a *here* and a *there*. We sense here what is over there. Perception involves an *inside* and an *outside*; we sense in here in the body what is out there, outside, "external" to us.

I call this the "perceptual split." The here-there generates a gap, the space between the *here* and the *there*. This space is supposed to contain everything that exists. To "exist" means to fill some part of that "external" space.

Only the "out there" is supposed to exist. What exists is considered *cut off* from any other living process because perceiving is the basic starting process. But being perceived is not supposed to affect real things. They are conceptualized as inherently cut off from living process. To be real they need only to fill the perceptual gap space.

For example, we tend to conceptualize even single-cell organisms as if they had perception, because they may have a "detector," a specialized part that provides something inside them which indicates something in the environment. Although single-cell organisms are not said to have perceptions, their relation to the environment is considered along the same lines as perception.[8]

The perceptual split makes for the distinction between body and environment, the body here detecting the surrounding environment out there.

I am not saying that people believe what I just laid out. I am tracing an underlying system of assumptions. As I state it head-on you probably don't believe it, and never did. People have been trying to get out of that system for a long time. Gallagher and Stuart are newly working on doing so.[9]

For example, no one says that the organisms that don't have perception are *dis*connected from their environment. But their environmental connection is conceptualized as if it were perception. We need different concepts for the more basic way in which bodies form as environmental interactions in the first place.

I ask my reader not just to agree that body and environment are "somehow" not split, but to notice that we can't say *how* they are more closely linked, because our concepts assume that they are two things in the out-there space.

I will show that this here-there "perception" is not a body's actual perception. It is an already analyzed cognitive kind of "perception." Originally perception does not just hang there like a picture floating alone. It develops as part of a behavior sequence. It need not be taken as the here-there picture which gives rise to the body/environment gap and the space-filling entities in our science.

But before we deprecate the current model even for a moment, let us be clear *why* science needs this perceptual split and these space-filling things. We make stable things and parts. I call them *units*. (I call it the *unit model*.) Everything from the wheel to computers consists of stable parts that we make and combine. Seven billion of us could not live on the Earth without technology, so let us not pretend we can denigrate science and its perceptual split and its units. We need them even to study and cure living things. The first sense of the word "environment" I define is the environment that science presents. I call it *environment #1*. Of course we will keep it, and keep developing it.

3. How We Can Get Out of the Split Perceptual Assumptions

The choice we have is to consider not *only* the science environment. Stable units are not alive. They are *made* things. But we can also study living things with a different basic conceptual system not modeled on things that are not alive. Such a second system is now developing. We can move back and forth between the two systems.

People have wanted to overcome the body-environment split for a very long time, but there was no alternative model. To get out of the unit model (while also staying in it, of course) we need a different conceptual model. If the one I offer isn't right in every way, I think it does move in a right direction.

We need not limit ourselves to already made things. We can also *ask about the processes that generate them.* We can conceptualize them as generative processes.

There are three different generative processes that need to be distinguished. If we don't distinguish them, then just one of them is assumed to explain everything else. The three are: first, the formation of the concrete living body; second, its behavior; and third, the patterning of gestures, art, language, and culture. Everyone knows these three processes, but let us consider them as *living and generative.* Then we can ask how they generate the environmental things *as objects of organisms.* Considered as living and generative, they have great explanatory power because they do in fact generate our objects. Let me say what I mean by taking them as living processes:

The formation of the concrete body is a living activity. The body is not only what is analyzed and arranged by observers. And it generates *objects.* By "objects" we mean specific parts of the environment to which the body responds with specific processes.

Second, behavior is not only motion. Motion is a change in position, location-change (locomotion), so it is a change from someone's here to there. I will show that behavior is not just a change of location. It is something like digging holes or building nests or eating. Behavior sequences alter and differentiate the environment and generate the objects with which we act.

Third, our bodies emit *patterns* such as gestures, waving hello to welcome someone. Or smiling. And speaking consists of sound patterns. Patterns come from the shape, sound, and feeling of the human body. The shape of the face affects us. Once we sense the patterns of the human body, all other things acquire *their own* patterns as profiles on our patterns. Then we divide and redesign them to make new objects, so many that it fills up the world's behavior space. But our most important patterning is not making things but generating our world of human situations. Situations are carried forward with visible gestures and sound patterns. Patterns create situations which are the main objects in our lives.

Each of these three processes can *explain* how different *kinds of objects are generated.* But to understand how this happens, we need a new conceptual system.

4. Some New Concepts and Distinctions

When we know where the here-there split comes from, we can consider an alternative model. This will be able to link body and environment more originally, and first of all in the process of forming the body.

The environment is not only what we observe and study. There is also the organism's own environment, or as Dreyfus phrases it, the environment "from the perspective of the animal" (*After Cognitivism*, 61). Of course, the phrase "from the perspective of" contains the unwanted assumption of here about there, but all our main words assume this. I say "we see" when I mean "we understand," as if understanding were something perceived in front of me. But what could we mean by "the organism's own environment"? What is the active organism's environment?

I propose that the active organism does something I call *implying*. It implies the environment. The environment may or may not occur somewhat as the body implies. Implying and occurring are two interdependent functions that create one process. *Instead of body and environment being two things, let us distinguish between* implying and occurring and spell out how their functions require each other. If what I have said about body and environment is true, then they cannot exist without each other because what each is involves what the other is. Together *implying and occurring-into* begin to conceptualize the inherent relation of body-environment.

Implying never exists separately, but only in some occurring. In a living process occurring occurs into an implying. *The body implies the environment. The environment occurs-into the body's implying.* This will allow us to begin with a single body-environment process (without the here-there split), but with new distinctions.

The body implies both one next environmental occurring and also a *sequence* of them. For example, hunger implies feeding. But feeding implies digestion and defecating, and resting, then getting hungry again. So hunger implies the sequence. But a sequence cannot occur all at once. The one next occurring will change the implying so that it implies the next occurring and the one after that. *A process is generated* when occurring changes implying so that it implies a further occurring which will further change it so as to imply still further occurrings that will change it further.[10] But what the body implies is never exactly what happens next. The sequence continues if what actually occurs *changes* the implying into *a* next implying. We call that special kind of change "carrying forward."

The first body-environment process is the formation of the body, the first of the three generative processes. I call it *body-constituting*. Body-constituting is a generative body-environment process (without the here-there split).

How a living body is generated and regenerated has been understood only as science presents it. Of course, we wouldn't want to do without what we know in embryology and biology. But there is more we can know if we consider body-constituting as a body-environment interaction process, not only as analyzed by a spectator.

The forming of the body is a generative bodily process. The body is not first just made and then turned on only when it is completed. The process that forms the body as a structure is a body-environment interaction *first*, before they can be two things.[11]

So I propose a distinction between environment#1 (the scientist's observed environment) and environment#2 (body-environment as a single identical occurring). The body is an environmental process. It *is* "environment" in this use of the word.

Everyone agrees that the body is made of environmental stuff, but it was assumed to be separate from the environment, merely perceiving and moving in it. But if we consider the body's formation as a body process, then the body *is* environmental interaction from the start. The body is identical with its environment in one body-constituting process.

And body-constituting continues as long as life lasts. Certain special kinds of body-constituting are part of every "higher" kind of process.

I will now discuss how the body-constituting process generates its environmental objects. This will show how a process can generate objects. I will then discuss how objects are generated in the other two processes.

5. The Body-Constituting Process Differentiates the Environment and Generates Objects

Certain processes become differentiated; they occur just with certain parts of the environment. This generates specific environmental objects.

I need to emphasize that bodies without perception generate objects. We can take organisms that have not developed perception as our more basic starting point and model. Let us consider them "from the organism" (not only as in science). Then I can show that such organisms differentiate their environment and generate objects.

Perception (behavior) is not the first kind of object-formation. The body is first constituted as environmental events and material, and some of this is always present in the environment. But some of it is *intermittent*; it disappears and reappears. For example, sugar, water, and light appear and are incorporated only sometimes. Then the body-constituting with these "objects" becomes separated from the rest of the process (if the organism didn't die in their absence). *Then the body has separate processes just for these parts of the environment. The moment they reappear, just these processes resume.* So we call these differentiated parts of the environment "objects."

But to think this we need to say that *when something implied doesn't occur, the body continues to imply it.* Until something meets that implying ("carries it forward," we say), the body continues to imply what was implied and didn't occur. If part of what was implied did occur, then only the part that did not occur continues to be implied. This *reiterated implying* is a basic concept. It explains how *objects in the environment become differentiated.* (We will discuss it further in the second half of this chapter.)

6. Perception Is a Part of Behavior; Behavior Is a Body-Environment Process

Now how does behavior generate its kind of objects? Let us not just assume them as already formed and merely perceived.

Perception arises as a part of behavior. Rather than assuming everything already in a here-there perception, we can consider how perception is first generated in a process. That process is behavior. I will show that when perception happens alone it is already a cognitively modified kind of "perception."

But I have to point out that behavior is not only motion. Motion is just change of location. Locations are the here-there space. Motion is a change from there to there, something observed before us. Behavior is not reducible to something in front of us. It can be understood as a special kind of body-constituting. If behavior were merely motion, the objects would have to be assumed as already formed. Let us consider the generative process that forms and re-forms them.

Behavior is a special kind of body-constituting. The kind of body-constituting that generates behavior involves *bodily-sentient perceptions* resulting from the organism's own doing. Perceptions and sensings imply each other and carry each other forward. The moment they fail to carry forward, the sequence stops (for a detailed theory, see *ECM*, chap. 6).

We cannot omit the bodily sentience that comes in each bit of perception. Only both generate the behavior sequence. Sentience is not just an added extra.

Sentience is consciousness. All animals (even worms and insects) have this behavioral sentience which is consciousness. Consciousness is not something merely added to unconscious experiences. When you drive home while thinking of something else, that is not unconscious experience. You couldn't do it if you were knocked out. The body must still feel the brake and the gas. The body is conscious. Consciousness is bodily, of course.

Consciousness (sentience) seems to be an essential relationship between one kind of implying and one kind of occurring-into, which forms a behavior sequence. Consciousness is not a thing, and it cannot just be added to another thing. It is not like shining a light on something that is there as well in the dark. It seems to be inherent in a certain kind of sequence, namely behavior.

What is striking about perceptions is that the body does *not* become them. Perceptions are not incorporated like water or sugar. The sentience in behavior is a special kind of body-constituting. This was always understood in a way. Behavior was explained as a postponed consummation; for example, when food search is "motivated" by eventual ingestion and digestion. But the behaving body soon develops very many new "consummations," *new bodily needs for behaviors*, and new results of behaviors. These are new body-constituting.

Behavior involves a special kind of body-constituting.[12]

I think Clark and Rowlands rightly deny that action (behavior) involves a "subjective" process which must then be bridged to the environment.[13] The environment is directly involved when we act. But the environment should not be considered *external*. It is not in the here-there space of perception. Primitive bodies without perception are identical with their own environment #2. Their body-constituting occurs in their body-environment #2.

The current authors who want to consider only the "external" seem to want just half of the perceptual split. What I think they really intend is not an externally viewed body, but rather *the always already environmental body*. I agree that the body is indeed always environment #2, both in body-constituting and in behavior. Now I turn to patterns.

7. The Patterns of Human Interaction: They Are Body-Environment Interactions

In hierarchical monkey societies each male monkey turns his back to superiors and receives the same gesture from those below him. They fight if one of them doesn't turn. When male animals of any kind get ready to fight, just the getting ready makes a huge change over their whole bodies. But among monkeys the simple turn takes the place of the whole fighting sequence and so they don't have to get ready for it. That huge shift happens in their bodies only if the other monkey doesn't turn. A huge bodily difference depends on a simple turn.

Originally the turn comes at the end of the fight when one monkey turns his back. But by doing the ending before the fight even starts, the gesture short-circuits the fighting-behavior. It changes the behavior possibilities as fighting would, but without that behavior sequence. We could almost say that the turn is like talking *about* the fighting rather than doing it. If there were a whole sequence of different *versions* of such turns, as in the human case, that would be a symbolic sequence. It would *be about* behavior possibilities, rather than behaving.

We see how symbols arise, *continuous with behavior* but changing the behavior possibilities without any actual behavior. Human symbols are different, but we can understand their bodily connection from considering these "animal rituals," as they are called. Animals have a few such body-shifting "rituals," but humans have several hundred thousands of them just in language, as well as many more. Imagine monkeys who cause not one huge bodily shift, but long chains of such shifts in each others' bodies.

Human patterns enable us to have long chains of bodily shifts and changed behavior possibilities just with patterns. Spoken language consists just of sound patterns. Written patterns are purely visual. The sound and the visual patterns come in separated sense modalities.

The fundamental role of patterns in human life has not been well recognized. Of course, our all-important language consists of sound patterns. But language is not the only kind of pattern that brings large shifts in our bodies. Art makes them with its patterns of lines and colors, light and dark, and textures that are only visual. Music creates bodily shifts just with sound patterns. The bodily shifts can be *versions* of events from a lifetime, all now implied from one sound pattern to the next. I call the process *versioning*.

Human life in situations always involves the patterned bodily changes of *versioning*. Our patterns create a different world, not just behavior possibilities. When we use patterns we might not behave overtly at all, except with the throat or the fingers. The patterns can change our behavior possibilities. But human behavior possibilities are different for being generated in the patterned spaces. We call those spaces "situations."

Patterns, situations, and bodies are inherently linked, and they must be understood together. They cannot be understood without each other. They must have developed together. A new language symbol must have developed to manage a new differentiation between situations. Human

IMPLICIT PRECISION

bodies produce visual and sound patterns directly from being in the situation. The patterns can change a situation. They involve large shifts in how the body feels the changed situation and newly implies what we will now do or say.

Spitz discovered that infants require human interaction with facial patterns for their normal body-constituting. He found infants in filthy jails with their mothers developing normally, whereas orphans in good hospitals died or were retarded. This is why today in maternity hospitals the nurses regularly pick up the newborns and relate to them face to face.

Gallagher reports that newborns respond to gestures with gestures—on the first day![14] If you stick your tongue out, the newborn will do the same thing back at you. Move your tongue to one side and you get the same thing back. They report other findings that show that gestural interaction is inherited in the body. Adults gesture in the dark (and on the phone). Waving is a gesture, not a regular behavior; you're not trying to grab something up there. Like hierarchical monkeys, we generate and feel the interactional effect of our body-looks and sounds. Wittgenstein wrote that "one can imitate a human face without seeing one's own in a mirror."[15] From the body we feel the pattern on our face; we can change it from inside. It is evident that symbolic patterns arise directly from the human body.

Stuart points to the crucial missing piece in most theories of language. What she calls *enkinaesthesia* is what I am here calling the sentient half of a behavior sequence and the sentience of patterned interactions which is the sequence of bodily shifts I call *versioning*.[16]

If we omit the enkinaesthesia, we cut language off from how it is generated and experienced by bodies in situations. Then language is considered an "external" system. Yes, individuals are born into a language, but it is generated only through individual chains of bodily shifts (the enkinaesthesia) from which they come.

How do words come? I open my mouth and they come, mostly saying what I wanted to say. What I wanted to say was not already in words. The words come directly from my living bodily in the situation.

The words come already arranged in phrases. They come arranged both grammatically and pragmatically. Of course always both, since they would not have their situational meaning without their grammatical patterning.

We have to wonder how it is that words come already arranged. Then we cannot fail to notice the role of the body. The dictionary doesn't know my situation. My body brings the words *directly* from living in situations, so they say something relevant to a situation.[17]

Human situations involve behavior of vastly many new kinds, as well

CHAPTER 6

as those few old ones we still share with the animals. We still eat and make love, but our appetite is spoiled if certain patterns don't obtain. We still fight, but now we do it in many new ways. Our behavior possibilities are situation-changes. We don't mainly feel the behaving we are doing; we mainly feel the situation and how we are changing it. That sentience implies the next thing we do or say.

Given this intimate bodily connection of signs and situations, we certainly cannot assume that our signs came about accidentally or by conventional agreement. Different patterns can develop in different places, but they develop in the same way and they are incredibly long-lasting. In *A Process Model* (VII-B) I have a long piece on how sound patterns *develop* and differentiate situations. The so-called "signifiers" were long thought to be arbitrary and unrelated to the "signified," but this is certainly not the case.

Why am I arguing about this? It is because I want to bring home that human patterns carry our body-process forward, and that this is neither subjective nor external. Pattern interactions change situations and differentiate our environment.

Our symbolic patterns are generated by bodily process, and bodily process is body-environment interaction, so the patterns differentiate the world. They should no longer be called "inter-subjective."[18]

What has been asserted in short form should now be filled in at a few points. I rely on some readers turning to my *A Process Model* to see the whole work.

8. The Three Body Processes Occur Directly in the Environment

If we consider the three living processes not as truncated by the hidden perceptual split, but as generative and explanatory, then they can explain the "background." It is always in process, always the present body-environment interaction.

We shift *from the implicit to implying*. The "implicit" is not a store of past things; rather, it is the present activity, a process, an imply*ing*. The great number of things people can find in a background are all functioning, but the present doesn't repeat old pieces; it *regenerates* the past. The present would not be what it is if the past had been different, but present living changes how the past functions now.

Present experiencing consists of implying and occurring into implying. The body implies the environment. The environment occurs directly into the body's implying and carries it forward into a further implying.

IMPLICIT PRECISION

The body lives *directly* in each of our situations.[19] This explains why our bodily implied situations contain so much more than could ever be enacted even in our thinking. What actually occurs—what we actually do, say, or think—occurs into the implying and further develops the situation.

All three living processes function to enable the body to imply so much. The body-constituting always continues and it is also a part of behaving. Both are involved in patterned human living, which is why we are *sentiently* sitting here, able to sense ourselves.

We are not *un*conscious of this bodily-sentient ongoingness. We would be shocked if we suddenly didn't feel it, with its familiar sense of "knowing what we're doing." The body has to be understood as at least all three of these living processes, always freshly reconstituting itself.

As Gallagher has pointed out, the body-constituting includes micro processes that are not themselves conscious but are directed by conscious behavior and gestural interaction.[20] The body-constituting is determined by action and speech; the muscles and nerves act to provide just what we want to do and say. The three processes are different, but they constitute one implying of one next environmental occurring. They occur directly into environment, which is thereby being regenerated.

So we need to distinguish another sense of the word "environment": we need to speak not only of environment #1 and environment #2. There is also the much larger environment that the body *goes on in* and regenerates by going on in it.

Let me set out four uses of the word that we need.

9. Four Uses of the Word "Environment"

Environment #1 is the scientific observer's view. We keep it distinct and move back and forth, developing it in reciprocity with the wider view.

Environment #2 is the one identical body-environment interaction. The body is made of environmental stuff and its organismic events happen in the environment. The body *is* environmental body-constituting. Body-environment is a single sequence of environmental events.

Environment #3 is the organism's own environment which it *goes on in* and thereby constantly regenerates. (The body transitively "goes its environment#3 on," you might say.) The present process *goes the past on*. Environment #3 is much larger than the body-environment#2. Many processes go across the dividing membrane.

Environment #0, though mentioned fourth, really comes before the others. Of course, the organism doesn't make its environment #2 and environment #3 just from its own implying. The organism *is* an interaction with the freshly unpredictable environment, unknown until it occurs. (It goes on "in reality," you might say.)

Even in the science environment#1 we cannot predict what really occurs. Of course, we test our logical conclusions with operations. Even if we predict correctly, much more than that happens. Every study brings more data than we expect.

So the past can never *simply* repeat. Even if we observe the same thing over again, even if it seems to have done the same thing in every generation for millions of years, now it occurs newly in environment #0.

Drawing them together, life process is analyzed and aided in environment #1, identical as body-environment #2, goes on in its own wider regenerated environment #3, and occurs in environment #0.

These distinctions will now help us to say more about body-constituting, behavior, and pattern process.

10. Body-Constituting and Object-Formation

I reemphasize that the most basic way the body forms objects does not involve perception or detectors that work like perception. The objects are differentiated in the process of body-constituting. All "higher" kinds of object-formation involve body-constituting.

In our model the body implies sequences. How do objects that stay the same arise *from sequences? How does our model supply an inherent connection between process and object?* This worked itself out in detail in *A Process Model* as chapters 4–6 grew slowly. If those arguments are not wrong, we *can answer*: as I said briefly earlier, when the environment cooperates, something like the implied sequence occurs. When there is no cooperation the body dies, or if enough of it can go on, it implies the unmet part over and over. If it goes on living, the body keeps implying the part of the process that did not occur. What is not carried forward becomes a *reiterative implying.*

Some missing aspects of the environment never return, but some come and go. The changing environment provides *intermittent* cooperation; for example, the sun sometimes shines and sometimes it is dark. When the sun rises, a plant does incredibly complex things. When water comes, its body expands. So we say that the plant *responds* to just these environmental aspects. It responds not by perceiving them but by incorporating them, doing its body-constituting with them. It doesn't need

IMPLICIT PRECISION

a separate perception or detection of the sun or the water *in addition* to incorporating these parts of the environment. The body *is* its body-constituting interaction with them. It is its environment #2, the body-environment interaction with them.

Because these body-constituting interactions were *constantly implied*, they suddenly occur when these environmental "objects" return.

The observer sees the plant doing complex photosynthesis in response to the sun. This complexity surely doesn't come just from the nature of sunlight and water. Obviously, the organism contributes actively to the interaction. It *brings* a background of reiteratively implying that specific process. Then the process *occurs* the moment there is light and water.

Distinct and separate processes have developed in relation to just these differentiated parts of the environment. These parts have become objects. This kind of "object" seems odd because the word usually means a perceived object.

We gave names to the two concepts we developed here. How a missing process is implied over and over I call *reiterative implying*, and when a carrying-forward object occurs I say that it *resumes* the process. This is a way to conceptualize that mysterious power of objects to elicit relevant processes from organisms. We conceptualize it as a body-constituting process.

In the observer's environment #1 it matters very much whether the implied object is familiar or new. We can do a lot about familiar objects. For example, we can provide water and artificial light. We can often improve the resuming objects. It is quite different for us when what is next implied is unknown. But for the body the resuming object is always new.

A reiterated implying is always new and regenerating. And it is always open to *whatever* will carry it forward. Even if what does carry it forward is new in the history of the world, we can say that it "resumed" what was implied but missing. For example, we have an unsolved problem as a reiterated implying of a next step in a process that does not continue. When a solution comes, we can say that the missing process has "resumed."

Here we see one way a background functions without representations. The body-constituting process doesn't need them to "recognize" light and water.

Now let us turn from body-constituting to behavior. I need to show that behavior generates *a "space" of behavior possibilities*. We perceive objects in the space of behavior possibilities, not in pictures that are just colors. Perception is first generated in behavior, not as just a picture here about something over there.

11. The Space of Behavior Possibilities

We perceive *in* the space of behavior possibilities. We perceive what we can do with objects. Objects are clusters of behavior possibilities. Many possible behaviors come with any object.

The objects exist not just in locations but *in* the space of behavior possibilities. *That is the behavior space in which we act and perceive.*[21]

Perception does not consist only of momentary intakes from the sense organs. We *perceive* objects *in* the wider space of behavior possibilities. The momentary sensations *come into* the wider behavior space.

The organ intakes are separate colors, sounds, and smells, and so on. The separate intakes *come into the behavior space. We perceive behavioral objects*, not just colors and sounds.

Yes, humans can also analyze their perceptions into colors just as colors, and sounds just as sounds, but this is a cognitive capacity. You can't get the dog to do it, and you can't get a human to do it, for example, while a car is coming. If we are hiking down the middle of the road and hear a car coming, we immediately move to the side of the road. What we heard was *the car*, not a sound. Once on the side of the road, yes, we can examine the sound just as a sound, as we do in language and music.[22]

Therefore let us recognize that the old reduction of experience to five separated kinds of sense data is an indispensable analysis, but it is a cognitive symbolic cultural product, *not the start of experience.* (Seeing this makes large changes in our theoretical assumptions which I cannot discuss here.)

The dog never sees colors *as* colors, sounds *as* sounds, or smells *as* smells. The dog sees me coming, sees *that* I'm eating food, and would like some.

Humans *can* perceive colors *as* colors, and sounds *as* sounds. Patterns are *just* visual or *just* auditory. Only with patterns that are just sound can we speak. But like the dog, we primarily perceive the objects. We perceive the food we could eat. We take it out of the oven and *see that* it is still not cooked enough and we have to put it back.

We perceive changed possibilities. We *perceive that* someone could walk in because the door was left open.

When what we could do with an object has just changed, we perceive not only the object but the fact that what we could do has changed. We *perceive that* we can't go for a walk now because it has begun to rain. We *perceive that* an object with which we could have done behavior X has just changed so that now we cannot do X, but now perhaps we can do Y.

We *perceive that* the steaming water is too hot to drink, that is, we perceive it *in* the space of behavior possibilities. We *perceive that* the dusty chair needs brushing off before we sit in it.[23]

IMPLICIT PRECISION

Because the body perceives objects as behavior possibilities, therefore we can do skillful actions with the body without first having a separate perception (a *just-perception*, I call it) to see how we can. Without first just perceiving how I will do it, my hands rotate the empty pot so I can grab the handles. Similarly, Antonio Damasio observed that before he perceived it, his body had switched his cup of coffee from one hand to the other so he could grab the banister.[24]

Even when we have no organ intakes from the things at our side, we *perceive that* they are still at our side. We perceive that we could turn to them. For example, I find my thumb sticking out to hold back the stack of papers next to me on my easy chair so they don't fall on the floor as I get up.

My thumb move comes because my body implies sequences. It implies how the space of possibilities will change as I get up. So my thumb moves as I get up. *Many* sequences function implicitly in the coming of any one next behavior.

We perceive the space and objects behind us (as Merleau-Ponty said, and I explain). *We perceive and walk in a space in which we could back up or turn around and go.*

We would be shocked if we suddenly perceived that there was nothing behind us, a sheer abyss into which we would disappear if we backed up.

If *perception* is defined only as the present organ intakes, then the behavior possibilities have to be considered "interpretation," something "only internal," therefore "subjective." But behavior possibilities are not subjective. The space of behavior possibilities is environmental interaction.

An intake in a single sense is never perceived alone; it *comes into* the space of possible behaviors with objects, and it modifies that space. Behavior objects are not constructed from momentary separate sense data alone.

The body implies objects because it implies behavior. In behavior the objects are implied in all five sense modalities. The body implies five-sense objects even when only one sense is coming from one organ just now. A behavior that is now forming can be modified by a single organ intake. If there is an intake from a second sense, it would also modify the ongoing formation, so it would join the first intake. This explains Gallagher's "intermodal" perception.[25] He has established the concept of "intermodality," but how the connections occur has remained a question because of the assumption that perception consists only of separate intakes from the different organs, although no neurological connector has been found. (Newborns connect the five modalities long before neurological connections develop.)

The analysis in terms of organ-intakes is valid and highly useful, but perception cannot be conceptualized only as organ intakes. We perceive in the formation of behavior.

Now let me show that the body implies a field of interrelated behavior possibilities in the formation of one next behavior.

12. The Field of Interrelated Behavior Possibilities

Let us ask: how are behavior possibilities interrelated? Each object comes with many possible behaviors (Gibson called them "affordances").[26] Behaviors are not mere motions, not mere changes in location. We perceive objects with the ways we could behave with them, for example hold them, or push them, eat them, sit on them.

If we consider just the things, they appear to be *side by side*. But the possible behaviors do *not* appear side by side. Let me expand this key point: behavior possibilities are not *side by side*. An object is perceived *in* a cluster of possible behaviors. Only the objects are spread out side by side in location space; the behavior possibilities (what we *can* now do) are organized in a different way. The behavior possibilities constitute an implicit space that is quite different from the space that consists just of objects. How are they organized?

As I said, *a behavior changes the other behaviors that can now be done and how they can be done.* If we kick the ball, we can no longer pick it up and throw it. If we kick someone, we can no longer fondle the person, or the fondling will now be a comforting. If we boil the eggs, we can't then fry them. *Each behavior is a change of the cluster of implicit "cans."* If we do *this* we can no longer do *that*, or not in the same way as before. On the other hand, after each behavior we can do some that we couldn't do before.

A behavior is not only itself, not only what occurs. A behavior changes the implying of the cluster of behavior possibilities. *It alters the cluster in which it occurs.* It occurs in the new cluster that its occurring has changed. Again we see: the past, the background, the "context" *in* which something new occurs is the regenerated context, not the past. The behavior occurs in the changed cluster.

Each of the other behaviors is also such a cluster-change when it occurs. Each of the many possible behaviors is a cluster that includes the one behavior which just occurred. If the behavior that occurred is new, each of the possible behaviors now has the new one in its cluster.

The many different consequences are necessarily taken account of in relation to each other. Each behavior possibility interrelates the consequences of the possible behaviors in its cluster. The one behavior that comes re-forms the cluster of all of them.

IMPLICIT PRECISION

We see the precision: each changes the cluster in its own precise way and not like any of the others. Each is a different change in how the others can happen. The cluster consists of precise interrelations.

The items that the background is said to contain are not independent items. As part of behavior possibilities each is a change in the possibility of the others. In later examples we will see that humans have many different situations, each of which is such a cluster.

13. Immediate Formation Is Forming-Into

Because a behavior *is* also the cluster-change, therefore the change is immediate, not first this which then affects that.

Now we can further explain the taking account of the past. Since the very forming of a behavior is also the re-forming of the cluster of behavior possibilities, therefore it is a taking account of the way the others have been possible. It is by changing them that the behavior takes account of them. How it *goes on in* the previous changes the previous.

Behavior *forms-into* the implicit cluster of behavior possibilities. *Therefore a behavior does not form without (what we called) "taking account" of the previous moves* (the cluster of other behaviors). Its forming and coming *is* implicitly also their re-forming.

This is the reason why the taking account happens in the very coming. The coming *is* the taking account of the other possibilities, because it is also their re-formation. So the behavior cannot form except by forming into them.

And a behavior cannot help but be a *precise* taking account of the others in the cluster that it forms into, and of which it is a present re-forming.

I want to have shown that the body implies a field of interrelated behavior possibilities in the coming of one next behavior. This is one instance of how the "background" functions, ever present and precise. The past functioned in the present process without needing to be reviewed. The present process implies and enacts the next behavior without needing a preview of it in advance.

Now I take up two examples of interrelated possibilities, both from humanly patterned interactions.

14. Implying and Taking into Account: Two Examples

Consider the special case when we work on a problem. At first nothing comes. If we are asked about the problem, we can easily say many things, why it matters, how it came about. Many old thoughts are implicit, but if we aren't asking about those, they don't come. Nothing comes to advance the problem.

This "nothing comes" is really quite smart. It involves the implicit knowing why the old thoughts have no chance of providing even a small advance on the problem. What does come can include very unlikely ideas that fail examination immediately, but the old answers do not come.

You can feel when a thought has the slightest chance of advancing the problem. It might be a big idea or only a little lead. What came might fail immediately, but if it came at all, it had some slight chance to move the problem.

Of course, the "nothing comes" is not plain nothing. It reproduces the problem over and over. It is the continually regenerated hold we have of the problem. If you get distracted you may lose hold of "it." Then you work to have your sense of the problem come back. "Oh, yes, there it is again." Any new thought goes on in this reiterative implying, and carries it forward.

You can observe in detail how your knowledge has implicitly functioned, if someone asks you about one of those old well-known thoughts. You are immediately ready to lay out quite logically why it won't advance the problem. You could show how each old answer about which you are asked has *functioned implicitly in not coming. Each* old thought you consider turns out to have functioned precisely and logically in not coming.

We can see how this *intricate process* has happened. No implicit store of old knowledge and experience has occurred. The actually functioning background is not the old products but a new *implying* which may produce a new *occurring*—or not.

Rather than repeating the past, the new implying *further develops the past* by implying something new. We have seen that the process accounts for each item from the past precisely, but we have not yet explained how it can do that. My next example should show how it can see the concepts and what they do.

15. A Second Example: Chess Masters

Dreyfus has pointed out that chess masters make new moves *without deliberating*.[27] They don't spend time considering each of the many possible moves. Only the new move comes to them. We are explaining this. Masters have spent years studying books of games; they know many possible moves at any point. Now they don't have to run through all those old moves (as the computer does). Those moves don't come to mind to be considered. We have just explained why nothing comes until a promising move comes.

The master doesn't deliberate when playing with ordinary players. When masters play each other, they want every minute of allotted time *to examine the move they are about to make*. Several new moves may occur to them, but certainly not the many old moves.

A new move has to be examined by seeing its consequences many moves ahead. The coming of the new move has already accounted for the consequences of each possible old move, and these consequences in relation to each other. Any of the old moves would result in problematic situations in which the new move is already more promising.

As in the previous example, we can see how all this has implicitly happened, if we ask the master about any one old move, "Why didn't you do well-known move *x*?" The master would be ready to reply by comparing the possible consequences of the old and the new move.

To compare old and new consequences many moves down would generate a new logical system. Of course, the system could not have been created before the new move came. The move is the source, not the result of that system. It compares the old consequences with the new ones that the move just brought. The new consequences are new units, implicitly created in the new coming.

If not asked about old moves, the master does not think those, but uses the time to examine the new move by generating its consequences one by one, separately. This might reveal some possibilities that need to be pursued or avoided. Here we can see how logic and implying expand each other reciprocally. The new move was *more* than the old units, but laying it out by generating new units from it makes *still more*.

Again we see the inherent precision with which the implicit background functions. A next occurring is precisely implied. Nothing occurs that does not carry this implying forward. The implying is the opening for the unknown occurring which will carry it forward. It does not have the form of a finished product; it is the continuing of the process from the finished products to something that has not yet happened. When it comes into the implying it will change the implying into a further implying. Then we can generate new units that can lay out how what came took account of what already existed.

This process happens not only in chess, of course.[28] A new thought can come in any situation, and when it does we examine what follows from it. We do that by generating the new units which are precisely implied in it, just these and just so.

Humans live in *many* situations. If you are reminded of another one, you can change your plans in it, or go to take care of something in it, then return to chess or the problem you were working on. We move between situations. Only some of them are problems, fortunately, but *each is an implying where new ideas come only if they carry our old knowledge forward.*

The problem we are working on is kept separate from all our many other situations. They are all *kept neatly separate* from each other, each in its own history and precise detail. They are *not merged*, but they do have multiple interconnections because some of their details are related to some other situations.

How can we understand this "holding" of the separate situations? The holding is the implying of a next which has not occurred. When it doesn't occur, the implying repeats over and over (if some of life did continue). We discussed this earlier and called it *reiterative implying*. What holds each situation is a reiterative implying. When we *act in* a situation, the reiterative implying is a kind of background that holds the situation so that we "know what we're doing" and which situation we're in, and so that we bodily feel how to meet the situation.

16. Carrying Forward Differentiates and Expands the World

Are cognition and behavior "really" in the world of body-constituting, so that we humans live on the plane of the bacteria, or are behavior and body-constituting "really" in the vastly larger cognitive world which humans discover? And the answer has to be: *both, of course!*

If we said only one or the other, we would have either the usual scientistic reductionism (we *are* our brains and tissues) or the old idealism in which reality was the order of thought. But our model can show exactly how they are in each other, resulting neither in reductionism nor idealism.

Gallagher has been saying that the body provides necessary structural events, but they are directed and shaped by the cognitive level: "When in the context of a game I jump to catch a ball, that action cannot be fully explained by the physiological activity of my body. The pragmatic concern of playing the game, even the rules of the game, may define how I jump."[29]

How the rules of the game exist in the muscles (how each "higher" process is in each "lower" one) cannot really be anything else than how the muscles exist in the patterned interactional world (how each "lower process" is in each higher). The rules *direct* the muscles because the rules are a training *in* the muscles, which is possible since human muscles grow in a patterned interactional world. There is only one implying which has to be said both ways. That the rules are *in* the muscles is the same fact as that the muscles are *in* a cognitive cultural world.

Human body-constituting and behavior now form in the patterned situations in which we live. The body implies its situations even when we sleep. Psychosomatic effects are not mysterious. And conversely: the pattern sequences involve a kind of behavior and body-constituting.

The fact that structural events are needed to jump in the game shows that we still behave and body-constitute, although all in one process with playing a game.

The three living and generative processes each differentiate the environment. What exists is differentiable.[30]

The pattern sequences with which we interact change the world. Things come onto our body patterns where they cast their profiles, which we then divide, analyze, move, and change with our scientific patterns.[31] The things are by-products of the pattern process which creates the human world of situations in which we live. *The pattern process of our inter-human situations differentiates the world.*

17. Conclusions

The background is not something that occurs separately; rather, it is always regenerated in what presently occurs.

We probably knew that the background can't work when a person is unconscious and that it is not an infinite number of actually occurring entities, nor a fuzzy merger. If the background were a fuzzy merger, it couldn't make for the relevant environmental responses that it is meant to explain.

We knew that the background functions *implicitly*, but how something implicit functions couldn't be explained, because we had concepts only for something presented before us (an appearance, perception, object, entity.) *But we can consider anything like that as a product generated by a process.* With a model of products *and process* we can explain how the background functions implicitly.

With our new distinctions using the word *environment* in four ways, we can specify in what exact way body-environment is a single process.

We can distinguish between implying and occurring-into, two interdependent functions which create that one process.

The process always *generates* the events. It does not consist of already-formed products that are repeated or rearranged. It always *regenerates* its past. And the organism is interaction with the actual environment, unpredictable and unknown until it occurs. The implying and the occurring into it regenerate the body-environment.

We cannot logically deduce the present from the past, but we can always find (and with new units exhibit) how the regenerating took account of the past. We saw the precision of this taking account, for example, when a new chess move comes. Then it can be shown logically and precisely why its consequences are superior to those of any one of the old moves that did not come. The not coming is the present implying and occurring. We can show this in thinking about any problem.

If the three processes we discussed (body-constituting, behavior, and patterned interaction) are considered as *both living and generative*, then they can *explain* what will otherwise be only asserted. But they have to be distinguished; no one of them can explain what the other two generate.

When we have distinguished them, we can see that body-constituting is an essential part of behavior and both are essential for patterns. The development of the three is also the development of the body. This is why the human body generates behavior and patterns. These three generating processes will always exceed their products. Finished products are alive only in the present process that regenerates them.

Notes

1. I want to thank Mary Hendricks, Kye Nelson, Rob Parker, and Zdravko Radman for very helpful readings and comments.

2. Dreyfus has for thirty years stayed with the extremely unpopular message that computers will never become able to replace human intelligence. He pointed out that humans don't have to run through their stored-up experiences as computers do, and are not then limited to doing one of those, as computers are. Here I quote his 2009 article: "It seemed to me, however, that the deep problem [for artificial intelligence] wasn't storing millions of facts; it was knowing which facts were relevant"; see Hubert L. Dreyfus, "How Representational Cognitivism Failed and Is Being Replaced by Body/World Coupling," in *After Cognitivism: A Reassessment of Cognitive Science and Philosophy*, ed. K. Leidlmair (Dordrecht: Springer 2009), 41. "The problem is an artifact from the perspective of the researcher rather than from the perspective of the animal. But, according to Freeman the cell assemblies are not just passive receivers of meaningless input from the universe but are tuned to respond *directly* to significant aspects of the

environment *on the basis of past significant experience*" (61, my emphasis). I think this answers his question only if we can also explain how "past significant experience" was possible in the first place, and then also how the past functions in the present without needing to be gone through, as a computer does.

3. See the book review by Shaun Gallagher, "Mark Rowlands's *Body Language: Representation in Action*," *Notre Dame Philosophical Reviews* (2007), http://ndpr.nd.edu/review.cfm?id=11183.

4. Michael Polanyi, *Personal Knowledge* (New York: Harper and Row, 1958).

5. See M. Rowlands, "Understanding the 'Active' in Enactive," *Phenomenology and the Cognitive Sciences* 6, no. 4 (2007): 427–43; A. Clark, "Memento's Revenge: The Extended Mind, Extended," in *The Extended Mind*, ed. R. Menary (Cambridge, Mass.: MIT Press, 2010).

6. See, for example, essays by S. Gallagher, J. Margolis, and S. A. J. Stuart in *Knowing without Thinking: Mind, Action, Cognition and the Phenomenon of the Background*, ed. Z. Radman (New York: Palgrave Macmillan, 2012).

7. H. M. Collins writes: "What is missing is any understanding of the difference between human and animals." "In the case of humans the main determinant is not the body but language. . . . The obsession with the body among the new orthodoxy is misplaced. . . . What is needed is to understand socialisation"; see Collins, "The New Orthodoxy: Humans, Animals, Heidegger and Dreyfus," in *After Cognitivism*, ed. K. Leidlmair, 80, 84. I agree with him that the human/animal difference has not been understood, but this applies as well to the human body. I don't agree with the rest of what he says, but he is the only one I know so far pointing to *the difference between* two of my generative processes.

8. Evan Thompson writes that the living body is "organized as a self-producing and self-maintaining network," and he calls this the "core form of biological autonomy"; see Thompson, "Sensorimotor Subjectivity and the Enactive Approach to Experience," *Phenomenology and the Cognitive Sciences* 4, no. 4 (2005): 407–27, quote on 407. But then he goes directly to saying that "this core form is recapitulated in a more complex form in metazoan organisms with a nervous system" (407). Thereafter the whole discussion assumes perception.

9. See, for example, essays by S. Gallagher, J. Margolis, and S. A. J. Stuart in *Knowing without Thinking:*.

10. Implying always implies many sequences, always *many in one*. It implies one specific next environmental event. Even the most primitive organisms and single cells imply many sequences, many processes. The implying is much more than could occur at once. Because implying implies sequences, therefore occurring into implying generates a more complex kind of time than just now now now, as if there were only occurring occurring occurring (see *APM* IV-B).

11. This is of course an odd use of the word. This "interaction" is prior to two separate things that would first meet in order to interact. I call it *interaction first*.

12. Developing more behavior involves body-constituting. In every species all the parts of the body are formed so that it can enact its behaviors. Obviously body and behavior formed together. We see body-constituting also in the finding that every species has "fixed action patterns," behavior that the body will eventu-

ally enact if no occasion for it presents itself for a long time. There is no doubt that behavior is inherited along with body structure. This definitely includes human gestures and the capacity for art and sound patterns. The fact of inheritance should not be used to explain behavior and patterns; it rather needs to be explained. It involves a body-constituting process that is part of the "higher" processes, behavior, and patterns.

13. See M. Rowlands, "Understanding the 'Active' in Enactive," *Phenomenology and the Cognitive Sciences* 6, no. 4 (2007): 427–43; A. Clark, "Memento's Revenge: The Extended Mind, Extended," in *The Extended Mind*, ed. R. Menary (Cambridge, Mass.: MIT Press, 2010).

14. Shaun Gallagher, *How the Body Shapes the Mind* (Oxford: Oxford University Press, 2006), 70.

15. Ludwig Wittgenstein, *Philosophical Investigations* (Oxford: Blackwell, 1953), 285.

16. See S. A. J. Stuart, "Enkinaesthesia: The Essential Sensuous Background for Co-Agency," in Radman, *Knowing without Thinking*, 167–86.

17. Stuart and the others are quite right to consider all this as interactional and inter-human. People are not in situations only as individuals, but always with others. I would only point out that this doesn't begin with culture. Many animals have very complex relations with each other. In many species their most numerous behavior is with each other and some of them clearly feel each other's experiencing. (For example, Jane Goodall in a personal communication described how when a young monkey was injured, his little sister held the two sides of the cut together and comforted him.) Bodily interpersonal sensing originates much earlier than humans and culture. Stuart recognizes this with her term "agents" which applies to people and animals.

18. I recognize that people intend this word to mean *not*-subjective, but it still assumes that human living is something alien in a real world modeled on our not being here. So it still makes the world we live in seem to be "inside" us.

19. The words *organism* and *body* differ, partly because the latter is still often used to denote only the body structure. I will argue for a structural-behavioral-symbolizing body nearly as wide as "organism," except that the latter can include the person. The person-body relation is a large topic I cannot go far into here. It involves a crucial variable: attention. Attention is being studied separately, but still in the old Gestalt model. See S. Arvidson, *The Sphere of Attention: Context and Margin* (Dordrecht: Springer, 2006). In our TAE (Thinking at the Edge) a kid asked: "*Am* I my body or do I *have* a body?" A fast answer might have been: "Neither, as you recognized or you wouldn't be asking. And good for you for seeing it! The answer is that it's *this* way, the way you have here. We don't have good concepts for it yet."

In this article I use both words. I follow current usage with "organism" but emphasize how *the body* becomes able to provide the implicit background. The body lives directly in our situations so that attention to the body can reveal more of me than I knew. See my "*Befindlichkeit*: Heidegger and the Philosophy of Psychology" (chapter 11 in this volume), and "Improvisation Provides," presented at the Society for Phenomenology and Existential Philosophy, New Orleans, October 1993; available at http://www.focusing.org/gendlin/docs/gol_2223.html.

20. Gallagher, *How the Body Shapes the Mind*, 37–39.

21. Current theory assumes "sensory-motor coupling." But I would predict that there won't be clear findings until behavior, rather than just motion, is assumed to be coupled to sensing.

22. Aesthetics will greatly profit if it is understood that pictures and music involve not just behavior and perception, but the purely human capacity to see colors as just colors and to hear sounds as just sounds. These are processes with patterns, only visual or only auditory. Patterns create and differentiate the many different situations as well as a world of art, music, and technology. Patterns make vastly many more versions of bodily sentience than behavior can. Pattern process is a versioning.

23. The fact that what we perceive is so much more than our momentary intakes is supported by the unexplained finding that only a murky 20 percent of the clear scene we see registers on the cortical measures at any one time. See M. J. Mahoney, *Human Change Processes* (New York: Basic Books, 1991), 100ff.

24. Antonio Damasio, *The Feeling of What Happens* (London: Heinemann, 1999), 129.

25. Gallagher, *How the Body Shapes the Mind*, 160.

26. J. J. Gibson, *The Senses Considered as Perceptual Systems* (Boston: Houghton Mifflin, 1966), 49.

27. Dreyfus, "How Representational Cognitivism Failed," 39–73.

28. Of course, chess rules form a conceptually limited scheme that is not changed by a new move. There is probably a limit on possible new moves so that the computer might eventually contain all possible moves and regularly defeat chess masters as it has sometimes defeated Kasparov. Our situations always remain open to present regenerating.

29. Gallagher, *How the Body Shapes the Mind*, 142–43.

30. See my "How Philosophy Cannot Appeal to Experience, and How It Can," in *Language Beyond Postmodernism: Thinking and Speaking in Gendlin's Philosophy*, ed. David M. Levin (Evanston, Ill.: Northwestern University Press, 1997), 3–41; and C. Petitmengin, "Listening from Within," *Journal of Consciousness Studies* 16, nos. 10–12 (2009): 252–84.

31. All patterns derive from the human body. Our bodies feel and enact the patterns of how the body looks and gestures or sounds in interaction. Human bodies imply patterns along with all implying. Because the tree comes onto our human body patterns, it reaches for the sky. It comes onto our chemistry and mathematics. *On our patterns* the things really have their own patterns by which they can be taken apart and altered. New patterns can be moved onto things that never had them. With humans the patterns of the world come loose.

7

A Direct Referent Can Bring Something New

In philosophy I introduce a new term, *implying*.[1] Other philosophers have talked about it, but how it functions in us has not been well understood. Here is a very initial understanding of implying.

1. Implying

Anything we ever observe or talk about has a great many characteristics that are not yet separately defined. No matter how many we have already separated, there is always a vast amount more that a living organism implies.

There is always an *implying further*.

So both what now "is," and what it further implies, are always more than any one set of already separated units. What is implied is as yet undefined, but may further develop and then become partly defined.

What we later call "was implied" is anything that carries the ongoing living process forward. By "carrying forward" we mean the bodily-experienced effect which indicates that something was carried forward so that (we can then say) it "was implied."

Implying usually leads to further implying, rather than constituting an immediate solution or a great new possibility right away. Carrying forward brings some development. But it is usually welcome because of the further implying to which it leads.

Implying and carrying forward differ clearly from something that merely happens to an organism. Implying and carrying forward are the organism's own process. When carrying forward has happened, we can recognize that "there was implying," if it was carried forward.

What *will* occur cannot be considered the same as what "was" implied, since the implying was not already defined. The implying happens now; it is not the future (see *APM* IV-B on a different understanding of time).

What *will* now carry implying forward is not predictable. But when something does carry forward, we can then say what it was that carried forward. Carrying forward is a *changing-into* the bodily-felt effect of what we can then say "was implied."

We can also explicate and analyze a carrying forward that has happened. New phrases come to us that say what had that effect. Explicating generates a new set of units, a new string of words that can come freshly from a carrying forward.

(In carrying forward, we cannot divide between a part that changed and a part that stayed the same. When we think only in "is"-units, everything must be either the same or different, but *carrying forward is neither the same nor different.* It is rather an ongoing re-generat*ing*, reconstitut*ing*. We can retro-analyze the effect of carrying forward. This is a different use of logic.)

2. An Example of the Implicit

Language appears to develop only in human beings, or we can say the development of language is also a development of being human.

When we use language to talk, think, hear, or read, our words themselves are each a universal, and they are general for all speakers of that language. But what you mean and want to say is particular and always bodily implicit.

Would you please check? Please ask yourself, "Is that right?" It may take a moment to realize that what you individually mean is always implicit and particular, even though you speak or think in words. What you individually mean is still always implicit. You always mean much more than we put into words.

To understand what language does in us, we need a set of terms. "Universals" are words. They create a general (dictionary definition) response in everyone. But they have another side: "particulars" which these words arouse in you. Your particular is implicit. In this way the words are always "dual," both universal and particular.

It may seem that language consists only of universal meanings and is quite independent of what you mean. But this is not the case. Language does not consist only of the universals. Your response to any words is always also particular and implicit. The words bring their dictionary meanings, and they also say your particular meaning that you want to say.

Language involves this "dual carrying forward." This dual nature of language has not been understood. When you use words, you want the words to carry forward what you mean and want to say, which is always still implicit, whatever the words.

At some rare times, you might feel that you mean exactly and only the words you said. But when you hear the other person's response, you usually feel that you no longer want to mean those exact words. You then have a more exact version to say.

When I finish a lecture in class, I usually feel that I said exactly what I wanted to say, that I was very clear, and that it was very good. If I go home at this point, I can keep that feeling. But if I finish my lecture no more than halfway through the class time, when people's hands go up and they tell me how they understood me, then I realize that I was nothing like clear and accurate. Now I have a lot more specific things to explain, and I am ready to say a lot more.

Something like the same thing happens when other people speak or write. What they say is in the words they have used, but what I understand them to mean (how that changes our situation) can implicitly be much more or much less and also different.

Whatever I hear myself say or think, and whatever I see that I write, if the words carry forward what I meant, then I have endorsed those words. If they do not, then I usually need to add something and keep adding until my implicit understanding of what I meant is carried forward.

To recognize this duality (the words themselves, and the bodily-implicit understanding of what I wanted them to say) is an ordinary, common experience, which I hope you find right now.

This dual carrying forward is both the words and the bodily implying.

If it were the case that there are only the words and no implicit sensing, then we would find that the words, as written, are different from the spoken sound. The visibly written is something visual, whereas the sound is something auditory. Currently there is a tendency to assume that language comes either in visual units or in auditory units. But this is a great error. Dividing between "visual" and "auditory" only divides different organ-sensations. It assumes that perception is mere input (see *APM* IV-A, VII-A, the derivation of consciousness).

Gallagher made a very important point in *How the Body Shapes the Mind* when he was so puzzled by the fact that newborns (both animals and humans) can connect seeing and hearing long before the neurological bridges between the visual and the hearing have developed.

An animal responds in a bodily way to something visual and also to something auditory. If one of these comes first, and then the other, the animal will incorporate both, along with a bodily sensing of its situation. It will sense one situation and both organs.

There is always a bodily sensing of the situation. If we hear words spoken or see words written, this does not happen without a bodily-implicit sense of how those words have affected the situation. Understanding a situation is always an implicit understanding, even though there may be spoken or written words.

The alternative happens only when we "are out of touch" with the bodily effect of the words, for example, when we have heard or seen the words, but *not attended* to what they mean, not engaged with what they mean, not let ourselves feel what they mean. Quite often we can hear but not "concentrate" on what is being said. In that case, we have to ask for them to be repeated for us.

So we cannot very well consider language to consist only of sounds and writing. Language involves those, but what they mean to you or me is something else.

When language is considered to be only the words (along with certain "rules" of syntax), such a theory of language does not account for what we mean. Nor can we simply divide this duality. Such a division would be something like the old division between mind and body. It would assume floating meanings. Actually, any use of language (speaking, thinking, or writing) of course involves words and meanings in one result.

The words separated from their meaning are no longer what we mean by "words." They only seem to become just sounds and visual patterns, but this is not what words are when we think or say them.

3. Two Different Precisions

The universal words and the implicit particular meaning are each precise. In what way can something be "precise" while it is still forming and never ultimately definable? We can easily see this kind of "precision" if we consider that we don't like to stop saying what we set out to say, as long as what we hear ourselves saying does not yet feel like what we wanted to say. This shows that what we wanted to say is in a sense already "precise." It can indicate that we have a felt sense of what we wanted to say even though we do not know what that is.

It is characteristic of the implicit that it is demandingly specific, even though we have not defined what it is. It can determine that we have not yet expressed what we wanted to say. I am therefore asserting a kind of precision that something implicit can have. It is as if the implicit knows exactly what does or does not satisfy the demand. This shows that what is implicit already has this kind of precision, certainly different from an already unitized and separated precision. But this implicit precision we use constantly when we are working in new ways. We would not want to deny how we use this kind of precision in all new conceptualizing and new research.

CHAPTER 7

From a carrying forward that has happened, we can retroactively generate new units in terms of which the carrying forward can be explicated. The new units can look as if they had already happened. But these new units did not happen until they came. The units that explicate a carrying forward are new and generated after the carrying forward.

To explicate a carrying forward involves a kind of logic very much related to our familiar logic. However, this retroactive logic is possible only from a carrying forward that has already happened.

The very possibility of a retroactive logic can open our thinking to a great many happenings. The usual logic and mathematics are limited to deduction, to repetition. In the usual logic, anything that happens at time 2 (t^2) has to be explained by something that happened earlier at time 1 (t^1) such that $t^2 = t^1$. The retroactive logic goes beyond those limits to many more and different precisions. They were not explicitly there at time 1, and so they were not predictable.

But we would not use only the retroactive unpredictability. We need to keep what I call "the unit model"—the usual logic, mathematics, and research procedures. In the unit model, everything is conceptualized only in terms of already-determined units that remain identical to themselves.

We need to use both the predictive model and also the wider process model. We need to use the models separately and know which model we are employing. Otherwise, for example, the very activity of adding up numbers might involve something implicit that would change the quantity of each of the items we are adding. If we were to mix them, the new model would make it impossible to continue to employ the old one, and the old model would freeze the new one.

[At the author's request, selected and revised passages from his unpublished essay "A Changed Ground for Precise Cognition" have been added here.—Eds.]

We can always easily say a lot from the implicit:

First I will discuss an easy way of access, then a more difficult way.

You can always easily say a ton of things about what you are already saying and why you are saying it. More words come when you are asked (or ask yourself) to say more of what is involved.

You might be asked: Can you say more? Why are you saying that? Why do you think this or that part of it? What are you really trying to get us to see? (to understand? to do?) Who agrees with this? How does it affect x or y or z? (There are an endless number of other issues.) You may or may not have good answers, but each time you can easily say something further.

I call this the "easy access" because whatever the words used, what an individual means is always also bodily implicit, and can develop.

Your responses were not formed until the questions were asked. Thinking and speaking always involve development. When you tell more and more, you can no longer distinguish just what was implicit from what has developed further. There is no such line. Speaking and thinking involve "carrying forward" (my concept for this kind of change, no line between what changed and what stayed the same). Carrying forward expands the thing in the telling, but doesn't change it into a different thing. So, in some sense the further developments "were" all implicit in what one already said.[2]

4. The Difficult Way of Accessing the Implicit

The difficult way involves the fresh coming of a direct referent, which may come in response to our directly referring to the whole of something without as yet defining it, and then waiting. When a direct referent has come, the words that can come *from* it can bring new ideas, new steps, and new meaning.

What the word "meaning" means is famously controversial. The words alone are not the meaning, nor is the meaning the implicit without words. We can say what "meaning" means if we keep both words *and* the implicit. We will further examine this *and*. We can say that "meaning" consists of the few words we say and the gigantic "all that" which can be bodily implicit in what we say and mean.

But can we ever have the implicit apart from the particular sentences?

Humans are never just without words because the whole language is implicit in our bodies.

Therefore words are implicit in any human experience. The word "preverbal" says rightly only that an implicit can be sensed without a particular string of words. We can sense an implicit "all that" in a bodily way, "kinaesthetically," like we sense our muscles and our being in motion.

When an "it" has actually come, then "it" is a direct referent. Then we can think "it" without as yet a particular set of words. This is a new kind of implying; "it" is still implicit although "it" has also occurred. This is the first implying that has occurred as this (implicit) "it."

Before a direct referent has come, I may be paying attention to a troublesome emotion or problem that I wish were not there. I seem to know what it needs, but I cannot do that (for instance, love myself). All this seems already defined and it engulfs me.

CHAPTER 7

After a direct referent (an "it") has come, what I call "I" feels freed and has "a little distance," a little breathing space from the problem. "I" can now relate to "it." Now "I" no longer wish "it" were gone. "I" can be interested in "it" and what "it" will bring further. The coming of the direct referent has also carried "me" forward.

There are many common instances in which a direct referent of what we want to say comes without as yet any particular words. Here are some examples:

Example #1 of a direct referent:
When we have said something quite well but the other person didn't understand it, we lean back and think how else we might say "it." Thereby we are letting a separate "it" come from the original set of words. But what exactly do we have at such moments? Here we can directly examine this. What do we have when our meaning is no longer only in the words we just used, and not yet in another set?

We see that we can refer directly to a bodily implicit "it" that may come without a particular string of words.

Since another way to say "it" may soon come, we see that this "it" contains implicit words even before an alternative statement has formed. And if we don't accept the statement that comes, another may come, and then still another. We can hold out for a statement that seems to us to say "it."

The implicit "it" consists of a lifetime of learnings ("all that"), but it implies "just this." We see that the precision of the implying is stubborn. "It" implies just this stubborn next step. "It" can make us reject many restatements that suggest themselves. The rejection shows the implicit precision. We reject a restatement if those words feel too far from what "it" implies. But we can know when it is too far, even though we don't have words for what it implies.

Different phrasings don't leave "it" unchanged, but they do not change it into something else; rather, they "carry it forward." So we see that "it" is not determined only by words, although each rephrasing can develop "it" further.

Example #2 of a direct referent:
There are other occasions when we try to refer directly to what we mean. For example, we may forget what we were about to say. We didn't have words prepared; we just knew we were ready to speak. Now we have a residual sense of the forgotten left, but it is closed so that we cannot enter

into what it "was."[3] If we refer to this left-over bodily quality (a nameless quality, "that, there . . .") and spend a little time there, it may suddenly open so that what we wanted to say floods back—still not in words, but now open ("nascent") and ready again to be spoken from. When it does ("Oh, I've got it back!"), it is still without words but a direct referent has come.

Example #3 of a direct referent:

The following is big and exciting: we can also use the same procedure when we sense a new step at any juncture of thought.[4] Although not something we already had and lost, a direct referent may come and then open into a readiness, a wordless "Oh, I know . . ." which can then lead to new concepts.

We cannot control, but we can invite a new direct referent, one next bodily implying, to come at any spot we are thinking or reading where we sense a new expansion. We may feel a "something" is already forming. Or at times, we may feel like we are standing in front of a gray wall, nothing distinct, although there is still something we do know and cannot yet put our finger on. We can await a bodily quality, as in the example of getting back what we wanted to say. We can invite the precise bodily quality by asking: "Is this more like heavy, or more like jumpy?" even though we know "it" is neither. Then we can wait or return, again and again, to the "it" that has not yet come. Soon we are not sitting with a blank, but rather with a new bodily "this." Then we can welcome whatever new has come, even something small or odd. It will soon lead further.

The bodily direct referent may come in response to our referring. We have to refer to it while it is not quite there yet. This is odd but one learns how to do it. At first it is a little fitful; it may come or not, and it has various degrees of distinctness at various times.

When a new bodily "it" comes and opens, we feel, "Ah, yes, this 'was' implied!" But actually "it" was not already there until "it" came. "Its" coming is a further development, a carrying forward. That is why many new further steps can come from "it," which could not come just in the easy saying.

Before a bodily-implicit direct referent has come, we might be tempted to infer an "it" only theoretically (because it "must be" so).

Up to here, we have tried to be consistent in defining the direct referent and in defining the easy access. But now, we need to say that our consistent definitions can be understood in two different ways: either as verbal and conceptual definitions or *from* and *with* the implicit.

For instance, near the beginning of this chapter I asked you to please check whether you agree that what you, personally, mean is always implicit, whatever words you have also used. You may have agreed that this is so only because it "must be" so. Or you may have agreed because you directly encountered something that you were implicitly trying to say.

Similarly, all our definitions of "direct referent" could be taken as only consistent verbal definitions, although you almost surely understood them by referring directly.

From here on in, new definitions will emerge in new terms coming from and with the implicit direct referent.

5. Implicit Language; How Words Come; Readiness to Speak

In both the easy and the more difficult access to the implicit we can ask: In what way is language implicit in the body? And how do the words come to us? I open my mouth—and they come. What is a readiness to speak?

Since there are no established concepts of "implicit language," "how words come," and "readiness to speak," let us establish new concepts. Let us allow these three to be concepts. But what do they mean? Well, first off, they mean what they do here: how they themselves are speaking from implicit language, from the coming of the words, and from the readiness to speak. Of course, we will say more and more with and from them; we will let them generate more specific phrases and concepts in which they can say more of themselves.

In how we think these three, we are already thinking with the implicit, not only with statements.

Now we can go on to redefine "human body" as always including implicit language, the coming of words, and the readiness to speak. This expands the meaning of these phrases to include what the word "body" has been doing in my discussion throughout. The human body is the externally observable structure *and* also the body sensed from inside. "The environment" is not something separate, located only outside the body; rather, the body is always already constituting itself of "environment" before it is separately definable (*APM* I). Body and environment are always interaction-first (*APM* IV). Actually, you have probably directly understood all the new process-concepts (*APM* I–VII).

Language is implicit in the human body but not as in a dictionary, where the single words themselves are each there. *Language is implicit as the ability to form sentences.* The particular words come only as we say or think them.

Words don't come singly as if we had to put them together. They come already appropriate to the situation. They come already-arranged in grammatical sentences to say *this* to *this* person in *this* situation. The words have arranged themselves implicitly in the body; by the time they come, they are all arranged appropriately. So we see that the body implicitly "knows" (has, is, implies . . .) the situation and the action (including speaking) implied to meet it.

But what is "a situation"? A situation is not just external facts, not only that there is a river over there, but that I need to get across, or that it protects me from pursuers, or that I could support myself by setting up a ferry here. A situation implies a way to meet it, a way that is not yet formed, has not yet occurred. To "meet" a situation means acting to change something, but not into a different situation, but rather into something this situation demands (implies). Only if we break up the situation have we changed it into a different one. An action that would meet it develops and reveals what the situation really "was." Here again we need our concept *"carrying forward"*: *a change, but not into something else.* We could derive "carrying forward" from this familiar character of situations.

The implied demand to meet the situation is something that we *might* or *will* do or say. So it is a kind of future that is here now. We need a concept for that kind of future.[5]

6. Occurring into Implying

A process always occurs into its implying. If an organism no longer implies, it has died. If it has not died, but cannot continue its process, it immediately enacts a new process (Merleau-Ponty, quoted in *APM* 76).

We can conceptualize all organismic processes (including the lowest) as occurring into implying. What occurs from the organism will enact something like what the organism implies. I say "something like" because the implying is not yet any particular formed occurring. An occurring forms only as a particular environmental interaction. Therefore the implying "was" never the same as what has occurred.

But the implying is not indeterminate; it is rather more determined than something that has only one form. An implying is more precise than anything that can ever happen.

For example, plants imply absorbing water; if there is no water and they didn't die, they imply a complicated different process involved in drying out. Mosses on rocks can dry out but can wait for water for a long time. When water comes, they become green again. Seeds can wait in the soil for hundreds of years and still become plants when light and water come. This happens if they have not died.

Bacteria imply complex further organismic processes from any present moment. It is their own implying, not only the scientist's. Even a slight change in the environment, if it doesn't kill them, enables them to "break out" in unpredicted new processes.

An implying implies one next occurring which may carry the implying forward. If it does, it will imply a further occurring which, if it happens, may again carry the implying forward to imply a still further occurring. Implying, and occurring into its implying, is a "process." We have derived a model of process in *A Process Model*, in which my theta diagram pictures how a process seems to go back identically to where it was, but then goes further back and then comes forward in a new way (*APM* 69).

In our model, "process" is never just occurring-occurring-occurring, never only formed events. "Process" always implies and occurs into its implying.

"Process" is not just change as usually conceptualized in science and as commonly understood. "Change" in the usual sense assumes formed and fixed units that can only be rearranged. If something new and unpredicted happens, it is assumed that we made some mistake. The units are assumed to be self-identical, so that they must stay as they are already defined. But "process" is successive as carrying forward.

"Process" is also not what we usually think of as "motion." In the usual concept, "motion" is only a change of the *location* of something that otherwise does not change.

Biology and biochemistry are still formulated only in the unit model. We want to keep what has been and can be formulated in the unit model, but the process model is wider. We can use the wider model to expand what we know in new ways. But what the wider model has said cannot be formulated in the old units. As we said earlier, we must use two models and keep our use of them distinct.

If process meant only change or motion (and this is all process often means), then we would lose our new understanding of the process of implying and occurring.

If we allow a direct referent to come, and "it" has actually come, then we can *think directly from and with* this bodily implying. Now we think by meaning *this* direct referent. This way of thinking is process understanding itself.

From the direct referent can also come many new concepts that can expand what we can say about the process. This will develop philosophy.

When we think from a direct referent that has come, the statements we say *from and with* it can look like ordinary statements. But we no longer mean the ordinary statements. We mean the direct referent itself.

As we think from and with a direct referent, we think of many different examples, applications, times when something like this happened. These are new topics to which this direct referent can "apply" (in this new sense of "applying"). Verbally they can seem to mean different topics, but now they each instance this direct referent. Although this direct referent is carried forward in many ways each time, the "many instances" are still also this direct referent again.

When a direct referent is carried forward, it does not "change" into something else. What it brings that is new "crosses" in what is then still "this direct referent." (Crossing is discussed in *APM* VII-B-e, VIII-f-9.) In this successive crossing, this direct referent opens new possibilities beyond what had seemed to be a limited number.

The concept of "degrees of freedom" (*APM* VI-A-h-2) assumes that reality is limited to a fixed number of already-structured possibilities. In contrast, the process model assumes that carrying forward brings new possibilities. We show that more determinants make for more novelty.

When a direct referent has come, we keep meaning *this* direct referent. Verbally each statement from it seems to say something different if they are taken just as statements. But since we mean this direct referent itself, it *instances* all its many applications, new topics, and ways of carrying forward. It is again one, although it is also many, but in a new sense of "one" and "many."

Each crossing is again "this" direct referent, and it is also its many instances of the direct referent. The many instances are each instancing every other instance. Now each of our different statements is an instance of this cluster.

I call this cluster "a monad." I say a direct referent "is monading" its many instances (*APM* VIII-f-3, app. to VIII).

In monading, we are thinking directly from and with this special implicit, a direct referent (it is the thinking I have taken up in *APM* VII).

In its usual meaning, each word seems to instance its fixed higher and lower classifications. It seems that a word is always subsumed by its higher classifications and always subsumes its lower classifications. And that word seems unable to escape its classifications.

A direct referent can, however, be the source of *new* classifications. This is because, as I said throughout, what we live and encounter is, for the most part, not already verbalized, not already verbally classified (see *APM* VIII-A-f-7).

CHAPTER 7

Our words need not always fall back into the old existing classifications. It is always possible to generate new classifications. A direct referent allows words to mean in new classifications that we sense before we can speak in them.

With pausing, we can invite a direct referent ("it" is still implicit) to come at any point in our thinking where we encounter something we sense but cannot yet state. A direct referent frees all words from their fixed classifications. It is exciting how our bodies' implying can open possibilities new to the world.[6]

Notes

1. As I have often said over the years, this model builds on Dilthey, Whitehead, McKeon, Heidegger, Merleau-Ponty, and Wittgenstein, as well as Plato, Aristotle, Leibniz, and a great many others. Elsewhere I have discussed my debt to them, and my way of going on from each of them. (See the many articles in the Gendlin Online Library at www.focusing.org.) Thank you to David Young for help in the revision of these pages.

2. A further distinction is needed: since the endless and easy further saying is a developing carrying forward, therefore we see that not all of what comes was implicit at first. As we say (explicate, carry forward) some of what was implicit, more and more becomes implicit. (See the term "held" in *APM* VII-A-o.) It follows that "everything" that the implicit "was" is not a finite number.

3. William James wrote: "Suppose we try to recall a forgotten name. The state of our consciousness is peculiar. There is a gap therein; but no mere gap. It is a gap that is intensely active. A sort of wraith of the name is in it, beckoning us in a given direction. ... If wrong names are proposed to us, this singularly definite gap acts immediately so as to negate them. ... And the gap of one word does not feel like the gap of another, all empty of content as both might seem necessarily to be when described as gaps. When I vainly try to recall the name of Spalding, my consciousness is far removed from what it is when I vainly try to recall the name of Bowles"; see William James, *The Principles of Psychology*, vol. 1 (New York: Henry Holt, 2009), 251.

4. See Eugene T. Gendlin, "Introduction to 'Thinking at the Edge,'" *Focusing Folio* 19, no. 1 (2000–2004). TAE was earlier called "Theory Construction."

5. Currently spoken of as "anticipation"; see Gallagher, *How the Body Shapes the Mind*. It is not recognized as the implying which is always part of body process and behavior formation. *APM* IV-B has the more intricate model of time that is implicit here.

6. In our practice of Thinking at the Edge (TAE), steps 1 to 8 will let you become able to state anything that you can sense but have no words for yet. The TAE steps are available in long and short form at www.focusing.org; click on the menu tab, "How to Think at the Edge," or go directly to www.focusing.org/tae.html.

8

The Derivation of Space

This essay is for Edward S. Casey. I write in the terms of my own philosophy about place and space as well as many other topics. I contrast two ways of thinking. We need both, and I will show exactly how we can use both. One way of thinking is narrow; the other much wider. Each is a way of thinking about what really exists, but the wider way can explain the narrow one, and can show how the narrow one is derived. I will derive it.

The narrow way assumes that everything exists in the space that has things in it. That space seems to be the reality in front of us and all around us. According to the narrow way, only what is in that space really exists. The wider way begins from *the activity we are*, the process, the happening, not just things that are before and behind us.

1. Location Space

The space of located things is familiar. In our Western culture it has seemed to be the original reality, what is "really" there. To exist has meant to fill space in some location.

This space extends to the galaxies. Each thing seems *located* in it. Something that fell off the table must now be down there, even if we don't find it. The old book is still there, on the shelf where I put it years ago, unless someone moved it. Now I want to look something up in that book. So I go to that shelf. There it is.

The located things are *there*, that's quite true; but every "there" is a *there from here*, seen and heard by someone here who points from here to there. The space we are examining is the gap between a *here* and a *there*.

The space of locations is a spectator's space. It is perceived but then the bodily *process* of perceiv*ing* is dropped out, so that only the perceiv*ed* things seem independently real. If that were so, there would also already be the space between them. But the process of perceiving is what is generating the percept*ions*! They are wrongly considered to exist by themselves.[1]

The dependence on the perceiving observer has long been well known. But the existence of this space was so thoroughly assumed, that *it seemed only a famous problem* that space depends on an observer or observers. The mistake really was to put the product before the process that is generating the product. We will change this assumption and reverse the priority.

Quantum physics is the only science that has rejected the old concepts, although without providing new ones. Using only mathematics and experimental operations, physics finds that the observer-space does not exist. *Well, of course it doesn't!* There would have to be only one observer.[2] More importantly, we and everything else would exist only in observer space. But we and the things don't exist only as observed from outside.

Sometimes we view ourselves as if we were "really" objects. Many people assume they are just physiological structures in space. But those are cognitive conceptual structures and perceptions which are being generated.

The located things don't exist by themselves. Even in physics the particles don't exist by themselves. Only their being generated and re-generated can be calculated and predicted. But the location space is still assumed in most other sciences and by most people. Most of our concepts are about structures in space. So we find ourselves falling back into assuming locations even when we don't want to. But with the wider kind of thinking, *we can have a different kind of conceptual structure.*

Let me examine location space a little further. It is a featureless space and assumes a featureless existence. Something exists if it fills some space. This featureless *existence* and this *space* are the same thing.

In modern symbolic logic one asserts that a thing exists by saying: "There is an x such that x is . . ." (followed by a statement of what it is). All the content is in the part of the formula that tells the "such that . . ." The assertion of existence is featureless, nothing but "there is an."

What "is" seems to be what is located. To continue just means is is is. If it continues, it fills successive time positions, now now now. The is is is and the now now now are located positions. There is no organic continuity between them. The continuity of generating a process is dropped out in favor of "relations" between separate things. But relations are not events.

When we assume the separate things first, then each seems to exist and fill a space of its own. To exist seems to mean filling a space that has no features. This space is just the gap between the separate things.

In the wider order we *live, act, and think with* an implicit intricacy, not only with what occurs explicitly formed. A process does not reduce to is is is and now now now, although we can derive those from it. A process is not only the formed occurrences that appear before us, not even when they are newly differentiated.

It is not a process even if the nows are stretched to include a little past and future (in Husserl's way). Even with the term "anticipation" we still place ourselves at some position in the is is is. But a process is something more.

Terms like "unfolding," "emergence," "background," and "implicit" have become common. But most people still consider them vague ideas with which one cannot go further. I offer a detailed conceptual structure *with precise concepts that can connect to an implicit kind of order.* These concepts will enable us to derive and go beyond location space, among many results of a wider understanding.

I need to introduce three further developments. I will explain them as I go on.

First, because bodies *are* body-environment interaction, therefore new forms are generated *immediately in* the environment. It is not the case that what happens at a later time must be composed of the same units as existed at the earlier time. A different kind of concept can explain the continuity across novel developments.

Second, in the living body the seemingly "lower" micro processes have the "higher" perceptual and cognitive processes *implicit* in them. I will offer precise concepts for how something implicit functions.

Third, the empty space derives from patterns, from communicating with seemingly simple motions and *just visual and just sound patterns* like language, art, and music. You wave to the people coming up the walk and they wave back. They know you are not reaching for something. Humans also make new things by moving just a pattern onto a thing that does not have that pattern from itself. When one moves just a pattern, one ignores everything between, as if it were empty space. But the patterns are not actually simple.

2. Body-Environment Interaction: Immediate Novelty

The concept "body-environment" says that we are always *part of* the environment, not that we have only perceptions of the environment. This much has recently been widely agreed on. We can go further.

Immediate novelty: Merleau-Ponty described a bug whose legs were cut, so that it walked in a new and more complicated fashion. Similarly, I observed an ant on my fuzzy rug, walking in a complicated wiggly way that was obviously quite new to the ant. In these examples we see that a new and more complex process can form immediately. We can explain it. Since the organism is always already part of the environment, the previous organization comes out in a new way in a changed environment. The ant doesn't gradually develop a new walk, doesn't first have to walk in its old way—indeed, it can't. Nor does it need random unorganized motions from which to select a new walk. If it walks at all, it will walk in a new way. If there is a change either in the body or in the environment, a newly organized way happens *immediately* (unless the change has killed the organism).

The new walk need not be a lesser part of the old walk. It can be more complex. Now the ant rebalances from side to side as it moves forward. What had been a much simpler walk occurs in this new way because the ant *is* an interaction with the new environment. Similarly, for example, if we fall into water, our walking turns into much larger thrashings.

The point is: *because* an organism is environmental, therefore it happens directly into the environment. In a changed environment it can only be different.

Here the theory of evolution can serve as an example. In the old theory of evolution anything new had to be constructed out of existing forms or random accidents. Billions of "mutations" were required for something new, but these have not been found. The theory is not universally believed, but it instances an assumption that underlies the usual concepts, that anything new has to be composed of already-formed parts. Now we can propose a better theory. In body-environment interaction a change can immediately be *newly organized*.

Of course, a new process comes from what existed before, but not from the formed units. A process is a more intricate continuity. We call it "carrying forward."[3]

In the wider kind of thinking we include something implicit and the continuity between this and the new occurrings that are being generated.

We will see as we go further that the universe exists implicitly as well as implying ever-new occurrings that carry it forward.

3. Implicit Organization

We can go another step further: what we mean by "embodied cognition" is not only what occurs, but also a great multiplicity of implicit events that are not separately occurring. The many implicit events imply one further occurring, and enact it if the environment permits.

Embodied cognition is more than old or new formed things and parts. It is regenerating the formed things and parts. To think with un-

THE DERIVATION OF SPACE

folding, emerging, implying, and occurring involves a more intricate conceptual structure. Let me discuss some examples:

Consider action or *behavior*. We *could* act in many ways with each thing. I could move that broken chair or I could carefully try to sit in it again. I could chop it up for firewood, or I could just leave it there. I could take that book down and look up the spot I want to see. In the laboratory we could perform one of many known operations or try out a new one. Each object "*affords*" us many possible actions, as Gibson said (and we noted already). In my way of saying it, we always have *many action possibilities*.

But while the objects are spread out before us, let me point out that action possibilities are *implicit, not spread out before us*. And every possible action also involves a host of detailed circumstances that are not spread out before us.

How do we *have* this familiar "what we could do"? Shall we say we *know* it? Yes, but this is an odd "knowing," not something in our thinkspace, but rather, an innumerable number. Shall we say we *feel* them? Yes, but it is a nameless "feeling," so much at once and changing all the while.

No common word says how we *have* our possibilities. Whatever words we use to talk about it will have to mean *this* familiar way we have them.

The implicit possibilities and their circumstances are intricately organized. Every action changes whether and how the others could be done. Some can no longer be done, but some are new possibilities. Any single action is a change in other possibilities, but each is a different change in them. Every possibility is a cluster of changed possibilities. An action is not only what occurs, but also a cluster of implicit clusters, an implicit intricacy.

Behavior happens in a space, but it is a *filled space*. Any actual behavior happens in this implicitly organized space.

The possibilities are not separate next to each other; rather, they are implicit in each other. They are not merged but have a very precise organization. What would actually occur is implied very precisely. This kind of organization is more organized than side-by-side things can ever be. Anything enacted emerges very exactly formed.

Language is another example of implicit organization. The several hundred thousand words of our language are fixed, but each has a great many different uses. These happen in phrases and sentences with other words. We have the uses implicitly, and can imply a new one.

When we are about to say something, we don't yet have the words. We have what we want to say—implicitly. Unless we have prepared the words in advance, they come as we speak. We speak directly from what we want to say. The words come grammatically arranged and they usually say pretty much what we wanted. But if we find that we were misunderstood, we go right back to what we implicitly want to say, and let fresh words come to say it.[4]

We could not act or speak without the implicit intricacy of possibilities and what we want to say. Implicit intricacy is more precise and has more organization than separate units can provide. The conceptual structure I have discussed here can connect with the implicit kind of organization.

4. Reciprocity: How the Analytic Retains Its Power and Also Develops

The narrow way of thinking consists of separate terms with logical relations between them. An analytic layout can help us immensely. Distinctions and separations enable us to do more and more in our lives, as well as to create the ever-changing technology without which seven billion of us couldn't live on the planet. Analysis creates separate entities before us and relates them clearly. We cannot do without this. An analytic layout carries our whole situation forward.

An analysis consists of a fixed set of terms. If we change a term in one spot, we must change it in every other spot. And since all the terms are logically connected, a change in one term necessitates changing the others. An analysis creates logical consistency, a great power which brings logical implications and clarity.

But the clarity which an analytic layout brings lies not only in the layout before us. It has an effect in the body. It brings an implicit whole-bodied *understanding*. "Aha!" we say.

If we turn from the layout to the implicit understanding which it brought us, new steps of thought may come, which could not have been deduced from the layout itself. From the bodily understanding we may think in a new way. Then there may be new facets to lay out. And if we succeed in an improved layout, it can bring us a new "aha!"—a further implicit understanding which may again give us new facets for a still further layout. Analysis and implicit understanding expand each other reciprocally. I call this "reciprocity."

We can allow analysis and implicit understanding to expand each other by alternating our attention between them. I call this "fresh thinking."

Fresh thinking is not at all illogical, since it generates ever-new logic with newly emergent terms. Its continuity differs from the continuity of a single logical analysis. That is the kind of continuity I call "carrying forward."

Carrying forward is the kind of transition that Fodor examined in trying to define how science progresses from year to year.[5] He found no logical series across the development, and this led him to reject the old idea that more complex sciences can be reduced to simpler sciences; for example, organic chemistry to inorganic chemistry and physics. Fodor showed how science develops ever-new specialties with new terms and characteristics. Where there were three terms, now there are thirteen, all of them different from the earlier three.[6]

With reciprocity we can employ the powers of both analysis and implicit understanding. Let us not make opposing ideologies of them. They inherently involve and expand each other. We can deliberately adopt the development that Fodor has found, and we can make concepts from this kind of continuity.

5. How Occurring and Implying Function

What occurs is always both explicit and implicit. The implicit happens only in an actual occurring, but the actual occurring changes the implying into a further implying. A whole sequence of occurrences is always implied, but an actual occurring changes the implied sequence.

Implying and occurring happen at the same time which they generate. A new occurring generates a new present time. Implying exists only in an actual occurring, but the occurring is a change in the implying,

Existence is implicit and implies and enacts the next explicit occurring. So existence can be called an "explicating" process. It does not consist just of is is is units. Occurring does not exist alone. It carries implying forward. The continuity of carrying forward happens within occurring, not only with logical relations between separate terms. But we can generate many separate terms and logical analyses from occurring and implying.

Regenerating the Now-Functioning Past

The explicating process generates a more intricate kind of time. Occurring generates time. Because what occurs is new, therefore it has generated a past for itself. The past is now not what it was, not merely moved to a different position. We grow old not because time passes; rather, it passes because of the changes which occur. Happening is real and makes time.

By *generating* a new occurring, the organism has generated a past for itself. The past functions implicitly in the present, since the present would not be what it is if the past occurring were different. But how the past now functions depends also on what is now occurring and regenerating the past. It does not now consist just of unchanged events that are merely moved to a different position on a line.

The present occurring generates time by generating present events so that they have a (new) past. The new occurring therefore has an implicit record of its past, whether or not there is also someone's conscious memory. The present occurring changes how the past now functions.

There is also a future that functions in the present. This future is not what will be present and then past, just not yet. Those are only positions on an observed timeline. The future that functions now consists of the real but implicit possibilities and circumstances, as I discuss in *APM* IV-B.

6. Three Processes Implicit in Each Other

Gallagher offers a breakthrough by showing that our bodily micro processes can be directed by our perceptual and cognitive processes. Behavior cannot be accounted for by physiology alone. Nerves, muscles, circulation, and digestion can act in accord with cognitive rules. As quoted earlier, he writes: "When in the context of a game I jump to catch a ball, that action cannot be fully explained by the physiological activity of my body. The pragmatic concern of playing the game, even the rules of the game, may define how I jump" (Gallagher, 142–43).

I can offer a further account of this. Organisms, even single cells, are enormously complex even without perception. They happen directly into environmental interaction and did so for millions of years before perception and cognition ever developed. In humans the micro processes still happen directly into the environment, but now they implicitly contain perception and cognition.

Only if we clearly understand and distinguish cognition, perception, and micro processes (see *APM* IV–VII) can we then also understand exactly how they are implicit in each other and cannot happen separately. Cognition and perception always occur as part of micro processes. For example, we cannot speak unless the muscles of the tongue provide the sound of d and s. To have human emotions the heart rate has to increase. To perform this, the whole language and all our situations are implicit in the micro processes. The bodily processes are never without implicit perception, thinking, language, music, and art.

If we attend directly to something we have implicitly, we can be in a place that is grounded in our much wider actual body-environment interaction, and we can think from there.

When we first form concepts from something implicit, we don't yet know what that something is, so how can we know that what we think at first is not what is implicit? We can know because the implicit stubbornly responds with "no, nothing budges." It does not carry forward—until at last it does! When this happens we feel the bodily shift. Even then we may not yet have the words. *The muscles and the cells know the language.* They produce and respond to what we say and think. And they produce and respond to perception.

To have something implicit to think from is very reassuring. We don't have to make something up in some arbitrary way. And it is exciting when we feel traction in response to our words. Suddenly we feel traction where something felt stopped before. Now we can think further into it.

Might we end up saying something quite wrong? Yes, and even if not all wrong, anything we say will be partly wrong, and also poorly said. But by attending to the implicit version directly, we don't mean only what we say. We mean *this* actual implicit.

So it is clear: how cognition requires the muscles and circulation is the same fact as how the muscles and circulation can function in accord with cognitive rules, as Gallagher argued.

With these concepts many old puzzles resolve, for example psychosomatic medicine, intuitive understanding, the complex agriculture of indigenous people, improvisation as in musical ensembles, and many others.[7] It requires the concept of an implicit intricacy which implies and enacts one occurring.

7. Movable Patterns

Humans live in an environment that includes our human way of making things by moving *patterns* from one thing to another. Of course, there are very complex patterns throughout nature. Plants also seem to have patterns. They turn to the sun and their roots grow toward the water. And animals also have patterns. How is the human way with patterns different?

For humans the patterns have come loose. We can move *just* visual or *just* sound patterns, or rather, they seem to be just patterns when we move them. Animals imply their objects in all the sense modalities even if they only hear or only see just them (as discussed in the section on "Separate Senses," in *APM* VII-A, VII-j-1).

We make artificial things by creating purely visual patterns and moving them. We put our furniture patterns onto the wood. We put the round shape on clay. Wood and clay don't have those patterns from themselves. "*Making*" *is moving a pattern* and imposing it on things that don't have that pattern from themselves.

To move a pattern onto something, we ignore that thing's own patterns and everything that lies between us and that thing. When we move a pattern, the space between here and there seems empty. That empty space is made by moving patterns. Then that space can seem to surround and precede everything else.

Humans do a lot of living just with patterns. We handle our situations mostly with the sound patterns of speaking. We are deeply affected by the sound patterns of music.

Our gestures are patterns. For example, when we wave to the people coming up the walk, we are not acting with an object up there in the air. The others recognize the gesture and respond back. Gestures are more complex than behavior although they appear to be simple patterns.

The human body responds to just patterns. If you stick your tongue out at a newborn infant, the infant's tongue will come out as well. Neurologists say the infant "*imitates*" you, but that notion misses something. The neurological structures involved are called "mirror neurons." Seeing someone do something rouses our own neurons that would be involved if we did it. But the notion of "mirroring" is insufficient. I say the infant is *responding* to you.

Moving just patterns is a special kind of behavior, more exactly, not behavior at all. A simple sound or motion carries the body forward and changes the situation. This is a special development that begins with a few animals. A certain simple move or sound can elicit a whole-bodied change; for example, getting ready for fighting or for sexual intercourse. In some species of social monkeys each male turns his back when a superior monkey comes by. If he fails to turn, or if he bares his teeth, both monkeys' bodies change drastically and get ready to fight. What appears like a simple motion changes the body and shifts the whole context.

We humans develop this much further. We generate long sequences of such patterned moves and sounds. These are complex bodily changes and shifts in the situation. We generate version upon version of our interhuman action context. This is speaking and thinking, as well as music and art.

Our use of just patterns is part of an implicitly intricate body-environment process, but the patterns seem simple, and as if we move them in empty space. For example, behavior is called "motility." The link between perception and action is called "motor coupling." But actions are not just motions. Motions only change locations from here to there. The simple motion and its simple space are actually a complex product. One cannot account for action in terms of motion.

Patterns and their motions don't happen alone. They are developed in and with the earlier processes. They don't consist just of the repeatable patterns. Yes, patterns are *inherently repeatable*. A "same" pattern can happen in many locations. Patterns are the origin of "universals," generalities, abstractions. A patterned thing can be the same each time, like minted pennies. Then the pennies can be differentiated only by a location. This penny here is the one we observed over there before. Only spatial location differentiates "particulars" that have no features, only the same pure pattern.

So we see that empty location space is a sophisticated creation. It is not the antecedent reality.

In our science we study organisms by plotting them on our patterns. We study what *they* really are, but we do it by mapping *them on our* conceptual grids and with findings on our instruments. This produces enormously valuable information, but on our patterns. What the patterns picture enables us to intervene, improve, and cure. But the patterns give us only a graph, a map, a picture that is presented before us. What is actually going on is implicitly much more and different in kind. Of course, we need the patterns and this kind of science. We can employ both the patterns and the implicit in their precise reciprocal effects.

8. Being in the Universe: Concepts Applicable to the Universe

Let us begin with our own ongoing. We are environmental interaction in the universe. Rather than assuming that human experience is not real, not part of the universe, that we are aliens where we live, *we* can begin from our living process. Then this "we" can immediately include the other animals, the plants, the microorganisms, and everything else that exists. They are all generative happenings.

We have been developing many precise concepts that let us think further. We keep them linked to the familiar implicit version to which we can attend directly. Thereby we always mean *this* which is implicit, not only what we say.

With the new concepts we need not try to understand ourselves and everything else only as spatial structures. We need not try to think that we "really" are only what space concepts can say. How we are is not possible within those concepts.

If we begin from how we are, we can see that what Casey calls "getting back into *place*" is prior, much more original than location space, and also where we live after everything, and where we want to be able to perceive, act, and think from.[8]

Since we exist, we can be certain that how we are is not impossible. But this question goes further. The concepts that apply to the universe cannot be limited to structures in space. Since some of the universe is us, the concepts of it must be such as can account for people, animals, and all other organisms. We are not just *located in* the universe; we are *part of* it. We may be very special, but it is capable of being us.

We do not need to conceptualize the universe as having the nature of a single logical analysis. Rather, we can liken it to the sequence of analyses that develop in reciprocity with the implicit. The concept of this kind of sequence gives us a wider understanding of the universe. Therefore its basic nature is not limited to spatial structures and units.

The universe can be thought of as existing implicitly and explicating itself by occurring. We can take it as an implicit intricacy, a multiplicity of precisely organized factors and strands that are not separate, but always imply one next happening.

It used to be assumed that "the body" is the thing that will be left when I die. But that is not the body. That will be a dead body. This "body" is alive. I argue that we "know" what a living body is because we act and speak and think from one of those.

Notes

1. The process was long thought to be "transparent," just an "-of" of the things; only the content of consciousness was considered real.

2. Of course, we do need one space so we can find each other in one world, and we use the sun as a fixed point.

3. See *APM* 25, 42f; Gendlin, "Implicit Precision" (chapter 6 in this volume); and Gendlin, "The Time of the Explicating Process," in *Body Memory, Metaphor and Movement*, ed. S. C. Koch, T. Fuchs, and C. Müller (Amsterdam: John Benjamins, 2012).

See also "recursive" in S. A. J. Stuart, "Enkinaesthesia, Biosemiotics and the Ethiosphere," in *Signifying Bodies: Biosemiosis, Interaction and Health*, ed. S. Cowley, J. C. Major, S. Steffensen, and A. Dini (Braga, Portugal: Portuguese Catholic University, 2010), 305–50.

4. Once in a while the words don't come and it feels almost painful for some minutes as the language rearranges itself in the body. But no wrong words come either. The body implies what we want to say.

5. J. Fodor, "Special Sciences and the Disunity of Science as a Working Hypothesis," *Synthese* 28 (1997): 77–115.

6. The development brings vastly greater insight, but it does not necessarily incorporate every insight, implication, or advantage of an earlier analysis.

7. See Gendlin, "Improvisation Provides." What comes *directly* from the bodily implicit is most truly one's own and may already have taken the others into account.

8. See Edward S. Casey, *Getting Back into Place* (Bloomington: Indiana University Press, 1993); and Edward S. Casey, *The Fate of Place* (Berkeley: University of California Press, 1997).

9

Arakawa and Gins: The Organism-Person-Environment Process

On the first page of their book *Architectural Body*, Arakawa and Gins write, "The organism we are speaking of *persons* the world"; my italics are to point out that *persons* is a verb here.[1] The book begins:

> Born into a new territory, and that territory is myself as organism. There is no place to go but here. Each organism that persons finds the new territory that is itself, and, having found it, adjusts it.... An organism-person-environment has given birth to an organism-person-environment. The organism we are speaking of persons the world. (*AB* 1)

1. Personing

The "personing" and the body are not the same thing, but they are also not different. Arakawa and Gins do not begin with the three separate things usually meant by "body," "person," and "environment." Their "environment" does not consist of unitized entities filling an external space. Their "organism-environment" is not the body-structure. They don't begin with things that are already observed and thought about. The three were not first separate and then combined. Their hyphenated birth*ing* is first.

This "inging" (as I call the birthing process) is not merely the sequence of birth*ed* events (the contents). I will talk about this inging process.

Arakawa and Gins recognize no line between the bodily and the "higher" functions such as perceiving, imagining, thinking, and building. The body relates directly to the universe: "Surely there has never been a sufficiently diversified approach to the study of the body in relation to the universe."[2]

Arakawa and Gins's creations are attempts to provide an access to the inging, so that we, too, can create in it, and speak from it as they do here. In these new uses, the words acquire new meanings. This shows that the nature of language and the body is such that we need never be captured by the already-existing meanings, patterns, phrases, and concepts.

Ongoing process is fresh organizing, not organized just within categories. This is a major agreement between Arakawa and Gins and my philosophy. Only within the category *father* does it follow that there *must be* a child. Any real father is *a much more intricate happening*, never just someone cramped into categories.

Of course the stable (repeatable) units and parts are indispensable for technology. Six billion people could not live on the planet without technology. But the units and parts are derivative, made and remade; they are not the given. We must keep a set of *explicit* units steady (or, more exactly, change them slowly over the years), but we can also recognize the ever-fresh intricacy of experienc*ing*. We are the inging, and this is a different *kind of order*.

2. The -*Inging* Process Is Not the Contents

Arakawa and Gins call the contents of inging "landing sites":

> A person proceeds by registering a "this here" and a "that there" and a "more of this here" . . . fielding her surroundings. Whatever comes up in the course of this fielding should be considered a *landing site*. (*AB* 7; my emphasis)

> . . . anything, a whiff of something . . . (*AB* 9)

Landing sites are not discrete units. They have an intricate inter-overlapping organization. But they are not separate things, which only then overlap. They "overlap" before some of them are separate.

Landing sites abound within landing sites. The corner of a desk can be taken as a full-fledged landing site, even while subsisting as part of the desk as a whole (*AB* 9).

One kind is imagined landing sites: "Imaging landing sites . . . determine the measure of *things to be*" (*AB* 13; my emphasis). They are a kind of future that is here now. The already organized multiplicity is also still open for further inging.

But what kind of order is this? Many landing sites originally overlap,

CHAPTER 9

are intricately organized, *and* are *also* still open, implying but not determining their future.

Since I am a philosopher, not an artist, I ask about this *kind* of order. I articulate it beyond what Arakawa and Gins say, but not beyond what their sayings imply. It is not an order of already determined things and places. Neither is it simply indeterminate. We are not designing in a void. The inging always re-generates, but it is not arbitrary, not just anything at all. *We are a very precise kind of ordering which is also an opening for further ordering.* The body-environment process carries itself forward. This is a more intricate kind of order than the kind that consists of already determined units in categories with logical relations, the kind of order that is currently still being assumed as the given.

The inging is a multiplicity of interdependent "units" that *could* be separated out but have never been separate. A few of these interdependent possibilities actually occur as we go. Most of "them" evolve in the going *without ever existing separately.*

Recognizing this order opens new possibilities. Every problem can seem insoluble, every situation can seem determined, if we take it to consist of discrete unitized factors. But no situation is actually made just of those.

But if the inging process is actually first, what is its source? Arakawa and Gins say: "Surely imaging capability derives from a mobile and sculpted medium of locatings . . . kinaesthetic and tactile landing sites, *the human body*" (*AB* 13; my emphasis).

The kinaesthetic and tactile locating *is* the body, more primordial than vision, earlier than perceiving something that is not us. But how can bodies have landing sites without perceiving?

In my philosophy this is explained as the earliest kind of body-process, an *organic "symbolizing"* by primitive organisms. If body-environment is one process, how can it have objects ("landing sites") without perception? Here is how it can:

When some aspects of the environment go missing, then the *whole* body-environment process cannot happen. If the organism doesn't die, if some life process does continue, then the body-environment process differentiates itself into what continues and what does not. Later, when the missing environmental aspects return, the stopped processes resume, and the observer marvels at how the organism "recognizes" its "object."

The observer perceives the object, but to the organism it *"means"* the body-environment process that it resumes. *The resumed process "organically symbolizes" without perceptions.*

In my use here the word *symbolize* acquires a new (more basic) meaning. Our human bodies also symbolize in this direct organic-environmental way, more basically than with perceptions or representations, although in humans these are always implicit as well. Our "higher" functions are not separate; they always involve the organic symbolizing process. That is why our perceptions and cognitions *implicitly involve* so much more than if we take them just as the forms before us.

And once they have formed, they continue to function implicitly even when we don't have them as such. And they develop further while they are functioning implicitly. This is why our thoughts from yesterday may contain more in the morning.

Every new behavior and cognition expands the whole body's implicit functioning, and then new thoughts, new phrases and actions can arise from the expanded implicit process in turn.

This reciprocal development has happened throughout human history, but now we can systematically employ the reciprocity. If we can access the implicit bodily functioning, and if we move back and forth between concepts and implicit intricacy, they expand each other reciprocally.

Some of our lives and situations are perceived before us; more in them consists of meanings, and messages from miles away.

We live all our situations with our bodies. Thinking and sensations are special processes that involve organic symbolizing.

On the basis of organic symbolizing, my philosophy formulates a derivation of behavior and then of cognition as two kinds of body-process that involve "*turning*" on itself, "*having*" itself. The plant does not *turn* so as to *have* (perceive) its doing; it does not behave *in* its perceptions as animals do.

And humans have a further "turning" and having, so as to "behave" *in* cognized "situations." And then—one more turn: turning to have and think *in* the specific implicit intricacy.

Philosophy always attempts to grasp its own thinking. Whatever topic it seems to be about (such as science, art, society, language), philosophy always concerns how such a thing as that topic can come to be and be thought *about*. Philosophy is not really about anything. It is about the about.

But philosophy has not usually grasped thinking. The many different answers since ancient times seemed always to be just concepts again, not the think*ing*, just products.

But if we also *think with the implicit intricacy directly*, we mean more than just the concepts. We can let them refer to their own emergence-from the implicit inging. They may be about a lot of other things as well, but what they say can refer to their own coming. As they come to us we can let them speak also about the coming. Their saying can instance the process of their coming.[3]

CHAPTER 9

For example, Arakawa and Gins *are personing* in their use of "an organism that persons." So "persons" can mean *this*. We needn't first define it; rather, we can define it from here. Then we don't reduce the "inging" to a mere concept of inging. On the contrary, we can also take the old concepts as referring to the bodily-implicit intricacy which they bring along.

In *A Process Model* there is a conceptual model that incorporates the relation between experiencing and formed forms, between "-ing" and "-ed." In the new model nothing just "is."

Every *occurring* is also an *implying* of further occurring. The implying is in the occurring; there is no separated implying. The implying changes *in the environmental occurring* so as to imply a further occurring. Or we can say that occurring changes the implying to imply a next occurring. This is what we call a "process." This is a new kind of model, but there can soon be better ones of this kind.

The conflicting philosophies and theories are different ways of carrying the implicit intricacy forward. We don't try to resolve the conflicts because we don't think them only as concepts; rather, we look for what they make emerge in the experienced intricacy. We can have all those discoveries; only their abstract implications contradict. There is no relativism between ways that reveal, expand, and carry forward this specific implicit intricacy. In this way we can use all models, theories, and approaches. We don't adopt *them*, but rather only what they make emerge from the specific intricacy of this situation in which we are working. Each model implicitly enriches it, and it is always still open to further implying.

Arakawa and Gins recommend "that nonresolvable issues be kept on hold—fluidly and flexibly on hold—right out there in the world where they occur . . . open still further to yield additional information about what is at issue" (*AB* 22).

In thinking the implicit intricacy directly, we find more intricate phrases and concepts coming, as well as more specific actions that reveal the implicit intricacy of the situation. Small moves can come: for example, making some phone call or having a bit of interaction with someone. Doing those does not solve the problem, but it can reveal the territory in much greater detail. Similarly in thinking; I say more about this below. When we refer directly to the ongoing process, then concepts and phrases don't box us in. They don't just mean themselves; they mean *this specific implicit intricacy*.

Now we must discuss how to gain access to the specific intricacy of each different situation.

3. Access

Where is the implicit intricacy? It is embodied. We find it in the body sensing itself from inside.

Arakawa and Gins can be misunderstood just as concretizing contradictions to interrupt our comfortable mental maps. They speak of "a path with built-in contradictions, a path that contradicts itself" (*AB* 87). But their art does much more than contradict and interrupt.

The aim of their structures is to let *us* discover that *we* can access and create in-and-from this intricacy. And they do this by building a structure that forces us to use our bodies even to enter and then to move in it.

"Bodily inserting every last finger of herself . . . she curls past what bars the way, bodily threading through . . . neck curving around an obstacle, head part of a different curve, midsection pulled in, one leg striding forward and the other positioned with a bent knee" (*AB* 90).

Sitting in my living room, I can imagine moving that glass door with its nine little sections into the middle of the room. I would see the fireplace through the grid of those little windows. And that shelf of slanting books, how would it look through those little glass sections?

When I only imagine this, what I perceive remains the same, but it all changes when I get up, or move a little. I can never walk into the room that I see from here. But Arakawa and Gins build, for example, a three-dimensional room structured in accord with two views, *both* from one spot *and* from the ceiling. In their creations there are several paths to go from any spot. Each requires ducking, twisting, and feeling our way around the other pathways. As we move and enact some series of actually occurring body-environment events ("landing sites"), we grasp that we *are* the process of event*ing* the environment. We are not caught in one mere "is." We are the *inging process*.

The access to which Arakawa and Gins point is through perceiving, imagining, and building, but they apply their theories to all human activity. I provide access through the ongoing process of speaking, thinking, and acting in situations. We can easily discover this access when someone asks us (or we ask ourselves), "What were you getting at by saying (or doing) that, just now? *Can you say more?*" These last four words immediately let us sense the implicit more. A whole chain comes, one thing after another. We find the implicit sourcing involved in anything we said or did. "*Can you say more*" opens an access to the specific implicit intricacy, always many many things.

We can also have a more direct access to these many things together—"all that"—by *turning* to attend in the middle of the body.

From merely experiencing we deliberately turn to pointing, sensing, and having "*this*" bodily-experiencing. We can point to the bodily-experiencing as "this," whether large or a tiny sub-aspect.

Thinking and feeling are bodily too, but if we let go of *what* we think and already feel, if we refer to the whole situation as "*all that*," we find that each situation makes a different quality in the middle of the body, something like heavy, jumpy, tight, or expansive—*this* quality.

At the first moment nothing may seem to be there in the middle of the body, just lunch or coffee, but after some seconds of bodily attention there is a specific bodily quality *of this situation*, "all that." (We call this a "felt sense.") If we keep touching this quality—it opens! "Oh, *that's* what this is!!" And then further little steps: "Oh, it's more exactly *that*." And "Oh, *that*." Many little steps come. We find how the body has been living that situation, and in the finding it develops further. It uncramps. Now it stretches out. Even if what we find is troubling, this process of finding it is a physical relief, an exhale, "Ahhh . . ."

The bodily quality and the bodily "ahhh . . ." show that action and cognition are bodily processes. We can access how the body lives each situation and each statement.

Our worldwide Focusing network (see www.focusing.org) teaches this practice of accessing. A second practice called Thinking at the Edge (TAE) lets new phrases and categories come from the Focusing.

The implicit intricacy is never arbitrary, never just invented. The implicit order of any "this" is *more precise* than an order of already-formed units can be. You can observe how precise it is when you are sitting with a felt sense that you can't yet express. Sentences come to you, but you reject them: "No, that's not exactly what I mean." You cannot say what you *do* mean, but that is because it is *more precise* than what these sentences say.

At last one comes that says this, but we don't take it just as a statement. We need not lose the implicit intricacy. On the contrary, *this* statement helps us to hold on to *this* precise implicit intricacy. There can always be other ways of carrying forward, but even one is valuable and hard to get.

4. No Capture

We need never remain captured within the existing concepts, perceptions, interpretations, and phrases. My philosophy turns to derive new terms in which to think about the nature of bodies, language, and situations such that this is possible. Language is far from being just a system of fixed phrases. From a specific intricacy quite new phrases can come, new metaphorical sentences that surprise us.

Arakawa and Gins certainly write in this way, actually fielding, siting, adjusting, birthing, or holding open. They write directly from the intricacy. We may not like or even understand their phrases, but we cannot take the words in the old way. If we do understand at all, we understand them in a way that instances the inging of which they speak.

We can invite and permit the coming of new phrases directly from a felt sense. When we have difficulty, it is usually because something cannot be articulated within the existing categories and patterns. Only fresh "crazy" (metaphorical) phrases can go beyond those.

In new phrases the words acquire new meanings. We discover that words are never just captured in old uses and meanings. They *bring* their old meanings, yes, but these can expand and change in new phrases.[4]

New metaphorical phrases also bring new patterns. Those are not combinations of old patterns. A new pattern is incipient before we can say it.

For example, after experiencing TAE in class, a child asks: "But *am* I my body, or do I *have* a body?" We answer, "Oh, I see, neither 'am' nor 'have' fits this. You and your body are not two things, and yet not just the same thing either. Stick with how you have it *right there*, what lets you know that neither fits. *That* can let you say something new. It might sound a little odd. What would you say?"

We are teaching TAE. The children love it because it lets them discover that they themselves can think. Focusing shows them where inside them new thoughts can come, and how to let new phrases come. TAE also shows how to articulate a new pattern from a new phrase. For some adult professionals, later steps of TAE go on to lead to logically interrelated terms—a formulated theory. It all comes from the specific intricacy, which you are-and-have, *right there*.

The implicitly intricate process is an implying of next steps. It is much more highly organized than any *deliberate deciding*. Of course, we never want to obscure or preclude it by arbitrary inventing. I urge letting the steps come from the body's implying *first*, then exercising choices as needed. And then again see freshly what comes in the body.

Notes

1. M. Gins and S. Arakawa, *Architectural Body* (Tuscaloosa: University of Alabama Press, 2002), 1. Hereafter this work is cited as *AB*.

2. M. Govan, S. Arakawa, and M. Gins, *Reversible Destiny: We Have Decided Not to Die* (New York: Guggenheim Museum Publications, 1997), 313.

3. See the "iofi principle" in *ECM*.

4. See my article "What First and Third Person Processes Really Are," *Journal of Consciousness Studies* 16, nos. 10–12 (2009): 332–62. Available at http://www.focusing.org/gendlin/pdf/gendlin_what_first_and_third_person_processes_really_are.pdf.

Part 3

On the Edges of Plato, Heidegger, Kant, and Wittgenstein

10

What Controls Dialectic? Commentary on Plato's *Symposium*

The world-dividers, those powerful axe wielders: to them the Earth's crust is nothing. With their axes they go several inches in, and they make furrows in the Earth, like those trenches with which one surrounds a camping tent to let the rainwater run off. Only the axers build cement and steel gullies of them. Future archaeologists, when they will dig and find these, will not know what they were for, and will no doubt say that they must have had some peculiar religious significance for us. This time they will be partly right, because people are mostly mystified by these divisions and feel that it is forbidden to cross over. A smart scoffer, on the other hand, will use them for trails.

Now, in contrast, the humble geographer does the Earth no harm. Wherever geographic lines are drawn, or planes passed through the Earth, whatever hemispheres are cut, however straight the lines, the geographers persist in explaining that the Earth is round and whole. The Earth's axis cuts far deeper than those three-inch gullies, it cuts right through, in fact, and yet it leaves the Earth undivided. Or take the plane that divides the northern and southern hemispheres: it leaves the Earth whole so that it can again be divided into eastern and western hemispheres.

It is true that it is of great importance to the geographer, once a line is drawn, to make the other lines at equal intervals from the first. Once all this is done, a very exact location can be given to every village on Earth. If you are even one three-hundred-and-sixtieth of a three-hundred-and-sixtieth off, you might be in an entirely different village than you intended, and you might be taken for an enemy or an infiltrator there. One can hardly say that these lines are not serious!

And yet, these lines are only one possible system of lines. The zero line goes through Greenwich in London. Had the English really had any conviction in the fact that London is the beginning of the Earth, they would have chosen the very center of London, surely. As it was, they thought it just as well to be off center, and take their observatory in

Greenwich as the origin line, thereby moving London westward by some miles. Don't say it doesn't matter; you wouldn't want to be lost in some of London's boroughs.

But we could make a worse mistake than to call *these lines* unserious—for example, when the geographers show that the Earth is round, we could tell them that they can't be serious in this instance either. If they wished then to prove it to us, and began to draw their lines to do a proof, we would catch them at it and reject the proof on the grounds that the lines were arbitrarily chosen.

Worse, we could take it as evidence for their lack of seriousness, that they themselves claim that an infinite number of different lines can be drawn even through some small space on the Earth, and that this nonsensical statement describes the Earth better than their own system of lines.

There are thus these two fundamentally different kinds of dividers, those whose divisions separate, and those whose divisions unite and help us get around better. Charted territory is more united or more easily uniteable by travel, and politically as well. We may even take the axers' divisions and use even them to get around, rather than to block us off. The serious has just one point of view; humor always juxtaposes at least two.

The division between the serious and the funny is the most fundamental axer's gully. All other axings are instances of it, only, whereas this one cut is really serious. If accepted, then thereafter anything serious isn't funny, and all humor is also lost on one, because anything serious is withdrawn to the other side and can't be hit.

Everything is then in one system of lines only, and cannot be made to be located differently viewed from another place. The Earth is then really taken to be flat, Moscow is never north of Chicago, the truth becomes flat and thereby wrong. So it is the axers who, in the end, render the Earth as a system of lines. The *Symposium* must be understood from the end forwards, and from the top down. At the end, Socrates argues that the genius of comedy is the same as that of tragedy. This tells us that what is said playfully, and what is said straight-facedly, are not fundamentally distinguished thereby. It establishes that whatever about Plato's dialogues is comic does not thereby make the dialogues different than if they had been written straight-facedly—well, different all right, but not less serious.

Thus there is not a type of writing that is inherently to be taken more seriously.

The comedy provided by Alcibiades near the end shows how absurd it is to say that "love" is most beautiful and the highest good. In making us laugh it convinces us more fully than Socrates's serious statement earlier.

And, of course, Plato wrote both.

Plato held that any piece of writing is inferior to a real dialogue, because the assertions made in it cannot talk back, if questioned, and are not equal to really ongoing thinking. We can take this in two ways: we can misunderstand it to say that Plato could have written what he really thought, but he was afraid to do so and therefore what he did write was less than what could have been written. Or, we can take him at his word that what he considered the real thing could not be written, because of the very nature of writing, and because of the very nature of real thinking and of reality. If we follow the second alternative, then the dialogic fashion in which Plato did write must become clear to us as being more real, than if he had written only assertions and only ones that were all consistent with each other.

There is still another misunderstanding possible. We can become very serious and dour about how reality is beyond comprehension, and we can interpret Plato's fashion of writing as merely telling us that. But that cannot be right either, since that can be written in one sentence, and, in fact, that *can* be written. Were the point merely that no matter how we think or struggle we cannot comprehend reality, no genuine progress can be made, it is clear that much work could be saved. It is in fact largely to save work, I think, that people hold this view. Especially in regard to Plato, the difficulty of studying his texts is entirely cleared up thereby.

The aim of this chapter is to reject those readings at least in regard to the *Symposium*, and to do it by making sense of it. One can surely make more sense of it, but not less.

We want to see how Plato's philosophy does at least as much as flat serious writings can, and then more. This means that there is at least a difference between having understood, and not yet having done so. Therefore it cannot be said that what he wrote cannot be univocally interpreted—only that there is more here than that.

Another way to put it: when a conclusion of Plato's is that we don't know something, I will show that there is a lot he has said, that we can know, up to that point, in fact that the point he calls not knowing is very highly informative specifically.

It is entirely false, and one of the misunderstandings I characterized above, to say that the great insight is that we don't know, that it is more sophisticated to know that one doesn't know, and no more than that. What this misses is the specific knowledge, many specific facets of knowledge, which go into any given respect in which we don't know something.

When a Platonic dialogue ends in what they call a "negative" result, this is what many readers miss. Actually, none of these dialogues have negative results. Rather, the dialectic in each dialogue consists of a series of positive assertions. After each, there are counterexamples and difficulties posed, which show not only *that* the assertion cannot stand, but give a very exact aspect or sets of aspects which are *why* it cannot. The next assertion in the sequence of positive assertions is not just any new try, but an assertion which states positively these facets which were discovered as the reasons why the last assertion couldn't stand. Therefore the point at which the last assertion was found faulty is a highly informative point. It gives information one didn't see when one first framed that assertion. Thus, if justice is paying what one owes, then if one owes weapons, returning them when the person is upset would fit the definition, yet it seems unjust. What is defined as just is thus unjust. This contradiction (*Republic*, book 1) gives information: What does one really owe the person who has loaned one something, if not the return of this something? Why, exactly, is it unfair to return what one borrowed, if the person is mentally deranged just then? Because he will harm himself with the weapons? That is sad, but why is it unfair, unjust? It seems clearly unfair. Why? Because when he loaned me the weapons he was doing me a favor, and when I return the weapons I am not returning the favor, just then. So it is a favor I owe, not weapons. And a favor is something that's good, therefore exactly, it would be unfair to return the weapons in that crazy instance. Later on, perhaps, we will say that it is always unfair to harm someone, but not here. That information is not here.

The next statement is not to be just any old good statement, but only a statement which arises directly from what we got as information, when the last statement was found faulty, and this was that it was unfair to bring harm to someone who did us a favor.

Therefore, had the dialogue stopped at this point, without a further definition (and I didn't phrase one here), it would not be "negative" and its point would not be that justice is hard to define, and that we don't know what it is. Rather, the point would be that justice has something to do with good and bad given and returned, rather than objects or money being given or returned. (The definition which follows is that justice is giving good for good, and evil for evil.)

This information is never again lost, once one sees it and has it. Giving good for good and evil for evil is also not a tenable definition, but the additional information we get from its troubles is cumulatively added to the information we got from the demise of the earlier definitions.

A "negative" dialogue happens not to stop with one of the positive assertions in the series. It happens to stop with the interstice. It is therefore if anything *more* positive because where it stops there is nothing that is incorrect, only correct specific information. One has the facets which will go into a next better statement, but not yet that statement. (When one gets it, other facets will be discovered by what is wrong with it. Hence if one stops with the statement, the dialogue would stop with some undiscovered flaws.)

The key to dialectic is to see exactly how the negativity—the faults found with statements—is specific information which can lead to a new statement. A new statement also will later be overthrown, but the specific information which led to it will never be abandoned.

To take such a next step, new concepts must be made. By "new statement" I mean the fashioning of new concepts, I do not mean just rearranging one's terms or fixing some oversight.

Plato and Aristotle were concept-makers, they therefore knew something about how concepts are made, rather than merely used. They saw that concepts are made from experiences, from certain ways of proceeding with experiences. Any instance can be made into a concept that has general application, but of course one then cuts up the world along certain lines. Other instances will also lend themselves to concept-making, but with different world-cutting lines. Aristotle chose certain ones as the best, and they were good indeed. Very much of what he used came from Plato.

Plato himself, however, found the power for concept-formation infinitely truer than any one set—not because that left an infinity of possibilities, but because he discovered what *controls* concept formation. That which controls concept-formation and keeps it from being arbitrary, corrects it and forces us to remake concepts when we find where they are faulty, *that* he called the truth.

Plato therefore did not characterize writing and set assertions as less than totally serious because the information or knowledge contained therein was unsure or relative or negligible or uninterpretable or not ultimately doubtless. Rather, it was exactly because by making concepts and then using them we discover further information, and this information is always sure, always concrete and experiential and there in the world, but when we come to conceptualize that further information, we are taking the first of three steps to discover more. This discovery of more comes about, not as further information making our earlier information untrue—but only as making our earlier statement untrue. The further information which makes that statement untrue is discovered by that statement.

The key here is that something controls what we can and cannot continue to maintain when examples from life make what we said seem false to us. This recognition consists of something other than our statements, concepts, definitions, and logic. With only these we could never sense the wrongness of anything that follows logically.

How is it that one can be forced to abandon one's best definition because of some conclusion that follows with perfect logic from it?

Clearly something functions, other than definitions and logic! What is that?

Plato's *Symposium* is about that.

Another way to formulate the above is in terms of contradiction. In the example cited, returning the weapons is just (by definition), and unjust (by some other access). For the same thing to be just and unjust is a contradiction.

In a contradiction both positive and negative formulations (with or without "not") fail. Something other than formulation must function. Therefore dialectic requires *a person*. Someone must check each step, and at least say "very true," or else when the words fail there will be nothing else.

Contradictions must not be taken as adding up to nothing. If how it is "unjust" were simply that how it is "just" is not true, nothing would be left. Instead, what one side means is not simply a denial of the other.

A way in which this error can be practiced is to make each side mean only its negation, so that one can say about Plato that he is simply not serious, because he said he isn't serious. Then, usually in a different part of one's essay, one can also maintain that Plato is just plain serious because he also said he wasn't being funny, that comedy has the genius of tragedy. Thereby, instead of having nothing to say, one can take the contradiction as purely flat, getting out of each side only the plain denial by the other.

The right way to take contradictions is to notice that the information contained on the two sides is different information. One side doesn't simply say the other is not. But to combine the informations requires a new concept, new terms, new ways of drawing lines on the world. Until that is done, if one is to say the informations in the old words, one can say only: "It is x, but also not-x." A better way to say it would be: it is x in certain respects, and not-x in other respects. These respects must make a new concept.

Every paradox is like that. A paradox expresses an insight while still using the words one had before that insight. It can therefore be stated only by using the old words twice, not in the same way.

Thus a person is required, and there are not only words but also what the person has there which can be different for the same words used in two ways.

If justice is not "paying one's debts," then we can miss the point by concluding that justice is the nonpayment of debts. We can discuss Plato as asocial; does he not say that we should disobey contracts? But since he also said it was just to repay, we must also later on call him a totalitarian and a statist. He had Socrates say that it was better to die because of unjust laws than to violate these laws.

Instead, we need to see that the information on the two sides isn't the same. One side says justice *is* a kind of obligation we do have, the other side says it is the return of a favor, not objects or money, but something good. The negating side thus tells us something more about what the obligation is.

Similarly, by taking only denials out of contradictions, Plato's view of knowledge becomes a kind of "activity therapy," because he says purely formal knowledge without the participation of much more in the person than the cognitive, isn't the highest kind. Or one can make Plato a formalist, the ultimate formalist, because he says such activity contradicts itself unless such activity, practice, education, politics, poetry, is guided, is really only imitations of eternal forms.

Again, one can say there is no knowledge, only ethics, for Plato, because he denies a true that isn't good. Or, there may be no ethics because only knowledge apprehends the good.

The assertion or definition which just then runs into trouble is in one sense retained and true, so one cannot throw it out, but where it runs into trouble is where one learns something more about it. This more, to be sure, forces a change in the formulation, but not a total change. It is a further differentiation, added in.

Thus Plato is first of all serious, and writes and makes conceptual formulations some of which are as good as Aristotle's (and some of these were taken over by Aristotle). But then, also, in addition and not in subtraction, Plato does more than make a good formulation. He also makes other good formulations in other connections and contexts. And, what is really more, Plato also shows a method of concept-formation, and thinks this method much closer to the truth than any one product from the method.

If the method did not result in serious conceptual formulations, neither formulation nor method would be worth anything. Since it does, the method is of a higher order than one of its products, or even all of its products. Just as, only because our obligations are serious, therefore it is important to see that the good, and not the objects, are owed, so also, because formulating is serious, therefore the method of so doing is even more serious than any one specific product.

The method is a process, a generating. By the method, as in recollection, the eternally same forms (about which, later) are regenerated in a moving activity by us. This is method, dialectic, philosophy, love, being drawn and controlled by eternal but always newly generative forms, as the animals give new birth to the same form's instances, in new individuals and circumstances. This method itself must be shown and given, says Plato.

CHAPTER 10

Thus Plato does more, not less, than give serious knowledge and formulations.

Of course, to say flatly in a formulation what the genesis-of-formulations is, what the method is, this can again be only one flat product. Therefore, what I said above about the method must itself be lacking in some regards. Not only are other equally good ways of formulating it possible with different lines drawn on the Earth, but also, any one formulation, because it is only a formulation, will be able to run into some difficulty and teach us more thereby than it says.

I cannot at the moment see what my rendition misses, but we will no doubt discover something further on.

Also, if one used what I said or Plato says only as formulation, then one would in a sense miss even the seriousness of the formulation. Thus while one must not dump out one side of a contradiction, one must also not keep it without its being informed by the other further step. Thus the most serious use of a formulation is in further thinking, especially that further thinking in which the formulation discovers new aspects by running into its own trouble with them.

The furthest one can get from Plato is to view his philosophy as a kind of relativism, or ambiguity with limited interpretability. This would omit the order, the steps, the necessity with which just this, and not just any old further item, is discovered by a given formulation. It would also miss the necessity with which the next and better definition or assertion is guided and controlled exactly by just what was discovered when the earlier formulation ran into trouble.

With respect to further steps not yet run into, the assertion might be open (though even these are convergent and polarizing toward one outcome), but with respect to this one already discovered difficulty of the formulation, only a next step that combines what we had with just this new facet we ran into, will do. We may not arrive at a formulation, but only at an understanding of a formulation we don't arrive at.

Thus, although the aim of a journey and of dialectic is present in each transition, the specific effect of its control is different at each step, and cumulative. This is because the truth or reality whose facets we run into when we draw lines and then run into trouble with them, can be called "the truth" or "reality," but it can also be taken as just this facet we just now ran into with this formulation. As "the truth" it is always the same, and every transition is controlled by it. As this facet, it is different and necessarily cumulative. We cannot find out more about what kind of obligation we owe until we have formulated "obligation," and cannot find out why we don't owe evil, until there is a formulation which says we do, when someone harms us.

A journey is like that, in the above respect. If the goal of the journey were equally present in each town we go through to get there, then there would be no point in leaving one town that isn't our goal, to get to another town which also is not.

This also means that it is false to say that we will never get to the goal, the point is in traveling about. They offer us poor consolation, who say that we can never achieve what we strive for, but the point is the trying. It is an inherent part of trying, that one can succeed. Busywork is something else. Yet Plato says both that we can get there (Diotima says so in the *Symposium*) and that we cannot. In one sense, "get there" means to formulate or be the aim, and this we cannot. In another sense, "get there" means to a formulation or life which is formed from the controlling truth, and this we can. Thus, the negation of "can get there" really tells us how we can, what more exactly getting there means. And in this sense dialectic is not like a journey, or rather, it is like a journey in which the aim is not only New York, but the good to be done there, or somewhere. This good we do isn't the good that controls. We can get to the good in New York (or, if we see halfway there, that it has to be done with someone else in Montreal, we will shift direction and get there). We cannot get to the good which makes what we do good, but to say this is very different from putting it into doubt whether there even is such a factor as makes what we do good, or not good.

Now we want to see more exactly how this control by the truth or reality works. It is not a "faith," not a general belief that we can get there, which makes going worthwhile, or makes it seem worthwhile. It must not remain some myth either, though to speak about that which controls as itself an object whose formulation it controls will be a myth. The control, in action, must be specific and unavoidable for us, so clear must it be.

To show this control in action is possible, of course, even easy. I did so above. But in the *Symposium* this control is shown in the very discussion about this control.

And we also said that the *Symposium* is about what makes that control possible for us, which is that in the person which is more than formulations and logic, and takes the two specific informations given by contradiction and forms a new concept from both.

Diotima, having shown that love is not good and beautiful, is now asked by Socrates:

> "What do you mean, Diotima," I said, "is love then evil and foul?"
> "Hush," she cried, "is that to be deemed foul which is not fair?"
> "Certainly," I said.
> And later:
> ". . . love is neither mortal nor immortal," Diotima says. (200e, 202d)

Plato can show his method by doing it and letting it work, to let us see how concepts arise in the method. Thus, whenever anything important is said, it is always self-illustrative. It is about the truth, but can be true only insofar as the truth is just then controlling the saying of it. When we have this control, it is because we are moving through a contradiction because only in the contradiction have we run into the truth so that it can control our formulations. We run into it because we formulated, and in running into it our further formulation is controlled by it.

When it is his turn, Socrates isn't even willing to begin without some responses from someone (which will probably lead to a contradiction). He doesn't make speeches alone. Then, where Agathon can't be taken further, then Diotima must be invented, and the person moving through the contradiction is Socrates. The contradiction got from Agathon is that love is beautiful and good because it desires those, but also not beautiful and not good because it desires what it wants and does not have.

Were these statements all we had, zero would be the result. But Socrates as pupil is more than just these terms. He *is* also the loving or wanting (207b).

Between beautiful and good on the one hand, and ugly and evil on the other, is not some midpoint, but the very process, movement, or method which makes new concepts, under truth control.

The contradiction good, beautiful, and mortal vs. their opposites, is in a sense *the* contradiction of all contradictions. In another sense every contradiction not only enables one to take a step to a better formulation, but also shows the method of doing so. Once you walk through the doors marked "x, but also not-x," you move by this method, and are controlled in this way. But between the terms good and not-good we may find better terms for the method which controls us in this special concept-making.

The content we seek to define, love, is what we call it qua content. Qua the actual movement it is philosophy, dialectic, inspiredness, concept-*formation*—not just a concept.

The "mean" between good and evil or truth and falsehood which now is formed out of what we learned on both sides of the contradiction, is not a midpoint, half-good and half-evil, but a new conception. Taken as wisdom and ignorance, the contradiction produces "right opinion," that which has a reason but doesn't contain the reason.

So with love, it has an object but doesn't contain it.

A "mean" is a middle, a proportion in Aristotle's sense, a ratio, a reason, a relation. It is also a movement through the contradiction, and in this instance *the* movement, *the* relation between the divine and the human. Between the opposites is the movement.

The movement has always already occurred, if the person has run into trouble with a formulation. Thus, says Diotima, Socrates believes love to be not a god, despite Socrates's claim that he believes love to be a god. Diotima can say this before Socrates gets to it, because Socrates has already run into the mortality aspect of love when he agreed that love was not good and fair, which the divine is.

We might have scoffed, earlier, that one could ever hope to get beyond the contradiction inherent in what love and philosophy are.

But the everlastingness of love's object was already there controlling the process of how we moved, when we said that love seeks everlasting possession of the good. Again Diotima (207a) takes as the source of the concept of eternity, how we already moved (at 206a).

In being drawn or controlled by what we run into, we already have in movement the information for the concept we wish to form from this movement. Concepts are its products.

There is no reason to take Diotima's picture of eternity (aspired to by the species which has its form ever renewed in each individual) less seriously than we take the same thing when Aristotle says it straight-facedly (*De anima*, book 2, section 4). The forms are ever the same and are knowable.

In Diotima's sense the eternal forms are of course quite different from the cosmic floating forms which are widely taken to be Plato's view. He ridiculed those in the first part of the *Parmenides*.

Recollection (which in *Meno* is defined not as memory but as continuing "inquiry," 81c) is similarly the ever-new genesis of Diotima's forms. Recollection is thus a genesis, a concept-formation, a making, but under eternal forms, controlled by the desired eternity.

Only knowledge, or recollection (inquiry) is a genesis controlled *directly* by the eternity which controls both the actual things and the animals. Therefore here (at 208b) Diotima can assert "with all the sureness of a sophist" that anything mortal partakes of immortality in this being-controlled way. So also, Socrates says here that love is the only subject he claims to know. Yet the genesis of visible things is only the lesser mysteries. Animals, great deeds, political and social institutions and the ordering of states and families, and the creations of Homer and Hesiod are here. All these can be made from right opinion or inspiration without knowledge, and are thus indeed controlled by the eternity which they instance, but not by a direct contact with it first.

The direct contact, the greater mysteries, goes only through knowledge: from one physical bodily form to many, to all, an empirical generalization enabling practice (210c) is moved from, as one moves to concepts, knowledges. From these, to one unified knowledge (and we saw how divergent pieces of knowledge lead to one further formulation, so the single science is dialectic) and from this to one's sense of that which controls and cannot itself be stated except as again only a controlled (as here, for instance).

Thus direct contemplation is not knowledge but not without knowledge, rather more than knowledge and on the shoulders of knowledge and dialectic. The direct contemplation should be taken at least as seriously as one takes it when Aristotle says the same thing.

But there is more here, for now Diotima, at this top point, is called a prophetess (where she was called a wise woman earlier). That which is beyond formulation—as we saw earlier—*is* what inspires poetry and animal love, and functions in every transition where a person *has more than could as yet be said.* Thus what guides and draws prophecy functions *before* knowledge, then also *in* each step of it, and then also *remains* beyond it as well.

This always gives Plato's discussion of this point an odd quality he uses ironically; the poet is in a sense ignorant and doesn't know what he says (like Agathon), but in another sense inspired by the same truth which guides and remains beyond knowledge. (Agathon is so guided, as we will see.) But we must not remain content with this as a comfortable statement, but see here exactly the difference, what each side of the statement says. It says here that there is a great difference (lesser and greater mysteries) between these two ways of being inspired. And Diotima says now that only through this approach via knowledge and the beyond which knowledge gives at each breakdown and at the top, can one "bring forth, not images, but realities" (212a).

Socrates, addressing Phaedrus, the love object to whom all the speeches are really addressed, says he addresses all men and not only him, thus instancing the point about moving beyond one physical instance.

Practice has come twice in the progression, before and after knowledge. Before, it included the ordering of states and families (209a) and laws and institutions (210b). After and from knowledge only does it include education. At 209b also, lover and beloved bring forth the creations of Homer and Hesiod and Lycurgus and Solon, but these are only images of beauty compared to the true virtue (of 212a) which can be created in a person only by someone whose inspiration is from and after knowledge, and thus both knowledge and more than knowledge.

It is in this sense that Socrates drinks: for drinking is a kind of inspiration and can be had both before and after knowledge. Socrates is not for abstinence, but from the same inspiration he is for movement.

What we *call* education, or practice, or drinking, or any of these activities can be done before as well as after knowledge, but then they are very different.

We saw that the inspiration is necessary, it cannot be dispensed with. Each step of coming to know requires this aspect of the person, this being-drawn by something one has run into which overthrows one's formulation (though it is discovered by this very formulation). Only the love of truth, so to speak, leads one on past the desire to retain one's proffered definition. Therefore there is no knowledge without this love. More exactly, one is forced, even if one verbally denies it, to assent inwardly to any difficulty one's formulation encounters, one really cannot help it. The control is so strong.

Without this personal aspect of being drawn and controlled, there can be no steps of knowledge. One could only repeat one's definitions and get them only from someone else. There could be no generating of concepts.

On the other hand, if one has got to the knowing apprehension of what controls knowledge one won't be bowled over by any physical instance of inspiration, a beloved person or alcohol.

Thus it is the eternal object, but really only via drawing us and forcing us, which controls knowledge, and does it only through love, i.e., through controlling the part of us that is inspired, that *"knows" before we can formulate*, so that we may formulate from what we have encountered already.

We must say a little here about this control, how it is in terms of beauty and the good, not only logic. I have made clear, I think, how the control exceeds logic, making us throw out a definition with which logically nothing is wrong, because it gives a conclusion which, in a given instance, is sensed by us or inspiredly felt by us to be the opposite of what our definition said it should be.

This control involves the good and the beautiful. Logical formulation *alone* can pretend to a kind of "true" that need not be good and beautiful—therefore it is constantly corrected as it leads, via being controlled, to further steps. We have a perfectly logical conclusion about this instance—and yet we may sense that this can't be maintained. This has to do with what is good or bad.

For example, if justice remains the paying of debts, which in many societies it does for unthinking people, that's bad. With a greater sensitivity for the good and beautiful, we don't want to maintain that it is "just" to dump what we came to return on the man's porch and go our way, self-satisfied.

Similarly, when an action was planned, many circumstances considered, and is then taken, we implicitly consider the action and its expected result good. We think of it as good in some way, perhaps not for others but at least good for us. When it then has results that we didn't want at all,

CHAPTER 10

we call it bad. But this has to mean that some of the facts we considered in advance were false, or that some true facts were missing.

Thus good and true are together exactly there where the control by reality occurs, i.e., in first having said or thought or expected one way, and then finding that what does follow feels wrong or bad. Thereby we have a truth or fact by the tail, though we may not yet know what this missing but indicated fact is.

Similarly, the beautiful is not just aesthetic form apart from true and good. Aesthetic form itself is some kind of resonance with our healthy bodies in nature as one system.

Joel Perlstein reported that when, after a year of studying soil erosion and conservation problems, he returned to the most beautiful places he had seen the summer before, they no longer looked beautiful to him, for he saw the erosion and the results of the lumbering.

This does not make Plato an ethicist or an aesthetician, but it does place the role that, in us, is inspired by beauty (and as desire) into the process of knowledge-making. And objects of knowledge control, or can control, this, and should, for only in this control of moving steps are the three together.

What is first to us is the process of being moved, from out of which we create the concept. What is first in nature (as Aristotle put it) are the most knowable forms and their way of being most knowable, but beyond knowledge, not themselves formulations.

This movement is through something more than logic, that in us which is inspired and desires.

Diotima shows Socrates (in the example cited earlier) that he already believes love to be other than a god and also, as I will show, each of the speeches contains a contradiction.

Now I need a case in which a speaker makes an assertion, and then something follows from the assertion with perfect logic, but is false or bad in the actual example. My own examples of this came from the *Republic*.

The only example of such a thing in the *Symposium* is Agathon's admission (199c), and now we see that even this example of dialectic is such that my assertion doesn't quite work here. In this example there is no logical conclusion which doesn't fit an example. Instead, Agathon's assertion leads to a logical implication by which it contradicts itself! It seems all done logically!

But now I recall that I also said, earlier, that the person is necessary not only for a step beyond contradiction to make new concepts to capture both informations, but also that the person is necessary to check each step, i.e., that the logical progression too requires the person. Even if the person only says "very true" all the time, this represents this checking, as the boy does in *Meno*, where the example is billed as an instance of recollection.

I was thus wrong to cut so sharply between logic and an instance in which a person senses something not yet formulated; this "inspired" aspect of such a person functions as well in logical steps. Without the insight at each step, nothing is achieved but verbiage.

Agathon is an inspired poet who attributes here to love the attributes (most of them right) of beauty. He attributes to love the attributes of its object.

Most of Agathon's assertions are of the form: love is like these objects, hence love is that. The form is "Love verbs what has these traits, therefore it is like them." Softness, youth, virtues, beauty, delicacy, goodness, grace are some of these. But "like" is not a good enough concept, for love is like these and also not like them. The verbs are different each time, but love is assumed to be like what it verbs: Love *flees* age, *moves* with youth, *walks* in what is soft, *dwells* among beautiful flowers, "like to like" Agathon says, love is like these.

But "like" is too crude a concept, love is and isn't like. Agathon does not distinguish between "is" and "of," or between "is like" and "is of."

Agathon also uses the word "of," and Socrates catches him in it. But Agathon could easily have avoided that one slip. Would he then have been contradiction-proof?

Agathon's speech is poetry and rhetoric. It is poetry because inspired—who could listen to it and not be moved? It is rhetoric and poetry in being inspired but not controlled along knowledge lines. What is mirrored here is right, what inspires is true. But what is formulated and asserted slips through the concept "like."

Agathon moves no further than "like," no further than likenesses. It is theater, appearance. (He called the present discussion "theater" at 194a, and Socrates calls his speech only an appearing to praise.)

In not having knowledge, Agathon doesn't get all of the attributes of the love object right. He includes luxury, no doubt because he feels it to be good. He has no way to discover that it isn't, to sort out what is right and what isn't, from this result of his unknowing poetic inspiration.

He identifies the being inspired with what inspires, that to which love is like and not like, and hence the contradiction runs throughout, for everything he says is true (with one exception) of the object of love but not of love. The contradiction did not occur only in the one phrasing where it is most easily visible.

Each of the speeches has an easily visible contradiction which is tucked in so that we cannot miss it, and which instances the more basic and hard-to-see contradiction that would lead to the next step.

CHAPTER 10

Agathon was going to tell of the nature of love itself (and in a way, did so, and in a way not, since he gave the nature or some inspired description of the likenesses of beauty) which the previous speaker failed at.

Aristophanes had said that love is not of intercourse, "but of something else which the soul desires and cannot tell, and of which she has only a dark presentiment." Love, he says, "is the desire and pursuit of the whole" (192b and 193a).

This is true and prefigures where we are heading, but his original unity is wonderfully physical. The gods split us, yet love is a god who unites. The gods threaten to split us again.

The union or whole here is at one point said to be more, but is otherwise said to be only the maintenance of the division. It is more and not more, than *a* person singly.

Much of this is an inverted farce of what Socrates says. Only the physical longing for personal union should be striven for (189c). The presentiment of more is after all only this. By putting the opposites together, Aristophanes gets no more than again a human.

Now, in a sense Aristophanes has more here than Eryximachus had. Aristophanes opens his speech, or rather, precedes it, with a quip at Eryximachus implying that Aristophanes has a hold of something higher about the human frame than just tickling and countertickling. Indeed he does, it is seeking after union and the whole, but he calls this both the union of two physical persons, and also not just this, falling back then into just this.

So Aristophanes must come after Eryximachus, but both "unite" opposites and get no more.

Eryximachus had indeed said that the union or harmony between the opposites is nothing more than just the right amount of each, so that a balance is made and they can be together. Thus the hiccoughs enable Aristophanes to exemplify, and to follow Eryximachus.

Eryximachus tells us his contradiction, when he discusses Heraclitus and says it is "an absurdity . . . that harmony is disagreement or is composed of elements which are still in a state of disagreement" (187a).

Eryximachus means by harmony only a certain quantity. Nothing new arises, only what might be infinite (or any amount) is made to have a limit—thus its sheer opposite.

But on the other hand, Eryximachus wants this harmony to be more than that. He wants to have cured the fight between the opposites and made the whole something more than the opposites were.

Thus he puts the harmonious love (which is already the opposites) into combination with the inharmonious love, and treats these two over again as if they were each one of two opposites. (This is just what Aristophanes does in a way, putting two people together to get, not more or something higher, but again a human.) The opposites are both in us, all right, but their harmony is something different than just the two pasted together.

Thus he differs from Socrates in not drinking very much and being a weak head, in this regard. Similarly, instead of moving through inspiration and desire and excitement, he limits the amount only.

Harmony, he says, consists of harmony and disharmony together.

This is always so, Plato thinks, when remaining on a physicist's level. It is all only about more and less, filling and emptying. But the sameness of harmony and disharmony is missed when it is reduced to such physical balancing (*Philebus* 186c, 207d).

But the pleasures which, in harmony, can be had on this level are, says Plato, partly pain, always. It is the pain being just then alleviated. Without this pain there is not the pleasure, and as soon as the pain is stilled, so is the pleasure. Therefore Eryximachus's contradiction is again not merely a matter of statement, but inherent in the pleasures of the physical, and inherently lead one, if one thinks, to the contradiction which, in turn, leads to something higher than merely tickling and countertickling.

Eryximachus had begun with Pausanias's "lame ending," as he put it. Pausanias had begun grandly with the distinction between the two kinds of love, just and unjust, worthy of praise or not. But Pausanias ended by again falling back from this insight, excusing and including all the evil people do for the sake of love.

In each speech we are faced with the contradiction so that we wince and can't help having a sense of something beyond what, as a whole, it says.

Eryximachus is a real step forward from Pausanias, there is some real science here, a knowledge of how much and what countermeasures are needed. Eryximachus can cure hiccoughs. He has a hold of the measure and balance which, in turn, would lead further.

Pausanias, on the other hand, is dealing entirely in terms of appearances, what people think, and how they view things. He finds, contradictorily enough, that lovers and beloveds are viewed both as good and as bad.

This is more sophisticated and further along than Phaedrus, who saw it as all good and only one.

Pausanias says, both, that to have the just and praiseworthy love one must love justly, and also that every manner of evil ways is excused and praised, if it is in the course of loving. He says lover and beloved "each of them have a law," and for the lover the law is "the entire liberty gods and men grant a lover" (183b and 184c). Even defenders of England's

CHAPTER 10

Charles I could not more vividly portray the contradiction, according to which honorable love is also dishonorable.

Similarly, on the side of the beloved, there is nothing dishonorable about being deceived, if virtue is what one aimed at. Thus virtue is also vice.

Thus, without knowledge, one cannot tell apart the real virtue from the appearance, and the appearance is enough for honor. There is no way to distinguish or set up tests for which is which, as is also shown by the tests of true love Pausanias cites, trials of strength and contests (184). Hearing this, how can we avoid thinking of better tests?

(Here, too, love is taken as the good thing, rather than what it is of, but that runs throughout and isn't yet what a contradiction directly points to.)

A good manner would make a bad action good, but by making it be a different action altogether, else no bad action is also good by being done in a good manner, or in the course of love.

But clearly, Pausanias is further back than Eryximachus, who at least knows how much badness to retain in a contradictory mixture or balance. Here the contradiction is flat, the bad actions are good if love makes them good, or rather, seem good.

Phaedrus, too, has a hold of something. While he misses the distinction between good and bad, he has the point, in a way, that love is to be evaluated by evaluating the object.

Therefore Phaedrus says that the beloved (which he himself is) is better than the lover: the lover only has the undeveloped beloved for his object, while the beloved has the superior love, namely of the lover.

But contradiction: he says the lover is so much better because he really loves, whereas the beloved does not have, or does not have much, love or desire.

Thus Phaedrus contradicts himself. Unavoidably, neither lover nor beloved end up looking so good: the beloved doesn't love; the lover loves someone who doesn't love. Each is both better and worse than the other.

We need a new term, when Phaedrus is done, to distinguish "better" and "worse."

Of course the ultimate point of the series of speeches is already here, the problem that love isn't the good, but of it, and love cannot double as both object and process. The two must not be confused, for one is the movement and the other the direction or control.

(Phaedrus's love is Heraclitus's and the earlier pre-Socratics', the primordial constructor, the universe being made up of love and hate, coming to be and passing away, or being put together and again falling apart. We saw how this theme requires something higher than just putting together, the ratio and cause at which the given construction "aims" in the sense of instancing it.)

In the introduction Eryximachus, the lover perhaps of Phaedrus, prescribes the topic and arrangement, but attributes the origin to Phaedrus, his love object, who then must speak first, as being truly the force that inspires the whole sequence.

In response, Appollodorus shows us something about the sense in which a step of knowledge is ultimate and serious, and the sense in which it is not. He says: "I pity you rich men and traders, you think you work when you are really idling. And I dare say you pity me as an unfortunate, which I *perhaps* am. But I certainly *know* of you what you only think of me" (173c). Here it is clear that with respect to the last step one comes from, one knows with certainty, whereas taken in respect of further steps one has not yet encountered, one must be unsure.

11

Befindlichkeit: Heidegger and the Philosophy of Psychology

In this chapter I will outline Heidegger's basic conception of the human feeling capacity and try to show the important implications of his conception. A new word is also needed because the usual way people think about "feeling" is greatly changed in Heidegger's way of thinking.

I will first offer a round delineation of Heidegger's concept in my own words, along with some discussion of the relation between philosophy and psychology.[1] This will enable the reader to understand the relevance of what I will next present: an excerpt and some observations from psychotherapy, and why a new concept is needed in psychological theory. A few remarks that are again on the philosophical level will conclude my preliminaries.

I will then present Heidegger in his own words (in section 2).

In this way I will give its application to psychology before I present Heidegger's conception itself in detail. I would like the reader to see the lack of the needed concept, indeed, to become hungry for it, to see where it is needed and what its outlines have to be. Then, after I present Heidegger, I will go on to further application in the more usual order.

I. Introduction to *Befindlichkeit*

Befindlichkeit is among the most frequently misunderstood concepts in Heidegger's work.[2] Certainly it is the most important among those that are frequently misunderstood. *Befindlichkeit* is one of Heidegger's three basic parameters of human existence (*Existenziale*) which are involved in most of his other conceptions. The other two basic parameters are understanding and speech. The three are inherently interrelated so that one can only understand them together. In outlining them we will therefore go to the core of Heidegger's philosophy.

Heidegger says that *Befindlichkeit* refers to what is ordinarily called "being in a mood," and also what is called "feeling" and "affect." But Heidegger offers a radically different way of thinking about this ordinary experience. *Befindlichkeit* refers to the kind of beings that humans are, that aspect of these beings which makes for them having moods, feelings, or affects.

But Heidegger thinks about this human being in a very different way than most people do, and so he also thinks about mood and feeling very differently.

Let me give a rough initial impression of Heidegger's very different basic conception, *Befindlichkeit*.

In German a common way of asking "How are you?" is "Wie befinden Sie sich?" This literally says "How do you find yourself?" One can also say to a sick person "Wie ist Ihr Befinden?" ("How do you feel?") The same form can also be used to say that something or someone is situated somewhere, or in some way. For example, one can say, "The White House *finds itself* in Washington, D.C.," or "I find myself in Chicago," or "I find myself in happy circumstances."[3]

Sich befinden (finding oneself) thus has three allusions: the reflexivity of finding oneself; feeling; and being situated. All three are caught in the ordinary phrase "How are you?" That refers to how you feel but also to how things are going for you and what sort of situation you find yourself in. To answer the question, you must find yourself, find how you already are. And when you do, you find yourself amidst the circumstances of your living.

Heidegger coined a clumsy noun from the German colloquial forms. To translate it, let us not look for an existing noun in English, since he found none in German. His noun is like "how-are-you-ness" or perhaps "self-finding."

The reason for being careful about these allusions, and for keeping his sense of the word, is because *Befindlichkeit* is a new conception and cannot be rendered in old ones.

To view feelings, affects, and moods as *Befindlichkeit* differs from the usual view in the following ways:

(1) Heidegger's concept denotes how *we sense ourselves in situations*. Whereas feeling is usually thought of as something inward, Heidegger's concept refers to something both inward and outward, but before a split between inside and outside has been made.

We are always situated, in situations, in the world, in a context, living in a certain way *with others*, trying to achieve this and avoid that.

A mood is not just internal, it is this living in the world. We sense how we find ourselves, and we find ourselves in situations.

Americans might say that "Befindlichkeit" is an "interactional" concept, rather than an "intrapsychic" one. But it is both and exists before the distinction is made. "Interaction" is also inaccurate for another reason. It assumes that first there are two, and only then is there a relation between them.

For Heidegger, humans *are* their living in the world with others. Humans are livings-in, and livings-with.

(2) A second difference from the usual conception of "feeling" lies in this: *Befindlichkeit* always already has *its own understanding*. (Here is Heidegger's second basic parameter of human existence: "understanding.") We may not know what the mood is about, we may not even be specifically aware of our mood; nevertheless, there is an understanding of our living in that mood. It is no merely internal state or reaction, no mere coloring or accompaniment to what is happening. We have lived and acted in certain ways for certain purposes and strivings and all this is going well or badly, but certainly it is going in some intricate way. How we are faring in these intricacies is in our mood. We may not know that in a cognitive way at all; it is in the mood nevertheless, implicitly.

This understanding is active; it is not merely a perception or reception of what is happening to us. We don't come into situations as if they were mere facts, independent of us. We have had some part in getting ourselves into these situations, in making the efforts in response to which these are now the facts, the difficulties, the possibilities, and the mood has the implicit "understanding" of all that, because this understanding was inherent already in how we lived all that, in an active way.

(3) This understanding is *implicit*, not cognitive in the usual sense. It differs from cognition in several ways: it is sensed or felt, rather than thought—and it may not even be sensed or felt directly with attention. It is not made of separable cognitive units or any definable units. When you are asked, "How are you?" you don't find only recognizables, but always also an implicit complexity. Certainly one can reflect and interpret, but that will be another, further step.

(4) Heidegger says that speech is always already involved in any feeling or mood, indeed in any human experience. Speech is the articulation of understanding, but this articulation doesn't first happen when we try to say what we feel. Just as *Befindlichkeit* always already has its understanding, so also does it always already have its spoken articulation. This doesn't at all mean that there is always a way to say what one lives in words. But there are always speakings with each other, and listening to each other, involved in any situation, and implicit in any living. Hearing each other, being open to each other's speech, is part of what we *are*, the living we *are*. And so it is always already involved in our living, whatever we may then actually say or not say.

So we see that, although Heidegger is talking about the ordinary experience of feelings, affects, or moods, he has given that experience a very different structure. We sense ourselves living in situations with others, with an implicit understanding of what we are doing and with communication between us always already involved. A feeling is all that. Our new conception of feeling has the structure I just outlined.

A Note on the Relation between Philosophy and Psychology

Certainly there is a difference between the theoretical structure of the concept of feeling, and a mere pointing to a feeling. *Befindlichkeit* names the structure, "feeling," "affect," or "mood," and these words can continue to name the ordinary event they always have. But the difference between philosophy and psychology is something else, not the difference between something and theory about it. After all, there is theory in psychology, too.

Philosophical discussion moves on a level from which all or many of the sciences are affected simultaneously. Philosophical discussion may, at some point, seem to be about people and sound, like psychology, or about society and sound, like sociology, or about matter and energy and sound, like physics. But not only a particular science but many other endeavors will be altered by a philosophical discussion. I will illustrate this shortly, in order to be clear.

Philosophy moves on a different level than science. One can say that it is one level more abstract than science. I will say this first in terms of kinds of concepts, and then in terms of kinds of beings, as Heidegger does.

A philosophy examines and sometimes alters *basic* conceptions. That is why there is no way to explain a basic conception in terms of other, more familiar ones. One can grasp a basic conception only by grasping it. It is a new conceptual structure, a new pattern. What I mean here by "basic" gets at the difference between philosophy and any science, and also the usefulness of philosophy for science. Let me be more specific.

Most people, scientists and others, do not usually think about what *kind* of concept they are using. The most current *kind is* modeled on ordinary things like stones. A stone can be moved from one place to another without changing. It is still the same stone, now in a different spot. A thing like a stone may relate to other things, of course; for example, it may hit and break a porcelain pitcher. But these relations are external and additional to what the stone is. Whether it breaks a pitcher or not, even if it just sits in one spot, it is a stone. It would not be usual to say that a stone is pitcher-breaking, or window-smashing, or any such interaction.

Without being aware of it or capable of examining it (for then they would be engaged in philosophy), scientists currently tend to use this *kind* of concept.

An "electron," for example, is a thing-like concept of this kind. In one puzzling experiment, one electron seems to go through two different slits in two different locations. While an electron differs from a stone in many ways, of course, the same kind of concept is involved in how both are thought of. An electron must be in one place or another, not both. Similarly, there is a puzzle in biology why given well-defined molecules suddenly assume highly important additional powers when in the company of certain other molecules in a certain tissue. As a thing with its own traits, regardless of anything else (as this kind of concept renders everything), this is not understandable. The molecule cannot *be* its different interactions, it has to *be* with certain traits all its own, and only with these is it thought to interact.

Psychologists, for example, use concepts like "self," "ego," "perception," "personal interaction," "feeling," or "affect," usually formulated in thing-like kinds of concepts. A self or an ego is like a thing in the person. A person is a larger thing in which the ego or self, as a smaller thing, resides like a stone in a box. Perception is a stimulus-thing making a representation-thing inside the box: personal interaction is a relation between two such boxes, each separate before they interact, like a stone and a pitcher. Feelings or affects are little things inside the box, sometimes within the self and sometimes in the rest of the box. People supposedly feel these inside feeling things directly, but can feel other people only by imagining an analogy with their own feelings.

Heidegger brings us an entirely different *kind* of concept. One might say it concerns a being that is its relating. But I say this roughly, and it is only for a simple contrast with the above caricature of the current kind. What interests me is the level of discussion, not a discussion of this topic or that. It is a matter of *kinds* of concepts. I would like to bring home the importance of differences in kinds of concepts for all sciences.

Note that it must have implications for any science to develop a different kind of concept, for example, some of Heidegger's concepts such as *Befindlichkeit*. It eliminates certain ways of making distinctions, and replaces them with others. In my simple four-point rendition of *Befindlichkeit*, we saw how the concept precedes and eliminates the distinction between *inside and outside*, as well as between *self and others*. Similarly, it alters the difference between *affective* and *cognitive*. Later I will show how it also alters the distinctions we are used to in space and time: here/there, and past/present/future. We will want to see exactly how Heidegger refashions all this, we will want to see a sharp and clear alternative structure to the one being eliminated, but it is certainly clear already that such basic changes in kind of concept must affect any science, not just psychology.

Let me now make the same point in a more Heideggerian way. (Of course, it is then not literally exactly the same point.)

Heidegger's philosophy is ontology. He is not directly concerned with kinds of concepts, but with kinds of being. (Of course, this leads to kinds of concepts, too.)

A tool, for example, *is* in a different way than a stone *is*; they are different kinds of being. Even if I use a stone as a tool; already it has a being like that of a tool; it *is* in a different way: now it lies ready-to-hand in my tool chest, and it *is-for*. It is for the use, to which its shape and weight fit it, for me. Now it is in a way that involves me and my activity. It is no longer in that way in which all of its being was just there, by itself. A tool *is* contextually; that is a different way to be.

People *are* different than either stones or tools. They live-in and live-with. They livein a world they themselves define with their living-in.

People, too, *are* not inside their skins, but *are* their living-in the world and their living-with others.

(In my terms, what kind of a concept is "living-in" and "living-with"? We will want to see this as a clear and sharp conceptual structure.)

Heidegger calls the human being "Dasein" (being-here.) This is again an ordinary colloquial German word. "Das menschliche Dasein" means something like "the human condition" or "being human." As with *Befindlichkeit*, Heidegger uses all the allusions of the colloquial form, both of "being" and of "here."

Humans are not at all some things among others, as dead bodies might be. Humans are being-here, they *are* in a self-locating sense. A stone can be here for me, but not for itself. This "here" is in the world, in situations, and situations are always with-others.

When Heidegger discusses *Dasein*, he is not discussing only humans, but also everything else that is for humans, or is accessible to humans. It lies in the nature of the human way of being that other beings *are* in relation to it. The stone may lie on the table, but the stone's kind of being is not an openness to something it lies on. A human observer positions stone and table in relation to each other in space and dynamics, but their being doesn't do that.

Therefore, how anything is studied in any science depends first upon the nature of humans as open to access to . . . whatever is studied. Mathematics is not just there; its units and series have to be constituted by Dasein. Physics isn't just there; human observation and measurement are certain specific modes of how humans *are* generating time and space and things. The basic ontological structure of Dasein therefore alters how we basically conceive of anything else, if we first consider that structure of Dasein.

If we speak of *Befindlichkeit* not merely as something about humans, but as basic to the way humans are open to anything, much more than psychology is affected. A basic method results, in which inquiry articulates what is at first only sensed, found implicitly. One must not forget that, as if to begin with sharp conceptions. The beginning is always how we sense ourselves, find ourselves already with . . . whatever we study, in an implicitly "understood" way, in our living.

Whatever conceptions are developed, in any science, they need to be related back to the implicit lived understanding we already have of the topic, and need to be viewed as articulations of that. Much changes if one employs such a method.

The structural parameters of this kind of concept (*Dasein, Befindlichkeit*), too, as I have already said, will importantly alter any science.

Both method and structural parameters will of course have important implications for psychology, among other sciences. Let me at last go into that now. Even so, I must ask my reader to follow me on both levels, philosophically as well as in psychology. For philosophy my discussion will be an example, an instance. For psychology it will be directly pertinent. Philosophically, notice the kind of concept, and kind of being. For psychology notice our need for this specific concept (not only the kind). Of course, we are talking about the same human being, and the same aspect of that human being, the structure of its "finding itself" in a mood, affect, or feeling. Philosophically, that is basic to how we *are* and anything else is. Only one of the implications of that is the kind of concepts we use, and one instance of this being, and this kind of concept, is in psychology.

Some Observations of Psychotherapy

During a psychotherapy interview, the patient quite often says something, then stops, senses inwardly for half a minute or a minute, then says: "No, what I said isn't quite right. I can't say how it feels, yet, but it's different than I said."

At such times it is quite clear that more than just thoughts and words are being worked with. If the patient had only thoughts and words, there would be nothing to check against, nothing to indicate that a statement that seemed right and true is, after all, not right. The statement may still be true, may still describe events, behavior, but the patient has something else there which is felt directly, and that cannot yet be said. Although the patient does not know what that is, it is definite enough to indicate with certainty that it is not . . . what the patient had just said it was.

The experience is somewhat analogous to forgetting someone's name. We then still have "a feel for" that name, which is quite sufficient to enable us to reject any number of other names. We know it isn't Smith or Jamison or Rostenkowsky, and we can also sense the specificity of exactly the name we seek. This specificity is in some sense "in" the "feel" of specificity of exactly the name we seek. This specificity is in some sense "in" the "feel" of the name, which we have.

If we, as it were, touch that "feel" of the name over and over, "touch" it with our attention, it may suddenly "open," so that the name appears. Then there is an unmistakable tension-release, a relief in the body, one exhales a long breath, whew . . . There is no doubt, then, that this was indeed the name one had forgotten. There is an unmistakable continuity between the erstwhile "feel" and this name.

The metaphoric language I am using is troublesome: the name is "in" the "feel," there is "continuity" between them, the "feel" "opens"; none of this is theoretically satisfying.

With Heidegger we could say that the name is part of the "understanding" that the *Befindlichkeit* has, our feeling not just of the name, but of all our living with that person.

Let me continue the example. We could have saved ourselves the trouble of remembering, and have picked any name, or perhaps the best-sounding name we can find. We could have insisted that that's the name, all right. After all, it is the best-sounding and most desirable name. Or, perhaps we might have found the name by matching a name to the person's presumed ancestry, cultural group, or for some other intellectual reason. We don't do that, because we know that that is not authentic remembering.

Everyone also knows the case when we are close, but not quite right. "It must be ____," we say, expressing our dissatisfaction and unease in that very phrase: "It must be." Although it sounds like necessary concluding, we have not really remembered.

In the following excerpt from a psychotherapy interview, the patient at each step senses that what she just said isn't right, although she cannot yet say what would be right.

It must also be noticed how different this process is from reasoning ("It must be . . ."). Once she is able to articulate what she senses, at each step, it makes perfect sense and we can think about it logically in a rational way. But the steps she actually takes differ from rational ones, though they are certainly not irrational.

What does seem irrational is the way in which each new step begins by contradicting the previous one. Each step says, "It's not what I just said, but rather . . ." Once we hear what it is, then that too makes sense. But the steps are not the reasonable chain that can be constructed in retrospect, after we have heard her. If we examine what we have at one step, we cannot, from that, get by reasoning or inference to the next step.

The sensing between each step and the next corrects her and changes the direction in a way that could not have been known in advance.

She says: "I'm late. I knew I would be. I have this magic way of saying 'It will be all right,' when I don't have any idea how. When I make a schedule or a plan I put more things in it than I could possibly get done. But I can't choose among them. I'm afraid of making the wrong choice, I guess."

There is a silence. Then she says: "It's not about making a wrong choice. I don't know what that is."

More silence. Then: "There's something there, like 'I want it all!' That's really childish, like kids wanting everything they see."

More silence.

"It's not wanting it all. It's not wanting what I'm supposed to want. My sister was the one that did all the right things. I couldn't do what she did, always fit in. I became the one that had secrets, and did the things that were dangerous and not supposed to be done. I still like to endanger myself, go out with men where I can tell it won't be nice. It's an excitement, like violence, it takes over your whole mind. Living dangerously. That's what that wanting is."

More silence.

"Well, I don't really want that. When I think of them telling us how we're supposed to be, then I get this feeling of wanting that violence and excitement. But, if I just think, well, what would I like, then I don't want that stuff."

In this example one can see what I call "content mutation."[4] First, the content is why she is late and how unrealistic her scheduling is. It seems to be about a fear of making wrong choices. Then it isn't that at all, but a childish wanting everything. Then it isn't a childish wish for everything, but a wish for excitement and danger, violence. Finally, it is a reaction to authority beyond which a different wanting emerges.

In retrospect the steps can make a chain of thought, but moving forward each step comes by contradicting the previous one. What does this contradicting? It is the "sensing" that happens during the silences between. She has the "feel" of it, and this feel is each time different than what she has said.

This patient took only a few minutes for this process. The same kind of process, often more slowly, is found in any psychotherapy when it is effective at all. (I say this on the basis of research findings I shall cite shortly.)

Psychological Theory: Why a New Concept Is Needed

Actually, the new kind of concept Heidegger makes possible is needed in many instances in psychology. I will pursue only the concept of "feeling" or "affect" and show how it needs to be restructured.

I will follow the same four points I presented before, now in relation to our psychotherapy excerpt.

(1) She consults a feeling between her statements, yet this feeling is of how she has been planning, living, choosing men and getting into situations. Although the feeling seems "internal" as she sits there, silently, it is of her living in the situations in which she finds herself, and of course with other people. A feeling must be thought of both as sensed and as in the world.

(2) She begins with a cognition ("I must be afraid of making wrong choices"), but the feeling has its own understanding. From the feeling emerges something ("I want it all") which seems childish to her. The feeling again has its own understanding (desire to "live dangerously"). She now has the cognition that she wants danger. Again, the feeling has its own understanding. (It's in relation to "them telling us how we're supposed to be.") A feeling must be thought of as containing its own understanding of how one is living.

(3) A feeling's understanding or meaning is implicit, first in the sense that it may not yet be known at all. Second, the meaning is implicit in a more inherent respect; implicit in that it is never quite equal to any cognitive units. There is always more to go. Third, it is a wholistic complexity: the feeling isn't just about being late, not just about scheduling, not just about choices, not just about men, nor these as separated things that happen to be together. Rather, there is a complex texture. Even in our short excerpt one can see how much was implicit in the feeling of—what seemed to be only—her chagrin at being late.

We also see (to be discussed later) the "lifting out" character of how cognitions are related to the feeling: at each step something is lifted out that is then both felt and cognized.

Furthermore, in the movement from implicit to being lifted out, the feeling itself changes. If it were not for this change, psychotherapy would not be effective. People would come to know much about themselves, but would not change. When psychotherapy is done by mere inferences, people indeed don't change. The felt understanding by which they live remains the same, and inarticulate. They seem to know why they act as they do, but not how to be different. In contrast, when feeling (as complex texture) leads to this "lifting out," there is a directly felt changing of the feeling at each step.[5] In our excerpt this is most visible at the last step, but that would not have been reached had the previous steps not each made its change in the feeling.

Thus feeling must be understood as *implicitly* meaningful, and as changing when there are steps of "lifting out," steps of explication or articulation. *To articulate is to live further.* To *go back* into how one *has been* living is *a forward-moving* step.

(4) The feeling knows how to speak and demands just the right words. The feeling, more exactly, is sufficient to bring the words to the person's speech. We can see that, if we compare what her next steps are, with what they would have been, had she pursued the implications of what she first said. No logic could have led her as she did in fact proceed.

We don't want to think that the words were *in* the feeling in the sense that pebbles are *in* a box. How language relates to feeling and living needs rethinking. But it is clear that just as in living she uses words as an inherent part of living, so also does the feeling-understanding already have the power to guide *speech*, even though at first it is only felt.

A series of research studies has shown that patients who engage in the kind of steps I described are successful in psychotherapy, while those who usually do not work in this way fail.[6] Success is sometimes measured by patient and therapist judgment after the therapy is over, sometimes by psychometric tests given before and after therapy.

How was it possible to *measure* the degree to which patients engage in this process? It turns out to be quite measurable. Patients are highly consistent in how they approach psychotherapy. Two four-minute segments from a tape-recorded interview are sufficient to give the same result as an analysis of whole hours. It is possible to pick out phrasings such as "I don't know what *that* is," as in our excerpt, statements that refer to something directly sensed but not known in a sharp cognitive way. It is noticeable that this kind of phrasing occurs between two quite different versions of content. There are also other signs, such as metaphoric language, often very original, that would have no meaning at all if it did not refer to what is sensed but not yet capable of being thought in usual terms. Raters of such tape-recorded segments arrive at reliable agreements. These scores correlate with the patient's, the therapist's, and the test's evaluation of outcome.

The older theories are remarkably poor for thinking about this observed behavior in psychotherapy. They are theories of what, rather than how—theories of what is supposedly *in* people, not theories about how the process I have described leads to change.

It is known that there is more *knowledge* in the person, somehow, than the person consciously possesses, but this is viewed as the "unconscious," a puzzling realm of internal entities. We have seen, however, that it is quite conscious and awarely felt or sensed, both while living and when attending to feeling.

It is known that complex implications and connections exist "beneath" any simple human event, but these are viewed as sharp and defined entities that are just like cognitions, only outside awareness. We have seen, however, that there is an implicit texture, a wholistic living.

It is thought that "feelings" are important for psychotherapy, but the word is taken to mean emotions. We need a new word that will distinguish emotions from what I call "felt sense," feelings as sensed complexity. Above all, we need a new concept! Really, such a new concept for feeling would also require changing most of the related concepts in our theories.

What matters most in psychotherapy is "feeling" in the sense of being unclear and sensing an implicit complexity, a wholistic sense of what one is working on. This can be very quietly sensed, or it may be very emotional, but that is not the crucial question at all.

Emotions—recognizable joy, sadness, or anger—any of these may be part of such sensing, or it may not. Even when it is, the felt sense is more complex and less well known than such a familiar emotion.

Explicit cognitions emerge from a felt sense, but this is not to say that *they* were "in there," in explicit form, in a layer beneath. An implicit understanding sensed in living, and its implicit capacity for speech, must be understood as living-in-context.

We need a new conceptual pattern for our concept of "felt sense," one which has the more basic unity preceding the inner/outer split, the self/other split, the affect/cognition split, and the acting/speaking split.

Philosophical Note

Human beings *are* with an implicit felt understanding, that is to say, they *are* "ontologically" because this entails an understanding of being—of their own being and the being of others, things, and tools involved in their own being-with and being-in.

Heidegger uses the word "ontic" for ordinary assertions of anything, and the word "ontological" for the understanding of the kind of being of anything. Thus, to say that I have a felt sense, now, of what I want to say, is an ontic statement. In contrast, to explicate the structure of how there is such an implicit sense of what I may later say at length, that would be ontology.

It needs to be clear that, although we distinguished the philosophical and ontological level from the ontic (for example, psychology), the two are about the same world, the same things, the same beings. One is an account of the basic structure of the other. If they were not about the same beings, there would have to be a separate realm of beings, just for philosophy to be about!

While Heidegger, when delineating *Befindlichkeit*, speaks of the basic structure of the human being-in-the-world, and thus of the world, and of any subject matter of any science insofar as humans have access to it, this *Befindlichkeit is* nevertheless the same feeling or sensing studied in psychology.

This is so doubly. First, it is so because the "ontic" and the "ontological" are two ways of considering the same being. Second, it is so especially because humans *are* inherently ontological. While one seems only to understand some particular living one is doing, one is always implicitly understanding one's own manner of being—as being human, that is to say, as being-in-the-world, always already in the midst of situations, with *how one is* quite open to events and in play, in the living itself as ongoing.

Heidegger says humans are "pre-ontological" (*BT* 32), insofar as this understanding of one's way of being is implicit, rather than articulated. Later I will give many implications that follow if we restructure the psychological concepts.

To be sure, Heidegger, whom we will now let speak in his own words, speaks on the philosophical level. As I said earlier, implications follow not just for psychology, but for any science, and for life. But it will also be immediately clear from what Heidegger says, how—and exactly how—we might restructure theoretical concepts in psychology, especially the concept of feeling or affect.

It is an error to make of *Befindlichkeit* something different than the way humans are feelingly, as if in addition to that there were some other, mysterious, purely philosophical something. *Befindlichkeit* has been little understood just because as a merely abstract principle it makes no sense. Heidegger is somehow not believed when he flatly insists that he is talking about how we live, and calling our attention to what we can directly sense. Then he is made to sound abstract and un-understandable.

Not only does psychology and any science study the same being that ontology clarifies, but also for ontology itself it is vital to begin with "Befindliches," with what is livingly sensed directly—and every statement of ontology lifts out something we can then directly sense, something which we already understood before in a pre-ontological way.

To understand Heidegger experientially (if I may call it that) is not at all to reduce ontology to psychology, it is the only way to do ontology, as he insists. The implications of so understanding him are of course much wider than just for psychology. To understand him experientially is to understand the inherent relation between living, feeling, understanding, and cognitions of any kind.

2. Heidegger on *Befindlichkeit*, Understanding, and Speech

> What we indicate *ontologically by* the term *Befindlichkeit* is *ontically* most familiar: the mood, or being moody. (*BT* 172)

> The different modes of *Befindlichkeit* . . . have long been well-known ontically under the terms "affects" and "feelings." (*BT* 178)

> Dasein is always in some mood. A pallid, flat being out of sorts . . . is far from being nothing at all . . . to be has become a manifest burden. One does not *know* why. (*BT* 173)

> *Befindlichkeit* has always already disclosed one's being-in-the-world as a whole. (*BT* 176) The possibilities of disclosure which belong to cognition reach far too short a way compared with the original and basic disclosure of moods. (*BT* 173)

> Even if Dasein is "assured" in its belief . . . if in rational enlightenment it supposes itself to know . . . all this counts for nothing as against the phenomenal facts of the case. (*BT* 175)

So we see the difference between how mood discloses the whole of one's being in the world, and how the mood stays "phenomenally," regardless of what one might say to the contrary. What one believes "counts for nothing" as the mood goes right on being what it is. The mood discloses much more fully than one knows. Let us now see how this disclosing and its understanding, differ from ordinary cognition.

> Disclosed does not mean known as such and such. (*BT* 173)

> *Befindlichkeit* always has its understanding, even if only in holding it down. Understanding is always moody. (*BT* 182)

> In *Befindlichkeit* Dasein . . . has always already found itself, not in the sense of . . . perceiving itself, rather as finding itself moody. (*BT* 174)

> Understanding is never free-floating, rather always *befindliches*. (*BT* 389) [There is] . . . an existential fundamental connection between *Befindlichkeit* and understanding. (*BT* 390)

We must now see how Heidegger delineates this "being-in-the-world" which is disclosed in a mood, feeling, or affect. How is it that people *are* the being-in-the-world?

> In clarifying being-in-the-world we have shown that a bare subject without a world . . . never is, and is never given. And so, in the end, an isolated "I" without others is just as far from being . . . ever given. The others are always already here with us in our being-in-the-world. (*BT* 152)
>
> The human being's "substance" is not spirit as a synthesis of soul and body; it is rather existence. (*BT* 153)
>
> The world of Dasein is a with-world [*Mitwelt*]. Being-in is being-with others. (*BT* 155)
>
> And even when Dasein explicitly addresses itself as "I, here," . . . this "I, here" does not mean a certain special point of an I-thing: rather, it understands itself as a being-in, in terms of the overthere of the world. (*BT* 155)

Humans are called *"Dasein,"* which means being-*here*. This *here* understands itself as a being-*in* the world in relation to the *overthere* of the world. Humans aren't just in space, as if space were just given. The being-here in relation to the overthere generates being-in-the-world. It is one structure, one pattern. And this is also the structure of feeling:

> In being in a mood . . . the pure "that it is" shows itself, the where-from and where-to remain in the dark . . . in everyday life the human does not "give in" . . . to moods, that is to say, does not go after their disclosing. (*BT* 173)
>
> Mood discloses in the manner of turning toward, or turning away from one's own Dasein. The bringing before the "that it is" . . . may be authentically revealing or inauthentically covering up. (*BT* 390)
>
> Dasein, as essentially *befindliches*, has always already got itself into possibilities. . . . But this means Dasein is . . . through and through . . . possibility. (*BT* 184)

Authenticity requires this bringing oneself before how one already is, how one is being-here as disclosed in a mood. Without going after what the mood discloses, one cannot be authentic. Authenticity is fundamentally grounded in *Befindlichkeit* and its understanding, and requires bringing oneself before how one is disclosed in the mood.

Being-here (that is to say, the human being) is the possibilities insofar as it is *befindliches*. As we will see now, one's authentic possibilities are only those disclosed in *Befindlichkeit*, for only *Befindlichkeit* and its implicit understanding (which it always already has) discloses how we are thrown into the situations in which we find ourselves (into which we have lived ourselves).

Befindlichkeit always discloses being-in-the-world "as a whole," and the familiar emotions are, for Heidegger, "determined modes" of *Befindlichkeit*. He discusses fear and anxiety. Fear is inauthentic because we attribute the cause to the external world. Anxiety is authentic because it brings us before our own being, and before the essential nature of our own being, its unsubstantial character.

> ... the phenomenon of the *Befindlichkeit* of Dasein shall be more concretely demonstrated in the determined mode of fear. (*BT* 179)

> In what way is anxiety a distinctive *Befindlichkeit*? *How*, in it, is Dasein brought before itself through its own being? (*BT* 228)

> Anxiety arises out of the being-in-the-world as thrown being toward death. (*BT* 395)

> The insignificance of the world, disclosed in anxiety, reveals the nullity of the things of our concerns, or in other words the impossibility of projecting oneself (*sichentwerfen*) on a can-be that is primarily founded in the things of our concerns. (*BT* 393)

> Fear has its occasion in being concerned with the world. Anxiety, in contrast, arises out of Dasein itself.... Anxiety frees *from* possibilities that are nullities, and enables becoming free *for* authentic ones. (*BT* 395)

Anxiety will thus be part (but only part) of authentic action, since the authentic possibilities will still be in the world.[7] If anxiety were all there is to authentic *Befindlichkeit*, death would be the only authentic action. But one "lives toward death" in a way that frees for authentic action *in the world*. *Anxiety is only one essential part of authentic action*, because it is always only one specific aspect of the wholistic *Befindlichkeit*:

> ... fear and anxiety never "occur" isolatedly in the "stream of experiencing"; rather, *they* always determine an understanding, or determine themselves from such an understanding. (*BT* 395)

> Understanding and *Befindlichkeit* are "equally original" and interlocked together. Understanding is never free-floating, rather always *befindliches*. The here is always disclosed equally originally through mood. (*BT* 389)

Understanding sketches out possibilities, or one can say (even in English) it "throws out" possibilities, as one throws out suggestions. The German word "entwerfen" means to sketch, to outline. Part of that word is "werfen," which means throwing. As we saw before:

> Dasein, as essentially *befindliches* has always already got itself into possibilities. . . . But this means Dasein is . . . through and through thrown possibility. (*BT* 183)

Let us now look more exactly at this "throwing" of possibilities, and the "thrown" nature of humans.[8] It is "moody understanding," or *"befindliches* understanding," which "throws" the possibilities, and as *Befindlichkeit*, we are always already "thrown."

> As thrown, Dasein *is* thrown into the kind of being which we call "throwing out" [*Entwerfen*]. (*BT* 185) Dasein *is* not something . . . which as an addition also possesses that it can be something; rather, it *is* primarily being-possible. (*BT* 182) Understanding inherently has the existential structure we call *throwing our* [*Entwurf*]. (*BT* 185)

> The character of understanding as throwing constitutes the being-in-the-world . . . as the here of a can-be [*Seinkönnen*]. (*BT* 185)

> Dasein *is* always more than it factually *is* . . . on the ground of . . . being constituted through throwing. (*BT* 185)

One is always already engaged, in the midst of trying something, striving for this or avoiding that, going about something. If we ask, "What are you doing?" it is never just the actual. We are trying to bring about this, or going to that, or making this point or trying to achieve something that is not yet. But this being possible, this way we are the possibilities, is not conscious planning, neither is it unconscious. It is implicit.

> Throwing [throwing out possibilities, *Entwerfen*] has nothing to do with relating oneself to a thought-through plan. . . . The sketch character of understanding does not grasp the possibility thematically, . . . such (thematic) grasping would deprive the sketching precisely of its character *as* possible, and would reduce it to *a* given intended content. (*BT* 185)

Heidegger doesn't mean by possibility and sketching-throwing a mere not-yet, that is otherwise fully and actually known. Rather, it is the understanding which mood always has, the implicitly lived understanding which is this possibility-sketching. We "know" what we are about, how we came into the situation, but we don't "know" it in a sharp way, in the kind of "cognition" that is cut off from "affect." We know it, rather, in that way in which a mood always already has its understanding, and in which understanding (as Heidegger defines it) is always moody.

We have seen that in Heidegger's conception the person is not an "I-thing," but a being-in-the-world. But have we lost the person thereby? Is this being-in-the-world not just an extroverted, internally empty way of being only in relation? Heidegger says that this losing oneself in the world is indeed a constant pitfall. To be authentically, we must continually bring ourselves back from being dispersed. It is in how we bring ourselves back that the authentic essential nature of the self becomes clear.

Authenticity has been largely misunderstood, in Heidegger's philosophy, just because *Befindlichkeit* has not been understood. Authenticity is frequently taken to mean nothing more than living by one's own originative possibility-sketching, rather than living by what the world says and the possibilities it defines. While this is true of authenticity, it lacks the essence. One could be merely capricious and still fit such a definition. Also, one could live oblivious to much of one's relations to others, and still fit the definition of authenticity. But Heidegger defines authenticity much more exactly, and his definition depends upon *Befindlichkeit*.

As we grasp his definition of authenticity, we will also understand feeling or *Befindlichkeit* much better. His conception of the person will emerge much more basically.

A human being is not a what:

> In understanding . . . the can-be is no what; rather, it is the being as existing. (*BT* 143 182)

> We designate "knowledge of the self" . . . not as a perceptual . . . viewing of a self-point, rather an understandingly grasping of the full disclosedness of being-in-the-world *through* its essential parameters, *on through* them. (*BT* 186)

A human self is not a thing but a process, and a "self" is not a what, but a reflexive structure, the phrasing of which always requires that the word "self" be used twice. In bringing oneself before oneself (or in covering up), the human self is. The self is not, like a point is.

> Existing being sights "itself" only *so* far as it becomes transparent to itself, the constituting aspects of its existence, equally in its being-alongside the world and its being-with others. (*BT* 187)

But how does this being, which is being-in-the-world, which is the sketching of possibilities that are in the world . . . how does it bring itself back from the world, how does it bring itself to itself?

Human beings cannot help being-in-the-world, for that is what they are. But we can continuously bring ourselves back from being lost in the possibilities themselves. But to do this is much different than just sketching out more possibilities. Then we would only be lost in those instead of these.

We are not the possibilities themselves, we are the sketching, the throwing, and also the being-thrown. Since we are the throwing and the being thrown, we are lost as soon as we identify with the possibilities themselves.

> And only *because* Dasein (being-here) is its here understandingly, can it disperse and mistake itself. (*BT* 184)

Since "understanding" means throwing out possibilities, and being this throwing, therefore it is possible to be lost in the possibilities.

> And insofar as understanding is *befindliches* . . . Dasein has always already dispersed and mistaken itself. (*BT* 184)

The mood is the possibilities we already are, as being thrown into them.

> *Befindlichkeit* and understanding . . . characterize the original disclosedness of being-in-the-world. In the way of having a mood Dasein "sees" possibilities from out of which it is. In the sketching disclosing of such possibilities it is always already in a mood. (*BT* 188)

"Always already." The possibilities we are, are always already in the mood, and only in the mood are they seen, or known. But the mood, *Befindlichkeit*, has a special power. *It brings the being-here before itself, it finds itself.*

> Being in a mood brings Dasein *before* its thrownness, in such *a way*, however, that the thrownness is not recognized as such, but rather is much more originally disclosed in the "how one is." (*BT* 390)

A special time relation is generated here. By going back to retrieve oneself one goes forward authentically.

We saw earlier how Heidegger views space not as a geometric container in which we happen to be, but as generated by the human being-here in relation to a there. Now we also see a new time-relation emerging, not the linear one thing after another, but a going back that is also a going forward, and the only authentic way of going forward.

All three times, past, present, and future are together, but not just merged. We must see the exact, sharp structure of their relations. Although the three are together, "understanding" grounds primarily in the future, as possibility.

> *Befindlichkeit* . . . temporalizes itself *primarily* in the having-been. (*BT* 390)

Being moody, we saw, *brings Dasein before* its thrownness.

> The bringing before . . . becomes possible only if Dasein's being constantly is as having-been. (*BT* 390)

That humans exist as having-been is just as true, whether we bring *ourselves before it or not, since we are moody, we already are the having-been*, we are it in the "how we are," as we just saw above. Heidegger says that this human way of existing as having-been

> . . . enables the self-finding (*Sich-finden*) in the manner of being *befindlich*. (*BT* 390) The basic existential character of mood is *a bringing back to*. (*BT* 390)

> The authentic coming-toward-itself . . . is a coming back to the ownmost thrown self . . . [this] enables Dasein resolutely to take over that being which it already is. (*BT* 388)

How is this "coming back" or "bringing back" of *Befindlichkeit* related to the sketching-forward of "understanding"? The exact relation of this "past" of the moody having-been, and the "future" of understanding, makes the authentic present. Let us see exactly how this is structured:

> The understanding is . . . primarily future . . . but equally originally determined through having-been and presentness. (*BT* 386)

> In running ahead, Dasein brings [*holt*] itself again [*wieder*] forward into its own can-be. The authentic *being* the having-been we call retrieval [*Wiederholung*]. (*BT* 387)[9]

> In resoluteness the present is . . . brought back from distraction with the objects . . . [and] held in the future and in having-been. [This is] the authentic present. (*BT* 388)

Past, present, and future are thus not merely serial, as usually viewed, as if they were positions in a line. Instead, each involves the others, and they make one structure together.

Going back is also bringing before oneself. One goes back to "how one is," how one is already existing. One goes back to it, it is always already. It is a having-been. Only in so doing does one retrieve one's authentic possibility-sketching, so that a present is made in which one is ready to act authentically.

Mere caprices, however they may originate from me alone, are not authentic because they don't arise from the being I already am. I must take this being over. If I leave it covered, nevertheless, I am that existing, but inauthentically.

I can only take over the being I already am, by finding myself in my *Befindlichkeit*, and moving forward from this going back and self-finding.

We have now found the person, not at all as some notion of oneself, not at all as some "thing" or spot, or steady entity, but as this finding oneself (in the inauthentic mode of not pursuing one's "how one is," or in the authentic mode of retrieving, going back to bring oneself before oneself).

It is the essential nature of Dasein not to be a substantial "thing," but rather a being-in and being-with, that is therefore fundamentally open to events. What we are is our living, the existing, and that is how we *are affected* differently than a stone is affected. A stone isn't affected essentially. It is a stone, and then it may be changed in this way or that, while its stoneness continues. Humans *are* being affected. Our being, in Heidegger's view, is always being affected and that is how we find ourselves. We *are* the living-in events with-others, our being rides on the events, is dispersed in what happens, is the being-in what happens. Only in so finding ourselves can we constantly retrieve ourselves, so that there is a present in which our capacity to be is again and again our own. That is authenticity.

Being-with is a fundamental aspect of being-in the world. Our situations are always with others. That we can hear each other is inherent in this being-with.

> Hearing is constitutive for speech . . . listening to . . . is the existential being open of Dasein as being-with. . . . Indeed, listening constitutes the primary authentic being-open of Dasein. (*BT* 206)

> Dasein hears because it understands. (*BT* 205)

> Speech is constitutive for the being of the here, that is to say, for *Befindlichkeit* and understanding. (*BT* 206)

> *Speech is existentially equally original with Befindlichkeit and understanding* [Heidegger's italics]. Understandability is always already articulated even before it is appropriately interpreted. Speech is the articulation of understandability. (*BT* 203)

Just as Heidegger uses the term "understanding" for the implicit sense of our mood, that is to say, for something much earlier that prefigures what we usually call by that name, so also he uses "articulation" (*gegliedert*) for the inherent speakability of mood and understanding, before we put it into actual words.

Articulation is not a good translation, however. *Gegliedert* means having interconnected links and parts, being structured, having interlinked links, not like a snail or applesauce but like a skeleton or an animal with articulated limbs.

It is clear that Heidegger means that, in how we are as *Befindlichkeit* and understanding-sketching, which is not just applesauce-like but has structure. This is the inherent precondition of actual speech, and is equally original, equally basic, inherent in *Befindlichkeit* and understanding. This characteristic of people is inherent in what humans are as being-with. Understandability means not only that I understand implicitly what I am doing, but with. Understandability means not only that I understand implicitly what I am doing, but that others do, and that I am understandable to them and they to me. Thus the basis of communication lies in the nature of our being as being-with, and without it there would be no world, no situations for us to be-in.

This concludes my quotations of Heidegger on *Befindlichkeit* and its implicit understanding and communicability.

Earlier I said that in addition to the conceptual structure with which we must think about feeling, in psychology, *Befindlichkeit* also has important implications for method generally. Again, what he says is philosophical and examines how we can know anything. Specific sciences are specific ways of knowing some specific topic. What he says also applies to the sciences, of course.

Heidegger on *Befindlichkeit* and Method

> *Befindlichkeit* is a basic existential way in which Dasein (being-here) is its here. It not only characterizes Dasein ontologically, but because of its disclosing, it is at the same time of basic methodological significance for the existential analytic. Like any ontological interpretation whatsoever, this analytic can only, so to speak, "listen in" to the previously disclosed

being of something that is. . . . Phenomenological interpretation must give Dasein the possibility of original disclosing, to raise the phenomenal content of this disclosing into concepts. (*BT* 178–79)

Here Heidegger says explicitly that *Befindlichkeit is* the disclosing on which phenomenological method depends. Without the "possibility of original disclosing" there is no phenomenological method, for that is what this method raises into concepts. If the disclosing of *Befindlichkeit* isn't there as part of the method, it will be free-floating, and not phenomenological.

Every statement or interpretation, every *logos*, must be in a direct relationship to this original disclosing of *Befindlichkeit* and its understanding. What we already sensed and understood, perhaps in the mode of covering it up, must be brought to concepts.

In explaining what phenomeno*logy* is, Heidegger discusses phenomena and then logos:

> The *logos* lets something be seen . . . and it does so either *for* the one who is doing the talking (the *medium*) or for the persons who are talking with one another, as the case may be. Speech "lets something be seen" . . . that is, it lets us see something from the very thing which the speech is about . . . making manifest in the sense of letting something be seen by pointing it out. (*BT* 56)

What phenomenological statements let us see is usually covered up, and emerges and shows itself only in response to such statement.

> And just because the phenomena are mostly not immediately given, phenomenology is needed. (*BT* 60)

> As the meaning of the expression "*phenomenon*," the following is to be firmly *held on to* [*ist daher festzuhalten*]: that which shows itself in itself. (*BT* 51; Heidegger's italics)

Thus phenomena in the primary sense of phenomenological method are not those which are immediately obvious anyway without method, but those which show themselves in response to the logos, the statement or formulation.

Heidegger, instancing what he is telling us, here gives a phenomenological interpretation of phenomenological interpretation. He has asked us to "*hold fast to*" the meaning of "phenomenon" as what shows itself on itself. Now he says:

> With a concrete having before oneself of that which was set out in the interpretation of "phenomenon" and "logos"; the inner connection between the two terms leaps into view. . . . Phenomenology means . . . letting be seen . . . that which shows itself, just as it shows itself from itself. (*BT* 58)

Thus phenomenological method involves something quite different from statements only, something that, once the logos lets it show itself, shows itself independently. It is possible to have only "free-floating" statements without such an independent phenomenal aspect showing itself, leaping before us, in response to statement. Also, even if there once was such a concretely present self-showing aspect, it can be lost as mere statements are passed on without ensuring that the self-showing aspect too is each time found by each person.

Every concept and sentence drawn originally in a phenomenological way as a communicated assertion has the possibility *of* degenerating. It *is* passed on in an empty understanding, loses its grounding and becomes free-floating thesis (*BT* 60).

Thus Heidegger insists that he is to be understood experientially with something concretely showing itself from itself, for every concept and sentence of his. The ontological structure of the human being, and all other subject matter that can be studied only in relation to it, can be grasped only phenomenologically, and never as "free-floating thesis."

> Only "*as phenomenology is ontology*" *possible.* (*BT* 60; Heidegger's italics)

It is often thought, wrongly I believe, that Heidegger's concepts and those of others, if repeated, are phenomenological or are phenomenology. Heidegger has himself said that this isn't so; they might be repeated as free-floating theses. Phenomenology is nothing if it is not method, the method of grounding each assertion in something that then stands out.

> "Phenomenology" names neither the object of its inquiries, nor does this title characterize the subject-matter of its inquiries. The word informs us only about the how of the presentation and mode of treatment. (*BT* 59)

3. Further Applications and Implications

Psychological

The essence of psychotherapy—when it is effective—is phenomenological, not perhaps in the conception of the therapist or the theory, but in the process of the patient.

As in the cited excerpt, any statements and interpretations are effective only when they lift out something from the directly sensed and preverbally "understood" felt complexity.

Even very sophisticated statements by patients and therapists alter nothing in the patient's living, unless there is the distinct effect of lifting something out. Many patients have gone to psychotherapy, so-called, for many years several times each week without much effect.

Such failure cases are found in all methods of therapy, and success cases are also found in all methods. The difference is not the ostensive method of psychotherapy, but whether the concrete experiential process described earlier occurs or not. Thus we can neither accept nor condemn one or another type of therapy.

In our excerpt, at each step, one could apply Freudian theory (or Jungian theory) and explain the patient in terms of the theory. However, no theory could have predicted the next steps to which she was led by directly bringing herself before her felt sense. Similarly, if we wish, we can render the whole chain, now that it is explicit, in any of the theories.

In retrospect, it is always possible to construct a logical account for such steps of therapeutic process. In the actual process the steps come first. The statements are a kind of "listening in," as Heidegger puts it, to what is already disclosed preverbally in the feeling.

There is a back-and-forth movement between statement and feeling. Having verbalized something, what then leaps up is not the same as before, and enables a new listening in, which leads to a new statement.

In this role, the theories can be highly useful. Of course any inference is only a guess, a try, an attempt. The anticipated aspect (*or some other aspect*) leaps up in response; if not, then even the best theoretical inference happens just then to be useless. Even when it is corroborated, the inference is not the therapeutic process. The inference has helped, but only insofar as a directly sensed phenomenal aspect arises. It then guides the next step, not what one would have expected to follow theoretically. Notice: even when the inferred statement is corroborated, the aspect lifted out as a result of it soon leads to something further and different than could be inferred from the very statement that led to it.

This being so, we see that the actual texture of living cannot be equated to any theory. All theory and language *can relate* to living (and to the feel of living), but cannot be equated to it.

Freud and Jung discovered depth psychology. They correctly saw that there is always a vastly complex texture involved in any human event, however simple and routine it might seem. In this they were right.

Freud and Jung erred in taking the symbolizations from a number of people (very much like the patient's symbolizations in my excerpt) and constructing from this a system of contents in terms of which we are all supposedly explainable.

The fact that there is more than one such theory should give one pause. All are effective to some extent, which contradicts the exclusiveness with which each is put forward. We cannot really accept any *one* rendering us. If we change the way they were intended to function, we can use them all, Jung's, Freud's, and additional theories. The more ways of articulating human experience one knows the better. At a given juncture one or another of these vocabularies may enable us to make a statement that leads to a lifting out. This way of using theories changes the very essence of what theory is: theory, taken phenomenologically, relates to what it is about not as an equation or a rendering, but as a logos which lets something be seen *which is then seen on its own*.

The nature of human nature, of living and feeling, is therefore of a much finer texture than any theory or system of sharp cognitions. This is the opposite of saying that experience is indeterminate or vague; it is always very demandingly just exactly how it is, how we find ourselves, but *more organized*, structured, "gegliedert," than any system can equal. Also, it is not given in little pieces, but as a wholistic texture of sensing and living.

In recognizing this, we do not give up on theory; rather, we restore theory to its proper relationship to actuality. This proper relationship lets theory have its own great power. For as we lift out, more and more becomes possible. Theory further builds the world, develops life and gives further structure to anything to which it is applied, but of course it does not do this by itself. Only if theory is put in direct relation with what it is about, does it show its power there.

Words can help the patient lift out something only if the words each have *their own* sharp meanings (even though what is lifted out then has *its own* character). Theoretical words too can lift out, and again only if they have their own sharp meanings. In no way, therefore, does what I say lead to a loss of theory or theoretical sharpness.

If one says that an ax shows its power only on the wood, or whatever is cut with it, this wouldn't imply that one doesn't need to keep one's ax sharp. How much more is this so for the subtle further living and building when theory lifts out something.

Phenomenologists have not well understood all this. There has been a tendency for phenomenology to fall back into descriptions of what is obvious on the face of itself and needs no lifting out, needs no phenomenology. It has become popular to deny not just the concept of the "unconscious" (which, as a conception, deserved to be denied), but also what this concept (clumsily) points to. The implicit complexity, at first only sensed or felt, emerges in the kind of process I am describing. Then something further is felt. There are steps of an explication process. Phenomenologists have felt compelled either to insist on only the face value of human experiences, a hopelessly inadequate view, or—when put to it—they fall into the other extreme and cannot find their way out of accepting one or another psychological theory. This happens frequently, when the phenomenological philosopher as a person enters psychotherapy (for then the power of these theories is experienced directly); and also when the philosopher at last decides to think about psychotherapy. Avoiding the topic, not especially of psychotherapy, but more importantly the topic of feeling, has not well served philosophy.

Feelings were relegated to "tertiary" status in the eighteenth century. They appeared in the rear of philosophy books as "the passions," and had little or no role to play in the constitution of objects and objective reality. Humans were thought to be in touch with reality only in two ways: through perception and through reason. Reason was thought to give order to incoming bits of perception. (Of course this was not ever the only viewpoint during any period.) This view still structures most of our concepts, so that even if we wish to say something else, we cannot do it clearly. Our concepts themselves are still part of that outlook. "Feelings" are held to be internal, rather than a sensing ourselves living. It is then puzzling why there is so much implicit wisdom in feelings. They are also confused with sheer emotions, as I explained earlier. Most philosophers have stayed away from them, instead of clarifying our thinking regarding them.

There has also been another reason for this avoidance. We want to avoid the erroneous view that philosophical questions can be resolved by arguing from psychological factors, wrongly placed underneath as if they could determine philosophy. Freud, for example, thought he could give psychological reasons why philosophers say what they say. But when philosophy assumes Freudian underpinnings, it is no longer philosophy, for it omits at least the examination of Freud's kind of concepts and conceptual patterns.

Psychotherapy is essentially phenomenological—this does not mean phenomenology is psychotherapy. Phenomenology is a far wider category, and its most important meaning is philosophical. Precisely, therefore, it can provide a critique and restructuring of the way we have been thinking about feeling in psychology and in everyday life.

Elsewhere I have presented a "Theory of Personality Change" in which I formulate psychological concepts along the lines I presented in discussing Heidegger.[10] As I cannot review them in detail here, one concept only will be mentioned. A "direct referent" (I also call it "felt sense" or "felt meaning") is both felt and interactional, the feel *of* one's living in one's situations. It has the organization of this living before and without reflection. Facets can be lifted out and symbolized, which "were" how one was already living. This "were" is in quotation marks, because one changes in authentic explicating. The very act of symbolizing is itself a further living and a further structuring. But only rare statements (and other kinds of symbolizing) have this lifting-out character. As I said earlier, research can measure the extent to which this is part of someone's manner of approach.

Let us change our fundamental way of considering psychological theory. If we see clearly in philosophy that the human way of being cannot be reduced to, or undercut by, any system of concepts—why leave psychology to that false assumption? A quite different kind of psychology is possible, one that studies the process, rather than imputing a content-system.

Even to study process, certain concepts must be formed and used. Philosophy will always be on another level, and will always examine how concepts are made, and what different kinds of being are. But from philosophy implications follow for what kinds of concepts are needed in psychology. We need and have recently formulated concepts to study steps of process and even to measure them. With such concepts we can make clear how there is "content mutation" through process-steps.

Theory must be considered in a new way. What I have said so far can be misinterpreted as if to imply that the differences between Freud, Jung, and others don't matter. Nothing of the sort follows! Words and theoretical concepts, too, have power only insofar as they are sharp and have their own clear structure and implications. Feelings without further symbolization are blind (and symbols alone are empty). The new view implies no denigration of theory and clear concepts—but a fundamentally new way of understanding what concepts and theory are, and how they may best be used in their proper relation and most powerfully. And that is in a process of steps of lifting-out.

Philosophical

Let me now turn to more philosophical implications, still bearing on this question. What is this "lifting out" relation between theory (and language) on the one hand, and living and feeling on the other? I ask this now not in the practical sense already described, but as the philosophical question of how this relation is possible.

In Heidegger's sense, living is always already linguistically patterned (*gegliedert*). Speaking is an equally original emergence along with *Befindlichkeit* and understanding.

In my way of saying it, we live in linguistically structured situations. Even though what we will further say is new, that emerges from living-in our contexts. These contexts are differentiated by speakings (although, not only in this way). If we imagine speech gone, then a whole host of differentiations and intricacies of our situations is also gone. New further living restructures this implicit structure further.

We must therefore grant feeling *more* organization than that of our poor theoretical systems, vastly more. Given that we do, we can then also understand the power of theory to structure further. This is no small power! Poetry in a very different, and more obvious way, has a power of that kind. One would not need to think that humans are *made of* the kind of entities of which poems are constructed, in order to sense why poetry is powerful. Such a view would trivialize the obviously creative power of poetry. Neither are humans made of the cut entities the theoretical systems contain, and yet theories are immensely powerful new languages for living further what we already are.

But this line of thought leads to the question: how shall we think of this much more organized implicit patterning—if the theories are not to be taken literally? So far I have spoken of it as a Persian rug, a fine texture, a capillary system (metaphors of intricacy, complexity, and fine patterning).

Homage to a great philosopher is best done by really seeing what the philosophy points to, and by going on further. The later Heidegger himself goes much further in this direction than he does in *Being and Time*, from which my quotations are taken. And his pointing becomes more powerful. For example, in "*On the Essence of Truth*" he writes that any true statement also hides truth, and formulation is thus also false. Ultimately, that cannot be denied. It will apply to Heidegger's own work and to anything I have said or will say.

Heidegger brought forward a line of development from Schleiermacher and Nietzsche through Dilthey and Husserl, the founding of our assertions directly on our living, as we experience. Having seen how Heidegger does that, let us notice: Heidegger always goes only one step, from the living experiencing to his formulation of the structure implicit in it. The reader thereby has lifted out some aspect that "was" already being lived, but was not seen as such. But other authors lift out other aspects, or one could say, they formulate "the same" aspects differently. Different aspects of these "same" aspects are lifted out. My interest here is not in reconciling different philosophies, but rather in the question I have been posing: how might we think about that much finer and different organization of living, such that "lifting out" is possible?

What is (or are) the relationship(s) between living and formulations, such that different formulations are possible? (And, such that each hides, as well as lifts out?)

As capable of giving explicit birth to these liftings out, the character of the organization of living is much more fundamental than even the structure in *Being and Time*. And it can be studied! This organization can be studied because we have transitions from one formulation to another, one mode of symbolizing to another, one step of this process of further symbolizing to another step.

Thus I said above that one could say either, that others lift out other aspects different than Heidegger's, or one could say they lift out "the same" aspects but somewhat differently and thus with different sub-aspects. One can see that our ordinary logical notions of "same" and "different" are offended by this situation. Put differently, what is lifted out by two systems is not the same, but neither is it just plain different. "Same" and "different" have to give way to a kind of order that doesn't consist of sharp units, the kind of units that are only the same *or* different.

My own work for many years preceded my reading Heidegger. I came to him quite late. Both the personality change theory mentioned above, and the philosophical work I will now mention, were written before I read Heidegger. But I had read those philosophers that most influenced Heidegger, and so I emerged from the same sources, at least to some extent. I had also read Sartre, Buber, and Merleau-Ponty, who were greatly and crucially following Heidegger. Hence my own work continues from Heidegger, and stands under his influence, although I did not recognize that until later. I have differences with him, too, but this is not the place to discuss them.

In *Experiencing and the Creation of Meaning* I develop a way of studying, not unformulated being or experience, nor formulations, but rather the transitions from one formulation (of something lifted out) to another formulation (of "the same" aspect lifted out).[11] It is easy to show negatively that in such a transition lived experience has no one scheme, and no one set of fixed units. Much more follows. Experience *in relation to further symbolizations* can be said to have quite an odd "structure." I call it the "metastructure." A different kind of "logic" arises to specify these transitions. There are a number of different kinds, each with specific dimensions. The resulting "characteristics" of experiencing in relation to further symbolizing are startling, and lead to a new way of thinking that can be sharp and clear, but with a very different logic.

Notes

1. Note added in 2006: Heidegger always urged people to go further from his new concepts. He would be glad that I am doing so. Without changing anything in his conception, I add the bodily-experiential dimension. Since he did not mean it in a bodily way at all, we should not attribute my concept of *Befindlichkeit* to Heidegger.

2. *Befindlichkeit* is translated as "state of mind" in Macquarrie and Robinson's English translation of *Being and Time*, but it is neither state nor mind. Nor can *Befindlichkeit* be translated either as *mood* or *attunement*, since Heidegger uses *Stimmung*, an old word, and nevertheless finds it necessary to create a new word, *Befindlichkeit*, as well.

3. Heidegger told Joan Stambaugh, an editor and translator of his works in English, that in his later work *Befindlichkeit* becomes *wohnen* (dwelling); personal communication from Joan Stambaugh.

4. See my "A Theory of Personality Change," in *Personality Change*, ed. Philip Worchel and Donn Byrne (New York: Wiley 1964).

5. I use the term "felt sense" for one's feel of a wholistic texture. This is to be distinguished from an emotion like joy or anger. Such emotions are embedded in a "felt sense"—the sense of all of one's living involved in being joyful now, or angry.

6. See Eugene T. Gendlin, J. Beebe, J. Cassens, M. Klein, and M. Oberlander, "Focusing Ability in Psychotherapy, Personality and Creativity," in *Research in Psychotherapy*, ed. J. Schlien, vol. 3 (Washington, D.C.: American Psychological Association, 1967).

7. "Equanimity [*Gleichmut*] . . . *is* also characteristic of authentic action" (Heidegger, *BT* 345).

8. This "throwing out" is translated as "projection" by Macquarrie and Robinson. This loses the inherent relation between the throwing-out of possibilities and being thrown.

9. Although *Wiederholung* can mean "repetition" in German, it is an unfortunate translation. Heidegger carefully constructs the term in the above sentence from *holen* (bringing) and *wieder* (again). I translate it as "retrieval."

10. See Eugene T. Gendlin, "A Theory of Personality Change," in *Personality Change*, ed. Philip Worchel and Donn Byrne (New York: Wiley, 1964); Eugene T. Gendlin, "Experiential Psychotherapy," in *Current Psychotherapies*, ed. R. Corsini (Itasca, Ill.: Peacock, 1973), 317–52; and Eugene T. Gendlin, *Focusing* (New York: Everest House, 1978).

11. See also "Experiential Phenomenology," chapter 3 in this volume.

12

Time's Dependence on Space: Kant's Statements and Their Misconstrual by Heidegger

Heidegger's *Phenomenological Interpretation of Kant's Critique of Pure Reason* reveals an unavowed difference with Kant concerning time, which has major implications.[1] It also turns out that in a very important way Heidegger preferred the second edition of the *Critique of Pure Reason*, even in 1928, contrary to what has always been thought.[2] These lectures are a beautiful running commentary on the "Aesthetic" and the "Analytic." It is a great privilege for us to sit, so to speak, in Heidegger's Kant class. Heidegger's step-by-step commentary is lovely, yet there are more distinctions in Kant—differences that matter a great deal to Kant—that are lost in Heidegger's treatment. Only if we first grasp certain specifics that are very important in Kant's basic view can we pinpoint the differences between the two views.

Therefore I will first discuss Kant alone.

I

For some years now I have been tracing the reasons for a brutal change Kant made in the second edition of the *Critique of Pure Reason*. Where he had five arguments for space, and five for time, neatly parallel each to each, in the second edition he removes one of the arguments for space. He sets that argument up in a separate, longer new section just after the numbered arguments. But for time he leaves all five as they were. The result could not be more lacking in elegance, and it is quite clear that something important is being achieved at this cost.

Later, in parallel with the new section on space, Kant writes a new section on time as well, just as if he had taken out the time argument. In this new section Kant says that this argument which he left in its original place "properly belongs" in this new section, but he left it there (these are his words) "for the sake of brevity [*um kurz zu sein*]."

CHAPTER 12

The new sections are called "Transcendental Exposition of the Concept of Space" and "Time," respectively. He has also given the old sections, now the four arguments for space and the five for time, a new title: they are "Metaphysical Expositions." What he means in the new sections by "Transcendental Exposition" is showing how space and time give rise to other synthetic a priori knowledge. For space this is geometry, he says, an a priori science of the properties of space. For time he first gives this puzzling reference to having left the argument under "Metaphysical" for the sake of brevity, and then adds in the same short paragraph that alteration is only possible in time, and thus the a priori doctrine of motion is the a priori knowledge which fits here.

Why it was briefer to leave the argument there does not appear at all.

The argument which was left there says that time has only one dimension, and that different times are not simultaneous but successive, as examples of apodictic principles concerning time relations or axioms of time. These cannot come from experience, since they are necessary.

Evidently Kant, in the second edition, did not consider that these axioms quite make up "other a priori synthetic knowledge" which could be cited under "transcendental." And yet he says in that later section that this argument is "properly transcendental." So they must be something in between.

Whatever the explanation is, the matter was of sufficient importance to Kant to disfigure his usual neat array, as well as to be deliberately puzzling. For the sake of brevity, he says, he is placing an argument in a different place than where it "properly belongs."

I looked this up some years ago in Norman Kemp Smith's *Commentary*—if you will forgive me this provincialism. Kemp Smith writes that "Kant left the argument where it was for the sake of brevity." I no longer own that commentary.

My excitement was great when I discovered that volume 25 of Heidegger's *Gesamtausgabe* is a commentary that follows the first *Critique*'s outline. Of course, Heidegger deals with what I have said so far. He attributes it to the fact that motion, for Kant, involves concepts, that is, belongs in the "Analytic." But Heidegger comes to conclusions about Kant which we can understand and evaluate only if we trace our way through the first *Critique* along the theme with which Kant is so very concerned here.

Kant's view is that time does not have its own science as space does. Heidegger does not say this, but while time is indeed presupposed in the science of motion, motion is alteration in space. The science of motion is not a science of time alone.

TIME'S DEPENDENCE ON SPACE

Now, as I thought about this, if geometry is the a priori science of space, I would have expected the a priori science of time to be arithmetic. But obviously, here, for Kant it is not. Is not geometry both quantitative and spatial, whereas numbers are ordered in a time-series only? Tracing through the first *Critique* where you would expect to find arithmetic mentioned gives odd and interesting results. Kant does not mention arithmetic—it is usually algebra he cites. Under "Axioms of Intuition," where the mathematics of extension is called "geometry," he also discusses "numerical relations" and manages never to say the word "arithmetic." He says here that there are no axioms of numerical relations. An axiom, for him, is one general rule covering may different constructions. But 7 + 5 = 12 is "only [a] numerical formula," although synthetic and a priori. Each number is single and made always the same way, differently from every other. Therefore there are no axioms, only an infinite number of different single formulae. On the other hand, rules like "if equals are added to equals, the wholes are equal" are **analytic**, merely conceptual! No new whole is actually made, the same thing is said twice.

In the "Introduction"—significantly in a section added in the second edition—Kant shows why "7 + 5 = 12" is synthetic. He writes: "We have to go outside these concepts (7 and 5) and call in the aid of intuition which corresponds to one of them, our five fingers for instance, or . . . five points" (*Critique of Pure Reason*, B 15).

There are no time relations without spatial points. And, near the end of the "Analytic," again in a section added in the second edition, he writes: The possibility of things as quantities . . . can be exhibited only in outer intuition, and . . . only through the mediation of outer intuition can it be applied also to inner sense. But, to avoid prolixity [*um Weitläufigkeit zu vermeiden*] I must leave the reader to supply his own examples of this" (*Critique*, B 293).

Now we are near the end of the "Analytic" (*Critique*, B 293). Why is Kant always so concerned with brevity when this topic comes up?

Before supplying our own examples, recall: he has already mentioned fingers and dots. A little past the last quote, he says: "the concept of magnitude seeks its support and sensible meaning in number, and this in turn in the fingers, in the beads of the abacus, or in strokes and points which can be placed before the eyes" (*Critique*, A 240, B 299).

The number series for Kant is impossible without outer intuition, dots, slots, beads, points, marks. If you want to check your memory that 5 + 7 is indeed 12, how would you?

||||| + ||||||| = ||||||||||||

That is our example he asked us to supply—however you did it, it involved some spaced-out slots.

CHAPTER 12

In his preface to the second edition Kant says that all the parts of the *Critique* hold organically together and that he has not changed any of it. Only in the manner of his exposition has he tried to deal with certain misunderstandings. What we are tracing is not at all a change in his system, but an effort to avoid a misunderstanding. And in a footnote to this spot he lists the "Refutation of Psychological Idealism" as "the only addition" he has made. Even this, he says here, was only a new method of proof.

Here we are looking at the footnote to the "Preface" to the second edition. Kant has added the "Refutation of Idealism" to the body of the *Critique* and has made the changes in the spots we cited (and in others) on this specific theme. He has also made the change in the numbered arguments on space. Now he has written the new preface and with all that done, here he is, adding a footnote to—the preface of the new edition—indicating that he is still worrying over the same issue! He writes:

> The empirical consciousness of my existence . . . is determinable only through relation to something which, while bound up with my existence, is outside me. . . . For *outer sense is already in itself a relation of intuition to something actual outside me*, and the reality of *outer sense, in its distinctness from imagination*, rests simply on . . . its being inseparably bound up with inner experience as the condition of its possibility. . . . The determination, however, and therefore the inner experience, depends upon something permanent which is not in me, and consequently can be only something outside me, to which I must regard myself as standing in relation. The reality of outer sense is thus necessarily bound up with inner sense, that is I am just as certainly conscious that there are things outside me . . . as . . . that I myself exist as determined in time.
> (*Critique*, B 12; my italics)

Please note, in the above, that Kant has said that outer sense is a relation to something actual outside me, something that is not me. He has thought about what "outer" can mean, and finds its basic meaning as outside me, that is, not me. And Kant says that any determination of time involves something outer.

So we see Kant drastically emphasizing the dependence of time-determination on spatial and outer intuition. There is no *determined* inner sense without outer. "Determined" means "of something."

In time alone nothing can be constructed. Let us understand this.

We can bring it home to ourselves if we grasp that there is always only one intuitional given, not two. Space and time are not two realms of different givens. They are two manifolds, which means two multiplicities, two ways of variation. You can get one multiplicity in space by looking around you. You can get another multiplicity by holding to one spot in space, and getting successive givens there, in different times. But anything given is always both in space and in time. Otherwise there would always be two intuitional givens.

Therefore time does not have its own realm, as space does. There is only one realm, the outer one. Without it inner time is pure flow, not successive takes of any *this*.

For Kant an imaginary line is also outer intuition, even though the event occurs entirely in inner sense. An event that occurs only in inner sense is purely imaginary. We know, and Heidegger emphasized, that Kant gave time priority over space in this regard. All appearances occur in time—some of them are only imaginary, only inner. But we see that Kant emphasizes that these too require something outer.

Outer Existing Space, Outer Existing Time

We are inclined to want to call it "quasi-outer," or at least to put the word "outer" in quotation marks in the case of the right-hand section, which occurs only in inner sense. But he insists that even when we do what is called "imagining only," there has to be something outer intuitionally present, and existing.

For Kant the phrase "only in inner sense" could be meant in two different ways: if it means without outer determination, then nothing determinate can be there, it is not even inner ***experience***. It would be mere flow, chaos (*Critique*, B 291). But we can also mean that the outer is there, but merely imagined. Then, of course, there is outer determination, and in that case Kant insists that something existing affects me. But what is this outer existing in that instance?

In the second edition's "Deduction," paragraph 24, he writes:

> Inner sense contains the mere form of intuition, but without combination of the manifold in it, and therefore so far contains no *determinate* intuition, which is possible only through . . . the transcendental act of the imagination (synthetic influence of the understanding upon inner sense) which I have entitled the figurative synthesis. (*Critique*, B 154)

Please note that by "figurative" Kant means spatial, outer. He writes:

> Even time itself we cannot represent, save in so far as we attend in the *drawing* of a straight line (which has to serve as the outer figurative representation of time) merely to the act of synthesis whereby we successively determine inner sense. (*Critique*, B 154)

CHAPTER 12

Thus the understanding, under the title of a *transcendental synthesis of the imagination*, performs this act upon the passive subject whose faculty it is, and we are therefore justified in saying that inner sense is affected thereby.

Kant carefully distinguishes between our activity and our being passive, even in the same event.

Imagination, he says, is that hyphenated event, the understanding-determining-intuition. And in regard to intuition we are always passive.

The figurative synthesis involves something outer and active. Without the figurative synthesis there is no determinate something there, in inner sense. In relation to it, I must be passively determined.

As he said earlier, I can know this affecting only through being affected; therefore I know myself as an empirical existence only just as certainly, not more certainly, than any other empirical existence.

Heidegger calls it "self-affecting," but not Kant. Kant does not use that term. For Kant it cannot be a singleness affecting itself. Something outer is always given through my being passively affected, even if this outer, as an event, occurs in inner sense only. Even then inner sense can count as experience, that is to say as determined, only via outer and via being passive.

Now why is this so important? We can imagine Kant with the 856 pages of the first edition before him on the table. He must have tiredly thought: "I cannot revise it all. I have to limit myself to clarifying the main misunderstanding." And we see him, in almost every clarification he inserts, concerned with *this* theme. The importance of this seemingly very technical demotion of time lies in the misunderstanding Kant struggled to correct.

In many places other than those cited, Kant adds something in the second edition that relates to our theme there.

Why this emphasis on the outer as capable of giving rise to a priori knowledge, while time does so only via the outer? Why this fear that time will be considered as though it could be determined alone?

Let us now go to that "Refutation of Idealism," which the preface said was his "only addition, strictly so-called" (rather than mere revision). There he is again, emphasizing that "outer experience is really immediate, and . . . only by means of it is inner experience—not indeed the consciousness of my own existence, but the determination of it in time—possible" (*Critique*, B 276–77).

But here the vital import of this point becomes quite clear. He says: "Idealism assumed that the only immediate experience is inner experience, and that from it we can only infer outer things" (*Critique*, B 276). Certainly the representation "I am" . . . immediately includes in itself the existence of the subject; but it does not so include any *knowledge* of that subject, and therefore also no . . . experience of it. For this we require in addition to the thought of something existing also intuition, and in this case inner intuition, in respect of which, that is, of time, the subject must be determined. But in order to so determine it, outer objects are quite indispensable (see *Critique*, B 277).

Finally, in a footnote to this "Refutation" he discusses "the question . . . whether we have an inner sense only, but no outer sense, only an outer imagination. . . . For, should we merely be imagining an outer sense, the faculty of intuition, which is to be determined by the faculty of imagination, would itself be annulled" (*Critique*, B 276–77).

Of course, he says, "whether this or that supposed experience be imaginary must be ascertained from its special determinations" (*Critique*, B 279).

In either case Kant requires not only imagination to figuratively structure an outer, or quasi-outer, but always also a being affected passively by something we can know only in its results. Even if the imagination is what affects us, it does so as something existing apart from the "I" that can know.

Insofar as imagination is also what affects us, we are passive and cannot see its active working, any more than we can see any other thing doing the affecting. We have the result of being affected only. That is why Kant so often stresses that we cannot see the imagination at work. It is said to be "a blind . . . function of the soul . . . of which we are scarcely ever conscious" (*Critique*, A 78, B 103). "This schematism . . . is an art concealed in the depths of the human soul whose real modes of activity nature is hardly likely ever to allow us to discover, and to have open to our gaze" (*Critique*, A 141, B 180).

When something outside is imaginary, the duality is maintained; we cannot see that which affects us, even though it is our own psyche as an empirically existing thing. Kant says we will fall into idealism if we do not maintain within the subject also that distinction between being affected by an existing thing, and the determining of that being affected which we then see. There is always something existing when we see something spatial (even if it be the psyche) that immediately affects us. Intuition is immediate; being affected means nothing between. We know our psyche only through the determinate outer picturing which affects us. Only on those conditions can there be an inner sense of something, in time.

We are embedded, inwardly as well as outwardly, in something existing that we can only know through being affected. That division is also within the subject itself, not only between it and the world.

Idealism would result if it were not so, because we could then have determinate inner experience without outer. There would then be no need to have any existing thing, not even we ourselves as existing, affecting our intuition. Imagination would be enough, rather than being only the determining of what is basically an outer receptivity called intuition.

But why is the outer the immediate one? Kant says we are unable to perceive any determination of time save through change in outer relations (*Critique*, B 277–78).

What is spatially there is immediate, and only through its change, mediately, do we perceive time-relations. The extreme nonsubstantiality of time is brought home—it simply is not anything but an aspect of changing outer givens. Time must not be thought of as a kind of plane that exists, upon which determinations are made. Anything we can look at bears no time aspects on its face. Time relations are only between it and some other given which again has no time aspects of its own. Furthermore, we need a fixed spot, so that there can be change at that spot. Time is then the differences of this same. Inner sense is not by itself a location in which change can be.

Time is therefore an ordering grid that is perfectly ideal, pure form. It is not in itself anything at all. I generate it in the act of apprehending something external, something not me, and only then. Without something external we do not apprehend anything. As we saw in an earlier quotation, number requires something external to be apprehended. Without that it is only a concept of the understanding, as Kant says: "Number is therefore simply the unity of the synthesis of the manifold of a homogeneous intuition *in general*, a unity due to my generating time itself *in the apprehension of* the intuition" (*Critique*, A 142, B 182).

We generate time in apprehending, and must have something outward if there is to be apprehension. That is why arithmetic is not a science of time alone. It goes to the very nature of time.

II

Heidegger, in 1927–28, lauds the second edition: "Only in the Second Edition did Kant explicitly come upon this basic structure of time as pure self-affecting, and he made use of it in the central pieces of his Critique. . . . With it, Kant won the most radical understanding of time reached before or after him. To be sure, with Kant it is only first glimpses" (*Kant and the Problem of Metaphysics*, 151).

Since Heidegger writes that Kant used this insight "in the central pieces of his Critique," that certainly includes the "Second Deduction," which most people think he rejects. Just there is where the self-affecting seems to be explicitly stated.

In 1962 the later Heidegger moved toward a space-time unity, and Sherover has already remarked that Heidegger was moved by this closer to the second edition.[3] But we did not know until the publication of these lectures that Heidegger viewed the second edition as especially and explicitly moving more toward Heidegger's own analysis of time.

In his first Kant book, Heidegger blames the second edition because in it Kant makes the imagination a function of the understanding, and he also condemns that in these lectures.[4] But he did not tell us in the first Kant book that in other respects he found support, especially in the second edition, for his view on time.

However, there is a large difference between what Kant says and how Heidegger takes him.

There are two differences, and Heidegger seems aware only of one. Heidegger wants one stem-function, imagination, not two or three as Kant has. That issue alone seems not really very important, since Kant means his various faculties as functionings anyway—and as functioning with each other.

Taken superficially, therefore, the difference could seem minor. Heidegger's first Kant book leaves the impression that there is no basic reason Kant could not emphasize the unity of the functioning, rather than the difference in the elements he separates. Heidegger attributes the difference to "the traditional teaching of faculties of the soul . . . their division . . . into intuition and thought which begins . . . with . . . aesthesis and noesis" (*Kant and the Problem*, 280). This is to say that there is no internal reason why Kant maintains the distinction.

For Kant the imaged outer is always the being passively affected by something existing, even when it is an unknowable aspect of us. Otherwise what intuition is will be abolished. Intuition is the passive element, it is fundamentally geared to something other than we actively make, something outside, that is, spatial. Only this is "a faculty as intuition." Otherwise it will be imagination, Kant said—and that is just what Heidegger calls it.

For Heidegger we are "self-affecting." He downplays Kant's distinctions both between intuition and imagination, and between inner sense and time. Heidegger, at the end of the commentary section on the "Analytic," summarizes as though summarizing Kant: "A pure intuition was sought for . . . one that determines . . . what it intuits. And we found this universal pure intuition to be time" (*Kant and the Problem*, 162).

Heidegger has chosen to emphasize time as the form of all determined experience, including imaginary ones that occur only in inner sense, but he ignores Kant's insistence that these must also be outer both as figurative and as affectedness from something existing.

Of the line gotten by self-affecting, Heidegger writes: "The self is here purely affected by time.... Time is therefore original pure self-affecting" (*Kant and the Problem*, 151).

Of this view Heidegger says that Kant came upon the basic structure of time only in the second edition and calls it the "groundpiece of the Kantian view of time" and "the key to the core problem of the Critique" (*Kant and the Problem*, 152). To interpret Kant this way is to read him just as he feared to be read. To avoid this he made most of the few changes he did make in the second edition.

For Kant, if determined inner experience can ever walk away from outer, if we can interpret the imaginary line as inner only and immediate, then the basic meaning of intuition is eliminated. If self-affecting is made to mean the opposite of what Kant meant, if it means an independence of inner over outer, then indeed there is basically no intuition.

Heidegger quotes Kant (again it is a passage added in the second edition) and stops the quote too soon. Kant says: "The form of intuition . . . can be nothing but the mode in which the mind is affected through its own activity (namely through the positing of its representation), and so is affected by itself, in other words inner sense in respect of the form."

Heidegger concludes: "Here it is said clearly: time as pure intuition is pure . . . transcendental self-affection" (*Kant and the Problem*, 392–93).

But Kant had continued: "The subject . . . can be represented through it only as appearance, not as that subject would judge of itself if its intuition were self-activity only . . . in humans this consciousness demands inner perception of the manifold which is antecedently given . . . and . . . must, as nonspontaneous, be entitled sensibility . . . it intuits itself not as it would represent itself if immediately self-active, but as it is affected by itself, and therefore as it appears to itself, not as it is" (*Critique*, B 68–69).

Heidegger speaks as if Kant had said that there can be determined experience that is in time only. "Only external appearances are spatial . . . [whereas] all determinations of the *Gemüt* fall into time" (*Kant and the Problem*, 147–48). But for Kant there cannot be determined appearances in time only. As we saw, Kant is at great pains to show us why there can be no experience in time alone.

Heidegger corrects his view of time in 1962, in "Time and Being."[5] He speaks of space-time. He says that the derivation of space from time in section 70 of *Being and Time* is incorrect. While he does not go into it, this must have had major consequences within his work, and for much that is said about time.

TIME'S DEPENDENCE ON SPACE

For Kant, time, the successive form, cannot be determinate at all except as an aspect of how we apprehend something that affects us from a source which is utterly unknowable in its activity.

In his first Kant book, as here, Heidegger discusses Kant's view of our finitude, with which he says he agrees. We have no *intuitus originarus*, no faculty that gives itself existing things. But Kant ensures this finitude by the utter division between intuition as affectedness, and understanding as determinative only of such affectedness. In that book Heidegger does not explain how he reconciles this finitude with his own assertion that there is one self-giving root. The Marburg lectures make it clear: Heidegger does not accept finitude in Kant's sense. "This root, the original capacity . . . does not apply to . . . what exists, which would be *ontically creative*. The *exhibitio originaria* of the imagination is only ontologically creative, in that it freely pictures the universal time horizon" (*Kant and the Problem*, 417).

Up to this point I have followed the texts painstakingly. Please notice how close I have stayed to the quotations. Let me now go a little afield.

Kant said idealism will result if this inherent otherness of the subject's affecting is destroyed. Inner experience will be determinable without outer.

The idealism Kant feared does not result in Heidegger, because like Kant Heidegger views all this as constituting the possibility, into which then something other comes, with which an existing object is made. Heidegger has not omitted Kant's utterly other with which we are affected and together determine something. Heidegger has omitted the utterly other only within the subject, within our own being.

With Kant we know ourselves, albeit only as our being affected by an otherwise unknowable aspect of ourselves. What becomes of this internal empirical otherness in our own being?

When later German idealism lopped off the noumenal aspect, it lost not only the otherness of things but also our own nature. Heidegger, of course, restores the otherness of the things we live among. But the aspect of our own being which actively affects us was forgotten.

Heidegger's horizon in *Being and Time* is in effect a nothingness, which exists only in the constituting of other beings. When the later Heidegger expands this view, the context, Being, *Ereignis*, becomes far richer, but our own being that affects us remains forgotten.

Heidegger's humans are not themselves part of the nature they confront and live with. They stand over against everything else as a nothingness, an originative projecting. Nature is only in front of us, nothing is behind us, in us.

Technology is, for Heidegger, the problem of our age. It is seen as a problem of regaining our belongingness, our in-dwelling in nature. He searches for and calls for a rediscovery of our original embeddedness. The problem has not been overcome in his later work, nor has it been rightly seen. Time and temporalizing cannot be freestanding, nor basic **to** experiencing, rather only lifted out from it.[6]

Notes

1. Martin Heidegger, *Phanomenologische Interpretation von Kant's Kritik der reinen Vernunft, Gesamtausgabe*, vol. 25 of *Gesamtausgabe* (Frankfurt: Klostermann, 1917). All Heidegger quotations are from this text.

2. Immanuel Kant, *Kritik der reinen Vernunft*, ed. Raymund Schmit (Leipzig: Meiner, 1944); English translation as *Critique of Pure Reason*, trans. Norman Kemp Smith (New York: St. Martin's, 1965). Hereafter cited in text as *Critique*.

3. C. M. Sherover, *Heidegger, Kant, and Time* (Bloomington: Indiana University Press, 1971), 280.

4. Martin Heidegger, *Kant and the Problem of Metaphysics*, trans. J. S. Churchill (Bloomington: Indiana University Press, 1962), 144 and 226. Hereafter cited in text *Kant and the Problem*.

5. Martin Heidegger, "Zeit and Sein," in *Zur Sache des Denkens* (Tübingen: Niemeyer, 1969), 24; English translation: *Time and Being*, trans. J. Stambaugh (New York: Harper and Row, 1977), 28.

6. See my essay "Analysis" (1967), as well as "Experiential Phenomenology" and *"Befindlichkeit,"* chapters 3 and 11, respectively, in this volume. I am indebted to David Brent for sharing an unpublished manuscript, "Heidegger on Kant," dealing with Heidegger's reduction of intuition and thought to a single root, and to Robert Scharff for a long and helpful discussion of my first draft.

13

What Happens When Wittgenstein Asks "What Happens When . . . ?"

Wittgenstein insisted that rules cannot govern speech, because they are formulated only from the practice of speaking, and only by it. He also rejected observational reports as a basis for understanding language. It has long been an open question just where Wittgenstein is speaking from.

Before we can consider this question, we must be concerned with a prior problem: it is generally agreed that Wittgenstein rejected the usual assumptions of objectivism with its basis in external observation, as well as the intellectualism which finds its basis in rules, convention, or construction. But most discussions of Wittgenstein involve some of these assumptions nevertheless, not because his rejections are missed, but because no other discourse is available.

As David Pears says, "Most recent accounts of Wittgenstein . . . start from the assumption that there really ought to be a definite rule dictating the use of every word."[1] Others assume that statements must be based on observation. The account of Wittgenstein then consists in saving as much of these assumptions as one can. Or, if they cannot be saved at all, Wittgenstein appears as if he were concerned with what cannot be said, something "ineffable." It seems that one cannot avoid beginning with assumptions he rejected, then trying to account for their rejection, always still in a discourse that assumes them. But this is not due to any oversight of ours. It is Wittgenstein who has made discussions about his work difficult if not impossible. He said he could not say, only show. He was convinced that what he showed could not be talked *about*. We must examine his reasons, but this requires the very discourse which they make impossible.

The problem is not only ours; it was also a problem for Wittgenstein. He knew that he was usually misunderstood, but he did not think it possible to speak *about* the showing he was doing. To do so, one would have to present language as if it were an object that could be presented. To substitute such an artificial representation would be misleading, and would miss how words actually work—not as representations, nor based on representations.

CHAPTER 13

Wittgenstein does his showing by means of language, of course. What mode of language is employed in only showing? This question must be asked, but Wittgenstein did not think it could be answered. He thought that language could not turn to talk *about* this showing use of language. He thought that the attempt to say would lose the showing mode.

In the first part of this chapter I will propose a mode of discourse that does not assume what Wittgenstein denies. With the aid of this I will return to the question of Wittgenstein's standpoint. Perhaps we can then at least begin to say where he is speaking from.

So far it has become clear that we face a dilemma: if we talk *about* Wittgenstein's showing, we exceed the bounds he set for himself, but if we do not, then we cannot make sense of his position. How to navigate between these two pitfalls is the problem. Rather than pretending to solve it, I will traverse the problem in very small increments, pausing at each juncture to examine exactly what in Wittgenstein we may have violated.

At no point do I intend to exceed Wittgenstein in just the way that he prohibited, by substituting representations for the actual working of language. I think we can develop another way. It would be something that he does not do, but it might enable us to say what he does do.

1. Affirmative Uses

First I will stay within what Wittgenstein does. The violation will consist only in selecting certain of his phrases; we will still use them only as he did. Later I will mark where we exceed what he was willing to do with them.

It is often said that Wittgenstein dispelled mistakes but did not assert anything. This is not quite so. He said that he could *only show*, but let us notice: he did assert that he could show. We also find him constantly asking questions and answering them with examples that involve quite affirmative statements. Let me call your attention to some characteristic phrases with which Wittgenstein asks and answers himself.

For example, while he denies that a concept or common feature governs the different uses of a word, he also *affirms* that they share only a family resemblance. This is obviously a metaphor. Later we will ask how it differs from the metaphors against which he constantly warns.

In a great many instances in *Philosophical Investigations* Wittgenstein asks, "What happens when someone says . . . ?" (*Was geschieht?*) and "Ask yourself . . ." and "Let us look and see what [this] really consists in."[2] There are many variants of this question. Then he cites many possible happenings.

He says, also affirmatively, that what happens is "more intricate" (*verwickelter, PI* 182) than a single referent would be. The greater intricacy of what happens is *shown* by the long series of examples. Later we can try to say what they show, but Wittgenstein did not think one could do that.

For the moment our only violence has been to select and set out certain of his phrases: "only show," "family resemblance," the question "what happens?" with the examples, and "more intricate," all of which are affirmative or at least not negative.

2. Using His Words to Speak about His Use of Them

Now let us move a step further. We will need some words with which to speak about his use of these words. Rather than importing a discourse other than his own, I will use only Wittgenstein's affirmative words for the next phase, and only in his sense. But let us be conscious that we are moving further than he would, as soon as we employ the words *to speak about* how they are used.

Let us ask what happens when Wittgenstein asks the question: "What happens when . . . ?"

We exceed Wittgenstein by turning the phrase to ask about its own use, but let us not exceed him in how we answer. Let us answer it as he would, and by using only these phrases. What happens? Well, ask yourself, and look and see what [this happening] really consists in.

To do as he would ask, let me cite two of his passages. In the first, Wittgenstein denies (as he does so often) that a meaning is a single object that exists and can be referred to. Here he takes up a case when the existence of a single meaning-referent seems almost unavoidable. When we struggle to find the right words to express something, isn't that a meaning-referent? We assume that we have the meaning there, since we are trying to find the "right" expression. But Wittgenstein asks:

> What happens when we make an effort, say in writing a letter, to find the right expression for our thoughts? This phrase compares the process to one of translating or describing: The thoughts are already there . . . and we merely look for their expression. This picture is more or less appropriate in different cases.—But cannot all sorts of things happen here? I surrender to a mood and the expression comes. Or a picture occurs to me and I try to describe it. Or an English expression occurs to me and I try to hit on the corresponding German one. Or I make a gesture, and I ask myself: What words correspond to this gesture? And so on. (*PI* 335)

Consider a second passage: Wittgenstein is arguing that there *may* be, but need not be, an inner process when we say we "expect" someone or something.

> "I am expecting him" would mean "I should be surprised if he didn't come" and that will not be called the description of a state of mind. . . . But we also say "I am expecting him" when I am eagerly awaiting him. We could imagine a language in which different verbs were consistently used in these cases. (*PI* 577)
>
> When I sat down on this chair, of course I believed that it would bear me. I had no thought of its possible collapsing.
> But, "In spite of everything he did I held fast to the belief . . . [that he will come]." Here is thought, and perhaps a constant struggle to renew an attitude.
> I watch a slow match burning, in high excitement follow the progress of the burning and its approach to the explosive. . . . This is certainly a case of expecting. (*PI* 575–76)

If we employ only Wittgenstein's phrases, and do so only in his fashion, we can minimally *talk about* how these phrases are used. What "happens" when he asks this? We can say he tells *what happens* (or the sort of thing that *may* happen) and this *shows* what "happens" means. So it also shows what "shows" means, and what "more intricate" means. Later we may become able to use other words to say *what* these words mean, but now we are only showing it (and only showing what "showing" means).

When Wittgenstein asks what happens when we use these expressions, he is far from denying what most people call "subjective" events. He does not consider them subjective, but he constantly answers his question by speaking of them. He *shows* that *what may happen* is *more intricate* than one categorizable inner process.[3]

Wittgenstein is even more interested in cases when *no* inner events happen, although we seem to refer to one, for example when we say that we "remember," "read," "expect." He brings this home by contrasting cases in which no mental events happen with cases in which they do. Wittgenstein clearly says that mental events *do happen* in some cases, not in others.[4]

Can we call Wittgenstein's array of what may happen "examples"? What do they exemplify? What do they have in common? So far, let us say only that each group of happenings may happen when we use the same expression (for example, "expecting"), but these uses share only a *family resemblance*.

So far we have answered always again only with his own words. Before we go further, let me say why it seems wise to remain for a while just with Wittgenstein's own words. Suppose we try saying more about what happens, for example *where* it happens. We might say it happens in a situation. Wittgenstein does sometimes talk of the situation (for example, *PI* 337), but this is easily misunderstood as something observed from the outside. We would need to argue that "situation" must be understood in a certain way, Wittgenstein's way. If we say that the happening happens "in situations," how could we bring it about that the word "situation" would be used in Wittgenstein's way? We would have to cite his examples (some of which are externally observable and some of which are not). So it would not help us at this stage to say that this all happens "in a situation," since this use of "situation" would still require the examples. We would have to define "situation" by what happens when Wittgenstein answers the question "What happens when we . . ."

Since any other words we might import here would require this return to the examples of *what happens*, we might as well use the original phrase about itself. Since other words would depend on the examples of what happens, we would gain nothing by importing them. Let us remain for a while with "what happens" and use the phrase itself to say (as Wittgenstein does not) how this phrase gets its meaning. We answer: *"What happens?" means the sort of things that the examples show.*

3. What Happens in the Examples and What Happens Here with Them?

Let us go a half step further simply by recognizing that we have answered two questions at once, when we just said that the examples show what may happen. We pointed to the happenings which are shown *in* the examples, but in doing so we also used the phrase to say what happens *here*, namely that the phrase gets its meaning from the examples. The latter is *what happens when Wittgenstein asks*, "What happens when we say . . . ?"

Our phrase works in two ways: it *says* what happens when we say "I expect him," and this is the only use of it that Wittgenstein undertakes. But we have also turned the phrase to ask how the phrase itself is used and acquires its meaning in Wittgenstein's use of it. Indeed, we cannot help but do both at once. Both happen if we merely say that the meaning of "happens" depends on Wittgenstein's examples. This already tells both what happens when we expect, and what happens when Wittgenstein tells what happens when we expect. But cannot all sorts of things happen here? To do as Wittgenstein does, let us really look and see what may happen here. We are being asked to look for something. We are given examples. We grasp that "happens" is to be *understood in terms of the examples*. We may appreciate the examples, and perhaps find ourselves thinking of other examples like these. We may be puzzled by the examples, not grasping what is being exemplified. Or we may think that we have grasped what they show, only to be horribly disappointed because the next example *cannot fit what we had surmised*. We may be frustrated and give up trying to find a thread through this diffuse series. At times perhaps much else may happen as well.

One might object that what happens when we read the text is not the happenings cited in the text. They are different, but not different in kind, and not on different levels. Words about words depend on the ongoing practice just as much as all words do, including the words of a text about words. Our phrases such as "understood in terms of the examples" and "cannot fit what we had surmised" are not different in kind from "expecting," or "trying to find the right expression for our thoughts." To be sure, it is in a doubled way that we ask, "What happens when he asks 'what happens?'" but the phrase depends on what may happen when we use it, and we must look for this in the same way here too.

Although we are using only his words, our use of them in discussing them adds a dimension to Wittgenstein which he did not employ. But there is no single line between what he did and what we are adding. Rather, we are traversing a zone. We selected his affirmative uses, then we turned to use these so as to speak about his use of them. Just now we saw that his use involves both what happens in the examples, and what happens here as they give meaning to the phrase "what happens." Now we will go further, but without leaving him behind. By using his phrases as he did not do, we are saying what he did.

4. Elevating the Redundancy: It Is a New Mode of Saying

Since we cannot help but speak about both the happening in the examples, and the happening of the examples, let us consider it as a positive mode of *saying*.

Since "what happens" acquires its meaning (like every phrase) from *what happens* when we say it, we find that "what happens" *says* how it acquires its meaning. The phrase *can be about* how it is used. Then it *says* how it is used.

Similarly, in this context, his word "show" *says* the showing by which it shows what it means. It can be used to tell *about* this showing, without substituting a representation for it.

Although we seem only to have gone around the maypole, this turn is more than Wittgenstein allowed himself to do. Although this use of words adds no information, the words can *say* how they are used and meant. They enable us to speak *about* how they work. Before we go further, let us repeat this turn with another of his phrases: Wittgenstein could not have failed to notice that he used "family resemblance" as a metaphor. Since he constantly warns against metaphors but did not refrain from this one, we can infer that his usual objection does *not* apply. Wittgenstein says that a metaphor is misleading when it presents *a picture* of something that is not actually there when we examine what happens. But a "family resemblance" is precisely not a picture. When you look at the pictures in the family album, there is a resemblance across them, but there is no picture of the resemblance, and there could be no picture of it, since that would only be one more. This has been well understood. The absence of a picture prevents this metaphor from being misleading, but a mere absence is not enough here. The use of words is not determined simply by *not*-being-pictured. Let us try to use "family resemblance" in order to *speak about* what "family resemblance" *does* mean.

The attempt to use the phrase about its own use can reveal something striking: "family resemblance" is itself a case of family resemblance! There is *only a family resemblance* between Wittgenstein's use of this phrase and its usual use.

If we ask what "family resemblance" *means*, the answer can be told in terms of "family resemblance." The answer would be: "You have the answer already, right here: A new word-use by family resemblance comes about just as it is doing here in the new use of 'family resemblance.'"

What we have found may seem obvious and redundant. It may seem obvious because family resemblance applies to all word-uses, and redundant because we seem not to find out more about how it works when we apply it to itself. We seem unable to say how it works.

Or we can let "family resemblance" *say* how it works. We can answer: "Look, it says that. And, in addition, you also have what you are asking about. It is *happening* right here, so you are in the best position to look and see what happens."

Is this only redundant? And is it something that we cannot say? Or is it a way of *saying* how it works, and moreover a way which also brings its working?

The double duty of "what happens" and of "family resemblance" comes because we are using these phrases to speak about what happens when we use them. Can we permit ourselves to do that?

On the one hand, one might object that I am doing what Wittgenstein warned against, namely speaking *about* language (about his use of his words). On the other hand, isn't this just the task we set ourselves at the start? It was our purpose to find a way which Wittgenstein admittedly did not give us, namely a way to discuss his standpoint in a discourse that would not assume objectivism or intellectualism. If this is possible at all, would it not have to be a discourse Wittgenstein did not undertake, and yet one in which one could say what he did?

But I can offer an even better defense in favor of allowing his words to speak of their use: we can ask why Wittgenstein was so opposed to speaking *about* language. Then we can see if we are making the mistake he warned against. It was that the attempt would ignore the fact that words about language are themselves dependent on the very practice they pretend to explain. Representations of language ignore the obviously ongoing language in which the rendition is attempted. And not only that. What the words would seem to say *about* language would be false and misleading. The words would be about referents which do not exist, as Wittgenstein strove to show.

Now it is quite clear that this is not what we are doing. When we let a word or phrase speak *about* how it is being used just then, this is not the *aboutness* which Wittgenstein opposed. The words are not about nonexistent things that the grammar creates. Such a misimpression is precisely what we avoid by letting the word be about how it is used just then, about what is happening.

But even so, did not Wittgenstein warn against any way of letting words be *about*? No, he was not opposed to the grammar that enables them to be about something, to *refer to* something. He only pointed out that this grammatical power of words *sometimes* seems to create referents that do not exist. For example, one might speak of *the* family resemblance as if *it* were a thing. We might then think of it as determining when a word can be used. But this is precisely what we do *not* do when we let "family resemblance" say what happens in the very use of it. Then we can look and see that the family resemblance is not there in advance; the word *comes* and is used. Only afterwards can we notice a family resemblance. The use of words about their use protects us from the kind of "about" that Wittgenstein opposed.

What Wittgenstein warned against does not happen because the *about* (the referring) is taken up with the ongoing working of the words, rather than being about a presented referent. This protection holds even when the grammar *would* seem to create a nonexistent referent, for example when we speak of the family resemblance as "it."

5. So Used, a Word Also Says Something about Other Words

Another objection can lead us to a further step. Someone may see something tricky in using a phrase about itself. It may seem reminiscent of medieval second intentions and mystifying Cretan, Russelian, and Richardian paradoxes. So it will be better always *first* to emphasize that *all* words mean what happens in the situation in which we use them, and only then say that "what happens" is no exception. Similarly, we can first emphasize that according to Wittgenstein the different uses of *any* word share only a family resemblance; then we can point out without mystery that "family resemblance" is simply no exception to this.

If we are asked to define what "intricate" means, we need not immediately answer that "intricate" means precisely how its own meaning is more intricate than a definition or a single referent. Rather, let us first say that what may happen with *all* words is *more intricate* than definitions or seeming denotative referents. Then we can add without mystery that this is so also with "intricate." It has no denotative twisted object. Rather, it means *and says* the intricacy shown by Wittgenstein's examples.

Why did Wittgenstein not apply his approach to itself? It would *not* have been the sort of thing he opposed. But of course, it would not have supplied what people asked of him, an explanation in other words.

I think Wittgenstein went very far, indeed further than we can easily follow even after years of study. So it is not surprising that he left it at "only showing," without asking how words could possibly show without also saying. We have now pursued this question and found that in his use "not saying" meant not giving a substitute version. We can now rescue the word "saying" from saying only the kind of saying he opposed. Why insist that "saying" can only say the misleading substitution of nonexistent referents? That is not what "saying" usually says in ordinary language.

Let us permit "saying" to say what happens when we say something. What Wittgenstein rightly avoided is only one kind of saying. Now we can solve the problem about *only* showing. When words show, of course they also say. If words acquire their meaning by how they work, of course this will be so also with words about how words work. If used about themselves, they show and say how they work.

In a recent book, Schneider shows in great detail how Wittgenstein constantly denies that categories underlie anything. It is misleading to map a pattern from one situation to another. "Wittgenstein warns us against concluding that if the grammatical forms (for example the subject-predicate form) are the same, the relations of the content must be the same."[5]

What do Wittgenstein's examples have in common? What do they exemplify? We fail to find a generalization to encompass them. But since they are *examples*, it seems that they must have the category *intricacy* in common. It would be a mistake to assume that intricacy must be a class or category. Indeed, it would be just *the mistake which he is trying to correct by using this very word*. So the phrase "more intricate" (*verwickelter*) says at least that we are not wrong when we find no commonality across his examples.

"More intricate" says something more intricate than a common class. We can allow "intricacy" to *say* a *kind* of kind that does not reduce to categories.

6. All Words about the Use of Words Can Say How They Work

Now let us take a large step further, still within the zone of discussing Wittgenstein in his own way. Rather than being locked into Wittgenstein's few affirmative words and their showing and happening, we will now see that a great many words—the whole language—can become free for this kind of saying.

Isn't it contradictory when I speak of a *kind* of intricacy that is not a kind? It is very like a grouping by a resemblance that is not a picture. Indeed, it is the same grouping. Wittgenstein's examples do of course have in common that they are all what might happen when we use the given expression (for example, "expect").

We can say that these are *examples* of what "more intricate" means, if we allow the word to say how they *do* function, although they do *not* form a common concept or class. We can also say more about how they function. They are the *kind* of variety we *find*, when we look and see what happens. But we can give this explanation only by letting the word "find" say this kind of finding in which we *find* this *kind* of happening. We can say this because "kind" (and every word) comes with this kind of grouping which is not conceptually identifiable by some pattern that is always the same.

If we were to insist that *saying* is only possible in the usual conceptual categories, we would seem to have only denials. We do *not* find the referents of the grammar; we find a group of happenings that do *not* constitute a kind. Then it seems we *cannot say* what happens in the examples, nor what happens here with them.

Wittgenstein repeats the procedure with many expressions. Each time we *do* find this kind of array of examples of "what may happen." The examples do their *exemplifying* in this way; they form a group of happenings of *this kind* of kind. So his words and ours *say* how they are used. Can "say" be used to *say* this *kind* of "saying"? Indeed it can; it is the ordinary kind of saying.

Now the word "say" says this saying which may be different in each *situation*. We can say this, since "situation" now says what may happen, including *all sorts of things*, some of which are called "subjective" because they are not observable from outside. Wittgenstein considers them part of the *situation*, just as words are part of a situation. "We make an effort to find the right expression for our thoughts," for example *"in writing a letter."* Now we can *say* that it is from *situations* that Wittgenstein speaks.

Each further word we use in this way is retrieved from other uses because it acquires its meaning from what happens *when* it is *used* here. The word "used" says what happened with it *when* it was used just *now*. Now the word "now" means a *kind* of *"when"* that is neither just momentary nor just timeless. It is not momentary since it will mean its use whenever someone reads these lines. On the other hand, this "when" is not eternity, but rather only those moments. If we look to see, we find a more intricate variety of times, just as with anything else. What kind of *time* (and what kind of *kind*) is it, if we say that this "now" says the times when someone reads these words, which might happen for hundreds of years, but only then? So there are more intricate *time characteristics* than any scheme of time. Wittgenstein finds that most anything is more intricate than the few schemes we usually attribute to it. Can this intricacy be *said*? But the intricacy is precisely what *is* said.

If we look to see what happens ordinarily, we find that this more intricate saying is of course understandable. Although an expression may never have been used that way before, in that situation it says *precisely* what it says, and not something else. Ordinary saying has this more intricate type of *order* which is not in accord with a scheme, nor is it always the same. But now the word "order" says something about what happens when we use an expression in a situation. Although it is not a conceptually definable order, neither is it an unknowable Kantian thing in itself which we cannot find. It is rather what we do find. We recognize Wittgenstein's familiar examples, and can devise our own. It is the more intricate kind of *order* that we find in our situations with other people in the *world* in which we live. And "world" . . . we could go on and on in this way, using and retrieving one word after another from the schematic assumptions.

Once a few words say their use, the further words we use to speak about them can also be taken as saying something from and about their own use. *Instead of falsifying the use of words by saying something else about it, we let the words say (some aspect of) the use which is happening just then.* In this way all words about the use of words can say something that their ongoing use instances, not only the few Wittgensteinian words with which we began.

Imagine a language in which what words *say* about the meaning of words *could always be something their use also instances*. What characteristics would such a language need? Words about words would need to involve two uses, so that one *could* instance the other. For this to be possible, we would need a language in which what words *say* depends on how they are used, so that what words say about the meaning of words would involve two uses. We recognize our own language, of course. Our vocabulary about Wittgenstein and the use of words is now the whole language.

I do not argue that words about words must always say what they also do, just that they can. Although they certainly cannot say everything about their own use, they can always say something from it. To let them do that, we forgo for the moment their capacity to say something else, which they would *merely* be about.

It is not true that what Wittgenstein showed cannot be said. It seems so because it cannot be said as a substitution in a theoretical language. Of course it can be said, but only in the language he uses to show it, the same language in which we normally speak.

Wittgenstein stands beyond the reach of what is currently called "the postmodern dilemma," since he employed nothing that postmodernism has undermined. What he showed depends neither on clean distinctions, nor on the assumption of something present and given, which we can represent. Wittgenstein points beyond postmodernism if we can go further in his way.[6]

For example, Wittgenstein can speak intricately about what is commonly called the "self" or the "subject": "*If someone has a pain in his hand . . . one does not comfort the hand, but the sufferer: One looks into his face*" (*PI* 286).

In this mode Wittgenstein can speak about the intricate way in which what is usually called "the self" and "the body" are related, without setting up theoretical terms for how it is that the one we comfort is not in the hand, or how that one has (owns, observes, feels, lives in, lives with .....) the hand, and that we find (reach, communicate with .....) the person in the face. No existing theory approaches the intricacy of what Wittgenstein's simple statement *says*.

Of course, there is nothing ineffable or unspeakable about what he showed.

And, of course, he said what he showed. One can say more in many further ways (for example, with the words in my parentheses), but only by what I call "naked saying," without covering it with a theoretical version which then claims to be what we *really* said.[7] Such a substitutional explanation is the only saying that is made impossible by what Wittgenstein showed.

Notes

1. D. F. Pears, "Wittgenstein's Naturalism," *Monist* 78, no. 4 (1995): 413.
2. See, for instance, Ludwig Wittgenstein, *Philosophical Investigations* (Oxford: Blackwell, 2001), 578. Hereafter this work is cited as *PI*.
3. Wittgenstein is often read as if he denied the existence of our obvious so-called subjective or inner experiences, for example pains, images, moods, and feelings, as if philosophy should not concern itself with those. Of course, Wittgenstein did *not* deny those obvious happenings; he constantly appeals to them to show that they are more various and intricate than the simplistic packaged entity that is imputed by the grammar: "Grammar tells what kind of object anything is" (*PI* 373; this is his notion of "theology as grammar"). "Expectation is grammatically a state (of mind)" (*PI* 572). "What gives the impression that we want to deny anything?" (*PI* 305). "Why should I deny that there is an inner process?" (*PI* 306). "Are you not really a behaviourist in disguise? Aren't you at bottom really saying that everything except human behaviour is a fiction?"—"If I do speak of a fiction, then it is of a *grammatical* fiction" (*PI* 307, his italics). Instead of these fictions, Wittgenstein appeals to us to attend to what happens. He refers directly to moods, feelings, images, and other inner processes to show that they are "all sorts of things," rather than one mental process.
4. When does something happen, and when not? Wittgenstein rejects categories and does not define kinds of cases, but he constantly contrasts different cases. I will point to four kinds of cases. This goes beyond Wittgenstein, although I will use only contrasts he actually makes. My distinctions seem clean only as long as we don't look at other contrasts that can cut across them.

There are at least three different cases in which Wittgenstein denies that a word like "expecting" or "remembering" has *the single inner process or referent* that its grammar implies:

(a) Usually, when we sit down on a chair, there is no thought or event that could be called "expecting" at all. To say "we expected the chair to hold us" is *an artificial statement* which only philosophers or psychologists would make. It is not an ordinary use. Similarly, it is artificial to say that one "remembers" one's familiar desk every morning. Such statements are not used.

(b) But even *the ordinary use of such expressions* usually involves no separate mental process or happening either. For example, "I expect him" usually means only that I will be surprised if he does *not* come. Or, for example, I may have a low "opinion" of Mr. N.N. in my dealings with him, without having spent time having distinct thoughts and feeling about him. The phrase "my opinion" refers not to mental events, but to Mr. N.N. (*PI* 573).

(c) But in certain cases we are *reporting actual thoughts or happenings*, for example when we say "I couldn't concentrate because I expected him all day." In such cases Wittgenstein argues that "*all sorts of things may happen*" and be called "expecting," rather than a single process that is always the same one.

(c-1) These obvious distinctions become difficult because of a further distinction within (c). Wittgenstein argues that the ordinary use of a phrase need not *refer to* those mental happenings, *even when they do happen*. For example, even if I have spent time actually feeling and thinking about Mr. N.N., what I usually call "my opinion" may refer not to my inner events, but to him (*PI* 573).

(c-2) If some feelings, images, or thoughts actually happen, *and if I am also reporting them as such*, then the phrase refers to them.

In most situations "I expect him" will still mean only that I would be surprised if he didn't come. It may not matter that I think of the person every few minutes, if that is not what I am reporting. Only if I am reporting that fact, is it a case of c-2. For example, I am reporting this if I tell someone, "I can't keep my mind on my work today; I keep on thinking of his coming" (*PI* 585). Wittgenstein says that "*this* is called a description of my state of mind." Similarly, it is a case of c-2 if I tell about my experience of watching the fuse burning toward an explosive (*PI* 576). But even if this mental process did happen, my statement might not refer to it, for example if the explosion didn't go off and I say "We prepared it very carefully, so I *expected* it to explode." Then the word does not mean that I was following the fuse; *although I did*. It only tells my surprise that it didn't explode. Wittgenstein says that it depends on "what led up to these words" (*PI* 586).

Wittgenstein shows that what happens is not of one kind, but rather one of "all sorts of things." Being unable to concentrate is not the same process as watching a burning fuse, although both are mental processes which did happen, and both were being reported in that use of "expecting."

5. H. J. Schneider, *Phantasie und Kalkül* (Suhrkamp, Frankfurt 1992), chap. 4; see especially *partnership*: 320, 350–51.

6. The insights of postmodernism are vital but they are upside down. The concepts and distinctions were never what gave our speech its *order* and its capacity to make sense. Therefore the inevitable breakdown of concepts and distinctions cannot prevent us from *saying* what we want to say. Only the pretended universals have broken down. The experiential and situational *order of saying* is not revealed by the contradictions and breakdowns of concepts and distinctions, and does not need to be revealed by them.

7. Eugene T. Gendlin, "Thinking beyond Patterns: Body, Language and Situations," in *The Presence of Feeling in Thought*, ed. B. den Ouden and M. Moen (New York: Peter Lang, 1992), 25–151. See also Eugene T. Gendlin, "Crossing and Dipping: Some Terms for Approaching the Interface between Natural Understanding and Logical Formation," *Minds and Machines* 5, no. 4 (1995): 547–60. It need not follow that the theoretical substitution of logic and science is impossible, or that our logical-mathematical science does not change our lives, only that its achievements do not underlie or explain experience itself. Rather, they must always be limited and modified *within the greater intricacy* of what we may become able to say in ordinary language.

Part 4

Thinking with the Implicit

14

The Responsive Order: A New Empiricism

The purpose of this chapter is to establish a new empiricism, one that is not naive. It will incorporate the insights of postmodernism and move past the dead end where postmodernism seems to stop. It will be an empiricism that does not assume an order that could be represented, and yet this will not lead to arbitrariness. We assume neither objectivism nor constructivism. The results of empirical testing are not representations of reality, nor are they arbitrary. Our empiricism is not a counterrevolution against Thomas S. Kuhn and Paul Feyerabend, but it moves beyond them.

The key is what I call the "responsive order," but this involves a new use of the word "order." To develop this new use, we have to understand and employ the capacity of words to make new sense, a power of words that Wittgenstein showed so well. I will need to refer to Wittgenstein and others, as well as to philosophical works of mine.

We will generate a kind of term that can enter into relations between the logical scientific order and the responsive order. A list of its distinguishable characteristics will show that the empiricism of the responsive order is useful in specific ways.

We can pinpoint the roles of the empirical, although it is not something separable. The assumption that empiricism requires a separate given has led many philosophers and scientists to conclude that empiricism is inherently impossible.

Section 1 shows why the things we study are not the same in different approaches, but the empirical contribution is not derived from the top down, from "history and language." We can state detailed characteristics of the responsive order. We and our procedures and concepts are within it.

In section 2 we discuss how the patterns of science change over the years. The change is not a logical progression. We consider the claim and the denial that they increasingly explicate what "was" implicit. Our new kind of term employs the relation, which is not an equation, between implicit and explication.

In section 3 we examine relationships between two kinds of explication, the logical and a greater order.

CHAPTER 14

In section 4 we ask how our thinking process can employ these characteristics. We recall two strands of philosophy that help us to do this: dialectic and hermeneutic. We can employ more than one approach simultaneously without relativism.

Section 5 shows how human beings can be understood by moving back and forth between the logical and the responsive order.

Section 6 outlines some broad implications of the responsive order.

1. The Responsive Order

An anthropology student returned from two years in the bush studying a primitive society. Now he was reporting his observations in my cross-disciplinary seminar. The group was intent as he talked, then alive with questions. In response to one question he said: "Well, we all know from postmodernism that I cannot claim that what I say about this tribe is actually so, anyway. So I can really say anything I want about them." There was silence. It stopped the discussion.

The rejection of representational truth must lead us to a more intricate understanding, rather than arbitrariness.

I meet a Nobel Prize–winning physicist and am eager to show him my critique of Einstein's relativity theory.[1] We arrange a meeting and I arrive with a list of points which I hope he will corroborate, perhaps with more details and findings than I command. He nods and approves every point. "Yes." "Yes, indeed." "Yes, perfect!" I feel very happy but I want to draw him out a little more on one of these points, so I ask: "But is this really tenable?" He answers: "Today, in physics, you can say whatever you want."

Many physicists now say that science is invented and arbitrary, but this is not quite what they mean. They lack the terms to articulate the changed outlook.

I begin by exhibiting two conflicting points which must be thought together:

Exhibit 1A: Different approaches lead to different findings.

All scientific findings seem determined by one of various alternative approaches (values, questions, methods, theories, hypotheses). Even the ordinary objects of perception involve many cultural assumptions, distinctions, organizing principles, and political influences. With another set what we perceive and what we find in science would be different. Currently many philosophers say that "nature" is a cultural idea. The scientific universe seems to be a mere "construction." If you do not like your findings, just change your hypotheses. Science is said to be just a game.

Exhibit 1B: Certain events can be brought about only with measurements and a precise combination of factors.

Since we arrive by airplane at our conventions, let us not announce there that science is a mere construction. While in the air, we have been hoping that factors such as the weight, speed, and amount of fuel have been correctly calculated in relation to the curvature of the wing. While we are in the air, science is not just a game.

To keep both points and think them together can lead to an empiricism that is not naive. On the airplane we know that the empirical plays some role. Let us see if we can specify its role:

(1) Many events (e.g., flying) can be brought about only by certain carefully measured procedures. This shows that what responds is stubbornly empirical. Empirical findings do not come just from hypotheses alone.

We can see that empirical results are also more than the hypotheses because:

(2) Whatever we study (nature, reality, the world, events, experience, practice .....) often gives back not only the precision we already know, but surprising and more precise effects which could not possibly follow just from the theory and hypothesis we had at the start.

This makes it quite clear that there is no mere construction, no one-directional top-down determination by history, theory, or a "horizon" of assumptions. Although the empirical and the approach are not separable, the determination moves in both directions.

(3) On the other hand, whatever we study also responds to other theories and procedures, but with a different new precision.

Since it responds to various systems, it cannot be how one system renders it.

(4) Whatever we study is very orderly indeed, but this cannot be the kind of order that conceptual systems have, since it can respond precisely to mutually exclusive systems.

(5) Since the findings exceed the hypotheses, they have objectivity, but since they are responses to various procedures, they have a responsive objectivity.

Although what I have said so far is obvious, there has been no way to formulate what is empirical and objective in science, because in our new sense of the empirical, it is a response to what we do. Let us see if our formulations enable us to think further.

Implicit assumptions such as our interests and our methodology partly determine what we do. They limit the validity of this responsive kind of objectivity. But just how do they limit it? We cannot be satisfied with the answer that this is a matter of degree. The demanding accuracy of the empirical is not a matter of degree. We fail completely if we are even slightly inaccurate. We must examine the interface between our activities and the responsive objectivity more exactly.

In what sense do we interact with a continuing thing, a stable referent, and in what sense does the identity of the referent depend on how we study "it"?

The problem cannot be solved along the lines of the famous story of five blind men examining an elephant from different sides. They report different findings depending on what part of the elephant they touch. That is not much of a problem, because the story assumes an elephant. If the world (events, experience, let us put "....." to indicate the many quite different words that might be used here) consisted of distinct things like elephants, the problem would not be difficult. One could have many attitudes, theories, and findings about "the same thing," and eventually reconcile them when the thing becomes more wholly known. But, as Austin put it, things don't come in "handy denotative packages." The thing does not remain the same.

For example, in animal psychology the Skinnerians study pigeons in a box. If the pigeon behaves in a certain way, it may be rewarded by a food pellet, or punished by an electric shock. Skinnerians have found that punishment quickly suppresses a behavior to zero, but as soon as the punishment no longer comes, the behavior rises to three or four times its original frequency. The finding has established that punishment is an extremely counterproductive mode of education. This is only one of their great findings.

Ethologists study animals in the wild. They find that all animals behave in very complex ways which were never learned. For example, a pigeon raised in isolation up to a certain age can later build a nest without ever having observed or learned it. A great many such inherited behaviors now make it plain that living bodies come with complex behavior sequences "built in" (as ethologists call it).

So far the story of the elephant could still apply. Isn't it the same pigeon studied from different angles? No, it turns out it is not the same pigeon.

Ethologists study each species. They find inherited behavior more complex in the next species higher on the evolutionary scale. In contrast, the Skinnerians are not really studying pigeons. The object of their study is the conditioning of **any** animal. The Skinnerians study a stable referent that is common to most of the animal kingdom.

But although the object of study differs, can we not still ask: isn't the physical thing in the space within the feathers the same? No, that is not so, either. The Skinnerians buy their pigeons from factories that breed pigeons just for science. For many generations **these** pigeons have only sat in cages. Most of the behaviors found by ethologists have been bred out of them. Science changes what it studies. Each group interacts with a stable referent, but it is not the same pigeon.

For many years the chemical LSD was administered to research subjects in small, whitewashed hospital rooms. The experimenter observed through a peephole in the door. Every precaution was taken to avoid confounding the effects of the chemical with other factors. But "it" is not "the same" when taken along with music and company. The chemical is not one thing with its own set of traits, nor is the human body. The assistants in a research program on human infants are instructed not to emit emotional responses that could affect the infant. A student tells me that his supervisor stands behind him and firmly holds his head by the hair, so that it hurts whenever he unconsciously nods to the crying infant. But other investigators study the capacities of infants that **are** responded to. They say that mother and infant are a single system, and that is "the thing" they study. The infant is not a single thing with one set of traits.

(6) The responsive order responds with "stable" referents, but different ones to different approaches.

If we can accept the difficulties, we can specify more characteristics of the responsive order. Alternative approaches develop separate **webs** of precise findings. Precision develops within each web, but they are not consistent with each other. Conflicting webs develop at the advanced edge of science. We can wish they would also develop at other points, so that we would not have to acquiesce to one "agreed-upon" monolith of science, since we know that alternatives are possible at any point. Perhaps they exist but we have not heard of them because they are being ignored by the scientific community. Perhaps we can regularly invite more of them.

Quine rightly saw that the order of nature cannot be just one of these "webs."[2] Although they can be internally consistent, they cannot be reconciled. Even if they could be, we know **in advance** that more of them will soon form. Since we know it in advance, we can assert it in advance: Nature ..... can **respond** with surprising and precise detail, but differently to different approaches.

The responsive order provides a "reality" (.....) to check against. We can check each approach (procedure, performance, set of experiments, measurements) against the feedback of an equally precise "reality." But there is no way in which we could "check" so as to decide between **these** "realities."

When philosophers deny the checking, they mean the second-order checking. But we need to change the question. Why should we continue

CHAPTER 14

to assume that there ought to be only one consistent system? Let us rather ask how to operate with more than one.

We need to raise the quality of the current debate. One side defends the insight that the second-order checking is impossible. The other side defends the first-order checking and its superiority over unchecked assertions. Both sides understand this difference, but they wrongly assume that empiricism requires a checkable reality to adjudicate between the variety. They both assume that a denial of second-order checking destroys the objectivity of first-order checking. Both sides believe that without second-order checking the result is the kind of thing I reported in my stories at the start.

Since the responsive order includes the production of the systems and pictures, it cannot be a system like them. It cannot consist of mutually exclusive systems, nor can it be a picture of inconsistent pictures. We need to think of it as comprising not only the systems, but also the procedures and we who institute them. Then we do not have the trouble of the impossible picture of pictures.

People readily acknowledge that pictures vary with different approaches, but then they still want one picture. They look for criteria to decide which approach to use, because this seems to determine which picture will be considered the true one. If there are no such criteria, the result seems to be relativism—and still a relativism **of pictures**. The possibilities of action and change are greater than the possibilities of a single picture or system. But objectivity is not therefore lost. It can be found in the orderly and regular character of the processes in which pictures and systems are generated. With this "responsive" kind of objectivity there is no reason why all interactive events should be determinable by one system of measurement, one grid of comparisons, one picture.

From within the responsive order it is not odd that different actions make different changes and enable different measures and precisions. This does not mean that we construct the infant; or that infants have no nature, or that we don't engage a real infant, although it (.....) can become a stable referent in many ways (the infant unresponded to, the infant + mother, or some other regular referent) in response to our approaches.

(7) Whatever we do engages what we study so that its changes are objectively its own responses, but they are responses in and to activity.

Let us now examine the various things we do and the responses to it. We engage in active procedures with actual findings. And we also formulate theoretical concepts. Procedures and findings are not separable from the concepts that define them. But let me show that procedures and findings do have a specifiable kind of independence from the concepts, which has not been sufficiently remarked upon.

(8) Theories can contradict each other, but findings cannot.

For example, the Skinnerians despise ethology. Naturalistic observation is not science at all, they say. What does it predict and control? On their side, the ethologists pity the Skinnerians. What can one learn about an animal, if one keeps it in a box? The poor Skinnerians see almost nothing of an animal's behavior. But despite the most intense rejection, neither can wipe out the findings of the other. Their theories are mutually exclusive but their findings are not. When punishment stops, the punished behavior will rise to several times its original frequency. Nothing the ethologists have found can keep this from being the result. And if you present certain things to a natural pigeon, it will immediately go into a long sequence of complex behaviors which it has never observed or learned. No Skinnerian finding stops the bird from doing this.

Findings cannot contradict each other, even when contradictory theories led to them. It shows that a finding is not just the creature of a theory. Something empirical about findings makes it impossible to discard them.

(9) A procedure can be instituted even if we reject the concepts. Procedures cannot contradict each other either.

Procedures also have an independence from concepts in another way: they arise not only from logical inference. Crease points out that experiments have the character of "performances."[3] What enters into a performance is more than the script or score. It includes a whole background of intuitive practices. All sorts of trials and errors, hunches, and wildly derived ideas enter into the design of experiments. In a laboratory many improvised moves occur. One may employ procedures that lack theory for years, as well as theory that lacks procedures.

(10) Procedures follow directly from concepts only after many retroactive revisions of both. Even then it may be wise to reject the concepts, and devise new ones from the greater intricacy that is involved in doing any procedure.

We see that although concepts are implicitly involved in all our activity, they need not determine the activity. Although findings and procedures are not separable from concepts, they do not function only within the "horizon" of the concepts, nor do they function like concepts. They have empirical characteristics which make them independent of the concepts that seem to define them.

Let us therefore undertake **a reversal of the traditional philosophical procedure** according to which doing (interaction, experiencing, procedure, finding, practice, ordinary speech, experiment .....) is considered derivative from preexisting determinants, (theory, history, language, culture, cognitive systems, comparison, horizon of conditions .....). Our reversal is a **second** insight. It comes after the hard-won insight that observation and experience are **inseparable from** all sorts of social and theoretical assumptions. **After** that insight, one can recognize that interaction (.....) **always again exceeds and precedes** the supposed determinants. Here I must refer to a longer work concerning this reversal (see my *ECM*).

Later I will show how "pure" logical inference can be examined and set apart, within the wider responsive order in which interaction has priority over logical consistency.

Let us now ask about the converse: do theoretical concepts have any degree of independence from the procedures? Of course, the concepts are not separable from past procedures and findings, but at a given moment suppose we sit back and think, for example, about punishment and reward. This refers to all animal organisms. If we change to thinking about nesting behavior, we refer to just a few species. There is an objectivity involved each time, but it is **responsive** to our referring. Our mere thinking and relating—i.e., comparing—constellates (creates, differentiates, synthesizes, lifts out, **refers** to .....) different referents, but their objective responses are not deducible from the mere identity determination. If in addition to this identity we still assume a separate single set in nature, we assume someone (the ideal observer?) who compares them. Referents can be constituted and reconstituted by mere comparison, but when given identity, they respond objectively and empirically, not at all arbitrarily. To think that there is no single set of individuated and located referent things has been considered the worst degree of relativism, as if it must destroy the objectivity of the responses. We can reverse this. Comparing and identity are less fundamental than empirical events.

Another activity of ours is similar. When we "only" measure, we are not disturbed by the fact that we have **constructed** the measuring scale, because we obtain the thing's objective measure on the scale. The trees don't compare each other; we bring the comparing. Nevertheless, this tree is **objectively** and **precisely** so much higher than that one. The fact that it is a matter of **length** depends on the measure, but this tree's length depends on the tree. On any scale we find objective precision. But different measures **compare** a thing within a different set of other things. The scale of length sets up all things that can have length. If we measure its atomic radiation, we **refer** to a different assembly of things. The referent-assembly can vary not only in extension (part of a cell, the tree, the ecological system), but on many dimensions of comparison. The variety does not destroy the objectivity of the empirical responses.

(11) **The measure is constructed, but the precision has responsive objectivity.**

Comparison is not really possible because earlier interactions are involved in anything, even if we are only thinking just now. Measuring is not supposed to change anything, but it involves procedures that may have interactional effects.

(12) Some interactions make some "mere" measurements impossible.

This forces us to notice that there are two different kinds of responsive objectivity: mere comparing brings the objective (and precise) empirical response of what we compare. On the other hand, actual events or interactions are active changes; they are an entirely different kind of objective response. We understand each kind, but there is a pitfall when we need both at once. Then we may wrongly assume that comparing and referent-identity must come before actual events. But comparing and localizing are **disturbed by** interaction; they **are not** interaction. We need them to define interactions, but that does not reduce interaction to comparing and referring.

Before Newton motion was considered "relative," merely a change in a thing's relations to other things in our location system. Then Newton's water bucket at the end of a twisted rope showed that there is something utterly different and empirically independent when a thing moves. But Newton continued to think of motion as if it were the change in space and time relations. So he concluded that the space and time relations (which are really just passive comparisons) have to be considered objective as well. Location became "absolute," so that the comparing was no longer something sharply different from empirical effects. But this was a shortcut that did not deal with **just how** space-time relations are objective—differently from how movement and interaction are objective.

Newton's space and time relations led directly to Kant's "conditions of any appearance." Comparing was given primacy over empirical events. The comparing process then became independent as Hegel's "movement" of differences. The comparing was no longer static, but it still seemed to determine everything else. Einstein modified but did not alter the claim of comparing to overarch events. The transformation equations still maintain consistent localization across quantum interactions. Relativity theory limits the greater number of solutions one could write for quantum mechanics alone. Physics may be moving past those restrictions. Logic and analyticity would not be lost, but localization would no longer have a status equal to interaction.

If one assumes that localization and reference must be the consistent frame, then the fact that interactions upset localization seems to be a loss of objectivity. But in a responsive order this rather indicates that something more than mere comparison is happening. Perhaps objectivity would be better supported by the ways in which interactive effects can be independent of comparison and localization. In a responsive order there is no reason why a consistency of comparative relations between points should encompass all interactional changes.

Changed relations are not changes. Positions don't relate to each other. They are results of comparing, referring. They are relations imposed from outside upon passive, merely referred-to entities. An observer gives them relations to each other. Their samenesses and differences are not their own unless we first reduce them to those relations. The comparing has no effect on them, unless we think of "them" as mere comparisons. The patterns are not events, only arrangements we place before ourselves. Localization assumes individuated entities that are only "there," only referred to, only related by position. Actual happenings and interactions are supposed to come second, and to leave such a system consistent and undisturbed. Even if one such picture stays consistent, why should we think of changes, interactions, and events as mere changes of the picture?

Many people accept the fact that comparison and interaction are inseparable, but then they conclude that interaction is only comparison. The empirical roles I have been setting out show that if we give priority to interactions over comparisons, we can understand the specific objectivity of both. On the other hand, if comparison is given priority over interaction, then the empirical disappears and we lose the objectivity of both. We have established a number of respects in which more happens (interaction, the empirical .....) than can be derived from comparisons. We have seen enough to refrain from reducing interaction to comparison. We were able to specify some independent empirical roles of findings and procedures (interactions), as well as of stable referents and precision (comparing). Within a responsive order both have objectivity.

2. Explication and Carrying Forward

If logical consistency does not determine the responsive order, what remains the same? And is it not nonsense to assert that the order of nature ..... is not what our assertions assert?

Exhibit 2A: Putnam asks: "Is water necessarily H_2O?"[4] Was it H_2O before this was discovered?

Since science changes over time, truth cannot be correspondence. But:

Exhibit 2B: Nature does not change when a law is discovered.

Our procedures *do* change nature. And new laws are rarely just new concepts alone. They come from, and lead to procedures. New laws can formulate ways in which we can now change nature so as to undo some of our previous laws of nature.

Our powers to change nature are ever increasing. New procedures bring forth more varied "things," new responses from nature ...... Human beings **are** nature still developing, and we also **make** fabulous nature-changing processes. "H_2O" allows us to separate H and O in ways that may not have happened before. We also produce water from H and O which could not be done before. Now we consider all the water in the world **as if someone had made it** by combining H and O. I will return to this "made" character that scientific patterns bring to things. We must reformulate exhibit 2B. **In what sense** does nature stay the same?

Putnam assumes that our world obeys something he calls "the laws of nature." He takes them as "physical laws" that are independent of whether we know them or not. We can be with him in spirit, but his carefully differentiated discussion makes no distinction between "the laws" and what does not change in nature, **whatever that is** ...... I will soon discuss the reason why Putnam and current thinkers refuse such a distinction. I think it would bring him closer to the realism he wants, if he made the distinction. If he had a term for the "....." (the responsive order), he would not have to use "the laws" for both. The unchanging order is not the same kind as a set of laws.

Science is a process of **retrospective revision**. The concepts that were derived **last** are put first (or the modifications that new findings require are put first), so that the findings follow from them. At a given date most of science (or each web) is arranged with logical consistency from premises, but **there is no logical consistency across the changed assertions from year to year**.

What we study (.....) seems determined by the laws of science; its behavior seems to consist of the latest factors and patterns. But since they will be different in a few years, its behavior is not actually determined by the current scientific patterns or by those we will assert in the future. **So the things are not determined by the conceptual patterns!** Can we face this conclusion, and is there a way to think further?

The traditional move is to sidestep the question, to deny that we can even speak of anything empirical as if we have only the sequence of changing patterns. "Constructivism" reduces everything to comparisons. Sometimes they are spoken of as if they did the comparing themselves. "Difference" happens. Events are thought of as "differences" happening. I consider this a kind of idealism. Hegel said "the differences march." Interaction is reduced to comparisons.[5]

Constructivism negates but retains the assumptions of correspondence and representation since it assumes that if they don't hold, then we have nothing but the sequence of assertions. On the other hand, if we develop terms for a responsive order, we can relate the sequence to something empirical, and we can examine the sequence in a different way. Hegel said that everything true is retained in science when it advances. Kuhn has convinced many people that science does not advance; it simply changes. Promising work is thrown out when there is a shift in scientific style. Certain questions are no longer asked. The hypotheses change and so do the findings. But Kuhn does not say that there is never any relationship between the changing statements, or that any and all proposed changes would be equally (un)justifiable. But why need we assume either that everything true is retained, or that nothing is? Rather than these popular simplifications, we can notice that **various relations** sometimes obtain. We may be able to characterize them more exactly.

For example, in later years there are almost always **many more terms** than earlier. Sometimes one cannot even find "the same" field. Where before there were three terms, now there are twenty-three, none of which are the earlier three. This recognizable relationship is neither logical deduction nor just difference.[6]

Naive empiricists say that the later versions "**make explicit**" what "**was**" (is now said to have been) "**implicit**" before. "Constructivists" deny anything to which the versions relate. But we can use these terms more intricately:

(13) In relation to the future we can always speak of something that is now implicit. But explication is not an equation. It does not displace the implicit: it carries the implicit along with it. The explication carries the implicit forward.[7]

Explication has parts, factors, patterns; whereas what "was" implicit did not. When we say that what we now assert "was" already so before (H_2O, for example), we must recall Wittgenstein's battle against reading a formulated rule back behind the performance which precedes it. The retroactive "was" is not the linear "was." But it is not just a lie or no relation at all. I have developed the recognizable marks of the term "explication" in other works. It is one among many relations that may obtain. Note that it is both a relation between two versions, and their relation to what (......) they carry forward which is not separable but noticeable in the transition.

The retroactive "was" does not move back; it is a carrying forward. It can generate a new, more intricate scheme of time which includes linear and retroactive time (see *APM* IV-B). Other terms of this kind have been developed: Next we discuss: shall we accept more-than-logical terms?

So far I have tried to show that our assertions are related to something that functions empirically. A discourse about this is possible if we do not assume that representation is the only possible relation to something empirical, so that its denial must leave everything arbitrary.

3. The Logical Order Employed within the Responsive Order

The uniqueness and singleness of logical inference must be retained. The responsive order shows itself in many different roles. Of course there are many kinds of logic as well, and they all involve many kinds of assumptions as well as the implicit effort to hold the implicit aside, to make "pure" logical inference possible. The actual process of logical inference and its assumptions can be studied within the wider order. But we must recognize that logical inference is distinguishable from any other process. Postmodernism merges the two orders and loses them both. We need both. We lose ourselves if everything is reduced just to what can follow from premises. But to deny the possibility of logical inference leaves philosophy helpless, while logic changes the world.

On the other hand, the responsive order is "more orderly" than a logically patterned system. But can the word "order" be used in this way? Some philosophers might argue that what we call "carrying forward" is nothing more than a paradox—i.e., neither the same nor different—just the sort of thing postmodernists delight in. Others will argue that something more-than-logical is simply "ineffable." They all assume that language is conceptually structured. But Peirce, Dewey, Mead, Dilthey, Heidegger, and especially Wittgenstein were already one step beyond this problem.

Wittgenstein showed convincingly that it is the logical models which must be put in question. What happens in ordinary situations is more intricate (*verwickelter*) than the artificial models.[8] He showed that one can use the same word in many new situations which give it **immediate** new meanings. The use of words is not arbitrary, but it is not governed or limited by logical patterns. Ordinary language and situations are an intricacy.

(14) **We can say that the responsive order is an intricacy. Words and procedures have immediate effects when they occur in interactions**.

Logical patterns are implicit in all human life, but they carry forward, they do not limit like premises. The concept "carrying forward ....." includes the linear time pattern of "forward," but the pattern is exceeded by the sense it makes in use. **So the word says the relation to the responsive order which its use involves**. The "....." is another term of this kind. We can put a "....." after any assertion. (We need not always write it.) Thereby we take any assertion not as an equation but as a carrying forward. Anything we study is thereby formally opened to being carried forward in other ways. Then "it" may acquire different parts, perhaps more parts. We can think it as implicit, as an **unseparated multiplicity** ....., more than can be reduced to individuated units. It is more intricate than a pattern; it can function in **multischematic** relationships. These terms bring a "....." which does what they say. When words are used to characterize the responsive order, they say and instance how their logical structure is exceeded.[9]

Let me cite some relations between logic and the more-than-logical order. For example, computers cannot recognize metaphors. But metaphors do not lack order! We may understand a metaphor **exactly**, yet find ourselves at a loss to convey it in logical terms. The sense it makes is **more precise**. When it expresses something about one thing in terms of another, it **crosses** them in a way that makes more meaning than either had before. It is easy to state many similarities. We can also find many differences to say what the metaphor does not mean. But we cannot easily state the crossing which is the metaphor. We must let the experienced crossing continue to function as such. Logic and metaphor cannot replace each other. Ordinary language is metaphor-like, an immediate crossing of words and situation.[10]

(15) When factors (forms, distinctions) function implicitly, they cross in the situation (......). The result is not their lowest common denominator. The crossed multiplicity is more precise than any logical formulations.

Now we can say how an unseparated multiplicity has more order: it makes more meaning than its crossed factors stated separately. In the crossing each factor changes what the others are. If we think of the changes in science in this way, we could say that the factors of science are not actually working as themselves; they are changed by other crossing factors that we have not (yet) discovered. And those, in turn, by others. The result is more orderly than could follow from explicit factors.

The implicitly crossed multiplicity is always prior; it is an **"original crossing."** Crossing a horse with a donkey produces a mule. The horse and the donkey must exist as themselves first. Only then can they cross. But in the responsive order **the mule comes first**. Creating parents for it is one way to carry it forward.

Mules produce no offspring, whereas crossing implicitly enriches each factor so that more can come from each, than if it remained itself. So this analogy would be an unproductive mule, if it could function only logically. But here it precisions (and is precisioned by) saying that the factors are "already crossed." So it enabled us to say something that it does not contain: "the mules come first."

THE RESPONSIVE ORDER: A NEW EMPIRICISM

In such a use the concept "already crossed ....." says how its logical pattern of crossing is exceeded by the crossing it says. "Crossing" might give the misleading impression that we think of events as consisting just of factors, although crossed. But factors always **work-in** a situation (experience, procedure, interaction, event .....). The "....." brings this working-in, and enables us to think from it. Crossing is one way we can speak about the responsive order as more orderly than a logical order.

Understanding anything exactly is a crossing. For example, a new statement must cross implicitly with a great many other things we know. As long as we must think the explicit statement, it obstructs the smooth way in which everything else we know **implicitly governs** our next thought and practice.[11] Let us now examine this kind of thinking process, and see if it can help us to enter into the assumptions which "pure" logical inference implicitly holds to one side.

4. Dialectic and Hermeneutic

In the history of philosophy, did no one develop a way of thinking with concepts that exceed their logical form, to move back and forth between logic and a wider implicit order? McKeon has shown that one ever-contemporary variant of philosophy uses a continual breaking of logical patterns as its very method.[12] Two examples come to mind immediately: dialectic and hermeneutic. Let us understand them in our terms.

We might retain much from Hegel's dialectic although we reject the assumption that everything true is always saved when concepts change. This would be nicely self-instancing—we would not guarantee that we retain everything Hegel was right about. But he shows us a kind of truth that does not depend on static statements—a truth that **may** be saved when terms change. But Hegel gave his dialectic a permanent formulation. There can be no formulation of how formulations change in explication.

Currently what is used of dialectic is only the constant possibility of contradiction and paradox. The rejection of Hegel has made people unfamiliar with other types and powers of dialectic. For example, Plato's dialectic should be resurrected; his was different each time. But most people know only a Plato who proposed eternal forms. Yet Plato makes fun of this view in the *Parmenides*. The only permanent "form" Plato proposed was the "idea of the good," which is not a form, he said. It is whatever makes some assertions untenable. Although there may be a violent refusal to admit it, people cannot help but recognize when Socrates cites an instance in which their argument implies something they do not want to mean. Stanley Cavell, in "Must We Mean What We Say?" has pointed to this implicit level of statements—which Socrates could inquire into—that illuminates what we had to have meant, and how we may want to change it when we have pursued some of its implicit import.

Meno tells Socrates the famous puzzle of Gorgias: "It is impossible to inquire into anything, because either you know what you are inquiring into, then there is no inquiry. Or you do not know it, then how can you know what you are asking about?" Socrates soon shows that nothing is fully known, nor is anything utterly unknown. The smallest bit of knowledge implicitly contains more, if one pursues it (*Meno* 86b). Knowledge does not come in individuated units or referents that stay the same, or become just different. But in dialectic the role of the implicit is subtle. How can one find it, to be led further?

We find it when our argument becomes untenable, because then we are not left with nothing. We ask ourselves "What was it that led me to say what I said?" **The good sense we were trying to make is still there, only now it is a "....."** since we now reject our formulation. But the "....." can lead to a new statement. This is not easy because **the "....." is now further crossed** because we saw a consequence of our previous statement. All consequences are not already implicit. There is no Laplacian system. Now a great many less than perfect statements may come to us, statements that do not carry what is new ...... forward. We may reject those and prefer to remain with ...... We see **how** an implicit kind of truth functions in transitions between statements.

(16) What makes implicit sense ..... can be carried forward into language.

Then new patterns can be formed from it, but this is harder. We may fall into old ones. Plato showed that discourse is not arbitrary, although every argument can be made to contradict itself. With our concepts we can notice:

(17) Logic does not generate its own contradictions, but it can always be made to contradict itself if some detail from the implicit situation is added into any unit.

This is a precise relationship between logical inference and the more than logical order. In dialectic the role of the implicit is not always recognized. In the hermeneutic process one cannot miss it. Dilthey developed a general hermeneutic from its role in elucidating texts, books, paintings, buildings—what he called an "expression." He says that one begins without understanding the parts or the whole very well. Only the whole gives the parts their roles and meanings. But of course we arrive at an understanding of the whole only part by part. A better grasp of any part can change the sense of the whole. So it should be asked how hermeneutic can ever get started. The well-known "hermeneutic circle" is often the only way we come to understand something, but how do we do it?

The meaning of the parts is not fixed; they must grow in meaning. With our terms we can articulate this. A hermeneutic circle would be vicious and impossible if we could think only with distinctions, parts, units, factors, patterned facts, formed things. We could only combine the individuated units that we already understand. Many theorists still assume that we can understand another person only if we have the same experiences. What a dull world that would be! With our new terms we can say: when experiences function implicitly, they cross with every new event. Statements bring an implicit mesh which grows even if the statement remains the same.

We understand a difficult text better after reading it many times. A sentence which was a senseless jumble before now plainly says something. We may later reinterpret it many times, but the sentence is never again a jumble. It shows how earlier understandings continue implicitly. But they cross; they do not limit our further steps.

Hermeneutic is a way of thinking which does not need unchangeable parts or individuated units. The parts neither stay the same nor become different. But this is not a contradiction; it is the relation we have called "carrying forward." It cannot long seem strange—it is the most ubiquitous kind of transition we find in thinking. We only lacked the terms to talk about it, and to think deliberately with it.

Dilthey held that we never really have the same understanding as the author had. If we understand a work at all, we understand it **better** than its author did. We must create the author's process out of our own, thereby augmenting both. In our terms we can say that they **cross**: some of each becomes **implicit** in the other. The author's statements do not change, but **implicitly** they now contain our own experience as well. So they constitute a "better" understanding than the author's. In the crossing our own experiences are implicitly precisioned so that they can form the author's **exact** meaning. We might render a point in other words and examples, yet render it exactly. Conversely, someone might repeat the author's words, and go on to a total misunderstanding. This use of the word "exactly" functions like "truth" did for us. It is like grasping a metaphor:

(18) **Exact understanding does not reduce to combined or rearranged units**.

Dilthey's point is largely lost today. People follow Gadamer who says that we always understand another person **differently**, as if understanding had to be the same or different. Gadamer does not mean that we can only misunderstand, but to say what he wants to say requires the kind of terms we are developing.

Meaning is not composed of individuated entities; it is an **order-for** continuation, an order-for carrying forward. From our own exact understanding we can make further moves that the author could not have made from the given spot. And conversely, when we turn the page we find the author going on as we could not have done alone. And yet we can follow the author's next move from our understanding of the previous one. Understanding is not composed of unchanged parts that we have in advance. It is an **implicit crossing** in which the "parts" can always be further reprecisioned. Therefore a new and **exact** understanding can be made in different people, that is to say from different crossed multiplicities. Then the meaning is exact, but different further moves are possible from each. Similarly, if we make a point, others can go much further.

(19) When we carry an implicit sense forward into language, the more unique and odd it was, the more universally significant it may become.

With our terms and hermeneutic we can now lead beyond relativism:

(20) Anything once found remains implicit and participates in our further steps of thought, even if we discard the approach with which we found it.

Mutually exclusive approaches can function in a crossing; indeed, there is always a welter of historically transmitted forms in any human moment. We can retain anything we found with one of them, even if we explicitly discard the whole approach. We can carry the implicit sense ..... forward with another approach. It will not be the same; "it" will lose and also gain. From the new ..... we can formulate some of the differences, although we rarely have time to do it. No formulation covers both previous formulations, but our next step is informed by both (though not by all of Hegel's kind of truth, perhaps). We can implicitly retain much of what both theories help find (bring, differentiate, synthesize, make, lift out .....).

There would be relativism if there were nothing but forms and formed things.

They would cancel each other, or we would always have to choose one. But when they function implicitly they do not function as a determinative horizon. In crossing each comes to imply more than could ever follow from its explicit form. We reverse the traditional way of reading formulations back as the basis of experiencing. Instead, the formulations are only relative, but relative **to** the more precise experiential (practical, situational .....) feedback of the responsive order. Hermeneutic shows this especially well.

There are two strands of hermeneutic: the older one grants science its logical methods and proposes only to examine the larger social context of science and its uses. The newer strand considers science itself as hermeneutic. We share much with both strands. We have shown much that is hermeneutical in science itself, but we cannot attempt to reject the special character of logical inference. In the next sections let us enter the context of science, and examine some of the assumptions which it is its essential feature to ignore.

Hermeneutic places the logical order **within** the wider implicitly crossed order. Hermeneutic involves the kind of truth and the carrying forward kind of continuity that does not depend on a congruence of form. It shows how the same statement can have more or less meaning, and how "the same" meaning can lead to a sequence of statements. It shows how a point once understood remains implicit even if we discard its formulation. Hermeneutic provides a process of thinking which moves back and forth between the explicit and the implicit, without reducing them to each other. We can employ logically structured statements that remain fixed, and also think with implicit meanings.

5. Science within the Wider Order

Science does not include its context. One result of this is that when it has a satisfactory analysis, it finds no reason to pursue the existence of anything it has not found. Then it claims to know all the factors. The caterpillars are eating the food plants and the trees. In the lab a powerful insecticide kills caterpillars. In application it kills great numbers of them, but the next year they are much more numerous than before. Wasn't it "the same" chemical and "the same" caterpillars? It takes a while to discover the parasites of the caterpillars. Then we find that the insecticide is relatively more effective against the parasites than against the caterpillars. When the unexpected happens, the difference is investigated, the factors are altered and the claim to know all the factors is reissued. The rub is that there is no finite set of "all" factors.

But what if we could **separate** just the known patterns, if those could be physically taken away from any others that might cross? There is a way. Suppose we build the known patterns of one thing into another thing, something else which does not normally have those patterns? Now our known patterns are not connected to the crossed multiplicity of the new thing. There will still be both, but not the unknown factors that cross in the first thing. Those can no longer be discovered because they have been left behind, while we are putting the patterns into a second thing.

CHAPTER 14

We separate the gasoline from the rest of the oil, and put it alone into smelted, separated, and purified metal so that it acts only with air and sparks. Is this familiar? **We have just derived—the machine!**

In terms of "crossing" we can define a machine as a set of known patterns separated from the thing in which other factors could cross with them. Now we can notice that science renders everything as a machine!

I said this earlier when I pointed out that H_2O makes all water seem as if someone had composed it. A machine embodies a set of externally imposed relations. Science transforms crossed internal relations into external relations between separable units.

Computers are the perfect example—they are embodiments of pure logical inferences and scientific patterns, but in a physical medium in which they can no longer cross with other factors, as they would in the actual situation we are studying. Once transformed into computer patterns, nothing internally related to it can cross.

Actual events are interactions, never just patterns and factors. In practice the computer people encounter all sorts of unexpected results when they first run a program. Only by running it can one find out what will happen. Even supposedly pure patterns are a crossing. This does not mean that the postmodernists are right to deny logic as such. Computer programs cannot be devised without logic. But the processes actually happen within the crossed responsive order. As characteristic #10 implies, only empirical trials and retroactive revision make machines possible.

We can think with the wider responsive order, as well as with the patterns themselves. In no way can we denigrate them! They lead to the wonderful technology which enables billions more people to live, and many of them better than ever before. We only want to relate logic systematically to its wider context.

The concept of "crossing" leads to a type of research that is now missing. For example, the cells that secrete a certain chemical in the human body can be separated and placed **in a dish**. Now they secrete "the same" chemical cheaply and easily. The porcelain dish will not bring what might sometimes cross with this process when it happens in the whole human body. Currently it is customary to test for all **the differences of which one can think**. If none of those are found, it is announced that there is "no difference." This violates the well-known principle that one cannot "prove the null hypotheses." One could find no difference between any two different things if one does not use the right instruments. And we know that new instruments will soon be developed.

But how can one test for differences one cannot even think of? We need to study the production and effects of such chemicals in the body over a long time and under various circumstances. Then we might find what occasionally crosses into this process. It would not be expensive. Rather than opposing all innovations on principle, or rushing to market, this kind of research would continue long after a product is put on the market. Therefore it might not be supported by either of the currently opposed groups.

Scientists are very concerned people, but there is no easy bridge between their concern and their science. We need to establish not just some research, but a whole new field on the interface between humans and machines.

For example, there is very little research concerning computer-and-user **together**. The research which develops word-processing computers rarely studies computer-and-secretary. IBM has changed the keyboard three times, but the odd and rarely used marks are still in all the convenient positions. The finger has to avoid the little-used slash after every sentence to find the period. Has there been no cheap study of (say) thirty typists typing for two weeks with various keyboards? When I inquired at one company I was told that the designer's assistants (not even the secretaries!) try out the keyboards.

The airplanes fly ever faster, but consider the seats. There seems to have been no research on (say) thirty people of varying sizes trying to sleep in various positions, so that the sharp edges could be designed to make sleeping maximally possible.

Studies of machine and human together are not considered part of the technological process. They are relegated to the business side. Called "operational research," they are only cost-benefit studies conducted by a business that uses the equipment, to devise its own most efficient personnel arrangements with existing machines. Such studies are not used as feedback in the next design.

Following Turing, there is a famous question: "*If* you were totally satisfied that a computer behind a screen produced the same conversational responses as a human speaker, would there then still be a difference?" The argument is that humans differ from machines only "metaphysically" (not really) if the behavior is the same.

Now it must be pointed out that the usual discussion of the issue assumes this *If.* You are invited to assume it, and then struggle for the difference, but it was already assumed that there is no difference. If there is no difference, would there be a difference? Obviously this makes any difference problematic.

Another fallacy: artificial intelligence buffs argue that desire is "only metaphysical," since they can produce a machine that seems to want something and to go after it. So purposeful behavior seems possible without any purposeful wanting. But of course there is a purposeful wanting in the case of the machine. It is the wanting of the designers who watch anxiously to see whether it will do what they wanted. Is this fallacy an oversight? Or is it rather that **in** the logical order one cannot formulate wanting, purpose, or humans?

In a science-fiction story a computerized robot-man realizes its condition and what is planned for him. (When it can **realize**—whatever "realize" is—the robot-man becomes a "him.") In the story he escapes and is caught. He has the reader's sympathy throughout. The story might seem to corroborate Turing, since it assumes that a robot could perform as a human can. But really it shows the opposite. Rather than showing that humans are machines (except in some metaphysical sense), it shows that if a machine could do **this** ....., then the machine would **be** human. The "this ....." is (among much else) wanting, feeling, realizing, appreciating ...... It would not matter whether it is **metaphysically** human or not; if it can feel its condition and want something else, it is no longer a machine.

Why are animals treated as mere raw material? It is because wanting, feeling, realizing, appreciating ..... drop out. If we articulate how animals appear in science, i.e., as machines, we can notice how people are rendered—in the same way: as machines.

In the hospital your leg is strapped up high and suspended. The doctor uses amazing technology to treat your leg. Of course you are attached to your leg, but we don't study that. For days you lie on your back staring at the ceiling—nothing there, not even TV. In a recent revolutionary study the hypothesis was that patients would get well faster when given the right to make a cup of coffee whenever they wish.

Humans cannot appear within the science that underlies our social practices. Even the difference between living and nonliving processes cannot be formulated. Of course, there are large segments of our society with other views of human nature, and they may seem culturally dominant. They can obstruct and delay technological innovations, but they cannot interact or modify science in a rational discourse. The bridges are missing.[13] The scientific patterns drop the human out. But since nothing can currently modify them, what else can our social policies eventually enact?

It can be important to know that the actual policies of one's society assume that one is a machine. We are in fact in the position of that robot-man, except that we don't quite yet appreciate our condition!

Wittgenstein would say "We don't comfort computers when they have trouble. We comfort people and animals." The actual quotation is:

"If someone has a pain in his hand . . . one does not comfort the hand, but the sufferer: One looks into his face" (*PI* 286).

"The human body is the best picture of the soul" (*PI* II, iv).

Without substituting theoretical terms Wittgenstein can speak about the intricate way in which what is usually called "self" and "body" are related. We are developing ways to move back and forth between the natural and the logical order.[14]

In the current polarized debates, only one group appreciates the power of logic, while the other is alone in knowing its limits. We need a society-wide understanding of the uniqueness of logic, as well as the irreducible roles of humans making sense.

A discipline moving between the two orders could do what I have outlined, and of course much more that cannot even be envisioned now.[15]

Now let us ask: exactly why must the logical order drop us out, and how can we deal with this fact within the responsive order?

6. Interaction versus Logic and Perception

It is a huge misunderstanding of our current world to denigrate logic. And quite apart from that, why would one want to? Or why slight positional patterns; for example, the beautiful clarity with which three little boxes across and **then** three down lead to the same spot as **first** three down and then three across? The same spot. Here at least we can define **all** the factors that make something the same. (This is where "the same" lives.) A problem might go through many pages and programs, yet come to the same answer that someone else obtains in another way. We can come to a total clarity on why we both arrive at the same answer—the only answer. And think of the excitement when what I just said doesn't hold, when the pure forms themselves lead to many wild logical problems that seem inherently answerable and yet we find no answer!

With logical patterns we constellate a wonderful world. Positional patterns are inherently movable and can be reproduced on any other thing. With them we generate a space in which they can be freely moved regardless of what else might be there. Our familiar **empty**, geometric space is the space of the mobility of patterns. Everything else now seems to exist within **their** empty space. In that space we can separate factors and rearrange them. We create a patterned, stretched-out version of what happens in the more intricate order in which we live (*APM* VII).

So one mistake is to miss the unique character of the logical order. Another is to assume that it must supervene over other kinds. Still another is that its relations are equivalent to events, actions, or interactions.

Patterns are mere proportions, repeatable samenesses and differences. They are comparisons. That is why they require the observer—the comparer—who (as Kant put it) retains the one while turning to the other. Without this there are no likenesses or differences. They are results of comparing. Samenesses and differences are passive products. They do not do anything. They cannot exist alone or determine anything.

Why is nature only said to "obey" laws? Why would "nature (what we study .....) not be active? Does it not consist also of active interactions, including our activities? Nature seems only passive because we use logic to study it, and logic consists of positional relations, external relations. The action of projecting those patterns and transforming everything into them cannot **appear** within them. We cannot appear in the world **presented** by science because something is presented to someone; it is something that appears to someone. How does the idea even arise that we should be something presented, something that appears—to whom? We cannot be appearances to an observer who is in turn only an appearance presented to us. The presented world comes from perception.

Philosophy cannot begin with perception. It has long been traditional to consider perception as the beginning and model instance of all experience. What has been said here leads us to challenge this ancient assumption, and to replace it by giving bodily interaction priority over perception. It is perception which has led to the whole problematic of space, time, and appearance—the conditions of appearance which cannot appear in the appearance.

Perception creates two dualities. The percept as "an appearance" splits itself off from the reality which it only indicates. Secondly, the percept also divides itself from the perceiver to whom it appears. The to-whom cannot appear. Since the percept appears and the to-whom does not, the percept seems to come first. The to-whom seems to be something added on. Percepts are flat, passive, seen, imagined, presented. Their to-whom drops out. The assumption that a location system must overarch empirical events can be traced to the assumption that experience is perception.

With the percept comes the whole familiar problematic of interpretation (and Nietzsche's puzzle: there are only interpretations; nothing to interpret). This problematic will surely arise if one takes perception as the basic model of experience (events, situations .....).

The world presented by science is made along the lines of percepts. The perceived order is "already there." Human interpretations must be brought to it. It has only external relations, and even these must be lodged in observers. The relations are between points, locations, positions. The number 14 is defined by its position between 13 and 15 in the order of counting. But the continuity which defines the positions happens only if someone counts. The positions do not relate to each other of their own accord. Science presented **organized** entities whose relations are given to them by an external observer who maintains the continuity of their relations.

In philosophy this problematic has long been traditional and accepted, as if there is no way out. But this is so only because perception is assumed to be the basic kind of experience. We should not begin with perception. If we do not, then it does not seem strange that an interactional order is wider than positional logic. Perception and logic are inherently products that point beyond themselves. They point to interaction. We can build on the work of Wittgenstein and Heidegger: we do not first interpret things; we live and act in them. We inhale, cry, and feed. We are **always already within interactions** (situations, practice, action, performance .....).

Scientific procedures are interactions, not mere interpretations projected by a floating human community of speakers communicating about meaningless objects. People from a different community might not interpret a cloud chamber track as a particle, but it is unlikely that they would build cloud chambers there, and **only interpret** their observations differently.

Can we put interaction first? Wittgenstein and Heidegger give us leads in this direction. We can say that every living species **is** a being-in its world. Its living activity "discloses" possibilities of the responsive order, which cannot emerge in any other way.[16] But Wittgenstein and Heidegger spoke from interaction in the human world. If we take this into account, we may be able to use their way to put interaction first.

Let us first understand the human version of "interaction first," and then transpose it.

For example, Wittgenstein writes: "Why cannot my left hand give my right hand money?" (*PI* 268). Here we can distinguish between perception and interaction. Certainly we can **perceive** one hand putting money into the other, but this is not what "giving money" means. Wittgenstein is not speaking as an observer of external objects, but where does he stand? Where does giving money happen? Wittgenstein (in *PI*) speaks from within situations and interactions.

Am I right that perceptions occur only within interactions, or can one still argue that the interactions are based on prior perceptions and interpretations? "Giving money" might seem to depend on a culturally shared interpretation. And since we frequently misinterpret events and other people, someone might argue that the interactions depend on our shared interpretations. But interpretations of what? In an interaction, what would be the object that we perceive and variously interpret? No, we have already lived interactionally to generate the events and objects which we then interpret. Printed bills are not first simply there, awaiting cultural interpretation. I do very often misunderstand my wife, but this is possible only within our marriage interaction. It did not happen so much before we were married. Perception and interpretation must be considered secondary within already ongoing interactions.

Of course, the scientific interactions do not seem to happen directly in Wittgenstein's situations. It might still seem that interaction with each other differs utterly from interaction with nature. Money and cloud chambers are too far apart. It might seem that money comes to be in interaction with others who respond to us as we do to them, whereas cloud chambers are constructed out of meaningless objects. Then the human interaction drops out of "nature," as I have already said. But this gap arises only if we accept how a logical order renders animals—as objects who do not interpret, upon whom all connections and interpretations must be imposed. Within science humans are no more than this, as we saw, but even outside science the human interpreters are left floating in empty space. We must reunderstand animal bodies in order to understand our own body (*APM* VI).

Our own animal body still functions and still comes with intricate behavior. Its ethologically "built-in" behavior has been **elaborated** but not replaced by history and language. Its roles in language can be deliberately employed and carried forward. Our bodies do orient in abstract empty space, but this is a less original capacity than how they sense and imply their situations. We live immediately in our human situations. Most of the day we perform most actions directly from the body-sense of each situation. Our bodies experience (feel, are .....) our situations, and imply our next actions and words. The phrases come to us to say, and change, a situation before we need to think about it. And if they don't come, we have to pause and wait for them—to come.[17]

So we can conclude that philosophy cannot begin with perception anymore than with patterns. We are always already in a wider responsive order which includes us and our comparing, and more importantly responds to us as doers, and as humans saying metaphorical phrases in originally crossed situations. A new empiricism which honors both orders can enable us to move between them in many ways.

Notes

1. Eugene T. Gendlin and J. Lemke, "A Critique of Relativity and Localization," *Mathematical Modeling* 4 (1983): 61–72.

2. W. V. Quine, *Ontological Relativity and Other Essays* (New York: Columbia University Press, 1969).

3. R. P. Crease, *The Play of Nature* (Bloomington: Indiana University Press, 1993), 68–71.

4. See the series of articles in Hilary Putnam, *Realism with a Human Face* (Cambridge, Mass.: Harvard University Press, 1990), 54–131. For Aristotle the referent of "water" did not include ice and steam, which were different elements. But Aristotle's procedure of using heat to convert elements still works, of course. Putnam points out that ways have been found to reconstruct the older referent (for example, commonsense "water") from the later more numerous terms. This is also a characteristic of explication. One can look back in many interesting ways which are not available in the forward direction. For example, Hegelian dialectic had no trouble arranging past advances, but a great many attempts have shown that it is nearly useless in further study.

5. The idealism is not intended today. The "movement" of difference is meant to correct the earlier view that science and discourse have their source in us as subjective "agents." But difference is comparison.

6. But isn't this relation the opposite of Occam's and Kepler's long-standing rule that the explanation with the fewest terms is the truest and most elegant? The two relations can be distinguished: someone may want to resurrect an older theory, but no one wants to go back to all the simpler versions of 1970. We do not call them all "more elegant." These are only two of many different relations we find—although each is stated as if it were the only one.

We can specify other relations: A sub-sub-detail of the situational intricacy of procedures or findings can generate a new overarching category. A detail may define new generalizations that alter the whole theory which first led to finding that detail. This provides another traceable relationship between later and earlier versions. It also allows us to reopen everything at those junctures when we think about a new empirical detail. A detail may be logically deduced from a set of conceptual patterns. But when it is found empirically, "the same" detail may implicitly contain and lead to further detail which may be inconsistent with that very theory. This is another way we can notice that an empirical detail is not the same thing as one deduced from a theory, although the same proposition may seem to state both. A new formulation may arise through the linkage of a deduced detail which—when found empirically—first "confirms" the theory, and then turns out to contain more than can follow from the theory. Attention to the implicit intricacy of the empirical detail may help one form new concepts.

7. The term "carrying forward" has been derived in other places in my work. But it is characteristic of such terms that they are derived in use. Therefore they can be derived from any fresh use they acquire. Those who know the term find it indispensably coming in a whole range of different contexts in which there is a continuity other than logical deduction. No single conceptual pattern determines its many uses. Language (the use of words) is a responsive order. See my "Thinking beyond Patterns: Body, Language and Situations," in *The Presence of Feeling in Thought*, ed. B. den Ouden and M. Moen (New York: Peter Lang, 1992), 25–151.

8. Ludwig Wittgenstein *Philosophical Investigations* (Oxford: Blackwell,

2001), 182; hereafter cited as *PI*. See "What Happens When Wittgenstein Asks: 'What Happens When . . . ?'" (chapter 13 in this volume).

9. See Eugene T. Gendlin, "How Philosophy Cannot Appeal to Experience, and How It Can," in *Language beyond Postmodernism: Saying, Thinking and Experiencing in Gendlin's Philosophy*, ed. D. M. Levin (Evanston, Ill.: Northwestern University Press, 1997). See also *ECM* and "Crossing and Dipping."

10. See my "Crossing and Dipping," as well as my "Reply to Mark Johnson," in Levin, *Language beyond Postmodernism*, 168–75, 357–58.

11. See "crossing" and "restored implicit governing" in my "How Philosophy Cannot Appeal to Experience" and "Crossing and Dipping."

12. Richard P. McKeon, *Freedom and History and Other Essays* (Chicago: University of Chicago Press, 1990); and McKeon, *Thought, Action and Passion* (Chicago: University of Chicago Press, 1954).

13. Patrick Heelan has a promising approach. He develops a single two-sided term consisting of the scientific rendering one side, and its location in the human world on the other. See Patrick A. Heelan, *Space-Perception and the Philosophy of Science* (Berkeley: University of California Press, 1983).

14. Wittgenstein planned to publish his *Tractatus* and his *Philosophical Investigations* under the title *Philosophical Investigations Set against the Tractatus Logico-Philosophicus* (*Philosophische Untersuchungen der Logisch-philosophischen Abhandlung entgengengestellt*). What an elegant way to contrast the two orders by juxtaposing one work on each! This title is discussed in Michael Nedo's volume introducing the new publication of Wittgenstein's works in parallel German and English. See Nedo's introduction to *Ludwig Wittgenstein: Wiener Ausgabe / Vienna Edition*, vol. 1 (Vienna: Springer, 1993), 42.

15. For example, a discourse that employs both orders could provide a context for bioengineering. It could define the kinds of research which one can formulate only with both orders. It would also enable the various interests to be represented at an early stage. For example, billions of dollars were invested in bioengineering as soon as a few applications became probable, before anyone could know what they would really be. Those billions are now a force that makes the new technologies almost unstoppable, but everyone including the investors might have liked to know the issues in advance. On not knowing the uses in advance, see Joseph Rouse, *Knowledge and Power: Toward a Political Philosophy of Science* (Ithaca, N.Y.: Cornell University Press, 1987). A structured discourse would also give the scientists a voice in deciding what is done with their discoveries. For example, one biochemist in a drug company developed a chemical that has the effect of lengthening the time before a cancer spreads. He does not know by how much time. Of course, it is the product department that decides about uses. It decided that testing the drug in relation to cancer was too expensive. Since the drug also darkens the skin, it is now used in the company's suntan lotion. This example does not show that the government requires too many tests, nor that companies are selfish. The department decided rationally within the bounds of what it is empowered to consider. My point is that no *other* agency is appropriately empowered to bring up other considerations. Such an

agency could share the risk of more research and perform other functions, if the science/human interface becomes a special field that develops beyond the current polarization. Currently one side views the market as an extension of evolutionary selection. The other sees only profits for a few corporations. But no general position can cope with these issues. The circumstances differ each time. The Monsanto company's soybeans are engineered to resist only Monsanto's herbicides. In this case it seems easy to decide for whose benefit the market works, but more information along several parameters might change our minds. Cows engineered to give more milk have swollen udders and fall ill more often. In the United States the same amount of milk as before will be produced by fewer farms. Many will go out of business. But perhaps in India these cows might be a blessing. My point is that there is a whole field here which the wider order opens. Another issue: evolutionary selection benefited the given species. Is it wise in the long run to engineer new animals without considering their benefit? For example, a combination cowpig was created a few years ago. It was in constant pain. This "evolution" was not in the interest of the creature. The purpose was an all-lean pig for the market. The farm organizations stopped this development, to keep one company from patenting a "superior" animal and eliminating everyone else who now raises pigs. But the creature's own interest could not enter in. Of course, it cannot even be conceptualized in logical terms. But could an interface discipline add something to the market, to approach evolutionary selection? In a similar way, much that matters to us about human beings is not detectable because of the inherent character of our scientific terms. With the responsive order we neither disorganize those, nor reduce everything to them.

16. On my use of Heidegger's "being-in," see "Befindlichkeit," *Review of Existential Psychology and Psychiatry* 16, nos. 1–3 (1978–79): 43–71. (This is now chapter 11 in this book.)

17. See my "The Primacy of the Body, Not the Primacy of Perception," *Man and World* 25, nos. 3–4 (1992): 341–53, and "A Philosophical Critique of the Concept of Narcissism," in *Pathologies of the Modern Self*, ed. D. M. Levin (New York: New York University Press, 1987), 251–304. For the psychological and social applications of this philosophy, see my *Focusing*, 2nd ed. (New York: Bantam, 1981), and www.focusing.org.

15

Introduction to *Thinking at the Edge*

(with Mary Hendricks)

Thinking at the Edge (in German, *Wo Worte noch Fehlen*), or TAE, is a systematic way to articulate in new terms something which needs to be said but is at first only an inchoate "bodily sense." We now teach this in a bi-yearly four-day course and are ready to distribute the steps in print and in a video production.

TAE stems from my course called "Theory Construction" which I taught for many years at the University of Chicago. Students came to it from many fields. The course consisted half of philosophy and logic, and half of the difficult task of getting students to attend to what they implicitly knew but could not say and never considered trying to say. It took weeks to explain that the usual criteria were reversed in my course. Whereas everywhere else in the university only what was clear counted at all, here we cared only about what was as yet unclear. If it was clear I said "We don't need you for this; we have it in the library already." Our students were not used to the process we call *Focusing*, spending time with an observation or impression which is directly and physically sensed, but unclear. All educated people "know" such things in their field of study. Sometimes such a thing can feel deeply important, but typically people assume that it "makes no sense" and cannot be said or thought into.

"Oh," one student exclaimed when he grasped what I was looking for, "you mean something about which we have to do hemming and hawing." Yes, that was just what I meant. Another asked: "Do you mean that crawly thing?"

How it is possible that something new and valuable can be implicit in a felt sense?

Of course, I know that it is a very questionable project to think from what is unclear and only a bodily sense. A rational person, and especially a phi-

282

losopher, will immediately wonder: why should such a sense be more than mere confusion? And if there were something valuable in it (say an organismic experiencing of something important in one's field), how would speech come from it? And if it sometimes can, how would one know whether what is said comes from it, rather than from reading something into it? Should one just believe whatever one said from such an unclarity, or would some statements be preferable to others?

These questions do not have single answers. They require entering a whole field of considerations. They require certain philosophical strategies about which I have written at length.

Since summaries of this kind of philosophical work are not possible, I can only refer to the works that lie behind what I will say here.

An internally intricate sense leads to a series of statements with certain recognizable characteristics. Statements that ***speak from*** the felt sense can be recognized by the fact that they have an effect on the felt sense. It moves, opens, and develops. The relation between sensing and statements is not identity, representation, or description. An implicitly intricate bodily sense is ***never*** the same thing as a statement. There are many possible relationships between the body and statements, and we have developed some precise ways to employ these relationships.

Every topic and situation is more intricate than the existing concepts. ***Every living organism is a bodily interaction with an intricate situation and with the universe.*** When a human being who is experienced in some field senses something, there is always something. It could turn out to be quite different than it seemed at first, but it cannot be nothing.

Here I would like to give an example: suppose you are about to fly to another city in a small plane, and your experienced pilot says "I can't explain it. The weather people say all clear, but the look of it gives me some odd sense of doubt . . ." In such a case you would not tell the pilot to ignore this sense just because it is not clear. I have stacked this example. Of course, an ***experienced*** pilot's unclarity has already taken account of all the clear knowledge that the profession uses, so that what is unclear is something more. We need not be certain that this "sense" is in fact due to the weather; it is enough that it may be. You decide to stay safely at home. But if the weather does become dangerous, then it is important to all of us to find out what it was that the pilot sensed, which escaped the weather people. The federal aviation people and the whole society would want that pilot to articulate just what was in the look of the weather which the unclear sense picked up. Adding this to the knowledge of the Weather Service would make us all safer when we are in the air. And so it is also with any person who is experienced in any field. But such a sense will seem to be beyond words.

We are all imbued with the classical Western unit model. We can hardly think in any other way. What we call "thinking" seems to require unitized things which are assumed to be either cleanly identical or cleanly separate, which can be next to each other but cannot interpenetrate, let alone have some more complex pattern. If, for example, there are two things which also seem to be one in some intricate way, rather than try to lay out this intricate pattern in detail, thinking tends to stop right there. We consider the sense of such a thing as if it were a private trouble. It seems that something must be wrong with us because "it doesn't make sense." And yet we keep on having this stubborn sense which does not fit in with what is already articulated in our field. It probably stems from a genuine observation which does not fit the unit model.

How it is possible for the same old words in the dictionary to say something?

The unit model is regularly the reason why some new insights cannot be said. But to reject the unit model in general is not possible, because it inheres in our language, our machines, and in all our detailed concepts. We fall back into it the moment we want to speak further. The new insight cannot be said in terms of the old concepts and phrases. In class I used Heidegger, McKeon, and my own philosophy, three critiques of the unit model, but as it turns out, the capacity for breaking out of the unit model cannot be imparted in this way. Critique does not prevent us from falling into the old model. Some say that it will take 300 years for the assumptions that inhere in our language to change. To a philosopher it seems unlikely that people can think beyond the pervasive assumptions. Therefore TAE can seem improbable.

On the other hand, Wittgenstein showed that the capacity of language far exceeds the conceptual patterns that inhere in it. He demonstrated convincingly that what words can say is quite beyond the control of any concept, preexisting rule, or theory of language. He could give some twenty or more examples of new meanings that one word could acquire through different uses. Building on this, we have developed in TAE a new use of language that can be shown to most anyone who senses something that cannot yet be said. This new way of speaking is the key to this seemingly impossible venture.

In my philosophy I have developed a new use of bodily-sourced language with which we can speak directly from the body about many things—especially about the body and language.

INTRODUCTION TO *THINKING AT THE EDGE*

Language is deeply rooted in the human body in a way that is not commonly understood. Language does not consist just of the words. The situations in which we find ourselves, the body, and the language form a single system together. Language is implicit in the human process of living. The words we need to say arrive directly from the body. I have a bodily sense of what I am about to say. If I lose hold of that, I can't say it. If I have the sense of what I want to say, then all I do is open my mouth and rely on the words that will come. Language is deeply rooted in the way we physically exist in our interactive situations.

The common situations in a culture each have their appropriate phrases, a cluster of possible sayings that one might need. The words mean the effect they have when they are used in a situation. Our language and the common situations constitute a single system together. However, this bodily link between words and situations applies no less when the situation is uncommon and what needs to be said has no established words and phrases.

All living bodies create and imply their own next steps. That is what living is, the creating of next steps. The body knows to exhale after inhaling, and to search for food when hungry. And in a new situation, new next steps come from the body. Even an ant on a fuzzy rug crawls in an odd way in which it has never crawled before. When we sense something that doesn't fit the common repertory and nevertheless wants to be said, the body is implying new actions and new phrases.

TAE empowers people to think and speak.

We find that when people forgo the usual big vague words and common phrases, then—from their bodily sense—quite fresh, colorful, new phrases come. These phrases form in such a way that they say what is new from the bodily sense. There is no way to say "all" of it, no sentence that will be simply equal, no sentence which will simply "represent" what is sensed. But what can happen is better than a perfect copy. One strand emerges from the bodily sense, and then another and another. What needs to be said expands! What we say doesn't represent the bodily sense. Rather it carries the body forward.

First it must be recognized that no *established* word or phrase will ever be able to say what needs to be said. The person can be freed from trying to "translate" the felt sense into regular sayings. Yet what a person wanted a word to mean can be expressed, but only in one or more whole sentences that use words in a fresh and creative way. In certain kinds of sentences a word can go beyond its usual meaning, so that it speaks from the felt sense. When one has tried several words and found that each of them fails to say what needs to be said, fresh sentences can say what one wished the word to mean. Now it turns out that each of the rejected words gives rise to very different fresh sentences. Each pulls out something different from the felt sense. In this way, with some further developments, what was one single fuzzy sense can engender six or seven **terms**. These terms bring their own interrelations, usually a quite new patterning. This constitutes a whole new territory where previously there was only a single implicit meaning. One can move in the field created by these terms. Now one can enter further into the experiential sense of each strand and generate even more precise terms. People find that never again are they just unable to speak from this felt sense.

Up to this point TAE enables fresh language to emerge. The last five steps concern logic, a very different power. But there is also an inherent connection between a felt sense and how we make logic. (See *APM* VII-A, VII-B-a, VIII.)

The new terms and their patterning can be given logical relations in a series of theoretical propositions. Now it becomes possible to substitute logically linked terms for each other. Thereby many new sentences (some surprising and powerful) can be derived. Expanding this can constitute a theory, a logically interlocked cluster of terms.

At every point in the process, we can see that explicating a felt sense is not at all arbitrary. Although it involves creating new terms rather than merely copying or representing what is already given, its implicit meanings are very precise. The various relations between sensing and speaking have not been well studied until now, because only representation was looked for. By using these very relations between sensing and speaking in order to study them, I have initiated this field of study and developed it in some depth. Here I only want to say that once one experiences this "speaking-from," the way it carries the body forward becomes utterly recognizable. Then, although one might be able to say many things and make many new distinctions, one prefers being stuck and silent until phrases come that do carry the felt sense forward.

TAE was envisioned and created by Mary Hendricks. The idea of making it into an available practice seemed impossible to me.

TAE requires a familiarity with Focusing. The participants in our first TAE were experienced Focusing people. This took care of the most difficult part of my university course. Nevertheless I expected it to fail, and I certainly experienced that it did fail. Some people did not even get as far as using logic, and most created no theory. Yet there was great satisfaction and even excitement. A great thing seemed to have happened, so I was grateful that I was saved any embarrassment. For some reason they did not feel cheated.

Later I understood. During the ensuing year many people wrote to us. They reported that they found themselves able to speak from what they could not say before, and that they were now talking about it all the time. And some of them also explained another excitement. Some individuals had discovered that they could think! What "thinking" had previously meant to many of them involved putting oneself aside and rearranging remembered concepts. For some the fact that they could create and derive ideas was the fulfillment of a need which they had despaired of long ago.

Now after five American and four German TAE meetings I am very aware of the deep political significance of all this. People, especially intellectuals, believe that they cannot think! They are trained to say what fits into a preexisting public discourse. They remain numb about what could arise from themselves in response to the literature and the world. People live through a great deal which cannot be said. They are forced to remain inarticulate about it because it cannot be said in the common phrases. People are silenced! TAE can empower them to speak from what they are living through.

People can be empowered to think and speak. We have come to recognize that, along with Focusing, TAE is a practice for people generally. They do not all need to build a theory with formal, logically linked terms. Thinking and articulating is a socially vital practice. In ancient times philosophy always included practices, and now philosophy does so again. One need not necessarily grasp all of the philosophy from which the practices have come. Nevertheless, I have accepted the fact that without the philosophical work no description of TAE can be adequate.

I need to make clear that with TAE we are not saying that thinking or any other serious human activity can be reduced to standard steps of a fixed method. When people said they discovered that they could think, they certainly did not mean these little steps which I myself couldn't remember exactly, at first. The steps help break what I might call the "public language barrier" so that the source of one's own thinking is found and spoken from. After that nobody needs steps. Precise steps are always for precise teaching so a new way can be shown and found. Then it soon becomes utterly various.

Steps 4 and 5 of TAE reveal a more-than-logical creativity inherent in the nature of language, which has remained largely unrecognized until now. Language is not the deadly trap it is often said to be. Language is often blamed when something exciting becomes limited and lifeless. Philosophers of many sorts hold that anything will fall into old categories

CHAPTER 15

by being said. This might be true when one uses only common phrases, but in the case of fresh phrasing it is quite false. *New phrasing is possible because language is always implicit in human experiencing and deeply inherent in what experiencing is. Far from reducing and limiting what one implicitly lives and wants to say, a fresh statement is physically a further development of what one senses and means to say.* Then, to write down and read back what is said can engender still further living. What one physically senses in one's situation is not some fixed, already determined entity, but a further implying that expands and develops in response to what is said. Rather than "falling into" the constraints of the said, we find that the effects of the said can open ways of living and saying still further.

Many current philosophers deny that the individual can think anything that does not come from the culture, from the group, from interaction. This view is an overreaction to a previous philosophy which treated the individual as the universal source. But both views are simplifications. Culture and individuality constitute an intricate cluster. Each exceeds the other in certain respects.

We have a language brain and we live in interactional situations. But language is not an imposition upon a blank. Even plants are quite complex, and animals live complex lives with each other without language. When the living body becomes able to carry itself forward by symbolizing itself, it acts and speaks from a vast intricacy. Of course, we get the language from culture and interaction. But we have seen that language is not just a store of fixed common meanings. Humans don't happen without culture and language, but with and after language the body's next steps are always freshly here again, and are always implicitly more intricate than the common routines. You can instantly check this by becoming aware of your bodily aliveness, freshly there and implicitly much more intricate than the words you are reading.

From the start I had the students in my class meet in listening partnerships during the week. They divided two hours, taking turns purely listening. "Just listen. Only say when you don't follow," I instructed them. "If your partner is working on a paper, don't tell about how *you* would write the paper . . ." They always laughed because they knew the problem. Nobody is ever willing to keep us company where we are stuck with our unfinished paper, so that we can think our way through. But in a Focusing partnership we do just that. We attend entirely just to one person at a time. This mutually sustaining pattern was always a main reason why students praised the course.

TAE has a *social* purpose. We build our inter-human world further. It is not true that merely developing as individuals will somehow change the patterns in which we must live. We need to build new social patterns and new patterns of thought and science. This will be a mutual product no single person can create. On the other hand, if we work jointly too soon, we lose what can only come through the individual in a focusing type of process. Nobody else lives the world from your angle. No other organism can sense exactly "the more" that you sense. In TAE for the first three days, one is constantly warned to "protect" one's as yet inchoate sense. We interrupt anyone who says "mine is like yours," or "yours made me think of . . ." or any sentence that begins with "We . . ." *We* may have uttered the very same sentence, but the intricacy that is implicit for you turns out to be utterly different from mine. These two intricacies are much more significant than what would come from this spot, if we articulate it together. There is an interplay which happens too soon and stops the articulation of what is so fuzzy and hard to enter. Because we are inherently interactional creatures, our implicit intricacy opens more deeply when we are speaking to another person who actually wants to hear us. But if that person adds anything in, our contact with the inward sense is almost always lost or narrowed. In TAE we provide the needed interaction without any imposition, by taking turns in what we call a "Focusing partnership." In half the time I respond *only* to you. I follow you silently with my bodily understanding, and I tell you when I cannot follow. I speak from this understanding now and then, but only to check if I follow. In TAE I write down all your exact words as they emerge (because otherwise they might be gone a moment later) and I read anything back to you when you want it. Then in the other half of the time you do *only* this for me.

Once the individual's sense of something has become articulated and differentiated enough, then what happens is something we call "crossing." Other people's insights enrich ours by becoming implicit in our own terms. If one first develops and keeps one's own terms, one can then cross them with others. Keeping one's own terms means keeping their intricate precision. Crossing enriches their implicit intricacy and power. At this point collaborative interaction can create a new social product right here in the room. This is of course the intent of the current emphasis on "dialogue" and Shotter's important work on "joint action," since we humans live fundamentally in an inter-human interactional space.[1] But we need the individual's unique implicit store of world-interaction and this requires articulating the individual's bodily-felt sense first. When many TAE theories cross, they need not constitute one consistent logical system. There is a different way in which they go together. They cross. Crossing makes the other theory implicit in the felt sense under one's own logically connected terms. Then we find that we can say more from our own felt sense, using the other theory and its connected terms. Implicit intricacy connects all the TAE theories in advance. Each theory opens an intricate location in the public world and in philosophy and science. It enables the implicit intricacy to be entered at that location. A TAE theory relates to many other locations not only through its felt sense, but also through logical connections to other things.

Logic and space-time science exist only within experiential explication.

Pure logical inference is retained in TAE, but we *also* find a certain "odd logic" in articulating a felt sense. We find, for example, that a small detail which would usually be subsumed *under* wider categories, can instead overarch them and build its more intricate patterning into them. Another example of the odd logic: we find that when more requirements are imposed, degrees of freedom are not lessened; more requirements open more possibilities. There is an odd logic of experiential explication (see *ECM*). Next we must consider regular logic.

In order to understand our reductive sciences within a wider experiential science, we must first appreciate the power of the unit logic. I need to laud what I call "graph paper," the units that logic requires. The little logical units are familiar to everyone from mathematics ($1 + 1 = 2 + 170 = 172$). The units of which numbers are composed are external to each other, next to or after each other. With Newton they became characteristic of space and time and therefore of anything that exists in space and time. If you imagine everything external gone, there still seems to be a space and time which is empty but still quantitative in this unit-measured way. The reality which science represents is constructed in this space and time. Science turns what it studies into nice clean logical units that can be used with mathematics. By calling this space and time "graph paper" I want to bring home that physics, chemistry, organic chemistry, biology, microbiology—every scientific specialty is an elaborate construction of little units on this kind of screen, such as molecules, cells, genes, neurons. The unit model is not the only possible model for science. Of course, nature doesn't really come in little units, but we can project it onto such a screen of units. We also enlarge it very greatly so that the units capture what cannot normally be seen. Then we can institute very specific operations with these units. We can test the results of these operations, and eventually create things that have never existed before. Among other things we also map **ourselves** onto these screens of units when we study ourselves. No, of course we are not these screens. It is a bad mistake to think that we consist just of these little units on all the screens. We are the ones who live and look at screens that we make. When I was young we were all supposed to be chemical. Then biochemistry and microbiology expanded vastly. Then, later, we were supposed to be neurology. Obviously there are many sciences; what they say changes every few years, and new kinds of screens are constantly being added. We are not little units on a screen, not the sum of all the current and future screens. But let us not pretend that we could do without the wonderful things that have been constructed from such units—for example, medicine, electric lights, and even this computer on which I am typing. Once we make a screen of units, logical reasoning and inference are very powerful and can lead us to places nothing else can find.

On the other hand, logic is not what creates the units. Only we create the units, and we keep on creating them. The solution of long-standing problems usually requires creating new units. Even Euclid proves a theorem about triangles only by extending one of the lines, or by dropping a new line from the apex to the base—in other words, only by creating some new unit.

When one is using a well-defined concept, if one enters the felt sense at that juncture one can find exactly how that concept is working at that juncture, its precise effect in that context. This will be much a much more precise pattern than the definition one had for that concept. A felt sense is a source of much greater precision and can enable one to generate new units.

The "complexity" theorists who make analog computer models still assume that the starting set of units must last through to the end. So their results are disappointing.

Logical analysis is being widely rejected even in analytic philosophy today, but giving up on logical analysis is a great mistake. It is true that logic depends on premises it cannot examine. Logic is helpless to determine its own starting position. But TAE shows that new logical inferences can be instituted at significant junctures with new units that are first arrived at by Focusing and TAE. The possibilities are greatly enhanced when we can give logical analysis an articulated way to determine new starting locations and to generate new units there.

From new experiences and new phrases that come, we can fashion new units for logical inferences. In this way we can build something in the world with articulated strands and terms. Then it is a new logic with new units. Then logical inference applies again, and leads again to new places, new insights, and new questions at which one cannot arrive in any other way.

What comes from a bodily-felt sense is often of an odd sort that doesn't lend itself to the little boxes of graph paper. And this "illogical" character is often the most important aspect of what we need to say. We can develop logically connected terms nevertheless. With TAE we have a way to let the "illogical crux" redefine all the terms, so that logical inference then lends them its power without losing an intricate new pattern or violating the life that the theory articulates.

When terms articulate a felt sense and **also** acquire logical connections, this duality enables us to move in two ways from any statement: once we have logically linked terms, logic generates powerful inferences far beyond what can be found directly from experiencing. On the other side, by pursuing the experiential implications we can arrive where logic would never lead. We need both.

For example, *A Process Model* employs both. In Focusing, new and realistic steps arise from the body, but this seems illogical. Focusing is possible, since we do it. But to conceive of a world in which Focusing is possible leads to a cluster of logically interlocking terms in which ***the living body is an interactive process with its environment and situation***. This is the case for plants. Animals require understanding how "behavior" is a special case of such interaction, and human language again is a special case of behavior.

In this way I have developed a conceptual model for physics and biology, which can connect to the usual concepts and data (as we must be able to do), but with conceptual patterns which are modeled on and continuous with living and symbolizing. This kind of concept can connect with the usual units, but also embodies what cannot be reduced. This model can let one reconfigure any concept. With such concepts one can think about all physical bodies in such a way that some can be living, and about all living bodies in a way that some can be human bodies (see *A Process Model*).

I can only indicate the philosophy behind the above. This philosophy is original with me, but of course I could not have arrived at it if I didn't know the history of philosophy and Dilthey, Husserl, Heidegger, Merleau-Ponty, Wittgenstein, Whitehead, McKeon, and many others.

My new way was to put the ancient concepts, strategies, and issues into a direct relation with implicitly intricate experiencing. I found that each philosophical approach can open avenues in the implicit experiencing, instead of canceling the others out.

Every major philosophy changes the meaning of the **basic** terms such as what "basic" itself means, what "is" or "exists" means, as well as "true," "understand," "explain," and all other such words. Each philosophy gets its changed meanings by entering into that bigger realm at the edge of thinking which is more organized than any system of concepts. But then the philosophy tells a story, its own story in its own terms about how it got its terms. It gives us only a conceptualized report about its entry and return. It doesn't enable us to do this. My philosophy lets us enter and return. It studies and uses what happens to language, and also (differently) what happens to logical terms when we enter and return.

There are ancient sophisticated conceptual strategies to think about how human beings live in reality in such a way that we can know something. It is after knowing many of these strategies and their pitfalls that I say: we don't just have interactions; we *are* interaction with the environment—other people, the world, the universe—and we can sense ourselves to be just such an interaction. What we sense from there is never nothing (see my article "Crossing and Dipping").

Note

1. J. Shotter, "'Real Presences': Meaning as Living Movement in a Participatory World," *Theory and Psychology* 13 (2003): 135–68.

Acknowledgments

This project has been a shared undertaking from the beginning. The two of us (D.S. and E.C.) have collaborated closely at every stage. We were assisted by the excellent advice of close students of Gendlin's thought: notably, Rob Parker, Robert Scharff, Kye Nelson, and Chris Honde. Special thanks to Greg Walkerden for his close reading of the "Introduction," and to Neil Dunaetz for his constructive criticism at several points. Lissa McCullough provided expert editing early on. Aaron Bernstein was indispensable in sleuthing out missing links early and late. Jane Bunker, the director of Northwestern Press, and Anthony Steinbock, the editor of the SPEP series, strongly supported the project from the start. Nathan MacBrien of the press marshaled the manuscript through the critical final stages. Throughout, Gene Gendlin himself gave generously of his counsel and inspiration. His partner and wife, Mary Hendricks, supplied an insightful contributory voice.

The essays in the volume were originally published in the following locations:

Chapter 1, "Two Phenomenologists Do Not Disagree," was originally published in *Phenomenology: Dialogues and Bridges*, ed. Ronald Bruzina and Bruce Wilshire (Albany: SUNY Press, 1982), 321–35.

Chapter 2, "What Are the Grounds of Explication? A Basic Problem in Linguistic Analysis and in Phenomenology," was originally published in *The Monist* 49, no. 1 (1965): 137–64. Republished by permission of Oxford University Press.

Chapter 3, "Experiential Phenomenology," was originally published in *Phenomenology and the Social Sciences, Volume 1*, ed. *Maurice Natanson* (Evanston, Ill.: Northwestern University Press, 1973), 281–319.Chapter 4, "The New Phenomenology of Carrying Forward," was originally published in *Continental Philosophy Review* (formerly *Man and World*) 37, no. 1 (2004): 127–51. Republished with permission of Springer.

Chapter 5, "Words Can Say How They Work," was originally published in Robert P. Crease, ed., *Proceedings, Heidegger Conference* (Stony Brook, N.Y.: Robert P. Crease), 29–35.

Chapter 6, "Implicit Precision," was originally published in Zdravko Radman, ed., *Knowing without Thinking: The Theory of the Background in Philosophy of Mind* (Basingstoke, Eng.: Palgrave Macmillan, 2012), 141–66. Republished with permission of Palgrave Macmillan.

Chapter 7 is previously unpublished.

Chapter 8, "The Derivation of Space," was originally published in Azucena Cruz-Pierre and Donald A. Landes, eds., *Exploring the Work of Edward S. Casey: Giving Voice to Place, Memory, and Imagination* (New York: Bloomsbury Academic, 2013), 85–96. Republished with permission of Bloomsbury Academic, an imprint of Bloomsbury Publishing PLC.

Chapter 9, "Arakawa and Gins: The Organism-Person-Environment Process," was originally published in *Inflexions* 6, "Arakawa and Gins" (2013): 222–33.

Chapter 10 is previously unpublished.

Chapter 11, "*Befindlichkeit*: Heidegger and the Philosophy of Psychology," was originally published in *Review of Existential Psychology and Psychiatry* 16, nos. 1–3 (1978–79): 43–71.

Chapter 12, "Time's Dependence on Space: Kant's Statements and Their Misconstrual by Heidegger," was originally published in Thomas M. Seebohm and Joseph J. Kockelmans, eds., *Kant and Phenomenology* (Lanham, Md.: University Press of America/Rowman & Littlefield, 1984), 147–60. Copublished with the Center for Advanced Research in Phenomenology, Inc.

Chapter 14. "The Responsive Order: A New Empiricism," was originally published in *Man and World* 30 (1997): 383–411. Republished with permission of Springer.

Chapter 15, "Introduction to *Thinking at the Edge*," was originally published in *The Folio* 19, no. 1 (2004): 1–8. Courtesy of the International Focusing Institute.

References

Arvidson, S. *The Sphere of Attention: Context and Margin*. Dordrecht: Springer, 2006.
Casey, E. S. *The Fate of Place*. Berkeley: University of California Press, 1997.
———. *Getting Back into Place*. 2nd ed. Bloomington: Indiana University Press, 2009.
Clark, A. "Memento's Revenge: The Extended Mind, Extended." In *The Extended Mind*, ed. R. Menary. 43–66. Cambridge, Mass.: MIT Press, 2010.
Collins, H. M. "The New Orthodoxy: Humans, Animals, Heidegger and Dreyfus." In *After Cognitivism: A Reassessment of Cognitive Science and Philosophy*, ed. K. Leidlmair, 75–86. Dordrecht: Springer, 2009.
Damasio, A. *The Feeling of What Happens*. London: Heinemann, 1999.
Dreyfus, H. L. "How Representational Cognitivism Failed and Is Being Replaced by Body/World Coupling." In *After Cognitivism: A Reassessment of Cognitive Science and Philosophy*, ed. K. Leidlmair, 39–74. Dordrecht: Springer, 2009.
Ellis, R. "Consciousness, Self-Organization, and the Process-Substratum Relation." *Philosophical Psychology* 13, no. 2 (2000): 173–90.
Fodor, J. "Special Sciences and the Disunity of Science as a Working Hypothesis." *Synthese* 28 (1997): 77–115.
Gallagher, S. *How the Body Shapes the Mind*. Oxford: Oxford University Press, 2006.
———. "Mark Rowlands's *Body Language: Representation in Action*. Book review. *Notre Dame Philosophical Reviews* (2007): http://ndpr.nd.edu/review.cfm?id=11183.
———. "Social Cognition, the Chinese Room, and the Robot Replies." In *Knowing without Thinking: Mind, Action, Cognition and the Phenomenon of the Background*, ed. Z. Radman, 83–97. New York: Palgrave Macmillan, 2012.
Gendlin, Eugene T. "Analysis." In Martin Heidegger, *What Is a Thing?* Translated by W. B. Barton Jr. and Vera Deutsch, 245–96. Chicago: Regnery, 1967.
———. "Crossing and Dipping: Some Terms for Approaching the Interface between Natural Understanding and Logical Formation." In *Subjectivity and the Debate over Computational Cognitive Science*, ed. M. Galbraith and W. J. Rapaport, 37–59. New York: Center for Cognitive Science, 1991. Also in *Minds and Machines* 5, no. 4 (1995): 547–60. https://www.focusing.org/gendlin/docs/gol_2166.html.
———. *Experiencing and the Creation of Meaning*. Evanston, Ill.: Northwestern University Press, 1997; first edition, 1967.
———. *Focusing*. New York: Everest House, 1978.

REFERENCES

———. "Improvisation Provides." Presented at a panel organized by Robert Crease. Society for Phenomenology and Existential Philosophy, New Orleans, October 1993. Available at http://www.focusing.org/gendlin/docs/gol_2223.html.

———. *Line by Line Commentary on Aristotle's "De anima."* 2012. Available from Amazon.com.

———. "The Newer Therapies." Chapter 14 in *American Handbook of Psychiatry* 5, ed. S. Arieti, 269–89. New York: Basic Books, 1975.

———. *A Process Model.* Evanston, Ill.: Northwestern University Press, 2017.

———. "A Theory of Personality Change." In *Personality Change*, ed. Philip Worchel and Donn Byrne. New York: Wiley, 1964. Reprinted in *Creative Developments in Psychotherapy*, ed. A. Mahrer. Cleveland, Ohio: Case Western Reserve University Press, 1971.

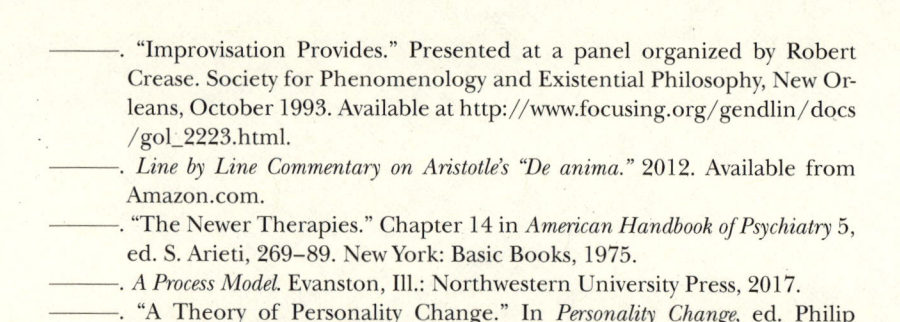

———. "The Time of the Explicating Process." In *Body Memory, Metaphor and Movement*, ed. S. C. Koch, T. Fuchs, and C. Müller, 73–82. Amsterdam: John Benjamins, 2012.

———. "We Can Think with the Implicit as Well as with Fully Formed Concepts." In *After Cognitivism: A Reassessment of Cognitive Science and Philosophy*, ed. K. Leidlmair, 47–161. Dordrecht: Springer, 2009. Also available at http://www.focusing.org/gendlin/pdf/gendlin_we_can_think_with_the_implicit.pdf. 23.

———. "What First and Third Person Processes Really Are." *Journal of Consciousness Studies* 16, nos. 10–12 (2009): 332–62. Also available at http://www.focusing.org/gendlin/pdf/gendlin_what_first_and_third_person_processes_really_are.pdf.

Gendlin, E. T., J. Beebe, J. Cassens, M. Klein, and M. Oberlander. "Focusing Ability in Psychotherapy, Personality and Creativity." In *Research in Psychotherapy*, ed. J. Schlien, vol. 3. Washington, D.C.: American Psychological Association, 1967.

Gibson, J. J. *The Senses Considered as Perceptual Systems.* Boston: Houghton Mifflin, 1966.

Gins, M., and S. Arakawa. *Architectural Body.* Tuscaloosa: University of Alabama Press, 2002.

Govan, M., S. Arakawa, and M. Gins. *Reversible Destiny: We Have Decided Not to Die.* New York: Guggenheim Museum Publications, 1997.

Heidegger, M. *Being and Time.* Translated by John Macquarrie and Edward Robinson. London: SCM, 1962.

———. *Sein und Zeit.* Tübingen: Niemeyer, 1927.

———. "Zeit und Sein." In *Zur Sache des Denkens*. Tübingen: Niemeyer, 1969.

James, William. *The Principles of Psychology*, vol. 1. 1890. New York: Henry Holt, 2009. Retrieved from https://archive.org/stream/theprinciplesofp01jameuoft#page/n5/mode/2up.

Jordan, J. S., and M. Ghin. "The Role of Control in a Science of Consciousness." *Journal of Consciousness Studies* 14, nos. 1/2 (2007): 177–97.

Mahoney, M. J. *Human Change Processes.* New York: Basic Books, 1991.

REFERENCES

Margolis, J. "Contesting John Searle's Social Ontology: Institutions and Background." In *Knowing without Thinking: The Theory of the Background in Philosophy of Mind*, ed. Z. Radman, 98–115. Basingstoke, Eng.: Palgrave Macmillan, 2012.

O'Regan, J. K., and A. Noë. "A Sensorimotor Account of Vision and Visual Consciousness." *Behavioral and Brain Sciences* 24, no. 5 (2001): 939–73.

Petitmengin, C. "Listening from Within." *Journal of Consciousness Studies* 16, nos. 10–12 (2009): 252–84.

Polanyi, M. *Personal Knowledge*. New York: Harper and Row, 1958.

Rowlands, M. "Understanding the 'Active' in Enactive." *Phenomenology and the Cognitive Sciences* 6, no. 4 (2007): 427–43.

Stuart, S. A. J. "Enkinaesthesia: The Essential Sensuous Background for Co-Agency." In *Knowing without Thinking: Mind, Action, Cognition and the Phenomenon of the Background*, ed. Z. Radman, 167–86. New York: Palgrave Macmillan, 2012.

———. "Enkinaesthesia, Biosemiotics and the Ethiosphere." In *Signifying Bodies: Biosemiosis, Interaction and Health*, ed. S. Cowley, J. C. Major, S. Steffensen, and A. Dini, 305–50. Braga, Portugal: Portuguese Catholic University, 2010.

Thompson, Evan. "Sensorimotor Subjectivity and the Enactive Approach to Experience." *Phenomenology and the Cognitive Sciences* 4, no. 4 (2005): 407–27.

Varela, F., E. Thompson, and E. Rosch. *The Embodied Mind: Cognitive Science and Human Experience*. Cambridge, Mass.: MIT Press, 1991.

Wittgenstein, Ludwig. *Philosophical Investigations*. 1953. Oxford: Blackwell, 2001.

Index

Adorno, Theodor W., xv
affordances, 128, 155
animals, 84, 104, 105–6, 112, 122, 135n7, 140, 159, 256–57, 259, 266, 274, 278, 281n15, 288, 292; insects, 153–54, 271; monkeys, 119–20, 136n17, 160
anticipation, 150n5, 153
Arakawa, Shusaku, and Madeline Gins, 164–71
Aristotle, xviii, 150n1, 179, 181, 184–85, 188, 279n4
Austin, J. L., 23–31, 47, 48–49, 50, 256

Befindlichkeit. See under Heidegger, Martin
behavior, 105, 115, 118–19, 135n12; behavior possibilities, 120, 122, 125–29, 155; behavior therapy, 74; explication and, 43
bioengineering, 280n15
bodily sense. *See* felt sense
body-constituting, 116–19, 123, 124–25, 132–34, 135n12
body-environment interaction, xvi, xvii, 104–5, 111–17, 119, 122, 146, 153–54, 159, 166, 292–93
body-mind split, xiv, xvii
Buber, Martin, 223

"carrying forward" concept, 86–91, 102, 106, 116, 118, 131–32, 138–39, 142–43, 147–49, 150n2, 154, 265–66, 279n7; hermeneutic and, 269–70; scientific progress and, 157, 264
Casey, Edward S., 151, 161–62
causes vs. reasons, 15–16
Cavell, Stanley, xix, 43, 268
Clark, Andy, 119

cognition, 31, 50, 132, 158–59, 167, 205; embodied, 154–55; limit of, 96–97
Collins, Harry M., 135n7
concept-formation, 179, 181, 184–85, 187
consciousness. *See* sentience
constructivism, 253, 263–64
Crease, Robert P., 259
creativity, 75, 287
crossing, 88, 91, 106–7, 266–67, 269–72, 289; crossed multiplicity, 102–3, 266, 270, 271; metaphor and, 266
culture, 85, 107, 113, 288

Damasio, Antonio, 127
Deacon, Terrence, xiii
degrees of freedom, 88, 91, 149
Derrida, Jacques, xiv, 93
determinism, 25, 48
Dewey, John, xiii, 265
dialectic, 267–68
Dilthey, Wilhelm, xiii, 47, 106, 150n1, 222, 265, 268, 269, 292
direct reference, xviii, 31, 56–60, 62–63, 66, 69, 76, 86, 143–46, 148–50, 221, 261
Dreyfus, Hubert L., 116, 131, 134n2

Einstein, Albert, 254, 261
Emerson, Ralph Waldo, xviii
empiricism, 253–58, 261–62, 264–65, 278
enkinaesthesia, 121
"environment" (in relation to self): #0, 123–24; #1, 114, 117, 123–25; #2, 117, 119, 123–25; #3, 123–24. *See also* body-environment interaction
experiencing, xiii, xiv–xvi, xviii–xix, 46–78, 81, 88–89, 122, 283, 292;

INDEX

interschematizable character of, 60–61, 64; multischematic character of, 60–61, 64; nonnumerical character of, xvi, 60–61, 64; phenomenological formulations of, 5–20, 33–34, 51, 61; verbalization of, 51–59, 64, 74, 288
Experiencing Scale, 72–74, 91n2
Euclid, 291
evolution, 154, 281n15
explication: grounds of, 22–23, 30, 33, 40–44; process of, 59–67, 72, 77, 139, 157, 264, 290

felt sense, xiii, 43–44, 49, 68, 86, 97–98, 104–6, 118, 122, 123, 140–41, 169–70, 205, 218, 221, 224n5, 278, 282–83, 286, 289–92; Sartre on, 38. *See also* direct referents; language and the body
Fenichel, Otto, 68
Feyerabend, Paul, 253
first-person perspective, xiii, xviii–xix
Focusing method, xviii, 170, 171, 282, 286, 287, 288–89, 291–92
Fodor, Jerry, 157
free will, 23–26, 48
Freud, Sigmund, 38, 68–69, 219, 220, 221
"fresh thinking," 85, 100, 156–57, 287
functional equality, 11, 12

Gadamer, Hans-Georg, 269
Gallagher, Shaun, 114, 121, 123, 127, 132, 140, 158–59
generative processes. *See* object-formation
Gibson, James J., 128, 155
Goethe, Johann Wolfgang von, 106
Goodall, Jane, 136n17

Hadamard, Jacques, 57, 69
Hadot, Pierre, xiv
"having," 167
Heelan, Patrick, 280n13
Heraclitus, 192
Hegel, Georg Wilhelm Friedrich, 7, 261, 263–64, 270; dialectic and, 267, 279n4; Sartre and, 35, 36
Heidegger, Martin, xiii, xviii, 5–8, 10, 33, 34, 35, 47, 50, 51, 80, 93–99, 150n1, 222–23, 224nn1–3, 265, 277, 284, 292; on anxiety, 209; on authenticity, 211–14; *Befindlichkeit* concept, xviii, 15, 94, 95–96, 194–201, 206–16, 222, 224nn2–3; being-in-the-world concept, 34, 38–39, 50, 207–12, 214; *Dasein* concept, 94, 104, 199, 207–10, 212–16; on Kant, 225, 232–35; on *logos*, 5, 216–17; the openness and, 93–94, 99, 100; on technology, 235; on "throwing out" and thrownness, 210–11, 212–13, 224n8. *See also* "moody understanding"; ontology; space; time
Hendricks, Mary, 286
hermeneutic, 268–71
Husserl, Edmund, xiii, 6–8, 33–34, 47, 153, 222, 292; on experience, 50–51, 54; on expression, 52–53, 59; on "natural attitude," 85; ontology and, 82; on universality, 17

idealism, 46, 132, 263, 279n5; Kant on, 228–32, 235
implicit governing, 91, 103–4, 106–7, 267
implicit intricacy, xvii, 83–84, 86, 88, 90, 104, 152, 155–56, 159, 162, 167–71, 196, 220, 279n6, 289–90
implicit multiplicity, xvi, 102, 266
implicit precision, 111–12, 129–32, 134, 141
implying, xiii, xvi, 11–12, 22, 90–91, 111, 116, 122–23, 135n10, 138–39, 159; accessing the implicit, 142–46; *Befindlichkeit* and, 196–97; experience and, 43–45; functions of, 100–104, 106–7, 111–13, 130; language and, 87–88, 98–100, 139–41, 143, 146, 150n2, 155–56, 288; linguistic analysis and, 27–28, 33, 42; occurring and, xvii, 90, 116, 118–19, 122–23, 131, 134, 147–48, 157, 168; reiterative, 124–25, 130, 132
inging process, 165–68, 171
intentionality, 11–12
intermodality, 127
intricacy, xiii, xiv, 81, 88–91, 246, 288; responsive order and, 265. *See also* implicit intricacy

INDEX

James, William, 150n3
Jung, Carl G., 219, 221

Kant, Immanuel, xvii, xviii, 96, 247, 261, 275; on imagination, 231–33; "Refutation of Idealism," 228–32, 235; on space and time, 225–35
Kemp Smith, Norman, 226
Kuhn, Thomas S., 253, 264

landing sites, 165–66, 169
language, working of, 94–95, 97–100, 121, 146–47, 170–71, 204, 237. *See also* implying: language and; metaphors; Wittgenstein, Ludwig
language and the body, 81–86, 89, 98, 105–6, 159, 162n4; TAE and, 284–88. *See also* "speaking-from"
Laplace, Pierre-Simon, 90, 268
Leibniz, Gottfried Wilhelm, 150n1
lifting out, 9, 102, 203–4, 218–23
linguistic analysis, 22–45, 47–49, 55
living-in, 105, 199, 205, 214, 222
localization, 261–62
logic, 82, 88–89, 90, 94, 106, 142, 275–78; "more-than-logical" concepts, 91, 265, 266–68; in Plato, 187–89; postmodernist denial of, 272; precision and, 111; responsive order and, 265–67; symbolic, 152; TAE and, 290–92

McKeon, Richard, 150n1, 267, 284, 292
Mead, George Herbert, 265
"meaning," meaning of, 143
Merleau-Ponty, Maurice, xiii, 39, 47, 50, 80, 106, 147, 150n1, 292; on adaptation, 153; Heidegger and, xviii, 223; space and, 127
metaphor, 58, 80, 81, 171, 266; Wittgenstein on, 238, 243
metastructure, 223
mirror neurons, 160
Mohanty, Jitendra Nath, 87
monads and monading, 149
Monsanto Company, 281n15
"moody understanding," 95–97, 99, 104–5, 207–8, 210–11, 215
more, the, 93–97, 169
motion, 115, 118, 128, 148, 160–61, 261

Nagel, Thomas, xiii
"natural attitude," 85, 86
newborns and infants, 121, 127, 140, 160, 257, 258
Newton, Isaac, 261, 290
Nietzsche, Friedrich, 222, 276
noesis, 51, 253

object-formation, 115, 116–18, 124–25
objectivism, 81, 237, 244, 253
objectivity, xix, 255–56, 258, 260–62
ontics, 205–6
ontology, 39, 82; Heidegger and, 199, 205–7, 215, 217
openness, the, 93–94, 99, 100, 106–7
order, standard concept of, xvi, 265
"organism" usage, 136n19
organism-person-environment process, 164–71

paradox, 180, 245, 265, 267
past and present relationship, 157–58
patterned human living, 120–22, 133, 137n31, 153, 159–61, 265, 288–89; aesthetics and, 137n22
Pears, David, 237
Peirce, Charles Sanders, 265
perception, 111–12, 117–19, 126–28, 151–52, 158, 167, 276–78; "perceptual split," 113–16, 119
Perlstein, Joel, 188
personality change theory, 221, 223
"personing," 164, 168
phenomenology, 5–20, 80–82, 220–21; *Befindlichkeit* and, 216–17; linguistic analysis and, 23, 32–40, 42, 44, 50; misunderstandings of, 33, 37, 80; "phenomenological basis," 51–52, 53; psychotherapy and, 70, 71, 74, 76–77; sentences and, 5–6; signposts of, 8. *See also* experience; explication
philosophy: psychology and, 197–200, 206, 221; tasks of, xv, 69, 91, 167, 292–93
plants, 104–5, 124–25, 147–48, 159, 167, 288, 292
Plato, xviii, 150n1, 175–93; dialectic and, 267–68; on love, 176, 183–85, 187, 189–92

poetry, 100, 186, 189, 222
Polanyi, Michael, 112
postmodernism, 80, 248, 250n6, 253, 254, 265
precision. *See* implicit precision
process model, xvii, 112, 122, 133, 142, 148, 168, 292
psychology. *See* philosophy: psychology and
psychotherapy, 43, 67–70, 200–205, 218–21; research in, 70–76, 204
public discourse, 12, 287
Putnam, Hilary, 263, 279n4

quantum physics, 152, 261
Quine, Willard Van Orman, 257

reciprocity, 156–57, 167
recognition, 57–60, 64
reference. *See* direct reference
relativism, 7, 106, 168, 254, 258, 260, 270; Plato and, 182
responsive order, xiv, xvi, xix, 81, 88, 253–78, 281n15
Richard, Jules, 245
Rowlands, Mark, 119
Russell, Bertrand, 82, 245
Ryle, Gilbert, 27, 43, 47–49

sameness and difference, 12–13, 276
Sartre, Jean-Paul, xviii, 7, 22–23, 34–40, 47, 80, 223; on nausea, 15, 38
Schleiermacher, Friedrich, 47, 222
Schmitz, Hermann, xiii
Schneider, Hans Julius, 245
science: findings and procedures, 254–59, 262–64, 271–78, 279n6, 280n15, 290–91; operational research, 273; patterns and, 271–72, 274, 275
scissiparity, 36
sentience, 118–19
Shapere, Dudley, 45n3
Sherover, Charles M., 233
Shotter, John, 289
situations ("patterned spaces"), 120–22, 132, 147, 160, 167, 170, 285, 288; *Befindlichkeit* and, 195–97

Skinnerism, 256, 259
space (and place), 126–28; 151–52, 160–62, 261; Heidegger on, 199, 208, 212, 229; Kant on, 226–32
"speaking-from," 83–87, 91, 105, 165, 283, 286, 287
Spitz, René, 121
Stambaugh, Joan, 224n3
Stuart, Susan A. J., 114, 121, 136n17
symbolization, xvi, xviii, 13, 60, 136m19, 166–67, 219, 223–24, 288

taking account, 111, 129–32, 134
Tezuka Tomio, 107n2
thinking at the edge (TAE), xiv–xv, xviii–xix, 150n6, 170, 171, 282–93; logic and, 290–92; social purpose of, 288–89
third-person perspective, xiii, xvi
Thompson, Evan, 135n8
time, 212–14; Kant and Heidegger on, 225–36
Turing, Alan, 273–74
"turning," 167, 169–70

unconscious, the, 69, 76–77, 82, 220
unit model, 114–15, 142, 148, 166, 284, 290–91
universality, 17–18, 139
universe, 161–62, 164
"unseparated multiplicity," 91, 266

Varela, Francisco, xiii
"versioning," 120, 121, 137n22

Whitehead, Alfred North, 150n1, 292
Wittgenstein, Ludwig, xvii, xviii, 47, 55, 95, 150n1, 237–48, 253, 264, 277–78, 284, 292; on the face, 121, 274–75; on inner processes, 240, 249nn3–4; on logical models, 265; publication plan, 280n14
words. *See* language

zigzagging, 90